A Short History of Sociological Thought

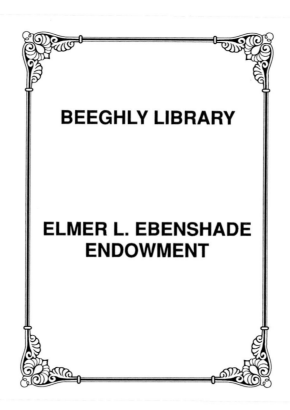

Also by Alan Swingewood:

Cultural Theory and the Problem of Modernity

The Myth of Mass Culture

Sociological Aesthetics and Poetic Theory

A Short History of Sociological Thought

Third Edition

Alan Swingewood

palgrave

First edition 1984
Reprinted twice
Second edition 1991
Reprinted five times
Third edition 2000

Published by
PALGRAVE
Houndmills, Basingstoke, Hampshire RG21 6XS and
175 Fifth Avenue, New York, N. Y. 10010
Companies and representatives throughout the world

PALGRAVE is the new global academic imprint of
St. Martin's Press LLC Scholarly and Reference Division and
Palgrave Publishers Ltd (formerly Macmillan Press Ltd).

ISBN 0–333–80190–9 hardback
ISBN 0–333–80199–7 paperback

This book is printed on paper suitable for recycling and made from fully managed and sustained forest sources.

A catalogue record for this book is available from the British Library.

10   9   8   7   6   5
09   08   07   06   05   04   03

Editing and origination by
Aardvark Editorial, Mendham, Suffolk

Printed and bound in Great Britain by
Creative Print & Design (Wales), Ebbw Vale

Contents

Introduction to the
Third Edition

This book is neither a history of sociology nor of sociological theory but a selective history of sociological thought from its origins in eighteenth-century philosophy, history and political economy. Sociological thought implies a body of concepts and theory which defines society as a system, or structure, governed by processes which involve both social institutions and human agents or actors. Eighteenth-century social thought was sociological in this sense although it failed to develop an adequate sociological concept of the social, too often assimilating it to political and economic elements. In effect, eighteenth-century social thought posed many of the critical issues of sociology without resolving them sociologically. In contrast, early nineteenth-century sociological thought sought to define the social both in terms of society as a complex structural whole and in its relation with specific institutions, notably the division of labour, property, social classes, religion and family. Society was industrial society and the broad themes of the early sociologists were those of social conflict, alienation, community, social cohesion and the problems of evolution and development. The task of social science lay in identifying the forces promoting historical change.

Early sociological thought was broadly optimistic: the certainties of the natural sciences could be applied to the social sciences unproblematically. Classical sociology emerges as a reaction to this form of positivist scientistic thought. The broad themes of classical sociology were pessimistic: industrialisation produces social structures which alienate the individual from the community, transform cultural objects into commodities and rationalise human life into bureaucratic systems of domination. Classical sociology becomes centred both on large-scale social changes and the role played by the agent in the making of change: 'voluntarism' and action replace the historical determinism of nineteenth-century positivism.

Modern sociological thought is characterised by a continual tension between this legacy of classical sociology, between a voluntarist model which emphasises the creative and active role of agents, and a structural model which focuses on institutions and processes which constrain and determine the course of action. The rise of functionalism as the dominant paradigm of modern sociology during the middle years of the twentieth century attests to the widespread influence of systems theory within sociology. In contrast, interpretive sociology, including phenomenology and interactionism, attempted a redefinition of the social by focusing on everyday social life as the basis of sociological understanding and analysis. By the 1950s these constituted the two major paradigms within sociology: Marx and Marxism were rejected as ideological. It was not until the 1960s that new schools of sociology – including phenomenology, action theory, structuralism, Marxist humanism and ethnomethodology – emerged to challenge the functionalist model.

For the third edition of this book I have sought to describe these developments and provide a extended discussion of contemporary developments in sociology especially the attempts to overcome its fragmentation into different and apparant contending schools and approaches which followed the breakup of functionalism as the dominant paradigm in sociological theory. I have also examined the influence of non-sociological thought, notably structural linguistics, post-structuralism and postmodernism. For this third edition I have tried to link the substantive theories and concepts of classical sociology, especially the preoccupation with modernity and its problems, with modern sociology and the contemporary debates around such issues as culture, identity, the de-centring of the subject, the postmodern turn in social theory, as well as those fundamental issues raised by classical sociology, the difficulties of integrating system, or macro analysis, with action, or micro analysis. The heart of sociological thought is a constant dialogue between the past and the present, the need to redefine concepts and to rediscover them.

Because Marx's thought played such an important role in the formation of classical sociology I have discussed both his methodology, basic concepts and substantive theories of social change, class and power. I have expanded on Marx's sociological analysis of social change and shortened the discussion of alienation and ideology and revised the chapter on Marxism, including both Gramsci and the Frankfurt School, in terms of their relation with Marx and classical sociology. Part II explores the development of modern sociology analysing the contribution of sociological functionalism and the attempts to develop a theory of the self and the interaction process. This section has been expanded to include the work of Goffman, while subsequent chapters examine the contribution of structuralism and post-structuralism, especially Foucault, to sociological knowledge, the current attempts to synthesise macro and micro sociologies and the problems associated with the postmodern critique of sociology and Marxism. I conclude with a brief discussion of new forms of sociological thought based on postmodern theory which raises questions about identity and self, action and culture.

The third edition is a substantially revised and, in many cases, new work. I have rewritten the chapters on Marx, sociological interactionism and structuralism; revised the chapters on Durkheim and Weber; shortened the material on early sociological thought and positivism and added new chapters on agency and structure, postmodernity and new developments in sociology. The development of sociological thought is the result of collaborative, communicative and dialogic interaction involving individuals, social groups and communities. Of all areas of the history of sociology this is perhaps the most complex and neglected although there have been valuable contributions by Coser (1971), Jay (1973), Clarke (1973), Schwendinger (1974), Therborn (1976), Smith (1988), Ross (1991) and Seidman (1998). This book is, as I have said, a selective history. At the end I have listed a number of works by chapter which refer the reader to further general discussion as well as more specialised studies. A history of sociological thought – from Vico to Bakhtin – can easily become a 'shopping list' of great names, a canon of mostly deceased writers, the holy trinity of Marx, Durkheim and Weber. I have tried to avoid this by concentrating on their relevance for modern sociology in terms of the complexity and richness of concepts and theory which have inspired later sociologists to debate with and develop 'old' ideas. Canons are always constructed and deconstructed, the sociological community constantly revising the value of the work of its 'founding fathers.' Marx, Weber and Durkheim have remained at the core of modern sociology not as founders of a discipline but through their intellectual depth, rigour of argument and the ability to raise disturbing questions about the nature of modern society. It is in this spirit that I have excluded the sociological thought of Pareto which I described in preceding editions as 'ultimately a dead end... less a sociological explanation of human society and its historically specific modes of development, than an all-embracing speculative philosophy of history' (Swingewood, 1991, p. 170). The history of sociology is never a history of a selective canon but a dialogue between the present and the past, how ideas born in different historical periods and cultures survive as active elements in contemporary sociological thought.

ALAN SWINGEWOOD

History of Sociological Thought

Origins

Eighteenth-century social thought (Vico, Montesquieu, Smith, Ferguson, Rousseau)

The development of nineteenth-century sociological positivism (Comte), sociological evolutionism (Spencer) and Marxism (Marx and Engels)

Classical Sociology

Weber, Simmel (the tradition of *Verstehen* sociology and critique of positivism and evolutionism)

Durkheim's critique of the positivist tradition

The development of Marxism after Marx involving a critique of materialism and evolutionism: Labriola, Gramsci, Sorel, Lukács and the Frankfurt School

Modern Sociology

Interpretative sociology (Schutz)

Functionalism

Mead and interactionism

Systems theory and Action theory

Post-structuralism

Parsons

Structuration theory

Structuralism

Reflexive sociology: Bourdieu

Habermas and communicative action

Part I

Foundations: Classical Sociology

1

Modernity, Industrialisation and the Rise of Sociology

Origins of Sociology

There was no sociology before the advent of the nineteenth century, if by sociology is meant a systematic corpus of knowledge, specific methodology and conceptual framework which clearly differentiate it as a distinctive discipline, with its own object of study, the analysis of human society, from the related studies of economics, history, philosophy and law. The term sociology was coined by Auguste Comte in the early nineteenth century although the study of society as an historical and empirical object had begun much earlier, especially in eighteenth-century France and Scotland, where a commitment to historical and scientific modes of thought and inquiry shifted the prevailing discourse of political and moral philosophy away from traditional concerns with the universal and the transhistorical to a grasp of the specificity of the social. This is not to suggest that eighteenth-century social theory constituted a sociology, rather it remained a peculiarly invigorating mixture of political philosophy, history, political economy and sociology.

The work of Montesquieu, Ferguson and Millar exemplified a sociology in the making. In discussing the development of sociology it is crucial to distinguish between those writers who discussed broad sociological themes within a non-sociological discourse and those genuine precursors who attempted both to provide a body of concepts and to define a method of inquiry or analysis of social institutions and social processes, analytically separate from political society.

Thus philosophers such as Plato (427–347 BC) and Aristotle (384–322 BC) defined society in holistic terms as an organism in which the constituent parts were necessarily related to the whole, a unified system, structured around social groups (warriors, tradesmen, middle class, the poor) the division of labour and social inequality.

Aristotle located the origin of society in an essential human nature which predisposes individuals to form groups and associations. Society was thus the expression of an inherent sociability, with social relationships the culmination

3

of this instinct. Aristotle's *Politics* is full of sociological insights into the nature of human society and contains one of the first systematic attempts to analyse and classify social phenomena, such as government, into broad types (tyranny, oligarchy, democracy). Yet it remains within the framework of traditional political philosophy and, as with Plato, there is no clear distinction between the state and society.

But philosophy based on fixed notions of human nature and a narrow static view of the social world could not generate concepts and a method to explain social change. It was this problem which dominated seventeenth- and eighteenth-century philosophers (Hobbes, Locke, Rousseau) who defined society in secular terms but as the product of human nature. Both Hobbes (1588–1679) and Locke (1632–1704) distinguished between a pre-social state of nature characterised by peace, good will and reciprocal relationships, the development of social conflict and diverging interests the result of the growth of private property and thus of social inequality. Both Hobbes and Locke grasped the secular historical nature of human society but assimilated this notion of the social to an underlying concept of a pre-social, transhistorical human nature: egoism for Hobbes, sympathy for Locke. In the eighteenth century Jean-Jacques Rousseau (1712–1778) further developed Locke's dichotomy of a sociable humanity existing in a state of nature and the corrupt, egoistic humanity of modern civil society; humanity as the product of nature versus humanity as the product of society and culture.

Although the writings of Aristotle, Plato, Hobbes, Locke and Rousseau contain substantive sociological themes – inequality, social conflict and social cohesion, the development of the division of labour and private property – the emphasis on human nature as the basis of human society and social order led to the view of the social as the expression of an immanent transhistorical process. There was no conception of society as a complex structure of economic, political and cultural institutions or the processes and mechanisms of social change.

The New Science of Giambattista Vico (1668–1774), first published in 1725, and Montesquieu's *Spirit of the Laws* (1949 [1748]) stand as the first major attempts to theorise society both as an organic whole and relate its varying cultures, values and institutions to specific stages of historical development.

Vico's *New Science* made history intelligible by defining it as a process characterised by three distinct stages of development – the age of the Gods, the age of the Heroes and finally the age of Men – and thus invested with immanent meaning. The theory itself is perhaps less significant than Vico's attempt to apply scientific concepts to the study of human history. His starting point was the affirmation of humanism – the creative, active role of the human subject. 'In the night of thick darkness', he wrote, which envelops the remote past 'there shines the eternal and never failing light of a truth beyond all question: that the world of civil society has certainly been made by men' (Vico, 1948 [1725], Section 331). Vico thus rejected the fixed concept of human nature which had characterised the social thought of Aristotle, Hobbes and Locke: the general argument of the *New Science* was that human society was historical, social institutions and human relationships defined as the product of action with history as an active, creative process made by humanity. One consequence of Vico's humanism is his argument that humanity can know only that which it has created itself: the true (*verum*) and the made (*factum*) are convertible. It was not, therefore, a question of passively recording, classifying and observing an external reality in the manner of the physical sciences, for 'the world of human society has certainly been made by men' and factual knowledge of the external world was clearly inadequate as the basis for human science since it eliminated the active core of human culture, diminishing the making in favour of the made.

But eighteenth-century philosophy remained unreceptive to Vico's humanist historicism. When Montesquieu visited Venice the *New Science* was recommended but there is no evidence that he either read or acquired the work. And it was Montesquieu, not Vico, who influenced the sociological writings of the Scottish School of Ferguson, Smith and Millar. What is characteristic of these writers is a commitment to one of the basic principles of sociology, that beneath the apparent chaos and randomness of social life there exists an underlying structure. Montesquieu (1689–1755) was not a specialist but a man of letters trained in classics and philosophy; his work combined the study of history, political science, criticism and political theory. Employing a richer and more detailed mode of historical analysis, more extensive and systematic than anything found in previous social theory, Montesquieu argued that although society presents itself as a chaotic and diverse phenomenon, beneath the surface exists a definite structure comprising regularities of behaviour, institutions and laws. Social institutions and processes are thus the product not of 'great legislators' (the standpoint of political philosophy) but of definite material conditions which can be discovered by empirical and historical analysis. It was this aspect of Montesquieu's thought that Emile Durkheim regarded as significant for the development of sociology: to accept the view that legislators alone framed constitutions and social customs was tantamount to denying 'any determinate order in human societies, for if it were true laws, customs and institutions would depend not on the constant nature of the state, but on the accident that brought forth one lawmaker rather than another' (Durkheim, 1965, pp. 11–12). Regular relationships exist between these objective forces. In his study of the Roman Empire (1965 [1734]) Montesquieu wrote:

It is not chance that rules the world. Ask the Romans who had a continuous sequence of successes when they were guided by a certain plan, and an uninterrupted sequence of reverses when they followed another. There are general causes, moral and physical, which act in every monarchy, elevating it, maintaining it… All accidents are controlled by these causes. (Montesquieu, 1965 [1734], p. 165)

All social phenomena are interconnected, 'every particular law is connected with another law'. Montesquieu's concept of society is thus couched in holistic, not atomistic, terms; societies are self-contained, integrated wholes.

Montesquieu's main concern was forms of government. But his types of government were effectively types of society. Law must accord with social context, but Montesquieu attempts to define context more precisely as a structure consisting of soil and climate, occupations, religious institutions, 'commerce, manners and customs'. The result is a concept of society as a system in which the various elements acquired meaning only in terms of the whole. The basic elements comprising this system were climate and geography: other writers had advocated physical factors as the basis of social analysis but Montesquieu was the first to analyse their contribution to the structure of society as a whole. His concept of environment, or milieu, implied the concept of a system in which the political 'superstructure' and culture express the spirit of the whole. Of course, Montesquieu overstates his case: suicide, slavery, marriage are all mechanically and causally related to specific climatic conditions and peculiarities of geography. But there can be no doubting the scientific spirit behind these arguments and the sociological core of Montesquieu's thought is undoubtedly the attempt to discover an underlying pattern of relationships between the different elements of society; beneath the apparent diversity and chaos of empirical reality exists a structure and system which, once clarified, illuminates the cause of diverse phenomena and thus generates meaning. His comment on the feudal system is apposite:

> The feudal laws form a very beautiful prospect. A venerable old oak raises its lofty head to the skies; the eye sees from afar its spreading leaves; upon drawing nearer it perceives the trunk but does not discern the root; the ground must be dug up to discover it. (Montesquieu, 1949, Book XXX, Section 1)

It was this task which fell to the Enlightenment writers Adam Ferguson and John Millar.

The Scottish Enlightenment and Modernity

During the second half of the eighteenth century a group of intellectuals working in Glasgow and Edinburgh advanced the scientific study of human society by raising critical sociological issues and problems analysing the social role of property, forms of government, the development of the division of labour and the alienation of industrial work. Such were the achievements of Adam Smith (1723–90), Adam Ferguson (1723–1816) and John Millar (1735–1801) that Edinburgh became known as the Athens of the North, compared only with Paris as the major centre of learning during the latter half of the eighteenth century. In effect the Scottish Enlightenment focused on the problem of modernity, the emergence of a radically new type of society based on new principles of social organisation: industry, science, technology, urbanism and the rise of modern cities and social class. Equally there was the sense that the pace of social change was accelerating, that there was evolution and progress. Society had a past, a present and a future.

The writers of the Scottish Enlightenment developed a core of sociological concepts and an empirical methodology subsisting within economic, political and historical perspectives. What is significant about the contribution of the Scottish Enlightenment to sociology is the clear awareness that society constituted a process, the product of specific economic, social and historical forces that could be identified and analysed through the methods of empirical science. Theoretical, or 'conjectural history', as the approach was termed – misleadingly, since the intention was a science of history and society, positive not conjectural knowledge and therefore theoretical in the best sense – was superficially similar to Montesquieu's broad comparative perspective. But the Scots were concerned above everything else with the problem of social change and the causes which lead to the transition from one type of society to another. As Millar wrote:

> In searching for the causes of… systems of law and government… we must undoubtedly resort… to the differences of situation… the fertility or barrenness of the soil, the nature of its productions, the species of labour requisite for procuring subsistence, in the number of individuals collected together in one community, their proficiency in the arts… The variety that frequently occurs in these and such other particulars must have a prodigious influence upon the great body of the people; as, by giving a peculiar direction to their inclinations and pursuits, it must be productive of corresponding habits, dispositions and ways of thinking. (Millar, in Lehmann, 1960)

Social diversity is thus explicable in terms of an underlying structure consisting largely of economic factors. Millar's comparative approach, however, sought to analyse diversity and uniformity in terms of the change from 'rude' to 'polished' society. Similarly, Ferguson related forms of government to property, social stratification, division of labour and social conflict. Ferguson's standpoint was civil not political society. Thus the Scots' typology of societies: savage, barbaric and polished (Ferguson), hunting, pastoral, agricultural and commercial (Millar, Smith), constituted forms based on the dominant mode of production in each.

For Adam Smith, the development of a commercial society produced a social structure divided into three clear classes, landowners, capitalists and labourers, 'the three great and constituent orders of every civilised society'. Like Ferguson and Millar, Smith did not employ the concept of social class, but there can be no doubt that in his work, and that of Millar particularly, a theory of class as a sociological category is articulated. The relation between Smith's three social 'orders' and the economic elements is unambiguous: the three groups derive their revenue from rent, from stock and from wages. Property forms the basis of social differentiation, 'the natural source of influence and authority' closely bound up with social change and pervading 'every corner of society'. Millar argued, indeed, that social development necessarily engendered social inequality, ceaselessly introducing 'corresponding gradation and subordination of ranks'. An economic interpretation of history is suggested:

> The distribution of property among any people is the principal circumstance that contributed to reduce them under civil government, and to determine the form of their political constitution. The poor are naturally dependent on the rich, from whom they derive subsistence; and, according to the accidental differences of wealth possessed by individuals, a subordination of ranks is gradually introduced and different degrees of power are assumed without opposition, by particular persons. (Millar, in Lehmann, 1960)

Both Millar and Ferguson, aware of the relation of social stratification to the division of labour, treated work specialisation sociologically. Their analysis represented a sharp break from Montesquieu who, while noting its economic significance, minimised the social effects wrought by the division of labour and failed to grasp its broad, structural significance. Thus Ferguson pointed out that the division of labour was a social as well as an economic institution separating those whose function commanded skill from those for whom work required neither thought nor the exercise of 'ingenuity'. Work thus becomes more efficient 'under a total suppression of sentiment and reason' and where 'ignorance is the mother of industry as well as of superstition'. In a famous passage Ferguson wrote:

> Manufactures... prosper most where the mind is least consulted, and where the workshop may, without any great effort of imagination be considered as an engine, the parts of which are men. (Ferguson, 1966, pp. 182–3)

Manufacturing occupations, unlike the occupation of philosopher, stultify the human intellect; the more minute the task, the fewer the ideas; the more that men work the less time they have for thought and study. Social development is indeed double-edged. As Millar wrote:

> As their employments require constant attention to an object which can afford no variety of occupations to their minds, they are apt to acquire an habitual vacancy of thought, unenlivened by any prospects, but such as are derived from the future wages of their labour or from the grateful returns of bodily repose and sleep. (Millar, in Lehmann, 1960)

One of the unintended effects of industrial development, the consequence of a 'polished' society, is that humanity increasingly resembles a machine, stripped of its mental powers and 'converted to a mere instrument of labour'. Social development inevitably brings with it dehumanisation and alienation. It is their analysis of the transition from one stage of social development to another which lies at the heart of the Scottish contribution to sociological thought.

Social change was grasped as a collective not individual phenomenon involving the combined efforts of groups and generations together with physical situation, economic and political organisation. Property was the key factor. Such a rigorously deterministic concept of social development circumscribes the activity of the human agent, and, while Millar introduced accidental causes and personalities into his historical schema, the basic tendency is mechanistic. Yet Ferguson continually emphasised the active nature of the human agent, the natural disposition to 'remove inconveniences' and improve the situation. Man, he wrote, was 'not made for repose... every amiable and respectable quality is an active power... and all the lustre which he casts around him, to captivate or engage the attention of his fellow-creatures... shines only while his motion continues'. In opposition to the utilitarian concept of humanity as pleasure seeking, Ferguson noted that 'the most animating occasions of human life, are calls to danger and hardship, not invitations to safety and ease'. Moreover, without conflict there was no society, no structure, no process. Without 'the rivalship of nations and the practice of war', Ferguson wrote, 'civil society itself could scarcely have found an object or a form'. Conflict functions to strengthen social bonds and the sense of community.

Vico's 'voluntarism' thus finds an echo in these formulations, but the dualism implied in the concept of an active agent and determining environment was never adequately resolved. The important point is the way in which social change was conceived, as a process involving both an objective structure – especially the mode of production – and active subject. Change is dialectical in that it emerges as the largely unintended result of human action. 'Every step and every movement of the multitude', Ferguson wrote, 'are made with equal blindness to the future; and nations stumble on establishments, which are indeed the result of human action, but not the execution of human design' (Ferguson, 1966, p. 122). 'Vico's 'incontestable truth', takes on a sociological meaning in Ferguson's analysis. It is precisely in these formulations that Ferguson, of all the eighteenth-century writers, approaches a modern sociological standpoint.

Like Montesquieu, the writers of the Scottish Enlightenment emphasised the structural nature of social phenomena rejecting the view of society as the product of a haphazard and accidental process. In their notion of the unintended consequences of social action they went beyond the static limitations of Montesquieu to embrace a concept of society as both structure and process. It is this complex relation between human agent and structure which lies at the heart of the Scottish contribution to social theory and while many of the insights developed in the work of Ferguson, Millar and Smith would be lost in the subsequent emergence of nineteenth-century sociology, Vico, Montesquieu and Ferguson had laid the foundations and posed the essential problems of a science of human society, culture and historical change, of the relationship between human action, objective social structures and historical change. The study of society as an organised system developing through definite laws and stages had been established. The real history of sociology begins at this point with the work of Saint-Simon, Comte and the positivist tradition.

Empiricism and Positivism

The relation of the Enlightenment to the development of sociology involved both a philosophical emphasis on reason, freedom and individualism and the secular concepts of society and social development as objective, collective forces. Three broad streams of thought can be identified as contributing to nineteenth- and early twentieth-century sociology: first, Vico's humanism with its emphasis on the creative and active human subject and rejection of any simple application of natural science methods to social analysis; second, the materialist social theory of Montesquieu, Millar and Ferguson, concerned with objective facts and the relevance of natural science to the study of society; and finally, the Enlightenment *philosophes*, Voltaire, Diderot and Rousseau, whose critical rationalism was dedicated to a scientific understanding of the social world, a rationalism that would free the individual from superstitious beliefs and intellectual error. Both the Scottish and the French Enlightenment were built around the principles of modern science, the rejection of metaphysics, the need to separate facts from values, and a belief in the possibility of objectivity. Science was positive, based on facts not conjecture. Hence positivism formed an integral part of the Enlightenment tradition: science and facts opposed metaphysics and speculation; faith and revelation were no longer acceptable as sources of knowledge. Sociological positivism dates from the early nineteenth century in the work of Auguste Comte (1798–1857), but as a philosophical and sociological movement positivism embraced a number of different meanings which included a belief in science as the foundation of all knowledge (scientism as it has been called), the employment of statistical analysis in social theory, the search for causal explanations of social phenomena and the fundamental laws of historical change or of human nature. Eighteenth-century Enlightenment positivism was essentially critical and revolutionary, its fundamental tenets of philosophical individualism and human reason largely directed against the irrational powers of the Absolutist state and organised religion. Social institutions, it was argued, should accord with the principles of reason.

The transformation of this critical positivism into nineteenth-century sociological positivism occurred in post-revolutionary France. From its beginnings it opposed the individualistic atomism of Enlightenment philosophy. It needs emphasising that with the exception of Montesquieu and Ferguson eighteenth-century social thought had failed to develop a theory of society as a system and objective structure. A theory of society as a totality is fundamental to sociology as an independent empirical science; the relation of parts to whole constitutes the methodological axiom guiding research into the social role and functions of institutions such as religion and the family. It was precisely this concept which could not develop within a rationalist atomistic framework. Enlightenment philosophy minimised the significance of institutions which the *philosophes* had labelled irrational. In particular, the problem of continuity within change could not be posed adequately given the prevailing emphasis on human perfectability and progress. So-called irrational institutions, such as religion, formed in the historical past, could not be conceptualised in their active relation with the present: lacking a concept of society as a whole, rationalist thought defined religious ideas as peripheral and residual exercising no significant and *positive* role in the maintenance of society.

The French Revolution had the effect of challenging these rationalist assumptions. Enlightenment philosophy was judged deficient in its analysis of those traditional institutions which effectively create the social bonds necessary for a functioning society. Edmund Burke (1729–97), Louis de Bonald (1754–1840) and Joseph de Maistre (1754–1821) were three influential critics of philosophical rationalism who rejected the individualistic concept of society developed by the Enlightenment philosophers, identifying its 'negative' and 'critical' principles with the collapse of traditional modes of authority and the organic nature of social bonds.

Society was defined as an organic whole in which 'irrational' and traditional elements played an active, constitutive role. Religion and the family were integral parts of the whole. The Enlightenment slogan of the natural rights of man and the rational principles enshrined in the social contract theory were rejected in favour of a concept of society which emphasised hierarchy, duty and the collective good. As de Bonald expressed it: 'The schools of modern philosophy... have produced the philosophy of modern man, the philosophy of I... I want to produce the philosophy of social man, the philosophy of we.' As an organism, society was defined in terms of its inner 'spirit' or 'soul', an essence fundamentally religious in nature. De Bonald and Maistre thus developed a concept of expressive whole, the various parts manifesting the inner essence and spirit. All elements of the organic whole were integrally linked as expressions of an irreducible essence.

Linked with this organic notion of totality was the ejection of empirical science as the means of analysing social forms. For Maistre and de Bonald society was apprehended through intuition, not reason or science. This belief in intuition and feeling is linked with attempts to discover a new source of political authority in the post-revolutionary world that followed the collapse of the old regime. Revolution and industrialism were creating a new form of society, one in which the old traditional values no longer held sway. The result was a concept of society which emphasised the creative role of the family, corporations and a hierarchical structure of authority similar to the rigid estate system of feudalism. It was through these institutions that the individual participated in the social whole, the 'I' transformed into a 'we'. The post-revolutionary critique of emerging industrial society was thus couched in terms of pre-industrial organic values: modern society was conceived as a calculating, individualistic system built around pragmatic, material values and interests with authority vested in formal rules and written contracts. Such a society could eventuate only in the collapse of social bonds and render problematic the organic relation of the individual to the collective.

Society did not consist in an aggregate of individuals: rather it was the expression of a whole culture, a collective concept which decisively influenced the sociological positivism of Auguste Comte. Only positivism, wrote Comte, provided the necessary basis for the new society pointing the way forward from 'the critical condition in which most civilised nations are now living'. Ideas were of paramount importance either governing the world or throwing it into chaos:

> The great political and moral crisis that societies are now undergoing is shown by the rigid analysis to arise out of intellectual anarchy... whenever the necessary agreement on first principles can be obtained, appropriate institutions will issue from them, without shock or resistance; for the causes of disorder will have been arrested by the mere fact of the agreement. It is in this direction that most must look who desire a natural and regular... state of society. (Andreski, 1978, pp. 37–8)

Comte's preoccupation with the question of social order and progress developed within a sociological framework that owed much to the work of de Bonald and Maistre, notably their emphasis on the nature of the social bond. The problems of the post-revolutionary age could be resolved only through the application of positive science and the principles of industrial organisation derived from the empirical study of social development. The work of Henri Saint-Simon was decisive in this process.

The Concept of Industrial Society: Saint-Simon

Saint-Simon (1760–1825) introduced the term industrial society into European social theory. He defined the process of industrialism as essentially pacific in contrast to the militaristic spirit of feudal society. Saint-Simon was particularly concerned with the transition from feudal societies, structured around consumption, to industrial societies centred around production. Saint-Simon's status in the history of sociology has always been ambivalent: on the one hand, his concept of industrial society emphasised the centrality of social classes, the importance of property and the structural significance of the division of labour in the process of class formation. His collectivist notion of society was broadly socialist and materialist; but, on the other hand, Saint-Simon's analysis of technology and the role of science and intellectual élites – mostly composed of scientists and industrialists – combined with his theory of moral crisis suggests a conservative standpoint close to the sociological positivism of Comte. In a very general sense Saint-Simon can be claimed as an influence on both nineteenth-century sociology and the development of socialism and Marxism. What is not in doubt, however, is that Saint-Simon's work represents the first serious attempt to address the problems of modernity, the emerging separation of state and civil society, the development of a public sphere consisting of economic, political and cultural institutions independent of centralised, bureaucratic administration. More emphatically than Adam Smith, Saint-Simon defined the state administration as parasitic and hostile to the needs of production and the newly emerging social classes engendered by the process of industrialism. By its nature, he wrote, mankind was destined to live in society, first under governmental or military regimes and then, with the triumph of the positive sciences and industry, under an administrative and industrial regime.

It was Saint-Simon who coined the terms 'social physiology' and 'social physics' to describe his 'positivist' method of analysis built around science and the growth of systematic social knowledge especially in relation to the laws which regulated the social whole. Saint-Simon's model of society was thus holistic: he defined a 'healthy' society as one in which the various parts subsisted in a state of functional harmony with the whole. Social health was closely identified with production and the role of the productive social classes. Saint-Simon described industrial society in terms of collaboration and consensus: under the old system force constituted the means of social cohesion, but industrial society creates partners not subjects and associated modes of co-operation involving labourers and the wealthiest property owners. The principles of free production generate moral solidarity. Saint-Simon contrasted the authority structure of feudal society, in which corporations symbolised coercion, with the unequal, hierarchical nature of industrial society arguing that industrial institutions were, by their nature, both functional and spontaneous. Society would become a vast workshop organised around the production of goods, and authority transformed from authority over individuals to authority over things.

Modernity had abolished the legitimating role of tradition and Saint-Simon raised one of the fundamental issues of later sociology – the problem of social integration in complex, highly differentiated societies. Traditional authority could no longer legitimise political forms: a moral vacuum therefore arose within modern society. Saint-Simon rejected the view of the political economists that the market worked to harmonise different and often conflicting interests into a social and therefore moral unity. Social cohesion would not flow from the free play of purely economic forces. Industrial society required a strong moral centre which he described in his last work, *The New Christianity* (1825), as a secular religion opposed to the egoism of philosophical individualism and functioning through a priesthood of artists, scientists and industrial leaders whose interests were identical with those of the masses.

Social regulation is thus described as a process directed from above by an élite of intellectuals. Although Saint-Simon's image of industrial society was one of co-operative enterprise, he defined industrial society as a system organised around the principles of functional hierarchy, rational discipline and selective leadership. Industrial society was not a communist Utopia but an hierarchical structure which produced a new governing class of scientists associated with the spiritual realm, and industrialists with the temporal, together creating the leadership and the values necessary for a functioning modern society.

There is, here, an authoritarian strand to Saint-Simon's thought, a distrust of democracy and representative institutions, a lack of confidence in the masses, or the people, to create for themselves a culture of self-government. His distinction between productive (industrial proprietors, investors and bankers) and non-productive, or 'idle' classes (the military, nobility, lawyers and those living off profits) is polemical rather than sociological, his main concern was always with those who produced and those who consumed. Those producing 'useful' things were the only valuable members of society and for this reason politics was defined as the science of production and the new society, emerging from the ruins of post-revolutionary Europe, industrial, technocratic and undemocratic.

Comte and Sociological Positivism

Saint-Simon did not develop a distinctive sociology. Auguste Comte (1798–1857) who, at one time acted as Saint-Simon's secretary publishing his early works under Saint-Simon's name, founded the first comprehensive system of sociology, one that was strongly influenced by the work of Saint-Simon and his belief in science and technology (elements found in eighteenth-century philosophers of history and champions of progress such as Turgot

(1727–81) and Condorcet (1743–1794)), and 'that immortal school' of de Bonald and Maistre with their concept of society as an organic, harmonious whole composed, like medieval society, of different and static social orders. Comte attempted to reconcile the anti-atomistic theories of de Bonald and Maistre with the rationalist concept of progress and notion of the perfectability of man. Like Saint-Simon, Comte's work was produced at a critical period of French history, the period following the Revolution in which the old regime had disintegrated and a new industrial regime was in the process of formation. Comte's sociological positivism was forged at the same time as Balzac was describing in fictional form the irresistible rise of the industrialists and the bankers within a French culture still permeated by the old aristocratic values.

Comte never held a full-time academic position. Sociology was not yet institutionalised; Frederic Le Play, who wrote a massive study of the European family during the 1850s and the leading French sociologist before Durkheim, attained an academic position but only as a Professor of Mining. Comte remained a marginal figure in French intellectual culture, ridiculed in academic circles, suffering from periodic bouts of madness and enduring the indignity of being listed as deceased in a contemporary bibliography. J. S. Mill, who corresponded with Comte, argued that his influence in the development of social science was greater than his actual achievements and that, while not creating sociology as a science, Comte's work nevertheless made it possible. Thus, although Comte's interpreters note his strong conservative bias and deprecate the influence on his sociology of Maistre and de Bonald as well as 'the illustrious Gall' (1758–1828), as he described the founder of phrenology, his place within the history of sociology is guaranteed by his attempts to explain the origin and growth of industrial society and his analysis of the social effects of the division of labour, increasing wealth and development of individualism and his rejection of metaphysics in favour of positive empirical methods in the study of social facts. Yet these elements had already been widely discussed by eighteenth-century writers such as Ferguson, Millar and Montesquieu: the Scots especially had provided a detailed empirical account of the emergence of industrial society, social class, social conflict, the division of labour and the mechanics of social change. Since Comte knew the work of Adam Smith and Ferguson, it is obviously important to grasp the ways in which his own approach differs from theirs and assess the extent to which Comte's sociological positivism assimilated and developed this proto-sociology.

Comte's attitude to the Enlightenment was ambivalent: although he accepted the theory of progress, especially Condorcet's notion of social evolution developing through the workings of specific natural laws, he rejected eighteenth-century philosophic rationalism abhorring its 'negative' attacks on the values of traditional authority and morality, on religious institutions and the family. In particular he rejected the Enlightenment view that pre-industrial society, especially the Middle Ages, constituted the dark age of civilisation. For Comte, Condorcet's one-sided devaluing of the past in his *Sketch for a*

Historical Picture of the Progress of the Human Mind (1794), was rounded out by the positive approach of Maistre and de Bonald:

> Right upon the subject were impossible... until full justice had been rendered to the Middle Ages, which form at once the point of union and separation between ancient and modern history. Now it was quite impossible to do this as long as the excitement of the first years of the revolution lasted. In this respect the philosophical reaction organised at the beginning of the century by the great de Maistre was of material assistance in preparing the true theory of progress. His school was of brief duration, and it was no doubt animated by a retrograde spirit; but it will always be ranked among the necessary antecedents of the positive system. (Comte, 1877, Vol. 1, p. 50)

Comte's *Cours de Philosophie Positive* (1830–42) is essentially an attack on the 'negative' philosophy developed by eighteenth-century individualistic philosophy. He agreed with Saint-Simon that the eighteenth century had destroyed rather than provided the foundations for a 'new edifice'. This new structure was to be directed exclusively in the interests of social order and social consensus. The 'essential aim of practical politics', he wrote, was 'to avoid the violent revolutions which spring from obstacles opposed to the progress of civilisation'.

From the beginning, the *Cours* set itself the task of social reorganisation: writing from within a society which appeared close to anarchy, it seemed obvious to Comte that 'true science' was nothing less than 'the establishment of intellectual order, which is the basis of every other order'. Comte's positivism, a science of stability and social reconstruction can thus be seen on one level as a response to the negative and critical traditions of Enlightenment philosophy by seeking to unite the notions of order and progress. The task of social physics would be wholly positive:

> Under the rule of the positive spirit... all the difficult and delicate questions which now keep up a perpetual irritation in the bosom of society, and can never be settled while mere political solutions are proposed, will be scientifically estimated, to the great furtherance of social peace... the positive spirit tends to consolidate order, by the rational development of a wise resignation to incurable political evils. A true resignation... can proceed from a deep sense of the connection of all kinds of natural phenomena with invariable natural laws. If there are political evils which... cannot be remedied by science, science at least proves to us that they are incurable, so as to calm our restlessness under pain by the conviction that it is by natural laws that they are rendered insurmountable. (Comte, 1896, Vol. 2, pp. 185–7)

On this definition, therefore, sociology prescribes a wholly passive and fatalistic orientation to the social world and contrasts sharply with Vico's injunction that the social world was the work of humanity. The active relation of human labour and thought to the development and transformation of social forms is effectively assimilated to a theory of objective, determining facts. The polemical thrust of Comte's positivism is thus clear: but what of his concept of science?

Sociology was defined in its relations with other sciences and Comte's stated aim was the synthesis of all available knowledge, a task facilitated by the law of three stages and hierarchical classification of the sciences. Both these conceptions had been stated by previous writers notably Turgot, Condorcet and Saint-Simon: in their beginnings, wrote Saint-Simon, all the sciences are conjectural but end by being positive, developing from the simple to the complex. Comte systematised these arguments, tracing the evolution of the sciences in great detail. All human thought, he argued, has passed through three separate stages, the theological, the metaphysical and the positive. In the theological state the human mind seeks for origins and final causes, analysing all phenomena as the result of supernatural forces; feelings and imagination predominate and Comte divided the theological state into three separate periods of fetishism (nature defined in terms of man's feelings), polytheism (a multitude of gods and spirits) and, finally, monotheism (the existence of one God and the gradual awakening of human reason with its constraint on the imagination). For Comte, each stage and substage of evolution necessarily develops out of the preceding one: the final substage of monotheism prepares the way for the metaphysical stage in which human thought is dominated by abstract concepts, by essences and ideal forms. In the final stage of evolution thought abandons essences and seeks laws which link different facts together through the methods of observation and experiment; absolute notions of causes are abandoned and the emphasis shifts to the study of facts and their invariable relations of succession and resemblance. Each science develops in exactly the same way passing through these separate stages, but they do so at different rates: knowledge reaches the positive stage in proportion to the generality, simplicity and independence of other disciplines. As the most general and simple of the natural sciences, astronomy develops first, followed by physics, chemistry, biology and sociology. Each science develops only on the basis of its predecessors within an hierarchical framework dominated by the law of increasing complexity and decreasing generality.

Sociology is particularly dependent on its immediate predecessor in the hierarchy, biology. The science of biology is basically holistic in character beginning not from isolated elements, as in chemistry and physics, but from organic wholes. The distinctive subject matter of sociology is society as a whole, society defined as a social system. Sociology is thus the investigation of the action and reaction of the various parts of the social system. Individual elements must be analysed in their relation to the whole, in their mutual relation and combination. As with biological organisms, society forms a complex unity irreducible to its component parts: society cannot be decomposed into individuals any more than 'a geometric surface can be decomposed into lines, or a line into a point'. Knowledge of the parts can flow only from knowledge of the whole, not vice versa.

Society was defined, therefore, as a collective organism characterised by a harmony between its individual parts and whole. The analogy between biology and sociology is constantly reiterated:

> in biology, we may decompose structure anatomically into *elements, tissues* and *organs.* We have the same things in the social organism... forms of social power correspond to the *tissue*... the *element*... is supplied by the family, which is more completely the germ of society than the cell or fibre of the body... *organs* can only be *cities* the root of the word being the nucleus of the term civilization. (Comte, 1877, Vol. 2, pp. 223–6)

Although Comte warns against pushing the analogy too far – cities are organic wholes themselves or aspire to be so – his theory of social order derives almost entirely from biology, especially his concepts of harmony, equilibrium and social pathology. Pathological situations develop within the social organism, for example, when the natural laws governing the principles of harmony or succession are disturbed by elements analogous to diseases in the bodily organism. Social evolution proceeds in accordance with biological laws and the general intent of Comte's positivism is to subordinate the study of society to biological concepts. The absence of a spontaneous harmony between the parts and the whole of the social system indicates the existence of social pathology. Harmony is consensus; conflict is equated with pathology. While Ferguson had rejected the biological analogy, Comte assimilated biological terms and models to his sociology arguing that the distinction between anatomy and physiology enabled sociology to differentiate structure from function, dynamics from statics, social order from social progress. All living beings exist under dynamic and static relations: statics investigates the laws of action and reaction of the different parts of the social system which 'normally' produce an equilibrium between parts and whole, a functional interrelationship of social institutions. Comte's notion of statics is concerned with clarifying the interconnection between social facts functional for a social system such as the division of labour, the family, religion and government and is clearly synchronic in nature. Dynamics is the empirical study of these interconnections as they change in different types of society and Comte describes this aspect of sociology as the historical method.

Comte describes the historical method as specific to sociology. It is clearly important to grasp what he meant by this term since it suggests a movement from analogical representations of societies to empirical analysis of social processes. 'If the historical comparisons of the different periods of civilization are to have any scientific character', he wrote, 'they must be referred to general social evolution' (Comte, 1896, Vol. 2, pp. 252–7). The comparative method belongs to statics, the historical method to dynamics. He defined the comparative method as:

> The comparison of different co-existing states of human society on the various parts of the world's surface – those states being completely independent of each other. (Comte, 1896, Vol. 2, p. 250)

The historical method links these states of society with evolution through the dynamic laws of social development which effectively relate to the growing solidarity and unity of society structured in the co-operative functions of the division of labour and the universal principles enshrined in religion and language. Social evolution, in other words, works through the existence of certain invariable laws which synthesise order and progress. It is in this sense that Comte repudiates empiricism. Sociology is not a science which accumulates mere desultory facts but seeks to interpret and connect them with each other through theory: facts are not strictly speaking based on observation but are constructed by the guiding hand of theory. Real knowledge can never be based on observed facts alone but on laws which connect all social phenomena through resemblance and succession. No real observation is possible, wrote Comte, 'except in as far as it is first directed, and finally interpreted, by some theory'. Observation and laws are 'indispensably connected' (Comte, 1896, Vol. 2, p. 243).

Comte's awareness that facts and theory are mutually connected makes him the first theoretical sociologist who was thoroughly sceptical that observed facts will, as it were, speak for themselves. But the theory which Comte developed was essentially a speculative theory of historical change, a philosophy of history. The result was a conception of the historical method, extremely abstract and non-historical: specific historical events, and the specifically historical character of institutions, fell outside the framework of sociological positivism. States of development are abstractly conceived, the sequences are conceptual and ideal, neither empirical nor chronological. One result of Comte's abstract formulations of the historical method and the distinction between static and dynamics was to separate the study of concrete events, or facts, from the study of social change as an historical category.

Positivism and Determinism

All social phenomena are subject to invariable laws and once these have been scientifically established humanity must, from necessity, submit to their dictation. Science makes possible social control and Comte defined 'true liberty' as the 'rational submission' of the individual to the laws of nature. Positivist sociology effectively abolishes 'the absolute liberty of the revolutionary school... and, by establishing social principles, will meet the need at once of order and progress'. From science comes 'prevision' and from 'prevision comes action', for 'to see in order to foresee is the business of science'. Eighteenth-century philosophy had laid the foundations of social science through the law of human progress, while the French Revolution had generated the need for order.

What Comte's 'wise resignation' means in practice is a submission to the facts of inequality within the emerging industrial society. The law of progress, as Comte described it, clearly affected social groups differently. Thus in his discussion of the role of the working class Comte described their 'inevitable lot' as existing on the 'precarious fruits' of labour and to suffer constant deprivation. Positivist sociology, while recognising this as a 'great social problem', would seek to ameliorate the workers' condition, but not at the cost of 'destroying its classification and disturbing the general economy' (Comte, 1896, Vol. 3, pp. 36–7). In his early writings of the 1820s Comte agreed with Saint-Simon's argument that the aftermath of the French Revolution had created a spiritual vacuum and absence of 'any moral discipline whatsoever'. The result was a state of 'anomie', a condition of normlessness, of deregulation. Saint-Simon's solution – an ethic of universal love – a new Christianity – in Comte's work became the Religion of Humanity, interposing itself as a remedial agency between the working classes and the governing classes. In this way the economic and political 'imperfections' of modern society, the products of 'intellectual and moral disorder' and the prevailing states of consciousness were resolved. What particularly concerned Comte was the maldistribution of wealth since it provided 'a most dangerous theme to both agitators and dreamers'. Only by convincing humanity of the superiority of moral over political solutions would these 'quacks and dreamers' relinquish their 'dangerous vocation'. The solution to inequality and class differences and interests was the organic society in which the positive concept of 'duties' replaced the negative concept of 'rights'. A moral education would inculcate an awareness of the individual's rightful social status: the subordination of the working classes to their employers would be seen as resting wholly on their less 'extensive actions' and responsibilities. And, once established, this gradation would be acceptable because of its clear principles and awareness that the working classes are 'privileged in that freedom from care... which would be a serious fault in the higher classes, but which is natural to them'. Following Saint-Simon, Comte conceived industrial society as a system dominated by the moral influence of a 'speculative' stratum of scientists and philosophers, in which capital is 'useful to society at large' thus rendering the distribution of property unimportant to 'popular interests' (Comte, 1896, Vol. 3, pp. 313–35).

Comte was particularly critical of previous social theorists who had minimised the crucial, constituting role played by these 'spiritual' elements.

Only morality provides an adequate regulation of economic activity, only morality can sustain social harmony. For Comte, the 'essential vice' of nineteenth-century political economy, for example, was its tendency to define social order in natural terms as the expression of market forces and thus free of regulation by artificial (positivist) institutions.

Yet although Comte disagreed with the *laissez-faire* principles of classical political economy, he accepted its pessimistic and largely negative conclusions on the social consequences of an advanced division of labour. Specialisation of work, while an essential element of an advanced society, tends to 'restrict human understanding' and promote ignorance and squalor among the working classes. Comte cited the example of pin manufacture: workers engaged in this tedious and routine labour cannot develop their faculties to the full with the result, 'a miserable indifference about the general course of 'human affairs' and a fundamental 'dispersion' of ideas, sentiments and interests. Comte drew a radically different conclusion from the political economists, arguing that the division of work necessarily entails moral regulation by external institutions.

Comte's solution to the problem of the division of labour was the institution of 'wise government' with its principles fundamentally religious and universal thus consecrating and regulating command and obedience. Civil society itself is judged incapable of generating from within its own spontaneously developed institutions the values necessary for social cohesion. Comte's distrust of democratic institutions is explicit; society is to be regulated from above. Humanity must learn to accept inequality and the natural laws of social subordination.

Comte's sociological positivism strips the division of labour of its *negative* effects and transforms it into an agency of social harmony although regulated by an élite of positivist intellectuals. Conflict relations engendered by the division of labour as constituting a source of social change was simply unthinkable. By emphasising the essentially religious nature of social bonds Comte advocated moral solutions that were conformist and ideological. Comte's positivism celebrates industrial society in its early capitalist form as the end of history: humanity must accept its place within the natural order of things and adapt to the necessary equilibrium between parts and wholes.

Like the socialists of his day, therefore, Comte accepted the structural significance of the industrial working class but differed from their analysis by his stress on the inevitable laws of social evolution which point to their integration into an unequal society. There was no question of class organisation and practice: the individual might 'modify' the course of social development and assert a freedom of action over 'blind fatality', but ultimately the natural laws of society are higher in their practical efficacy than human action. Social evolution, which for Comte was the progressive development of the human mind as it finds its expression in the three stages, is thus a process without a subject, a universal history of humanity which claims the importance of knowledge for the ends of social reorganisation, but subordinates the individual to the inevitable 'realities' of social life: the needs of order and progress.

Evolution and Sociological Positivism: Mill and Spencer

Comte had laid the foundations of a sociological positivism which was to remain the dominant paradigm during the course of the nineteenth century. But the positivism which developed after Comte took two forms: first, the widely accepted view that the methods of the social sciences were no different from those of the natural sciences involving the establishing of laws, the employment of experiment and observation and the elimination of the subjective element in social analysis – society was defined in terms of an organism evolving through the workings of specific natural laws. And second, the increasing awareness of empirical method and the value of statistics in the framing of hypotheses and modes of validation. Both forms of sociological positivism emphasised the necessity of eliminating philosophical concepts such as free will, intention and individual motives from social science and establishing sociology as an objective science.

Thus John Stuart Mill (1807–73) in his *System of Logic* (1976 [1843]) accepted Comte's basic sociological principles, the theory of stages, the distinction between dynamics and statics, the historical method of analysis and the concept of consensus. Comte's main conclusions, he wrote, were in all essentials 'irrefragable'. He also agreed with Comte's scientism arguing that there was no fundamental difference between the methods of the natural and the social sciences.

Unlike Comte, however, Mill believed in the importance of psychology and to this end he advanced the claims of ethology as the science of the laws of human nature. Psychology was not part of Comte's hierarchy of the sciences; he believed that Gall's 'cerebral physiology' explained the source of thought and mind in terms of its physical location in the brain. But Mill argued that all social phenomena were structured in the laws governing the drives and motives of human nature. Describing his approach as the 'inverted-deductive' method, Mill argued that social science consisted of the empirical laws of sociology, demonstrated in statistical studies and surveys, the laws of psychology, derived less from empirical studies than philosophical reflection, and finally, linking the sociology and the psychology, the laws of ethology, the fundamental laws governing human nature:

> The laws of the phenomena of society are, and can be, nothing but the laws
> of actions and passions of human beings united together in the social

state... obedient to the laws of individual human nature. Men are not, when brought together, converted into another kind of substance with different properties as hydrogen and oxygen are different from water. (Mill, 1976)

Human nature is thus fixed: the socio-historical context constantly changes so that the task of positivist social science lay in explaining empirical observations and sociological laws by deductions from the universal law of human nature. In effect, Mill proposed a reduction of the specifically social to the psychological:

All phenomena of society are phenomena of human nature generated by the action of outward circumstances upon masses of human beings. (Mill, 1976)

If human thought and action are dependent on fixed laws then clearly all social phenomena must conform to similar fixed laws. From this standpoint it is not surprising that Mill failed to develop either a systemic concept of society or an adequate sociological theory of social structure, social institutions and social change.

In contrast to Mill's positivistic nominalism the positivist organicism of Herbert Spencer (1820–1903), combined, within a broad evolutionary model of social development, a notion of society as both system and as an aggregate of individuals. Spencer's main focus lay on the evolutionary growth of social structures and institutions not mental states. Comte, he wrote, accounts for 'the progress of human conceptions... ideas' and seeks to interpret 'our knowledge of nature'; in contrast, 'my aim' is to account for 'the progress of the external world... of things' and to interpret 'the genesis of the phenomena which constitute nature'. Comte is criticised for emphasising subjective over objective. Nevertheless, as Comte sought to unify all knowledge in his hierarchy of the sciences, so Spencer aimed to unify all knowledge in his concept of evolution. The evolution of humanity was Spencer's theme in which society constituted a special instance of a universal law. 'There can be no complete acceptance of sociology as a science, so long as the belief in a social order not conforming to natural law, survives' (Spencer, 1965, Ch. XVI).

Spencer's model of society was organismic. Societies were like living bodies which evolve out of a state of undifferentiated unity to highly complex, differentiated structures in which the individual parts, while becoming more autonomous and specialised, nevertheless come increasingly to depend on each other. This interdependence of parts implies integration; for 'unlike parts' are 'so related as to make one another possible' and come to form an aggregate 'constituted on the same general principle as is an individual organism'. In simple societies the lack of differentiation means that the same individuals are both hunter and warriors. Society thus develops through progressive changes in the *structure* and *functions* of its basic institutions;

social evolution does not depend on individual intentions and motives. Thus, from a state of homogeneity, human society *naturally* develops to a state of complex heterogeneity, a process which Spencer saw as characteristic of the inorganic world of matter, where evolution begins, the organic world of nature, and finally the living organisms in society, the last stage of evolution.

Spencer identified three laws of evolution: the law of 'the persistence of force' or the conservation of energy, from which is derived the law of the indestructibility of matter and the law of the continuity of motion. The notion of the persistence of force forms the basis of Spencer's deductive system: the universe is characterised by a continual redistribution of matter and motion in terms of the processes of evolution and dissolution. Spencer noted four secondary propositions to these three laws: that laws are uniform in their workings; that force is transformed never lost; that everything moves along the line of least resistance or the greatest attraction; and finally, the principle of the rhythm, or alteration, of motion. All these laws and propositions are governed by the law of universal evolution which states that with the integration of matter, motion is dissipated and as matter becomes differentiated motion is absorbed: 'Evolution is an integration of matter and a concomitant dissipation of motion during which the matter passes from a relatively indefinite, incoherent homogeneity to a relatively coherent heterogeneity and during which the retained motion undergoes a parallel transformation' (Spencer, 1965).

The evolution of society is defined by Spencer as the gradual socialisation of humanity, a process occurring independently of human practice. The actual origin of human society is located as the result of population pressure which compelled individuals to enter the social state and thus develop both social organisation and social feelings. But having identified the genesis of society Spencer analysed social formations in terms of the biological analogy. As with Comte the historical dimension of society disappears; the organismic analogy has the effect of emphasising synchronic rather than diachronic analysis.

Spencer's ahistorical and anti-humanist perspective is especially brought out in his frequent defence of the concept of the social organism which he sometimes defined as a useful analogy and at other times as a reality. Thus in *The Principles of Sociology* (1969b [1873]) he writes that it is the character of both living and social bodies 'that while they increase in size they increase in structure', that as they acquire greater mass their parts multiply and differentiate. And in his article, 'The Social Organism' (1969a [1860]), he defined society as a 'thing' which grows, evolving from small 'aggregations' so simple 'in structure as to be considered structureless' in which there is 'scarcely any mutual dependence of parts', to complex, differentiated structures in which the separate parts acquire mutual and functional dependence: society is a structure characterised by co-operation between parts and whole. Should anything 'disturb' this consensus, Spencer adds, the equilibrium of the whole system is endangered (that is, if government artificially interferes with the workings of economic and social life). Although noting the differences between the biological organism and society – the parts are more dispersed and independent from the centre of society, individual members may die but the whole persists, in the biological organism the elements exist for the good of the whole while in the social organism the whole exists for the good of its members – Spencer tended to equate the two:

> While comparison makes definite the obvious contrasts between organisms… and the social organism, it shows that even these contrasts are not so decided as was to be expected… Societies slowly augment in mass; they progress in complexity of structure; at the same time their parts become more mutually dependent… The principles of organisation are the same, and the differences are simply differences of application. (Spencer, 1969a, p. 206)

Spencer distinguished 'militant' from 'industrial' societies in terms of this holistic approach. Militant societies were defined as lacking complex structural differentiation, dominated by a centralised state, rigid hierarchies of status and a tendency towards conformism; industrial societies, developing through the general law of evolution, were more complex and structurally differentiated and characterised by a multiplicity of beliefs, independent institutions, decentralisation and a tendency to individualisation. The organismic analogy, however, prevented Spencer from grasping the contradictions and conflicts of interest which industrial society actually engendered: unlike Ferguson, who rejected the organismic analogy, he failed to integrate the dialectical elements of social change into the holistic model, that evolution creates both differentiation of structure and differentiation of interest, that parts become independent through collective social organisation and the development of a common awareness by the members of different specialised organisations, and that their interests differ from the interests of others. Spencer had no conception of interest as a collective phenomenon, as class interest, group interest, and so on. Rather, interests were conceived strictly in terms of *laissez-faire* individualism, that although society consisted of different, atomistic interests they nevertheless harmonised into a unity through the operation of a 'hidden hand' which synthesised private interests with the common good. Individuals seek private ends but because such actions take place within a complex society built on the interdependence of institutions, the human agent unconsciously and unintentionally serves the higher needs of society as a whole. In this way Spencer attempted to reconcile his sociological individualism with his collective concept of the social organism.

One consequence of this argument was a rejection of social regulation as conceived by Comte and the forms of state intervention which Spencer saw increasingly dominating industrial society. For Spencer, society was regulated adequately if individuals were allowed to pursue their own interests free of collectivist intervention. Hence his hostility to state education, state medicine, the provision of free public libraries: institutions which 'artificially' preserve its 'feeblest members' lower the moral and intellectual standards of society as a whole. Spencer remained rigorously individualistic in his conception of human society. In *The Principles of Sociology*, discussing the controversy between nominalists and realists, he argued that society was essentially 'a collective name for a number of individuals' and that there 'is no way of coming at a true theory of society but by inquiring into the nature of its component individuals' (Spencer, (1969b [1873]), Ch. VI). In one important sense, therefore, Spencer's positivistic organicism and sociological individualism failed to develop much beyond Mill's psychological reductionism: on the one hand, society constituted the sum of individual actions and sociological analysis must focus on the biological and psychological characteristics of individuals; on the other hand, society was a system, a complex, highly differentiated structure consisting of phenomena that had evolved at the superorganic level. Spencer's sociology could not resolve this dualism, the conflict between a biological and evolutionary determinism and a profound belief in individual human action as the source of unity and social harmony. As Peel has observed, 'Spencer had no real sense of either the historical actor, or the sociologist, intervening or participating in the flow of events'. The pattern of evolution could not be changed by 'any "extra-evolutionary" action' (Peel, 1971, p. 164).

Spencer's sociological system, his concept of evolution as a cosmic process, his sociological individualism and organicist holism had no deep, lasting effects: some of his ideas crossed the Atlantic and found a congenial reception within early American sociology, but European sociology, in the general reaction against positivism at the close of the nineteenth century, debated with Spencer's theories (especially Simmel and Durkheim), only to salvage such basic sociological concepts as structure, function, system, equilibrium, institution. Nevertheless, the anti-historical bias of Spencer's sociology influenced the later synchronically oriented sociologists and deflected attention away from those structural elements in societies which, through conflict and differential interests, promote social change. Spencer's organicist positivism, however, did succeed in grasping society as a structure, a system, and he was one of the first social theorists to identify industrialism with a new, decentred mode of social organisation. In this respect he differed sharply from the centralising notion of society developed by Comte. Indeed, Spencer's lasting contribution to sociological theory may well be his notion that an advanced society – industrial society – built around increasing differentiation of structure and differentiation of function and reciprocal relations between different institutions as well as between parts and whole, necessarily lacks a single, dominant centre. Comparing the social and the biological organism he noted that 'while in the individual organism there is but one centre of consciousness… there are, in the social organism, as many centres as there are individuals' (Spencer, 1969a, p. 282). Spencer expressed the concept of decentred structure in atomistic terms but it is, nevertheless, an important insight. The implicit focus of Spencer's sociology is on civil society and its separation from the state. Of course, his synchronic, individualistic approach prevented a profound theorisation of the historical, systemic and contradictory nature of modern industrial society, that as industrialism expands the framework and frees the institutions of civil society, it simultaneously generates centralising trends within the state itself. Spencer's concept of industrialism and social differentiation could be said to be deficient in one important respect: that it failed to grasp the historical specificity of industrialism as class structured, as a capitalist process.

2

Marxism: A Critical Science of Capitalist Development

Comte's theory of historical change had emphasised the concept of determinate laws, that history necessarily moved through a succession of stages culminating in the scientific epoch of positivism. For Comte, as with Montesquieu, Smith and Ferguson, social change was not a random process dependent on purely subjective and accidental elements, but the result of an underlying structure of forces – material and moral – that generated both direction and meaning. As was argued in the previous chapter, many of Comte's fundamental ideas were derived from Saint-Simon, but Saint-Simon's writings contain both positivistic and socialist elements. The development of socialism as both an intellectual current and socio-political movement owed much to the influence of Saint-Simon's followers. The Saint-Simonian school, in particular the writings of Enfantin and Bazard, argued that production must be socially organised, run by the producers themselves (not the parasitic 'idlers' and 'unproductive classes'), and society develop from rule by government and military organisation to administrative and industrial rule. During the 1830s this notion of the socialisation of production, and therefore of private property, became the cornerstone of socialist theory: employed for the first time by the Saint-Simonian Pierre Leroux in 1832, socialism demanded the abolition of private property rights, the elimination of poverty, the assertion of equality and the organisation of production through the agency of the state.

Positivist sociology and socialist theory thus share a common source even though both socialism and sociology, as theories of social and political organisation, existed before they were named. But it was only during the crucial period between 1789 and 1830, in response to rapid political and economic changes, that the intellectual and institutional basis of sociology and socialism were laid as expressions of a developing opposition to the dominant ideas of political liberalism, individualism and the market economy.

Nineteenth-century socialism and sociology emerged after the intellectual consolidation of classical political economy largely in response to its doctrine of the immanent rationality of individual interests: sociologists and socialists both agreed that the private pursuit of interests must eventuate in the collapse of social and moral solidarity; the anarchy of the market place could not lead to social cohesion and stability. Comte's solution was authoritarian moral leadership; the Saint-Simonians demanded a socialised system of production. But socialist ideas made little impact on the nascent labour movement which developed rapidly after the ending of the French revolutionary wars. In England working-class leaders worked closely with the bourgeoisie, advocating liberal rather than socialist ideas in opposition to the political domination of the aristocracy. The success of the 1832 Reform Act had the effect of separating the working-class movement from the bourgeoisie and instituting a distinct socialist alternative – Owenism and the Chartists in England, the Saint-Simonian school and Fourier in France. Both Robert Owen and Charles Fourier insisted on the necessity for co-operation not competition as the means of social organisation, advocating the development of communities in which the worker would enjoy 'the fruits of his labour' to the full.

The early socialists tended to offer a moralising and Utopian critique of industrial capitalism, that as labour constituted the only source of value everyone, apart from the 'unproductive' workers, should work together and produce a society based on mutuality rather than private gain. The capitalist was effectively depriving the worker of that which was his own, an action clearly immoral and socially divisive. The solution was thus social transformation through moral criticism and action, a standpoint which led Engels to characterise Owen, Fourier and others as 'Utopian' not scientific socialists. In the sense that pre-Marxist socialism lacked both a theory of social change and a grasp of society in terms of the relations between economic organisation and the social and political system then it was Utopian, basing the necessity for socialism on changes in human nature. And, of course, it was precisely the scientific grasp of social change that Engels admired in the work of Saint-Simon, especially the concept of historical laws, the necessary historical conflict between social classes – feudal and bourgeoisie, idlers and producers – and the central argument that changes within the political system depended, not on moral actions, but on economic institutions. Equally significant for the development of Marxist socialism was the assimilation of the Saint-Simonian doctrine that socialised production was possible only through the organisation of a centralised state. The emphasis on the ethical component of socialism, which plays such an important role in the work of Owen and Fourier, disappears in the socialism of Marx and Engels: the moral element is entirely dependent on the structure of the economy and polity.

The development of Marxism is thus organically bound up with a burgeoning labour movement – especially in England and France – the rapid growth of industry and the new social relations of capitalist production. Equally important was the critique of this new social order by 'dissident' intellectuals influenced by classical political economy, especially the labour theory of value, and the revolutionary trends associated with democratic republicanism. During the course of the 1840s and 50s Marxism emerged as the first sociological theory which identified scientific analysis with the interests of a specific social class, the industrial proletariat; a theory of historical change grounded in the struggle between social classes and the priority of economic factors in the shaping of social and political structures. In effect the scientific study of historical development disclosed the necessity of socialism as the resolution of internal conflicts generated by capitalist production: Utopian socialism had disclosed no law-governed process in history, no historical necessity, and thus had ended with moral appeals in which socialism was defined as an ideal state realisable through education and co-operation.

The Development of Marxism

Marx's first writings (1841–5) were largely philosophical, concerned with the problem of human alienation and freedom. It was only with *The German Ideology* (Marx and Engels, 1964 [1846]) that Marx 'settled his account' with his 'philosophic conscience' and developed the first outlines of what later would be called 'the materialist conception of history'. Co-written with Engels, *The German Ideology* advanced a sociological concept of society as a definite structure built around antagonistic social classes, division of labour and forms of private property. Ideas themselves are rooted in specific material contexts and have no independent existence apart from the social formation. Specific modes of production characterise historical development: society develops through different stages from slave and feudal, to capitalist. In the works which followed *The German Ideology* – *The Poverty of Philosophy* (1961 [1847]), *The Communist Manifesto* (1962 [1848]) and *Wage Labour and Capital* (1849) – these themes were further developed within Marx's general historical theory, that social change occurs through conflict and struggle and more precisely through the contradictions existing between the productive forces of any society and its social relations. There is thus a pattern, a meaning to historical development located within the necessity for modes of production to develop towards higher social formations: socialism is thus given a scientific basis in necessary social change.

During the 1850s Marx produced a number of historical studies dealing with the problems of socialism and the working-class movement in Europe, *The Eighteenth Brumaire of Louis Bonaparte* (1962 [1852]) and *The Class Struggles in France* (1962 [1860]), which focus on the relations between political institutions such as the state and collective actors such as social classes. In these works Marx deals with the problem of action, the ways in which human actors influence the structure of society. But his most important work was the massive study of the economic foundations of modern capitalism, the *Grundrisse der Kritik politischen Ökonomie (Outline of a Critique of Political Economy)*, which remained unpublished during his lifetime becoming widely known only after its publication in East Germany in 1953. The importance of the *Grundrisse* in the development of Marxism lies in the continuity which it establishes between Marx's early writings on the alienation of labour and the concept of the active human subject, and the later, supposedly more scientific work, in which capitalism is defined as a social system governed by specific laws of motion and development. Nevertheless, while Marx employs the concept of alienation in the analysis of economic forms there are significant differences between the *Grundrisse* and the earlier works: the term labour-power replaces the concept of labour (labour power had been noted in *The Communist Manifesto* but only in a general sense); production is emphasised at the expense of exchange and the basis laid for the theory of surplus value, capital accumulation and economic crisis. These are the themes which dominate *Capital* (1867) of which only the first volume was published in Marx's lifetime. Yet the theory of alienation and dehumanisation are central issues in these later largely economic analyses and Marx remained faithful to the essential principles of humanism to the end of his life: capitalism was conceived as a system of production structured in contradictions, a social system which transformed human values into external things. In analysing Marx's sociology therefore, it is important to begin with Marx's own starting point.

Alienation of Labour

In the *Economic and Philosophical Manuscripts* (1843–4) Marx defined labour as 'man's self-confirming essence', the activity which political economy had succeeded in transforming into an object, an external thing. For classical political economy the worker was 'an abstract activity and a belly... increasingly dependent upon all the fluctuations in market price, in the employment of capital, and in the caprices of the rich'. Human activity is thus defined in terms of the non-human.

But the concept of alienation was not part of political economy's conceptual structure and it was from Hegel's dialectical philosophy that Marx derived the theory of alienation. In Hegel's *Phenomenology of Spirit* (1807) human culture was assimilated to the concept of 'Absolute Spirit' which progressively unfolds throughout history in a series of dialectical contradictions, eventuating in the expansion of human consciousness and increased self-knowledge; the ultimate stage is the assimilation of 'Spirit' to the 'ethical world'. History was thus defined as enclosing an immanent meaning in that it embodied a ceaseless activity and drive towards unlimited, total consciousness. 'Spirit' was, of course, humanity and the specific historical situations which constitute historical development are analysed by Hegel as 'moments' which, in their material form, embody the dialectical development of 'Absolute Spirit' from an unreflective unity to an organic and conscious unity with culture (the Renaissance, the Enlightenment, the French Revolution).

But as 'spirit' unfolds dialectically it is confronted by each specific moment as part of itself, something its own activity has created; it thus experiences this activity as external and alien. 'Spirit' seeks to recover these alienated moments thus creating the movement which drives it towards total unity and thus a non-alienated consciousness.

Marx inverts Hegel's idealist account arguing that such speculative history ignores real individuals and real conditions; through his grasp of political economy Marx defined labour as the basis of human culture. Culture is no longer the expression of a supra-historical force but the product of human activity through labour. Alienation becomes a process in which humanity is progressively turned into a stranger in a world created by labour. Marx analyses alienation in terms of the division of labour arguing that it succeeds in creating vast accumulations of wealth at one pole of society, an increase in the value of things achieved only at the cost of a progressive devaluing of human life itself. Human labour becomes an object: 'This fact implies that the object produced by labour, its product, now stands opposed to it as an alien being, as a *power independent* of the producer. The product of labour is labour which has been embodied in an object and turned into a physical thing; this product is an objectification of labour.' Marx distinguishes objectification from alienation arguing, against Hegel, whose philosophy embraced both as synonymous terms, that objectification is a process through which humanity externalises itself in nature and society, producing tools for example, and thus necessarily entering into social relationships; alienation, however, occurs only when humanity, having externalised itself, encounters its own activity, its essence, operating as an external, alien and oppressive power. For Marx, objectification was unavoidable and as such not identical with alienation. By assimilating objectification to alienation, Hegel had concluded that humanity (the 'Absolute Spirit') must remain forever trapped in alienation as its essential and ultimately tragic condition. But by locating alienation with economic and material elements Marx defined it as an historical not universal state.

It is capitalism which alienates humanity from its own activity as man's 'self-confirming essence'. His labour, turns increasingly against him, becoming a 'forced activity', a denial of his being, serving to stunt his faculties, induce misery, exhaustion and mental despair. Work is wholly instrumental; a form of activity which is specifically human, becomes an oppressive necessity, alien and external in which the individual feels free only outside work in leisure or with his family. Capitalism effectively defines the worker as possessing a saleable object, labour, which is thus purchased by 'another' so that his activity is no longer his own.

Marx's early writings thus propound two basic themes: first, that while humanity creates the social world through its own activity, the world is experienced as alien and hostile; and second, that human relationships are experienced not as relations between persons but rather as relations between things, as reification:

It is self-evident that political economy treats the proletarian... [as] a worker. It can, therefore, propound the thesis that he, like a horse, must receive just as much as will enable him to work. Political economy does not deal with him in his free time, as a human being... but... conceives the worker only as a draught animal, as a beast whose needs are strictly limited to bodily needs. (Marx, 1963, p. 132)

As the most alienated social class in capitalist society the proletariat exists on the basis of private property, itself the source of alienated labour. It is for this reason that Marx identifies the working class as a universal class 'for all human servitude is involved in the relation of the worker to production and all types of servitude are only modifications or consequences of this relation'. It thus follows that the whole of society is alienated, from capitalists whose life is dominated externally by the demands of profit, to writers and artists who sell their creative talents to the highest bidder. A total revolution is thus called for and the spearhead is the modern industrial proletariat, a class which constitutes the 'effective dissolution' of capitalism, for its demand that private property be abolished is only 'a *principle for society* what society has already made a principle *for the proletariat* and what the latter already involuntarily embodies as the negative result of society'. The dehumanised relation of capital to labour saturates the entire social structure; 'an inhuman power' rules everything.

Political economy could probe no further into the structure of alienated labour and explain the contradiction generated by an alienated social world and increasing material affluence. Political economy ended by celebrating bourgeois society and bourgeois thought as the close of history and as universal activity. The contradictions, the negative elements generated by this process, were simply eliminated: 'Political economy conceals the alienation in the nature of labour in so far as it does not examine the direct relationship between the worker ("work") and production.' Alienation is thus a denial of creative human potentiality, the dehumanisation of the subject and an obstacle to the building of a truly human community.

In Marx's early writings alienation is conceived both in socio-historical and philosophically abstract terms as, for example, the 'fragmentation' of labour and the 'fragmentation' of the human essence. It is important to note that Marx develops a concept of the whole man whose human stature is diminished by the external power of capital; man thus needs to be returned to a non-alienated state, reunited with nature, other men and society. As late as 1846, in *The German Ideology*, Marx could describe communism in terms of these Utopian elements arguing that the division of labour would not function merely to allocate individuals to specific occupational roles but allow them 'to hunt in the morning, fish in the afternoon, rear cattle in the evening, criticise after dinner... without ever becoming a hunter, fisherman, shepherd or critic' (Marx and Engels, 1964, Part 1). Nevertheless, there is, within this particular text and those which followed, a shift of emphasis and the argument that the concept of alienation in the *Grundrisse* and *Capital* is identical with that of the *Economic and Philosophical Manuscripts* suggests the untenable view that, while Marx's theory of society and social change underwent extensive revision and development in the post-1845 works, the theory of alienation remained at the conceptual and empirical level of the earlier texts. By the 1850s Marx's economic theory, together with his political outlook, had changed considerably. Thus from a purely logical standpoint those concepts retained in the later writings clearly imply radically different meanings from their earlier usage. The present appeal of the *Economic and Philosophical Manuscripts* undoubtedly lies in their depiction of humanity as the ultimate arbiter of the social world and man as an active subject duplicating himself and his powers through his actions. Yet the picture which emerges from these writings does not suggest the voluntaristic theory which has often been claimed for them, for if alienation dominates the social world to the extent of wholly debilitating humanity's creative and natural powers, transforming the individual from an active subject into a passive object, then how is it possible for change to occur? How is praxis possible? Marx's concept of alienation suggests the impossibility of radical human action, for consciously planned change. It is this contradiction between the notions of *active* subject and *total* alienation which leads Marx to posit communism as an ethical ideal which humanity ought to strive for, and the proletariat as the universal class which negates capitalist alienation. Marx's humanist concept of alienation is ultimately deterministic, philosophical and speculative lacking the sociological and economic framework of the later *Grundrisse* and *Capital*.

Between writing the *Economic and Philosophical Manuscripts* and *Capital* Marx developed a more historical and materialist approach arguing that research must investigate not man in general but man in society and society as a system structured around laws of change and development. But Marx did not abandon humanism. In *Capital* the concept of alienation is sparingly employed but the related notions of the 'fetishism of commodities' and reification are frequently discussed and form an important part of Marx's analysis of capitalist economic structure. In the *Grundrisse*, for example, the emphasis shifts to production; labour is defined as labour-power, a unique commodity found only within the capitalist mode of production. In the early writings Marx had followed Smith and Ricardo in defining labour as 'abstract general and social labour', an approach which succeeded in mystifying the precise relation between the creation of value (expressed in money, for example) and human activity (expressed in labour). Labour-power constitutes a commodity; labour in general does not. The creation of wealth is possible only through the exploitation of labour-power, the transformation of labour from an affirmation to a denial of human values. Thus in *Capital* Marx argues that commodity production entails the separation of two specific kinds of value, exchange and use value, values which either command a price or satisfy a human and social need. All commodities embody both values but it is only capitalism as a system of commodity production which aims at the expansion of exchange value.

Human activity increasingly becomes subordinated to the external compulsions of exchange value. Money becomes the objective bond of society, the real community in a system dominated by exchange values. When in the first volume of *Capital* Marx refers to 'commodity fetishism' he describes a process in which human subjects no longer control the objects of labour as their own. The worker exists only to satisfy the demands of the economic system; material wealth does not exist to satisfy the needs of the worker's development. The social process of production effectively negates the need for community, co-operation becomes alienated and replaced by compulsion. Human relations become 'atomised' assuming a material character independent of human control and conscious activity. This process is especially expressed by the fact that products take the form of commodities (Marx, 1958, Vol. 1, Ch. XXVI).

In a society dominated by exchange value, the real social foundations of the unequal relation of capital to labour is hidden. In a famous passage Marx writes of the commodity as 'a mysterious thing' which disguises the social character of labour presenting the relations between the producers and the totality of their labour 'as a social relation, existing not between themselves, but between the products of their labour'. Social relations within capitalism are wholly inverted, 'every element, even the simplest, the commodity for example... causes relations between people to appear as attributes of things'. The social world of modern capitalism is a perverted world, the products of labour generating an apparent independence, in which objects begin 'to rule the producers instead of being ruled by them', while those engaged in production 'live in a bewitched world', their own relationships appearing to them 'as properties of things, as properties of the material elements of production'. Humanity becomes dominated by a world of things, by processes its own activity has created but which, through the workings of the capitalist economic system, turn against them, as objective independent processes (Marx, 1958, pp. 72–3). In the *Grundrisse* Marx writes that 'social wealth confronts labour in more powerful portions as an alien and dominant power... a monstrous objective power which, created through social labour belongs not to the worker, but... to capital'. The emphasis, Marx notes, is 'not on the state of being *objectified*, but... of being *alienated*, dispossessed, sold' (Marx, 1973, pp. 831–2). And, in almost identical language, he writes in *Capital*:

We have seen that the growing accumulation of capital implies its growing concentration. Thus grows the power of capital, the alienation of the conditions of social production personified in the capitalist from the real producers. Capital... as a social power... no longer stands in any possible relation to that which the labour of a single individual can create. It becomes an alienated, independent social power, which stands opposed to society as an object, and as an object that is the capitalist's source of power. (Marx, 1962, p. 259)

The extraction of surplus value, the control over labour-power invested in the individual capitalist and capital, results in the development of a social world which progressively degrades human values and exalts the world of objects and things. In the *Economic and Philosophical Manuscripts* Marx had analysed this tendency: 'The worker becomes an ever cheaper commodity the more goods he creates. The devaluation of the human world increases in direct relation with the increase in value of the world of things.' The relation between the early and later writings is thus clearly stated; in a world dominated by commodity production and exploitation the worker's labour-power is quantified, measured as precisely as possible, treated entirely as an external thing. The analysis of capitalism as a system in the *Grundrisse* and *Capital* is based on similar concepts employed by Marx in his humanist critique of capitalism of the early writings. But in both the early and later writings reification is depicted as a process which so penetrates human and social relations that individuals comprehend the products of their labour as autonomous, objective forces unconnected with human activity.

This process of reification manifests itself most sharply in consciousness: those who comprehend the social world through reified categories emphasise the externality and inexorable *natural* determinism of a world apparently governed by blind laws beyond the control of human beings, a world in which things constitute the only active elements. In pre-industrial society, where use value was not dominated by exchange value, social relations were clear and unequivocal based on personalised ties and obligations, unequal relationships grounded in custom and tradition. The social structure of capitalism, however, is built around impersonal relationships based on the dominion of exchange value. In societies where exchange value has replaced direct use value a formal equality masks class relations; the world of capitalist commodity production appears as a world of equals bound by freely negotiated contracts. The exchange between capital and labour bears the illusion of a free exchange of equivalents (labour for wages) and it is at this point that the mystification of social relations occurs: the worker acts as if labour-power is not exploited, that in return for 'a fair day's work' there will be just reward. Capitalist inequality is thus defined as natural and therefore essential for the adequate functioning of society. The worker fails to understand that he has become part of capital itself and is but a special mode of its existence:

Hence the productive power developed by the labourer when working in co-operation is the productive power of capital. This power is developed gratuitously, whenever the workmen are placed under given conditions, and it is capital that places them under such conditions. Because this power cost capital nothing, and because, on the other hand, the labourer himself does not develop it before his labour belongs to capital, it appears as a power with which capital is endowed by Nature – a productive power that is immanent in capital. (Marx, 1958, p. 333)

Marx's theory of alienation has thus become more empirical, historically specific and sociologically grounded in economic structures. In his early writings Marx had written of the 'inhuman power' dominating social life, frustrating humanity's essential powers and transforming him/her into an object. In *Capital* the concept of alienated subject is retained but within a theoretical framework which defines capitalism as an objective system and alienation in terms of the inner and contradictory movement of capitalist production, an alienation embodied in the transformation of labour-power into a commodity.

Base and Superstructure: Materialism and the Role of Ideas

In the *Grundrisse* and *Capital* Marx advanced a radically different concept of society from that of his early writings. Society is defined as a system structured in the workings of specific, objective 'laws of development'. This is Marx's macro level of analysis which focuses on elements which generate an underlying pattern to human society. However, unlike Comte and Spencer, Marx is not advancing a 'grand theory' built around ahistorical abstractions and ahistorical laws: the core of his sociological thought lies in the principle of historical specificity and it is this which establishes a continuity between the early and the later writings. In the *Theses on Feuerbach* (1962 [1845]), for example, Marx rejected the ahistorical notion of a fixed human nature or essence arguing that humans make themselves through their labour and within definite social contexts and relations with others: history is 'the continuous transformation of human nature, the production of the individual through labour'. Thus 'the relations of production of every society form a whole' and can be understood only in this sense.

In analysing society as a system Marx distinguished between its 'real' foundations in the mode of production which include the forces of production (everything which enhances control over nature including raw materials, technology, science, human skills as well as industrial and technological institutions), and the superstructure, the cultural, ideological and political practices and institutions. Relations of production (the ways in which production is socially organised through the division of labour, authority, law) involve links between different social groups and classes, hierarchical structures of domination and subordination (authority relations in factories for example). Relations of production are objective and exist independently of individuals (relations between wage labour and capital for example). Marx's materialistic model of society thus assumes an homologous connection between forces and relations of production with the latter serving the interests of production as a whole. Hence the young Marx's statement that 'the handmill gives you society with the feudal lord; the steam mill society with the industrial capitalist' (Marx, 1961, p. 109). However, in his mature writings Marx frequently departs from such rigid functionalist models, emphasising that in the production and reproduction of social life ideas play a critical role. Thus in *Capital* he notes that 'Protestantism, by changing almost all the traditional holidays into work days, plays an important part in the genesis of capital' (Marx, 1957, p. 276). The so-called 'ideal' features of society contribute actively to social reproduction as material forces.

It is this relation between the ideal and the material aspects of society which present problems for Marx's sociology. By materialism Marx refers first to the economic and social elements which condition and set limits to the scope for human action and practice; and second, he argues that all forms of production necessarily involve ideas, knowledge, skills and thus involve active relations between those individuals involved. Marx's sociological thinking thus embraces both material and ideal dimensions of social life. Discussing the concept of production he argues:

We presuppose labour in a form that stamps it as exclusively human. A spider conducts operations that resemble those of a weaver, and a bee puts to shame many an architect in the construction of her cells. But what distinguishes the worst architect from the best of bees is this, that the architect raises his structure in imagination before he erects it in reality... He not only effects a change of form in the material on which he works, but he also realises a purpose of his own. (Marx, 1958, p. 178)

In both these comments, on Protestant culture and the practices of architects, Marx proposes both an active role for ideas and their realisation in a creative, imaginative agent. However, while rejecting the dualism of idea and materialism (and by extension, the dualism of agency and structure) Marx never successfully integrates this standpoint into his broad social theory: the result is the existence of two Marxs, one who stresses the partial autonomy of ideas, the other who analyses ideas as the reflections of external, material forces.

This problem is exemplified in Marx's model of society as consisting of a material 'base' (its economic infrastructure) which necessarily generates a 'superstructure' (specific forms of thought). Society is explained not through ideas but rather ideas through society: ideas have no history other than as elements of society and history. In *The German Ideology* (1964) Marx and

Engels postulated a strict, causal and mechanical relation between thought and the social world defining ideas as expressions of class interests. This theory of ideology therefore assumes a relation of correspondence between social structure and thought systems; ideas are merely the passive reflections of an external economic order. Knowledge is epiphenomenal, the product of objective social interests, and thus incapable of exercising an active role in society and social change.

In this formulation ideas are mere 'reflexes and echoes' of the 'life process':

> The phantoms formed in the human brain are... sublimates of... material life-processes, which is empirically verifiable and bound to material premises. Morality, religion, metaphysics, all the rest of ideology and their corresponding forms of consciousness, thus no longer retain their semblance of independence. They have no history, no development; but men, developing their material production and their material intercourse, alter, along with this real existence, their thinking and the products of their thinking. Life is not determined by consciousness but consciousness by life. (Marx and Engels, 1964, pp. 37–8)

This thesis of a strict causal relation of economic base and ideological superstructure reappears in Marx's 1859 text, *A Contribution to a Critique of Political Economy*, in which it is argued that the forces of production 'constitute the economic structure of society, the real foundation on which arises a legal and political superstructure and to which correspond definite forms of social consciousness. The mode of production of material life conditions the general process of social, political and intellectual life' (Marx, 1971, pp. 20–1).

This functionalist model thus assumes that ideas correspond directly with economic structure and class interests; bourgeois law thus functions to legitimate bourgeois society. But, as I have noted, there is another less symmetrical model of base and superstructure in Marx's work which emphasises the active interplay between culture, ideas and the economic infrastructure. Marx's base and superstructure model is not meant to correspond directly with reality but constitutes a method of analysing society at both the 'macro' or system level and the 'micro' level of human action and ideas. It is the relations between these two levels which constitutes the major problem in Marx's work affecting his overall methodological perspective and his substantive theory of social change.

Marx's Method

Marx's early writings, although employing Hegelian categories such as alienation, had rejected the metaphysical abstractions and methodology of the larger philosophy. By 1858 Marx now described Hegel's *Logic* as rendering in an accessible form 'what is rational in the method which Hegel discovered but at the same time enveloped in mysticism'. This is the distinction Engels made later between Hegel's *method* and his *system*, the necessity to extract 'the rational kernel within the mystical shell' and develop a materialist dialectic. To achieve this Marx adopted the category of totality, not as a speculative, philosophical principle, but as a methodological instrument which grasps the relations of the simple to the complex, the part to the whole.

Thus Marx begins *Capital* with the simple form of value, the exchange of one commodity for another, arguing that the commodity contains the basic contradictions of capitalism. But the commodity is also a *part* which must be related to a *whole*, a totality, capitalism as an economic, political and social system. Marx's method, therefore, opposed the atomistic approach of method-ological individualism (for example utilitarianism, rationalism) as well as those philosophies which defined the concept of whole as the simple sum of its parts: for Marx, totality is structured in the interconnectedness of phenomena, facts are not isolated and external data but internally related elements existing in a necessary relation to the whole although enjoying inde-pendence from it.

Much of the confusion which has surrounded Marx's sociology is linked to a misunderstanding of his methodology which involves both grasping society as an objective system and the ways in which subjective, ideal elements enter the analysis. In the 'Preface' to *Capital* he writes that 'in the analysis of economic forms neither microscopes nor chemical reagents are of use. The force of abstraction must replace both', and in the *Grundrisse* he argues that while the correct scientific approach superficially begins from 'real and concrete elements', actual preconditions such as population or the world market, such a procedure is wrong for the apparently concrete is in reality abstract:

> Population is an abstraction if, for instance, one disregards the classes of which it is composed. These classes in turn remain empty terms if one does not know the factors on which they depend, e.g. wage, labour, capital, etc. These presuppose exchange, division of labour, prices, etc. for example, capital is nothing without wages, labour... value, money, price, etc. If one were to take population as the point of departure, it would be a very vague notion of a complex whole and through closer definition one would arrive analytically at increasingly simple concepts; from imaginary concrete terms one would move to more and more tenuous abstractions until one reached the most simple definitions. From here it would be necessary to make the journey again in the opposite direction until one arrived once more at the concept of population which is this time not a vague notion of a whole, but a totality comprising many determinations and relations. (Marx, 1971, pp. 205–6)

Scientific method in the study of society is therefore the opposite of factual observation which always begins from the concrete and works towards the abstract; scientific inquiry does not adopt the standpoint of the raw material itself but seeks the 'inner structure' of the object by beginning from the general categories. Thus classical political economy was correct to start with population but wrong to define it as a concrete fact rather than as an abstract whole, which necessarily approximates to an ideal, general form emptied of complex and chaotic empirical material. To advance 'from the abstract to the concrete is simply the way in which thinking assimilates the concrete and reproduces it as a concrete mental category'. Thus the study of capitalism as a system must begin, not from particular capitals, competition and other elements which constitute its historic reality, but from 'capital as such', 'capital in general'. 'The introduction of many capitals must not interfere with the investigation here. The relation of the many is better explained after we have studied what they have in common, the quality of being capital... Capital in general as distinct from particular capitals does indeed appear:

1. only as an abstraction; not an arbitrary abstraction, but one which grasps the specific differences which distinguish capital from other forms of wealth...
2. however, capital in general, as distinct from particular real capitals, is itself a real existence'. (Marx, 1973, pp. 517, 449)

Capitalism is thus studied as an abstraction, a pure form, leaving out all the complex, historically specific complicating features, the 'appearance' as opposed to its 'inner essence or structure'. Marx's holistic methodology therefore assumes an ideal capitalism, one which is never actually present in reality, a model which is employed throughout his analysis of social change, class formation and social structure. The analysis of production, for example, is usually thought of in terms of specific persons or historical periods, but all stages of production share common features: '*Production in general* is an abstraction, but a sensible abstraction in so far as it actually emphasises and defines the common aspects and thus avoids repetition.' Marx argues that some features are found in 'the most modern as well as the most ancient epochs', but the 'so-called *general conditions* of all and every production... are nothing but the abstract conceptions which do not define any of the actual historical stages of production' (Marx, 1971, pp. 189–93). The relation between production, distribution, exchange and consumption can be established only by isolating the inner nature of production, the determinations common to all its forms and grasping the ways in which the historically specific elements depart from the general since in this lies the secret of their development.

Marx's method is thus to begin from a pre-given whole, such as population, production, the state, and so on, and to abstract further the elements comprising the whole; then, through a process of successive approximations, relate these elements organically to the whole itself. When he writes that 'the subject, society, must always be envisaged… as the pre-condition of comprehension', Marx implies that no category, by itself, can constitute an adequate starting point for scientific social analysis. Both explanation and comprehension, the historical and genetic determinations of an object, together with a grasp of its inner structure and relations with the whole – the diachronic and synchronic – are unified within Marx's dialectical methodological framework. Thus, in the first two volumes of *Capital*, Marx abstracts and simplifies capitalist society to one basic relation, of capital to labour, its inner structure, arguing that if this constitutes the dominant relation then it becomes possible to determine the existence of laws, trends and the possibility of prediction. It is for this reason that any account of Marx's sociology of class, conflict and social change must relate to his discussion of methodology.

Class Formation and Class Consciousness

In the *Philosophy of History* (1822–31) Hegel had argued that scientific understanding presupposed the ability of science to distinguish the essential from the inessential. For Marx, the 'leading thread' of his socio-historical-economic studies during the 1850s led him to identify and isolate the mode of production as the basic determinant of social structure, class formation, class conflict and ideology. Marx's earlier writings had not accorded production a central role in the analysis of class formation and, in general, a simplified two-class model is postulated which derives its force, not from the concept of surplus value, but from a speculative, philosophical view of social development. In *The Communist Manifesto* the logic of capitalist economic development is described in terms of a sharp polarisation of class forces: 'Our epoch, the epoch of the bourgeoisie, possesses… this distinctive feature; it has simplified the class antagonism. Society as a whole is splitting up into two great hostile camps, into two great classes directly facing each other: Bourgeoisie and Proletariat' (Marx and Engels, 1962, Vol. 1, pp. 34–5).

In his polemical writings Marx frequently advanced this oversimplified model of capitalist stratification; in his more scientific and historical studies, however, this simplistic, dichotomic structure is repudiated. In his *The Eighteenth Brumaire of Louis Bonaparte* (1852), for example, Marx distinguished between the financial, industrial and petty-bourgeoisie, proletariat, landlords and free farmers, while in other studies of France and Germany he noted the existence of bourgeoisie, farmers, peasants, agricultural workers, lumpenproletariat (the 'dangerous classes') and feudal lords. Marx describes some of these categories as 'transition classes' their existence contradicted by the necessary historical development of capitalism, a standpoint which comes close to asserting that only bourgeoisie and proletariat constitute the essential structure of capitalist social formations. But, in general, Marx never articulated a simple two-class model as an *historical* fact, emphasising rather the *complexity* of class formation and structure within capitalism.

Marx's second theory of class develops the concept of plurality of structure in which the category of middle class is especially important. The middle classes are defined as variegated groups comprising small producers, petty-bourgeoisie (employers of small fractions of labour), those engaged in the 'circulation of commodities' (marketing, buying, selling), the middle men (wholesalers, shopkeepers, speculators), those who 'command in the name of capital' (managers, and so on) and their assistants, supervisors, book-keepers, clerks, and finally 'ideological classes' embracing lawyers, journalists, clergy, state officials such as the military and police. In his historical studies the simplified model of the earlier philosophical writings disappears and Marx argues that the basic tendency of capitalism is not necessarily towards class polarisation but towards augmenting the middle classes especially those performing important 'social functions' such as professional groups, since they exercise significant roles in the maintenance of bourgeois society. As capitalism develops its productive forces, this class increases in size and influence and Marx suggests that 'the constantly growing number of the middle classes which, situated between the workers on the one side and the capitalists and landlords on the other side, [living] mainly and directly on revenue... press like a heavy burden on the labouring class, enlargening the social security and power of the upper ten thousand' (Marx, 1964–72, Vol. 2, p. 573).

These statements clearly contradict the view that Marx's theory of class is dichotomic for he accepts Thomas Malthus's statement, in his work on political economy (1836), that the growth of the middle classes and a constant decrease in the working proletariat is in effect 'the course of bourgeois society'. But to understand these statements it is essential to relate them to Marx's methodology. The analysis of capitalism was based initially on a 'pure' model purged of all complicating historical factors such as foreign trade, monopoly, colonialism, trade unions, the role of the state, a model dominated by the capital–labour relation. In the course of analysis, throughout the three volumes of *Capital*, more and more empirically specific and complicating features are reintroduced so that the model increasingly approximates to a complex, rich, concrete, historically specific capitalism.

In *Capital* Marx was mainly concerned with English capitalism as the most highly developed form in the nineteenth century and his comments on class are particularly significant. He identifies three broad social classes, the owners of labour-power, capital and land, their sources consisting of revenue, wages, profit and ground rent, arguing that they constitute the 'three big classes of modern society based on the capitalist mode of production'. In England, Marx adds, although the economic structure is highly developed, 'the stratification of classes does not appear in its pure form. *Middle and intermediate strata* even here obliterate lines of demarcation'. The tendency of capitalism in its pure form is to concentrate property in fewer hands, force the middle classes downwards into the proletariat and transform all labour into wage labour. But in reality capitalist development produces a complex structure of classes and class relations. Class is never a single homogeneous unity but rather a cluster of groups, or fractions, sharing a similar work function, values, aspirations and interests. This complex structure leads to frequent conflicts within the class itself, between the differentiated interests, as in the case of revenue derived from ground rent which is common both to landowners, mine-owners as well as property owners. Thus the dominant class is never a simple homogeneous whole but consists of fractions representing different economic and political interests, such as industrial and financial bourgeoisie, officials of the state apparatus and the leading 'ideological classes' within civil society, the law, politics, journalism. Similarly, the working class is differentiated through the various branches of industry, different skills and pay, and the weight of traditions. But Marx was insistent that a class is a class only when it is conscious of its interests and organised for pursuing those interests through its own institutions. This is the meaning of his remarks on the French peasantry:

> Their mode of production isolates them from one another instead of bringing them into mutual intercourse... In so far as millions of families live under economic conditions of existence that separate their mode of life, their interests and their culture from those of other classes and place them in opposition to them, *they constitute* a class. In so far as there is only a local connection between the small-holding peasants, and the identity of their interests *begets no community, and no political organisation*, they do not constitute a class. (Marx and Engels, 1962, Vol. 1, p. 334)

The working class is thus only a class when organised for class action: 'There is one element of success the workers possess: its great numbers. But numbers will weigh in the balance only when united by organisation and guided by knowledge.' But in many ways the actual historical evolution of nineteenth-century capitalism suggested that revolutionary class consciousness would be sapped by 'complicating' elements such as Engels noted with the reformist policies pursued by trade unions. Marx's abstract, pure model of capitalism excluded any possibility of social mobility which would clearly function as a stabilising process in a context of class inequality. In Volume 3 of *Capital*, as the analysis of capitalism approximates more closely to historical reality, Marx noted the possibility that numbers of propertyless individuals, by their own efforts and through their ability, accede to the capitalist class: 'Although this circumstance continually brings an unwelcome number of new soldiers of fortune into the field and into competition with the already existing capitalists, it also reinforces the supremacy of capital itself, expands its base and enables it to recruit ever new forces for itself out of the substratum of society... the more a ruling class is able to assimilate the fore-most minds of the ruled class, the more stable and dangerous becomes its rule' (Marx, 1958, p. 587).

How then is change possible? The simple class conflict model postulated an inherent conflict of interests between bourgeoisie and proletariat leading inevitably to a heightening of class consciousness and the possibility of revo-lutionary practice. But if the course of capitalist development negates the development of a polarised class structure does this suggest that revolu-tionary consciousness is impossible, or at least extremely unlikely? To answer these questions it is necessary to examine Marx's theory of class in terms of his larger analysis of capitalism as a system dominated by objective laws of development.

Laws of Development: The Problem of Social Change

Marx, defined capitalist society as a system, a structured whole dominated by the mode of production and the contradictions generated between privately owned economic forces and collective, social relations of production. This law, which attributes social development to internal contradictions within the 'base' 'superstructure' model, is expressed in terms of the dichotomic struc-ture of class forces in *The Communist Manifesto* (1962 [1848]), and capitalist society is characterised as splitting into two 'hostile camps' with irreconcilable interests. In *Capital* Marx discusses class at the end of the third volume and only then in fragmentary, unfinished form. His comments here will appear strange if his methodology is misunderstood, for, as I have argued, Marx is seeking the 'essential structure', the 'secret' of capitalist development, in the first two volumes of *Capital*. Marx's two-class model, 'the working class, disposing only of its labour-power, and the capitalist class, which has a monopoly of the social means of production', assumes that the 'laws of capi-talist production operate in their pure form' and therefore:

1. With the labour-capital relation as the dominant element which structures the development and form of the capitalist social formation the analysis of change eliminates any active influence of the 'superstructure'.

2. The capital-labour relation is reduced to its simplest form, capitalists and workers defined as standard types 'the personifications of economic cate-gories, embodiments of particular class relations and class interests'. The capitalist is thus portrayed as 'fanatically bent on making value expand itself' and 'ruthlessly' forcing humanity to produce for the sake of produc-tion and the development of the productive powers of society.

The first volume of *Capital* operates at a high level of abstraction, the macro analysis of 'capital in general' with its assumption of society consisting solely of capitalists and workers; Volume 2 deepens the analysis as Marx discusses the accumulation of capital, its reproduction and circulation, while in Volume 3 'capital in general' becomes 'many capitals', their relationships and thus capitalism as an historical-empirical reality. The abstractions underlying the first volume – commodities exchanging according to the cost of production in standard man-hours, the absence of monopoly, the appropriation of the entire economic surplus by the capitalist class (the state taking nothing), the two-class model, (classes as standard types) and so on – produce laws which must not be taken as concrete predictions about the future since they may be 'modified' by 'other circumstances' that comprise the specifically historical.

Marx's model of capitalism is a complex system in which the 'superstructural' elements exercise an increasing role in modifying the generalisations of the first volume. This is particularly the case with Marx's concept of capitalist crisis which has frequently been interpreted as the historically inevitable consequence of economic laws working with 'iron necessity' towards intensified class conflict and social breakdown. It is true that in *Capital*, Volume 1, there are many passages which support this historicist interpretation, but when the concept of crisis is integrated within the context of totality a radically different view emerges:

> From time to time the conflict of antagonistic tendencies finds vent in crises... momentary and forcible solutions of the existing contradictions... violent eruptions which for a time restore the disturbed equilibrium. The contradiction... consists in that the capitalist mode of production involves a tendency towards the absolute development of the productive forces regardless of the value and the surplus-value it contains, and regardless of the social conditions under which capitalist production takes place; while on the other hand, its aim is to preserve the value of the existing capital and promote its self-expansion to the highest limit. (Marx, 1958, pp. 243–4)

The law of the falling rate of profit can thus co-exist with the expansion of total profit and clearly Marx does not postulate a simple breakdown theory. Yet this was Engels's interpretation in his definition of historical materialism as historical explanation which seeks the 'ultimate cause' of the economic development of society in changes within the modes of production and exchange, division of labour and differentiation of society into antagonistic social classes. Engels defined Marxism as economic determinism, the ineluctable workings of the infrastructure of society and the abolition of the creative human agent. This is clearly an inadequate interpretation in terms both of Marx's methodological standpoint in *Capital* and his insistence on the active role of the superstructure, and thus of ideas (as noted above), on the course of social change. Social development is not inevitably mapped out by the workings of economic laws since historical laws exist only through individuals, through collective human action. Of course, socio-historical laws can be analysed as objective results of extra-human forces; but such mystification and reification is foreign to Marx's thought. Marx's concept of diachronic historical laws is not positivist for while the positivist trend in nineteenth-century natural science exerted a powerful influence on socialist thought it was mainly Engels, not Marx, who rejected the active role of agents in favour of economic determination in the last instance.

Marx's theory of social change cannot be assimilated to this positivist reading: the active and creative role of the agent remains at the heart of his theories of class formation, conflict and consciousness. Unlike Comte's sociological positivism, Marx depicts humanity as the active producer of the social world which transforms the external world as it transforms itself, not as isolated individuals, or individual wills, but as members of social groups and classes. And although he argues that the course of social development hinges on the objective application of science and technology to production, it is humanity which ultimately changes the world. In the *Grundrisse* he writes:

> Nature builds no machines, no locomotives, railways... These are the products of human industry; natural material transformed into organs of the human will over nature, or of human participation in nature. They are organs of the human brain, created by human hand; the power of knowledge objectified. (Marx, 1973, p. 706)

In the same humanist spirit he describes the development of west European agriculture:

> Not only do the objective conditions change in the act of reproduction, for example the village becomes a town, the wilderness a cleared field, and so on but the producers change too in that they bring out new qualities in themselves, develop themselves in production, transform themselves, develop new powers and ideas, new modes of intercourse, new needs and new language. (Marx, 1973, p. 494)

It is impossible to understand the relation of Marx's 'iron laws' of capitalism – the concept of capitalism as a system existing independently of the individuals who comprise it – to his emphasis on the creative, individual producer – a collective agent organised in groups – unless analysed in terms of his theory of civil society. Marx describes capitalism as effectively liberating civil society from the domination of the state and fostering the creation of separate and independent spheres in which the new industrial classes, the bourgeoisie and the proletariat develop their own distinctive institutions, political organisations and modes of activity. Capitalism as a mode of production made possible an enlargement of human practice enabling individuals to become reflexive and active within their own distinctive institutions: trade unions, political parties, cultural and economic organisations. Implied here is the concept of modernity: the relation of active, reflective agents to new forms of social organisation and society as a complex developing system.

Marx's theory of social change, therefore, functions on three distinct but related levels:

1. The system level comprising the laws of motion internal to capitalism (the laws of the accumulation of capital, centralisation of capital, falling rate of profit) which produce structural contradictions between exchange and use value and between the private appropriation of property and the centralising and socialising logic of capitalist production. All societies are characterised by a fundamental contradiction: feudal society comprised a contradiction between the agrarian landowning nobility and the nascent, growing bourgeoisie concentrated in towns and engaging in forms of production and exchange which demanded a market-oriented competitive society. This is Marx's 'womb' theory of social change as new forms of production come into contradiction with old traditional forms: in capitalism socialised production and the exploitation of labour contain the womb of a new social order based on collectivism and socialist political organisation.

2. The social structural or intermediate level comprising institutions, social classes and social struggles.

3 And, finally, the action level which focuses on the capacities of individuals to engage in reflexive consciousness, innovative and purposive practices.

Marx noted for example that it was 'conscious life-activity' which distinguished 'man from animal life-activity.' By including this micro level Marx introduced a 'probabilistic' element into his theory of social change: for if social change occurs solely at the system level then it works through determining laws which allow for prediction on outcomes. But if human action is included then change is far less deterministic and predictable (Sztompka, 1993, pp. 156–7).

Marx, then, has defined society as a system in which objective laws operate independently of, and frequently against, the will of individuals; yet, as Marx emphasised, capitalism makes possible human practice, control and planning, the active intervention of the human subject in historical development. Marx's concept of laws, of course, differs sharply from Comte's: laws are man-made and not natural and thus open to drastic change through human intervention. While Marx's sociological model is one which incorporates human action and practice into a systemic structure of collectivist and historically necessary forces it is the latter which tend to dominate his theory of social change.

This is the contradiction which lies at the heart of Marx's dialectical social theory illuminating the problems of the democratic strands in the theory of civil society – that change evolves through the collective, democratic actions of ordinary individuals seeking to develop their own social, political and cultural institutions – and the strongly collectivist elements of the capitalist social and economic order which suggest the eclipse of individuality and representative institutions. Marx failed to resolve the contradictions in his thought between the historicist notion of economic necessity and his humanist sociology.

Marx's Theory of Domination

Marx was not the first writer to emphasise the class nature of industrial society or the conflicts generated between dominant and subordinate classes. 'What I did that was new', he wrote, 'was to prove:

1. that the existence of classes is only bound up with particular historical phases in the development of production
2. that the class struggle necessarily leads to the dictatorship of the proletariat
3. that this dictatorship itself only constitutes the transition to the abolition of all classes and to a classless society'. (Marx and Engels, *Selected Correspondence*, p. 86)

In this formulation (itself made during private correspondence and therefore never intended for publication) Marx advanced a dogmatic notion of the centralising role of the state in the transition to socialism. And in *The Communist Manifesto* Marx and Engels described the modern state as a 'committee for managing the common affairs of the whole bourgeoisie', defining political power as 'the organised power of one class for oppressing another'. The implication in this formulation is that power flows from the ownership of economic resources and is simply a reflection of class interests. Class domination is thus the product of class antagonisms based on economic inequality, and while Marx emphasises that economic inequality and exploitation were characteristic of all modes of production beyond simple tribal communism, it was only capitalism which transformed all social relations into economic relations. In precapitalist society the social relations of serf and landowner, for example, functioned through a personal as well as an economic nexus: the class domination of the landowner was based on feudal ties of bondage and vassalage, personal elements which capitalism destroys, 'the motley feudal ties that bound man to his "natural superiors"', leaving only naked self-interest as the bond between individuals. It is in this sense that Marx wrote of class relations under capitalism becoming 'simplified' and 'universalised', with the result that power was increasingly concentrated in the major economic and political institutions.

Marx distinguished between three modes of domination: economic, social and political. Economic and social domination refers to the ways in which *capital* determines the functioning of institutions generally, while political domination refers to the ways in which the state creates and maintains the legal framework for bourgeois rule. Although Marx never used the term 'ideological domination', it is implicit in his analysis of ideology, referring essentially to the need for legitimation within capitalism with the rise of democratic institutions.

In *Capital* Marx depicted capitalist society as a system in which capital acts as an independent force, the capitalist class directly appropriating the whole surplus labour and surplus product in ways which augment the 'domination of capital over labour'. Like Saint-Simon, Marx argued that political institutions expressed basic economic interests; a relation of strict functional correspondence characterised economic and political institutions. Thus in *The Communist Manifesto* a simple, reciprocal base-superstructure model of political power is advanced in which the state – 'political society' – is conceptualised as an ideological institution which supports and defends the rights of private property. The state is a class state. But, in his later, historical writings, especially those analysing contemporary British and French history, Marx developed a more complex model of power, distinguishing between the different fractions within a dominant class and suggesting that the state apparatus was often controlled, not by the bourgeoisie, but by what he called 'a governing class'.

Thus in his analysis of the British political system Marx argued that although the Tory party remained the party of the nobility, it nevertheless carried out the policies of the bourgeoisie: 'The whole aristocracy is convinced of the need to govern in the interests of the bourgeoisie; but at the same time it is determined not to allow the latter to take charge of the matter itself' (Marx and Engels, 1962, pp. 351–8). The dominant class consists of its ruling and non-ruling fractions: the ruling class – the governing class – exercises power through the state on behalf of an economically dominant class such as the nineteenth-century English bourgeoisie. In a similar way Engels describes the German Junkers as the governing class of a Germany which was industrialising and transforming itself into a modern bourgeois society: the conflict of interests between the rising bourgeoisie and the emerging proletariat were overcome by raising the state apparatus over the whole society.

In the *Grundrisse* Marx noted that this internal complexity of class existed at the economic level also: as profit consisted of two separate forms of revenue, the existence of financial and industrial capitalists 'express nothing other than this fact' (Marx, 1973). The dominant class is therefore never a homogeneous whole but a structure of different and potentially conflicting interests. There is no simple mechanical relation, therefore, between class power and economic dominance: power is mediated through political institutions which, developing at a different tempo from the economic forces, succeed in exercising an autonomy in respect of class interests.

The State and Class Domination

From certain of Marx's writings the theory of domination appears as unproblematic: power is the reflection within political society of economic interests. But in analysing the theory of domination as it developed within Marx's work, it becomes clearly essential to distinguish Marx's polemical writings such as *The Communist Manifesto* from his scientific and historical studies *The Eighteenth Brumaire of Louis Bonaparte* (1852), *The Class Struggles in France* (1850) and his analyses of the Paris Commune (1871–72). He originally intended to complete his study of capitalism with a final volume devoted to the state but died before finishing the economic analysis. In this sense, therefore, there exists no theory of the state in Marx's work or any analysis of the state system comparable to Marx's economic analysis. Perhaps for this reason it is a relatively simple task to find a number of different concepts of the state ranging from the notion of state as class power to the state as autonomous institution. Bearing in mind, therefore, that Marx failed to develop a coherent theory of capitalist domination the theory of the state can best be approached by focusing on two related, although contradictory themes: that human emancipation depends on civil society being independent of state domination; and the argument that the abolition of capitalism necessarily involves centralised authority.

In Marx's early writings the state is separated from civil society: the state expresses the condition of civil society and is indeed described as its 'official expression'. In his essay, 'On the Jewish Question' (1843), Marx accepts Hegel's concept of civil society describing its creation as 'the achievement of the modern world' but he criticised Hegel for defining the state as the institution, together with bureaucracy, which produces social cohesion. Although Hegel's notion of civil society had been largely derived from the writings of the eighteenth-century historians and political economists, he was particularly critical of Adam Smith's depiction of civil society as an harmonious sphere in which conflicting individual interests were synthesised into a unity by the workings of a 'hidden hand'. Hegel defined civil society rather differently as comprising institutions which, by themselves, were incapable of producing social order and unity. Some of these ideas passed into Marx's theory of the state and civil society; Marx's early writings depict the working class as wholly alienated, outside society, their integration possible only through a total revolution and, by implication, the workings of a beneficial state. In *Capital* Marx drew a different picture: the industrial working classes succeed in developing their own characteristic institutions which mediate the

relation of class and state, institutions centred in civil society and democrati-
cally organised. Marx's analysis of the social relations of capitalism thus
suggest the possibility that the working class, through its democratic institutions, can lay the basis for socialist transformation.

It is this latter theme that indicates an anarchist element in Marx's thought
and his writings on the Paris Commune are particularly eloquent in
defending this standpoint. Nevertheless, the influential Marxist theory of
the state, the bourgeois state as embodiment of class power which can be
changed only by the centralised socialist state – Marxist-Leninism that is –
derives more from Engels's writings than from Marx. Engels declared
unequivocally that in 'the last instance' the economic is decisive, a reductionist argument which leads him to characterise the state as the embodiment, in a highly concentrated form, of 'the economic needs of the class
controlling production', its historical development the automatic product of
economic forces. The modern state, he argued, is the organisation which
'bourgeois society takes on in order to support the external conditions of the
capitalist mode of production against encroachments of workers as well as
individual capitalists'. For Engels, the state was simply 'a capitalist machine,
the State of the capitalists, the ideal personification of the total national
capital' (Marx and Engels, 1962, Vol. 2, pp. 148–9). In the 'last instance' the
state reflects the economic needs of the class which controls production, an
external, coercive apparatus for maintaining class domination.

Engels's formulation suggests that in capitalist society the state is fully and
consciously controlled by the economically dominant class. The political
structure, therefore, enjoys no autonomy but is simply an epiphenomenal
form of the economic order. Similar arguments inform Marx's own writings,
especially *The German Ideology*, which describes the historical evolution of the
modern state in terms of the division of labour and mode of production, the
separate spheres of administration (law, army, police, civil service) which
emerge from the increasingly specialist division of work creating a sense of
national unity, an 'illusory community' which seeks to conceal the facts of
class struggle and conflicting material interests: 'The state is the form in
which the individuals of a ruling class assert their common interests... [it]
acts as an intermediary in the formation of all communal institutions and
gives them political form' (Marx and Engels, 1964).

By the end of the 1840s Marx had yet to work out his theory of social
change, surplus value and exploitation: the analysis of capitalism turned on a
polarised model of conflict between two classes. This dichotomic model of
class structure and social formation underwent profound change in his work
of the 1850s and 60s. One of the most significant historical developments
which occurred during the course of the nineteenth century, especially in the
advanced capitalist countries, was the increasing centralised nature of capitalism as a system. Marx integrated these developments into his theoretical
model of capitalism. He argued that although previous revolutions, such as

the French Revolution, had embraced the ideals of freedom and democracy against authoritarian power, the actual results were always 'a perfecting' of the state. The centralised state machine had originally been forged during the period of absolute monarchy 'as a weapon of nascent modern society in its struggle of emancipation from feudalism, and although the French Revolution had sought to create national unity necessary for the growth of bourgeois society, this development could be effected only by enlarging the powers of the institution which the ideals of 1789, liberalism and freedom, opposed (Marx and Engels, 1971, p. 149). In the years between the publication of *The Communist Manifesto* and the analysis of the failure of the Paris Commune, Marx gradually abandoned the reductionist standpoint adopted in the *Manifesto*, with its implication that in socialist revolution the working class would simply take over the existing state machine and use it for the task of reconstruction. In the Preface to the 1872 German edition of the *Manifesto* two crucial changes are apparent:

1. The rapid development of the labour movement resulting from the growth of capitalism had created the potential for democratic change from within civil society itself, through the institutions of the working class.
2. Because of the increasing centralisation of capitalism as an economic system, the state itself becomes more centralised so that the task of socialist transformation is not the reform of the state but its abolition: 'The working class cannot simply lay hold of a ready-made State machinery (as different factions had done in their ascendence to power) and wield it for its own purposes'. (Marx and Engels, 1971, p. 270)

Marx's hostility to the state now becomes total: in his writings on the Paris Commune he describes the centralised state machine of modern society as enmeshing 'living civil society like a boa constrictor', functioning as 'a parasitic excrescence on civil society', 'unproductive and mischievous', an 'incubus' which must be 'smashed' (Marx and Engels, 1971, pp. 149–70, 202–3). Whereas in *The Communist Manifesto* and the *Address to the Communist League* (1850) Marx had argued that socialism would necessarily produce further centralisation now he advocated a decentralising transition to socialism.

These political themes are closely bound up with Marx's theoretical analyses of the state as a separate sphere from civil society, partially autonomous from the dominant class yet necessarily linked with it. The bourgeoisie must develop a centralised state structure to facilitate capitalist progress (the state being responsible for communications, education, taxation, foreign trade and law) but because 'the real life' of the bourgeoisie lay in the sphere of civil, rather than political society, the state is always more than a mere agent of this class. This aspect of Marx's theory of domination is especially brought out in his analysis of Bonapartism: in 1851 Louis Bonaparte abolished the parliamentary institutions of the French bourgeoisie, arrested deputies, deporting socialists and republicans and outlawed free speech and a free press, all in order to safeguard bourgeois interests from socialism. The bourgeois class consisted of two large factions, the big landed proprietors and the financial and industrial bourgeoisie; the internal divisions of this class, however, obstructed the development of an autonomous, united class-conscious ruling bourgeoisie. Marx attempts to show that the state was not a simple reflection of social forces but rather an example of the separation of the state from society: under the rule of the second Bonaparte, Marx wrote, the state seems 'to have made itself completely independent' so that all classes 'fall on their knees before the rifle butt'. Executive power embraced a broad stratum, state officials numbering as many as half a million, and Marx depicts this bureaucratic state machine as an 'appalling parasitic body which enmeshes the body of French society like a net and chokes its pores'. State power soars 'high above society'. This mode of domination emerges historically 'when the proletariat is not ready (or able) and the bourgeoisie has lost the facility of ruling the nation' (Marx and Engels, 1962, Vol. 2, pp. 331–2). Marx is arguing that when no single class enjoys social and political dominance, the state emerges to act as mediator:

> The bourgeoisie confesses that its own interests dictate that it should be delivered from the consequences of its own rule; that, in order to restore tranquility in the country, its bourgeois parliament must, first of all be given its quietus; that, in order to preserve its own social power intact, its political power must be broken; that the individual bourgeois can continue to exploit the other classes and to enjoy undisturbed property, family, religion and order only on condition that their classes be condemned along with the other classes to like political nullity; that in order to save its purse it must forfeit its crown. (Marx and Engels, 1962, Vol. 2, p. 288)

In sharp contrast, Marx analysed the events surrounding the Paris Commune to argue that the institutions thrown up spontaneously by the working class organising themselves against the bourgeoisie represented the only authentic alternative to the centralising trends of the modern state. The Paris Commune was essentially the political form of proletarian emancipation, direct democracy characterised by the recall of political representatives, a people's army and militia, 'the reabsorption of the State power by society as its own living forces instead of as forces controlling and subduing it, by the popular masses'. The Commune was the 'glorious harbinger' of a new type of society, the people acting for itself by itself. And only the industrial working class could invent and put into practice the concept of Commune, of workers councils (Marx and Engels, 1971, p. 153).

Nevertheless, Marx was sharply critical of the policies pursued by the Commune describing its lack of socialist leadership and coherent socialist ideology: it was not socialist, 'nor could it be'. Subsequent generations of Marxists drew the conclusion that a successful proletarian revolution required more than self-governing working-class institutions, but a disciplined revolutionary political party, Marxist theory and a centralised socialist administration. A close analysis of Marx's writings on the Commune, however, suggests that although he saw the events of 1871 as doomed to failure by muddled and incoherent leadership, he nevertheless regarded the Commune as embodying a struggle against the state and the centralising trends of modern society, a reassertion of the independence of civil society.

The Commune's policy of democratisation – election to administrative posts, the power of recall and equality of pay – was defined by Marx as part of a process which sought to reverse the historical trend, set in motion by revolutions of the past, which invests the state and its apparatuses with control over civil society. But in works such as *The German Ideology*, *The Communist Manifesto* and the *Address to the Communist League* Marx had emphasised that the state, founded historically on the division of labour, class interests and class conflict, was effectively the 'official form of social antagonisms in civil society': thus in the transition from capitalism to socialism greater rather than less centralisation would be necessary. A broadly similar standpoint emerges from his criticism of the Marxist programme of the German Social Democratic Party – the Gotha Programme of 1875 – in which he scornfully rejected the concept of 'free state', arguing that the issue was rather one of elaborating the social functions of the state in socialist society analogous to their functions in capitalism. In writings such as these the state is clearly defined as the instrument of class forces, as an integral structure of society: in socialism, therefore, the state, as the dictatorship of the proletariat, will dominate civil society disappearing only with the advent of communism. The state and its organs of repression remain firmly anchored within society. It was only after the experience of the Paris Commune that Marx began to shift his position and hesitantly advance the standpoint of state versus society and emphasise the necessity for civil society to absorb and abolish the distinct organs of political society and reverse the historical trend of increasing centralisation.

But this radical, libertarian strand remained muted: in their published writings both Marx and Engels tended to identify the domination and centralisation of *capital* as the critical issue, the 'despotism of capital' rather than the despotism of the state. This is particularly brought out in Engels' article, 'On Authority' (Marx and Engels, 1962 [1872]), written polemically against anarchist socialism, in which he explicitly rejected democratic, decentralising forms of authority. 'Wanting to abolish authority in large-scale industry', he wrote, 'is tantamount to wanting to abolish industry itself, to destroy the power loom in order to return to the spinning wheel'. Large-scale industry and social development are impossible without authority: Engels argued that authority was neither good nor bad but relative to the specific social situation. Socialism will effectively transform the political functions of the state 'into the simple administrative functions of watching over the true interests of society'. Engels's formulation asserts the centralising trend of industrialism: authority is imposed from above over civil society and not 'reabsorbed' into its institutional framework (Marx and Engels, 1962, Vol. 2, pp. 636–9). Marx's unpublished writings on the Commune can be seen as a further deepening of his analysis of the relation between the creative and reflexive nature of humanity and the developing democracy of civil society. Here lies the link between the modernity of the Scottish and French Enlightenment and Marxism.

3

Critique of Positivism I: Durkheim

Durkheim and the Development of Sociology

Emile Durkheim (1858–1917) has the distinction of being the first professional, academic French sociologist to be appointed to a Chair in Sociology (Paris, 1913). For Durkheim, sociology was a vocation. Almost single-handed he forced the academic community to accept sociology as a rigorous and scientific discipline. In both his teaching and his research Durkheim laid down the standards whereby sociology was to be judged. In 1895 he published the first major methodology study of sociology in which he observed that none of the nineteenth-century sociologists – Comte, Mill, Spencer – 'hardly went beyond generalities concerning the nature of societies, the relationships between the social and the biological realms' and were largely 'content... to make a cursory inquiry into the most general resources that sociological research has at its command' (Durkheim, 1982, p. 48). Durkheim set himself the task of defining the object of sociology and the methods appropriate to it. His contributions to the study of industrialisation, suicide, religion, morality and the methodology of social science aroused enormous controversy, but their influence on the development of sociology as well as other areas of social science, especially anthropology, have been far-reaching.

Durkheim began his career in sociology at a time when the French educational system was being expanded and modernised. This was the period which followed the national humiliation of defeat in the Franco-Prussian war (1870–71) and the German annexation of Alsace-Lorraine. The intense nationalism of the third French Republic formed the ideological context for the secular reforms carried out by the state throughout the higher educational system. Durkheim's sociology has been described as contributing to the formation of a new civic ethic, a modern republican ideology which rejected both traditional French Catholicism and a deeply entrenched social conservatism. Thus the educational reforms of the 1880s and 90s were mainly designed to free the French university system from the grip of traditional ideological influences, especially those associated with residual, pre-bourgeois social groups.

In 1887 Durkheim took up a teaching appointment at the University of Bordeaux, which was the first French university to provide organised courses in the field of the social sciences, especially sociology. The teaching of social science had a practical basis in supporting the modernising ideals of educational reform. Durkheim's first courses, for example, were specifically addressed to teachers and covered an impressive range of topics from ethics, social change, suicide, the family and education to socialism and the history of sociology itself. Durkheim was particularly concerned to clarify the scientific status of sociology and clearly differentiate it from socialism. In late nineteenth-century France sociology was often regarded as synonymous with socialism and therefore hostile to bourgeois culture and values, to religion and the family and peaceful social change.

In the years between 1887 and 1902, when he became Professor of Education at the Sorbonne, Durkheim produced a series of studies which defined the nature of a scientific sociology. *The Division of Labour* (1964 [1893]), *The Rules of Sociological Method* (1982 [1895]), *Suicide* (1952 [1897]) together with *The Elementary Forms of the Religious Life* (1961 [1912]) are works in which Durkheim set out his conception of sociology as 'the science of institutions, their genesis and their functioning' (Durkheim, 1982, p. 45) in opposition to the eclectic, individualistic and often crudely journalistic approaches of other contemporary social scientists. In particular Durkheim sought to distinguish sociology, as the science which studies the objective reality of 'social facts', from psychology which he defined as the study of individual consciousness. Sociological explanation dealt with collective, not individual forces. The concept of social fact became one of Durkheim's 'fundamental principles' referring to all objects of knowledge which have to be built up, not through mental activity, but from observation and experiment. Social phenomena were external things reflecting a reality very different from the reality conceived by an individual. In the genesis of a social fact, Durkheim argued, individuals exercise a role but 'in order for a social fact to exist several individuals... must have interacted together' (Durkheim, 1982, p. 45).

Durkheim's definition of the field of sociology – the study of external social facts – does not necessarily imply a thoroughgoing positivism. Social facts were not simple objects, or things, existing independently of human consciousness and action and therefore objectively 'visible' to the observer. A social fact was a collective entity – family, religion, professional organisation – characterised by an underlying order, or structure, hidden from ordinary perception. Durkheim's sociology was an attempt to establish the pattern which lay behind all observable phenomena. Thus Spencer's 'individualism' contrasts sharply with Durkheim's 'methodological collectivism'. Social facts were defined by Durkheim as structures which, through their manifest forms, constrain and regulate human actions. External to the individual, social facts are 'invested with coercive power' which enable them to 'impose' their influence on individuals even against their will: 'We can no more choose the design of our houses than the cut of our clothes – at least, the one is as much obliga-tory as the other' (Durkheim, 1982, p. 58). Thus language is a social fact in Durkheim's sense, a system of rules which determine the nature of individual utterances, although the speaker has no knowledge of the rules governing ordinary speech performance.

Social facts thus become internalised and rule individuals 'from within' becoming 'an integral part' of the self. In this way society enters the individual as a moral force. Sociology was, therefore, not the study of external facts but of the ways in which social facts are saturated with moral elements. In *The Division of Labour* (1964) Durkheim described morality as the 'least indispen-sable, the strictly necessary, the daily bread without which societies cannot exist'. Sociology was concerned essentially with social cohesion and social order, forms of social solidarity, the ways whereby individuals are integrated into a functioning social whole.

Thus although committed to the ideals of objective, empirical science Durkheim's work, especially in *The Division of Labour*, falls firmly within the Grand Theory Tradition of nineteenth-century social thought. His theory of the development of society from a 'mechanical' to an 'organic' type is similar to the philosophy of history which underpins the sociology of Comte and Spencer. Beginning from philosophy Durkheim was frequently brought back to its central issues in his later work; he remained extremely sensitive to the relation of sociology to philosophy, his many discussions and analyses of concepts such as anomie, social change and the division of labour are satu-rated with philosophical implications. It was not a question of extracting ethics from science, he argued, but rather of establishing 'the science of ethics', treating the facts of moral life according to the methods of the positive sciences. Although the study of reality does not necessarily imply any reforming commitment 'we should judge our researches to have no worth at all if they were to have only a speculative interest'. Social science must study the 'state of moral health' in relation to changes in the environment. The result, Durkheim argued, is not intellectual indifference but 'extreme prudence'. Social science governs practice in that science provides 'the rules of action for the future', and, by establishing the laws of society, distinguishes the 'normal' and 'healthy' forms of social organisation from the 'pathological' and 'abnormal' (Lukes, 1973, pp. 87–8).

In many important respects, therefore, Durkheim remained a faithful disciple of Comte's positivism. He rejected Comte's theory of the unity of the sciences and the law of three stages as metaphysical speculation, but accepted Comte's notion of consensus and the sociologism and scientism that underpinned the fatalistic concept of the human subject. Durkheim defined society as the sum total of social facts, objective, thing-like elements, moulds 'into which we are forced to cast our actions' which resist all attempts to change and modify them by individual volition. Humanity is thus deter-mined by things which stand outside itself for 'even when we succeed in triumphing, the opposition we have encountered suffices to alert us that we are faced with something independent of ourselves' (Durkheim, 1982, p. 70). But in what sense do social facts control human actions? As we have seen, Durkheim argued that the individual experiences objective reality subjectively acting in conformity to its constraining nature. But this formulation assumes a passive relation of subject to object, a position which Durkheim does not sustain in all his sociological studies notably *Suicide* (1952), where he comes close to accepting that action which follows the constraining influence of social facts does so because the individual, the subject, has interpreted the external facts in specific ways. Nevertheless, there is a strong, mechanical element in Durkheim's sociology as, for example, when he argues that 'states of consciousness can and ought to be considered from without and not from the point of view of the consciousness experiencing it', a standpoint reiterated in his brief discussion of Marxist methodology:

> We consider as fruitful this idea that social life must be explained, not by the conception of it held by those who participate in it, but by the profound causes which escape consciousness; and we also think that these causes must be sought chiefly in the way in which the associated individuals are grouped. We even think that it is on this condition, and on this condition alone, that history can become a science and sociology in consequence exist. (Lukes, 1973, p. 231)

Durkheim's sympathy towards mechanical materialism was clearly related to his attempt to rid sociology of the atomism inherent in other contemporary social theorists such as Taine, but the result was a conception of society less the product of collective human action than as an external constraining structure. Durkheim's epistemology has the effect of splitting society into two separate structures, 'social milieu as the determining factor of social evolution' enabling the sociologist to establish causal relations, and the subjective state defined as a passive process of socialisation.

In Durkheim's writings the concept of milieu plays a crucial role. The term itself characterised virtually all forms of nineteenth-century positivism (Taine, for example) but was never adequately theorised. Durkheim's usage derived also from the natural scientist, Claude Bernard, who employed milieu as the key to analysing the internal system of living organisms, the blood system, its various fluids, their functional relations in the maintenance of a constant body temperature and thus equilibrium. It is not surprising that Durkheim's sociology enjoins the methodological principle of externality with the concept of society as an inherently equilibrating organism.

Durkheim firmly rejected utilitarian atomism as an adequate perspective for social science. Social solidarity could never flow from an atomistic concept of individuals freely pursuing their own private interests: social reality could not be defined in terms of individuals who exchange goods and services and thus contribute to social cohesion. For Durkheim society was constituted through social bonds which functioned to links individuals together in a variety of social groupings. Through these social relations individuals were linked with society as a whole. Without social bonds and a network of social relations there could be no social solidarity, only temporary, fleeting interactions and individual experiences between separated individuals. Thus in his analysis of primitive religion Durkheim raised the question of how the Australian aborigines, scattered into numerous tribes, remained as a society. His answer emphasised the existence of institutions and practice (totems, rites and beliefs) which produced a powerful collective notion of society as an enduring and permanent structure. Durkheim's conception of social solidarity was clearly opposed to the influential work produced by the German sociologist Ferdinand Tönnies (1855–1936), *Gemeinschaft und Gesellschaft* (1887) (translated as *Community and Association*), which advanced the view that modern industrial capitalism, a society increasingly dominated by purely economic forces, was losing the authentic naturalism of earlier, pre-industrial social formations. Tönnies' depiction of modern society was one in which the cash nexus penetrated all spheres of social life determining the basic forms of social relationships. For Durkheim, Tönnies' concept of society, which largely derived from the writings of Marx and the German socialist, Lassalle, represented everything in their darkest colours, a simple dichotomy being established between the assumed spontaneous social solidarity of pre-industrial village life and the atomised, egoistic individualism of modern urban culture (Tönnies, 1971, pp. 245–7). Tönnies' analysis suggested that social cohesion and social regulation were possible only through the intervention of an external institution, namely the state.

While Durkheim agreed with Tönnies in rejecting Spencer's notion of an immanent harmony of individual interests that by themselves promote a spontaneous cohesion, they disagreed on the role which centralised authority must play in a modern industrial society. In this sense Durkheim's sociology was opposed both to Comte's authoritarian positivist church as the means of promoting social solidarity, as well as Marxist socialism with its central tenet of a centralised state functioning as the prime agency for social reorganisation and development of human communities.

It is this latter emphasis which has led some critics to argue that Durkheim's sociology was merely an attempt to combat 'the positions of the class-conscious socialist movement' which had developed during the latter half of the nineteenth century (Therborn, 1976, p. 269). During the 1890s many of Marx's important writings appeared in French translation and a distinctive Marxist intellectual and political culture emerged. French university students formed reading groups explicitly to study *Capital* while many of the leading academic journals discussed Marxist ideas, reviewed books on Marxism and posed the whole question of the scientific status of Marxist theory. Durkheim criticised Marxism for the class bias of its theory noting, in

1899, that the 'malaise' within modern society was not something centred on a particular class 'but is general throughout the whole of society', affecting both employers and employees although taking different forms in each case, 'an anxious and painful restlessness in the case of the capitalist, discontent and irritation in that of the worker'. State socialism was not the solution, for the crisis of modern society was not one of conflicting material interests but essentially a matter of 'remaking the moral constitution of society' (Lukes, 1973, p. 323).

Durkheim rejected, therefore, the political assumptions and theory of revolutionary socialism, insisting that class conflict derived less from any basic structure within capitalism than from the necessary transition from traditional to industrial society, involving the disintegration of one set of values without their replacement by other cogent values: property ownership was secondary to this problem as were the forms of class tension. Both Marx's theoretical and revolutionary socialist conceptions, although widely discussed in French intellectual circles especially through the work of Georges Sorel (1847–1922) who at one time sought to synthesise the work of Marx and Durkheim, exerted little influence on the development of Durkheim's sociology. Nevertheless, Durkheim was acquainted with Marx's writings and followed the debate between Marxists and other social scientists with great interest, although inclining to the view that the value of *Capital* lay in its 'suggestive philosophical perspectives' rather than its 'scientific' conclusions. Durkheim's understanding of Marxism, however, relied almost entirely on secondary sources and these tended to be mechanistic and positivist. The Marxist and socialist movement which developed in both France and Germany during the latter part of the nineteenth century has been described as intellectually shallow, simplifying and vulgarising Marx's theories into a crude economic determinism. Contemporary Marxism in fact made no lasting contribution to the development of sociology being largely defined as a mistaken, although useful doctrine against which the genuinely scientific claims of sociology could be tested.

Durkheim's main thrust against Marxism was its emphasis on centralised authority as the only viable foundation of social order and therefore the assimilation of the social and the political to the economic. By 1902, in the second edition of *The Division of Labour*, Durkheim was advocating occupational associations centred within civil society as the most effective means of regulating the anomic state of modern industry, arguing that with 'the establishment of an occupational ethic and law in the different economic occupations, the corporations, instead of remaining a confused aggregate, without unity, would have to become again a defined, organised group... a public institution'. It was only through such collective institutions that the individualistic and particular interests of modern society might be subordinated harmoniously to the general interest: 'A group is not only a moral authority which dominates the life of its members; it is also a source of life *sui generis*. From it comes a warmth which animates its members, making them intensely human, destroying their egotisms.' The relation of state and corporations, state and individuals is 'intercalated', mediated by 'a whole series of secondary groups' close to the individual and thus able to integrate him/her into 'the general torrent of social life'. It is the 'density' of these occupational groups that enables them to exercise a regulative moral role and fill the void, for without such a system of organs 'the normal functioning of the common life is found wanting' (Durkheim, 1964, pp. 26–9).

Thus the division of labour effectively replaces the collective conscience as society evolves from mechanical to organic forms of social solidarity. Mediating institutions come into being generating the necessary social bonds to integrate individuals into the social whole.

Durkheim's Method: Social Facts and Society

Durkheim's sociology was initially conceived within the evolutionary theoretical framework of Comte and Spencer. Society constituted an organic whole in which the various elements functioned to maintain equilibrium. Durkheim rejected Spencer's version of methodological individualism and its utilitarian postulates, as well as the prevailing atomism of contemporary French social scientists such as Gabriel Tarde. Sociological explanation, he argued, must be independent of psychology and subjective consciousness. Writing in the 'Preface' of the second volume of *L'Année Sociologique* he advocated techniques of social investigation that would establish types of laws and the interconnectedness of facts:

> The principle underlying this method is… that religion, juridicial, moral and economic facts must all be treated in conformance with their nature as social facts. Whether describing or explaining them, one must relate them to a particular social milieu, to a definite type of society. (Wolff, 1964, p. 348)

Wholes cannot be analysed sociologically in terms of individuals: the unit of analysis is 'milieu', the collective forces and facts which thus constitute the object of social science. For Durkheim, the social was irreducible, a *sui generis*, and thus the psychological element was irrelevant. Durkheim's social realism was clearly opposed to those social scientists who adopted a voluntaristic, subjective and psychological standpoint. In his debate with Durkheim, Tarde wrote: 'I am a nominalist. There can only be individual actions and interactions. The rest is nothing but a metaphysical entity, and mysticism' (Lukes, 1973, p. 313). In *Suicide* Durkheim explicitly took issue with Tarde's sociological atomism arguing that social facts were objective data, things which exist independently of individuals, of individual psychology and human interactions: social facts can never be reduced to another order. In 'affirming the specificity of social facts' he was following the Comtist sociological tradition: 'No further progress could be made until it was established that the laws of society are no different from those governing the rest of nature and that the method by which they are discovered is identical with that of the other sciences. This was Auguste Comte's contribution.' The social constitutes the true object of sociology and must be rigorously distinguished from other levels of human existence: the social is 'a reality *sui generis* in society, which exists by itself and by virtue of specific and necessary causes, and which, consequently, confound themselves with man's own nature' (Lukes, 1973, p. 68).

To distinguish sociology from the other social sciences Durkheim argued that sociology had its own specific object, 'a reality which is not in the domain of the other sciences', the domain of social facts. In defining the specificity of the social Durkheim identified three groups of social facts:

1. those related to the morphological structure such as the volume and density of population, territorial organisation, technology (buildings, machines)
2. social institutions, such as family, religion, political and economic institutions, involving beliefs and practices (the normative sphere)
3. currents of opinion, collective representations, involving moral concepts, religious dogmas, political and legal rules.

Social facts are external structures realised socially through individuals while remaining independent of them. Social institutions, for example, socialise both existing and future generations by inculcating and maintaining traditions and practices.

For Durkheim, the morphological level represented the most basic, constraining structure of any society, severely limiting the possibility of human choice. But as society evolves historically the expansion of institutions enables the individual to achieve varying degrees of autonomy. Collective representations further underline Durkheim's concept of social facts as modes of interaction between individual and society. To treat social facts as things, therefore, does not imply that they are things. Social facts constitute a synthesis of different elements which combine to produce what Durkheim called 'emergent properties'. When phenomena interact with each other they produce characteristics which differ from the phenomena which constitute them (thus gas, hydrogen and oxygen combine under the right conditions to produce water which has the characteristic of liquidity missing from the component elements). Emergent properties are the product of a chemical and not mechanical process. Similarly society is no mere aggregate of social facts but rather an organism which combines chemically not mechanically its various elements into a higher, dynamic reality than that of individual experience. Society is structured in 'emergent principles': the interaction of individuals with institutions produces a collective phenomenon, social solidarity, a *sui generic* reality transcending the individual spatially and temporally.

The analysis of social facts demanded a sociological method both comparative and historical:

> For instance, by comparing the curve which expresses a suicide trend over a sufficiently extended period of time with the variations which the same phenomenon exhibits according to provinces, classes, rural or urban environments... we can succeed in establishing real laws without enlarging the scope of our research beyond a single country... When, on the other hand, we are dealing with an institution, a legal or moral rule... which is the same and functions in the same manner over all entire country, and which only changes over time, we cannot limit ourselves to a study of a single people. (Durkheim, 1982, pp. 155–6)

What Durkheim called 'the supreme instrument for sociological research', the method of concomitant variations, established the principle that if two or more social facts varied together a causal relation was involved. Thus the causes of the division of labour are certain variations in the social milieu such as increasing moral density (heightened social interaction between individuals) and growing population density. For Durkheim the same effect always corresponded to the same cause. Thus 'if suicide depends on more than one cause it is because in reality there are several kinds of suicide'. Whether comparing social facts within a single society or tracing their development over time the method of concomitant variation derived causal relations internally not externally, demonstrating that 'they are joined by some inner bond'. Durkheim stressed that the sociologist should study general not isolated variations and having proved 'that in a certain number of cases two phenomena vary with each other, we may be certain that we are confronted with a law' (Durkheim, 1982, p. 151).

In these formulations Durkheim adheres to a positivistic model of sociological method, the search for causal relations and laws which exclude, as part of this process, the active involvement of human agency. At the heart of Durkheim's method is the assumption that what happens must happen: there is never any sense that some other course of action might have occurred, no possibility of alternative paths. Thus although describing social facts as modes of interaction and differentiating his method from 'materialism' through its application of the spiritual principle' to the study of social life, Durkheim failed to develop an open-ended voluntarism. The emphasis lay rather in the ways human action contributed to maintaining a given society.

Nevertheless, Durkheim's positivism is not that of Comte. From *Suicide* onwards he grapples with the problem of autonomy and agency, the role of ideals and morality in social life. In his account of social solidarity, for example, the key element is the autonomy of moral action. Durkheim's sociology is permeated by rationalist principles that lead away from his dogmatic positivism. In *The Division of Labour*, for example, he argues that 'a mechanistic conception of society does not preclude ideals', for demonstrating that things happen in accordance with laws, it does not follow that 'we have nothing to do'. Durkheim never satisfactorily solved this dualism of the autonomy of the moral act and the determinism of social facts and his later sociological work revolves around this problem of human action and a constraining milieu. Comte had remained insensitive to the human dimension of social evolution, Vico's injunction that the social world was the work of man; Durkheim's positivism grapples precisely with this problem.

Both Comte and Durkheim argued that the social system necessitated social regulation and as early as 1886 Durkheim wrote that society must be bound together by strong social bonds that were moral in nature. The point here is that although society is an organism it does not spontaneously produce equilibrium. Its normal, healthy state is one of harmony between its various elements, but Durkheim emphasised that in the absence of a strong moral centre society must inevitably collapse into anarchy and destruction. Sociological positivism defines society as a system, a structure of social facts in which unity develops only through moral action. It is in this sense, therefore, that Durkheim's sociology is rationalistic, in that social cohesion is less the product of the workings of social milieu than the moral dimensions of social facts themselves. Pessimistic about humanity's possible sociability, with its insatiable appetites and egoism, Durkheim argued that there was nothing 'within an individual which constrains... appetites'; they can be constrained effectively only by external forces. If these are absent from the system then the result is general 'morbidity':

> What is needed if social order is to reign is that the mass of men be content with their lot. But what is needed for them to be content, is not that they have more or less but they be convinced they have no right to more. And for this, it is absolutely essential that there be an authority whose superiority they acknowledge and which tells them what is right. (Durkheim, 1958, p. 200)

Social solidarity is not spontaneously produced by the internal workings of the social system. Durkheim's solution was a sociology which sought to integrate the subjective factor within his general positivist methodology. Durkheim defined social facts, for example, as collective phenomena which resisted change through individual intention and will, a positivist standpoint which implied that ideas held by individuals had no reality of their own and could exercise no influence on change. But in the latter part of *Suicide* Durkheim argued that social life was made up of 'collective representations', collective symbols through which society becomes 'conscious of itself.' Society can be constituted only by the creation of ideals which 'are simply the ideas' through which society sees itself. A mechanistic, purely external concept of society he now argued, tended to eliminate its 'soul which is the composition of collective ideals' (Durkheim, 1952, pp. 312–16). Social facts are objective entities, Durkheim emphasised, but they also contain a significant subjective element which, combining within the individual's consciousness, forms representations of the social world. Collective life – social life – is thus reflected in these representations which effectively 'become autonomous realities independent of individuals' (Durkheim, 1953, pp. 23–6). Durkheim emphasised that collective representations differ from individual representations: for example, the conception of religion is more than individual feelings, rather a system which unifies states of mind, 'a characteristic way of thinking of collective existence'. In his essay, 'Pragmatism and Sociology' (Wolff, 1964 [1913]) Durkheim noted democracy and the class struggle as further examples of collective representations, authority which imposes itself on the different members of the social group. Collective representations thus constitute the source of all human action for humanity is never motivated entirely by purely physical needs and desires but rather by residues from the past, 'habits', 'prejudices' all of which exercise an active role in social life.

Durkheim's positivism is thus shorn of its empiricist trappings: social facts were not mere external things; social reality is saturated with moral elements. In his essay, 'The Determination of Moral Facts' (1953 [1906]), he identified morality with the universality of religious belief, arguing that social life itself can never 'shed all the characteristics it holds in common with religion' (Durkheim, 1953, p. 48). Morality and religion are inextricably interwoven: there has always been 'morality in religion, and elements of the religious in morality'. It seemed to follow that moral life, and thus social life, possesses a 'sacred character' which inspires respect, awe and obedience. 'In the beginning, all is religious', wrote Durkheim, in opposition to the Marxist thesis that social and cultural life constituted mere derivatives of economic forces, with social change the automatic product of material conditions. Social life is more than this, a moral structure consisting of universal precepts built around religious values and ideas.

Durkheim's concept of the social realm is one which diminishes the productive role of social life in the genesis of culture and ideology: as an 'organism' society is theorised ahistorically and abstractly. Hence his distinction between the 'normal' and the 'abnormal', social health from social disease. A social fact is normal if found in a society 'at the correct phase of its development' either as an effect or as an adaptation of the species to the specific conditions. Thus crime, statistically omnipresent in modern society, is normal since it functions to maintain solidarity by reinforcing collective attitudes to morality and law. The normal are those forces promoting social health, social integration with the collectivity, while the pathological reflect the breakdown of social solidarity. Durkheim's concept of sociology as a science of morals, his concern with social regulation and the possibility of community is central to his studies of the division of labour and suicide.

Division of Labour, Social Cohesion and Conflict

The Division of Labour develops a theory of historical evolution in which societies pass from a state of mechanical to organic solidarity, a process necessarily determined by the structure of the division of labour. In the preface to the first edition Durkheim noted that the origins of the division of labour were bound up with the relation of the individual to social solidarity:

> Why does the individual, while becoming more autonomous, depend more upon society? How can he be at once more individual and more solidarity? Certainly these two movements, contradictory as they appear, develop in parallel fashion what resolves this apparent antinomy is a transformation of social solidarity due to the steadily growing development of the division of labour.

The relation of the division of labour to social solidarity is conceived in moral terms, for although fulfilling specific material needs, its existence is bound up with relations of friendship and community: Durkheim writes that the 'true' function of the division of labour is 'to create in two or more persons a feeling of solidarity'. Mechanical forms of social solidarity are defined as essentially pre-industrial; social organisation is highly undifferentiated, characterised by similarity of functions, resemblances and a common consciousness. Its morphological structure is segmental, small groups and tribes consisting of different organs co-ordinated by and subordinated to a central authority, a low level of interdependence and weak social bonds, a low volume of population and material and moral density. Collective sentiments and beliefs predominate and the individual consciousness is scarcely identifiable; the social and religious are unified so that religious ideas saturate the whole society. Law is repressive, expiatory and diffuse, functioning not through specialised institutions but the whole society: 'In primitive societies... law is wholly penal, it is the assembly of the people which renders justice' (Durkheim, 1964, pp. 37–8, 56, 76). The essence of Durkheim's concept of mechanical solidarity is well summed up in a passage employing the collective pronoun to good effect: 'When we desire the repression of crime, it is not that we desire to avenge personally, but to avenge something sacred which we feel more or less confusedly outside and above *us*' (Durkheim, 1964, p. 100).

Mechanical solidarity is defined as a structure of resemblances linking the individual directly and harmoniously with society so much so that individual action is always spontaneous, unreflective and collective. In contrast, the basis of organic solidarity is the division of labour and social differentiation; the social structure is characterised by a high level of interdependence, industrial development and a high volume of population and moral and material density. Solidarity through social likeness is replaced by solidarity through difference and a strengthening of social bonds. The individual is no longer wholly enveloped by the collective conscience but develops greater individuality and personality. In this situation it is necessary that:

> The collective leave open a part of the individual conscience in order that special functions may be established there, functions which it cannot regulate. The more this region is extended, the stronger is the cohesion which results from this solidarity... each one depends as much more strictly on society as labour is more divided; and, on the other, the activity of each is as much more personal as it is more specialised.

Initiative and individuality create a society 'capable of collective movement', one in which 'each of its elements has more freedom of movement'. Durkheim compares this form of solidarity with that of the 'higher animals' in which each organ 'has its special physiognomy, its autonomy... the unity of the organism is as great as the individuation of the parts is more marked' (Durkheim, 1964, p. 131). Thus the term organic solidarity refers to a system of differentiated and specialised functions unified by the relations between its various parts; the individual depends on society through a dependence on the parts which comprise it. Law is restitutive and co-operative; social norms create the legal rules which permeate civil law, commercial law, administrative and constitutional law, all of which operate through specialised organs such as administrative tribunals and an autonomous magistracy. While repressive law 'corresponds to the heart, the centre of the common conscience', restitutive law is less central and more diffuse (Durkheim, 1964, p. 112).

Durkheim's main focus in *The Division of Labour* was on the social problems engendered by the transition from one social order to another, and the problematic nature of the social bonds which united individuals with each other and with society as a whole. He praised Comte for recognising that the division of labour was more than an economic institution but was sociological and moral in its necessary relation with social solidarity, even though its practical workings had the effect of creating social disintegration and moral deregulation. Durkheim was particularly critical of Spencer's individualistic concept of the division of labour and his argument that if left to itself the mechanism of specialisation would lead to the unity of the whole. Durkheim rejected Spencer's contractual theory of society since its atomistic individualism failed to grasp that every contractual relationship involved both third parties and antecedent social norms which regulated the relationship. For Durkheim, the advance of science and industry, in the absence of universalising moral norms, must eventuate in anomie, a moral vacuum. The evolution of societies from mechanical to organic forms of solidarity would not result in the harmonious social differentiation envisaged by Spencer, but rather 'extreme moral disorder' and 'egoism' if the process remained unregulated by a consensus of moral beliefs.

Durkheim argued, against Comte, that this 'moral vacuum' was not the result of the inherent nature of the division of labour but rather the absence of a moral consensus regulating the division of labour: normally the division of work produces social solidarity, social reciprocity and shared moral values which then regulate the various branches of industry and social life generally. It is only through what Durkheim called its 'abnormal forms' with its dispersion of interests that organic solidarity is undermined. Durkheim's concept of the abnormal refers essentially to modern industry, capitalist forms of the division of labour exemplified in economic crisis and class conflict. Durkheim identified social inequality as the major source of the abnormal form arguing that 'external inequality' has the effect of threatening organic solidarity by no longer enabling natural ability to correspond with social status. For Durkheim, a normal mode of production was one in which the work of each employee of an organisation was functionally co-ordinated and unity achieved. The point here is Durkheim's assumption that given 'normal' circumstances organic solidarity is self-regulating; but if abnormal forms predominate social order is clearly threatened.

There is, however, more than structural instability within the system: although agreeing with Saint-Simon that the social crisis was essentially moral in nature, Durkheim accepted Comte's one-sided view of human nature, that humanity is basically in need of control because of 'insatiable appetites'. In *The Division of Labour* and *Suicide* Durkheim couched his theory of anomie, 'normlessness', in Hobbesian terms although with one crucial difference. In the course of the eighteenth and nineteenth centuries the function of egoism in social theory changes from its polemical standpoint in Hobbes, as a criticism of residual feudal elements and ideology in favour of capitalist enterprise and values, to a moral-evaluative and negative standpoint in Comte and Durkheim. The glorification of capitalist values embodied in the concept of egoism demanded a one-sided characterisation of human nature which, in the writings of late eighteenth-century thinkers, became increasingly problematical. Adam Smith, for example, conceived egoism and altruism as two distinct components of human nature which he treated separately, egoism in *The Wealth of Nations* (1970), altruism or sympathy in the *Theory of Moral Sentiments* (1976 [1759]), a division which prompted the so-called 'Adam Smith problem' in academic scholarship based on the failure to integrate these polarities into a unified whole.

But egoism as a conservative and universal precept develops only at the end of the eighteenth and beginning of the nineteenth century in the work of Burke and Comte in which it is identified as the source of the disintegration of social bonds. Durkheim's description of modern society in terms of a 'malady of infinite aspirations', 'a thirst [for] novelties, unfamiliar pleasures, nameless sensations' and an absence of 'a healthy discipline' is moral-evaluative and not scientific, a philosophical and conservative analysis which identifies egoism with conflict and normlessness. The problem of reconciling a biological concept of human nature with a sociological concept of regulation persists throughout Durkheim's work and is particularly acute in his studies of class conflict and suicide.

In *The Division of Labour* (1964) the anomic and normless condition of modern society is linked with trade and industry, a sphere of life in which deregulation is most pronounced. Yet to describe nineteenth-century industry as 'normless' seems hardly credible: the evidence adduced by Durkheim, that an anomic division of labour was responsible for class conflict and industrial crises replacing organic solidarity, can easily be interpreted as evidence of working-class solidarity and cohesion mediated through specific working-class institutions (trade unions) expressing opposition to capitalist regimentation and inequality. A strike of nineteenth-century industrial workers constituted a 'healthy' and normal rather than 'morbid' and 'abnormal' form of social activity. That Durkheim interprets industrialisation in these terms is somewhat surprising since the basic thrust of his argument of an increasing organic solidarity in modern society suggests that co-operation and mutuality are precisely the characteristic effects of the 'true' functioning of the division of labour. Indeed, he argues that the values of individualism ('the culture of the individual'), generated by the French Revolution and Enlightenment philosophy, constitute part of the movement towards organic solidarity: the progressive emancipation of the individual from a centralised authority and culture implied a strengthening, not a weakening, of the social bonds. Thus individualism progresses in proportion to the diversification of labour and is not necessarily to be identified as egoism since the breakdown of the social bond flows only from one form of individualism. The nineteenth-century labour movement clearly represented individualism in the form of wage-labour, labour which was free and dependent on market forces; it was necessarily combined with collectivism and mutuality and the strengthening of social bonds within the working-class communities.

Anomie

What, then, does Durkheim mean by anomie? Anomie is identified with the goals sought by the individual and their possible realisation; these goals, desires, are partly biological, partly social. In general Durkheim analysed nineteenth-century industrial society as one in which norms regulating the 'getting' were either weakly institutionalised or absent. It is this absence of norms which Durkheim analysed as anomie, a situation occurring when 'society is disturbed by some painful crisis or by... abrupt transitions... In the case of economic disasters, indeed, something like a declassification occurs which suddenly casts certain individuals into a lower state than their previous one'. For Durkheim, anomie is clearly centred in the economic structure: in the sphere of trade and industry social life is in 'a chronic state' since economic development has severed industrial relations 'from all regulation', from the discipline exerted by religion and occupational associations. Appetites have thus been freed 'and from top to bottom of the ladder, greed is aroused', aspirations are no longer effectively contained, no one recognises 'the limits proper to them'. With the growth of industrialisation desires multiply and 'at the very moment when traditional rules have lost their authority, the richer prize offered these appetites stimulates them and makes them more exigent and impatient of control. The state of deregulation or anomie is thus further heightened by passions being less disciplined, precisely when they need more discipline' (Durkheim, 1952, pp. 252–4).

For individual passions can be checked only by an authority which everyone 'respects' and to which they yield spontaneously. Only society itself possesses the power 'to stipulate law and set the point beyond which the passions must not go... It alone can estimate the reward to be prospectively offered to every class of functionary, in the name of common interest'. In the 'moral consciousness' of society the limits are vaguely fixed and generally accepted: the worker usually knows his position and 'realises the extreme limit set by his ambitions and aspires to nothing beyond. At least if he *respects regulations* and is docile to collective authority, that is has a *wholesome social constitution*... Thus an end and a goal are set to the passions'. Not that these goals are rigidly defined for some improvement is always possible but the point remains 'to make men contented with their lot while stimulating them modestly to improve it' (Durkheim, 1952, pp. 249–58).

Durkheim's discussion of anomie, organic solidarity and individualism suggest a theory of compliance with the existing society in terms of its basic institutional structure. At the same time he was critical of the failure of industrial society to achieve a 'normal' division of labour which might adequately regulate human passions and establish a 'normal' relation between natural and social inequality. Durkheim's idealised concept of the division of labour has the effect of eliminating all relations of conflict from analysis and assimilating contradictions to an underlying unity. To conceptualise social development in terms of ahistorical abstractions – mechanical and organic solidarity – is to empty sociology of historical specificity and define society less as an empirical whole but as the expression of an inner essence – the 'normal' state from which modern industrial societies deviate in terms of their lack of regulation. Thus Durkheim's sociology of industrial society oscillates between two distinct poles: on the one hand, it outlined theoretically the development of complex, multi-layered social structures in which the collective forces enabled individuals to become increasingly autonomous; and on the other, it failed to grasp that this process of structural differentiation is effectively a democratisation of culture, an expansion of civil society and its institutions which enabled individuals, collectively organised into unions, political parties and professional associations to articulate specific interests which bring them into conflict with other groups, classes and the state itself. Structural differentiation in effect allows for greater participation, democratisation and activity within the institutions of civil society: anomie is thus an expression of the increasing autonomy of the human subject struggling against social forces which seek to control and repudiate his/her interests.

Durkheim had no adequate theory of the subject. He conceived evolution from one type of society to another largely as the product of impersonal natural laws; equally, he failed to understand that structural differentiation itself flows from human action, the pressures exerted continuously from 'below' the major, 'official' institutions of society, from within the culture of the broad masses. But like Comte, Saint-Simon, Marx and his contemporaries, Pareto, Michels, Weber and Mosca, Durkheim mistrusted popular democracy and feared the consequences of that process of democratisation which industrialism and the division of labour had set in motion, and which his own analysis had disclosed.

Suicide and Social Solidarity

Durkheim never analysed social stratification in ways which would have filled out or modified his general social theory. Instead the concept of anomie is illustrated, statistically, through his study of suicide. He intended this analysis not simply as a closely argued monograph on a specific sociological problem but as a general contribution to the analysis of the culture of industrial society.

Suicide, one of the most private and personal acts, was studied by Durkheim because although superficially a phenomenon more suited to psychological, not sociological explanation, the act itself clearly related to the problem of social cohesion and the social bonds holding society together. There was, too, the practical issue of a falling birth rate and the possibility that the family might decline in significance. 'A high suicide rate', Durkheim wrote in 1888, could indicate a regression of 'domestic solidarity' in which the 'cold wind of egoism freezes... hearts and weakens... spirits' (Lukes, 1973, p. 195). Suicide had been widely studied in France, Belgium and Germany, first as a moral and then as a social problem with correlations established between the suicide rate and numerous social factors which included rapid social change, economic depression, socio-economic status and urbanism. But the originality of Durkheim's discussion, as Anthony Giddens has pointed out, was to develop a systematic and coherent sociological theory of differential suicide rates within a sociological framework that assimilated the existing empirical findings (Giddens, 1977, p. 324). The language which Durkheim employed in his study reflects this sociological concern: the causes of suicide are linked to the state of society, currents of opinion, excessive individualism and pessimistic currents within the culture – an emphasis on notions such as 'forces' and 'currents' which tend to disguise his concern with the socio-psychological conditions for social health. This aggressive sociological language, Lukes has suggested, 'was altogether less suited to what he wished to say than the language of "social bonds", attaching individuals to social goals and regulating their desires' (Lukes, 1973, p. 216).

Durkheim identified four types of suicide – egoistic, anomic, altruistic and fatalistic (this latter type is not discussed in any detail and is noted simply as resulting from 'an excess of regulations'). The types are closely bound up with Durkheim's theory of morality and social solidarity, that the degree of cohesion present in a society will generate a tendency to certain forms of suicide. Suicide is social and collective; suicide proneness exists only in relation to specific social conditions. Thus the suicide current is defined externally, a social fact related to certain types of social structure. Egoistic and anomic suicide, for example, are mainly found in modern industrial societies, in social structures characterised by an absence of strong regulative norms and lack of integration. It is the currents which determine the suicide rate and in this sense Durkheim's sociological explanation was not designed to account for individual suicides. This has led many critics to point out that both the rate of suicide and the specific individual act must flow from the same cause and therefore Durkheim's account is, and must be, both an explanation of the collective as well as individual acts of suicide. Yet he insisted that the causes of suicide must be determined 'without concerning ourselves with the forms they can assume in particular individuals'. It is psychology which studies the question of *who* commits suicide; sociology studies the broad social concomitants, the social currents that determine suicide as a collective force. Durkheim was surely right to argue that in order to explain suicide as a social phenomenon, as a unified structure with permanent and variable features, analysis could not begin from the individual suicide since such a procedure would never account for the specific statistical distribution of suicide as a whole. The individual only exists as an individual within the framework of a social whole: 'We start from the exterior because it alone is immediately given, but only to reach the interior' (Durkheim, 1952, p. 315). But while establishing suicide as an external structure, *Suicide* is, in effect, a complex and subtle study of the relation between individuals and the social whole and the mediations involved in this process, of the institutions which function to integrate individuals by attaching them to certain social ends and values, thus moderating their biological desires and appetites through social and moral regulation.

In *Suicide* Durkheim established a number of correlations between the suicide rate and specific socio-cultural elements and values. Catholic countries enjoy a lower suicide rate than Protestant countries although both religions condemn the act itself. The suicide rate decreases during wartime and in periods of political turmoil (an example of what Durkheim termed, 'acute anomie'). Married women have a lower suicide rate than single women of the same age although married women without children are more likely to kill themselves than unmarried women (an example of 'chronic anomie'). A higher 'co-efficient of preservation' characterises married women with children than childless marriages. Thus the suicide rate varies inversely with the degree of religious, political and family density. Durkheim concluded that the suicide rate was closely connected with the presence of society within individuals: anomic forms of suicide result from the failure of social norms to restrain individual passions.

He argued, then, that 'suicide varies inversely with the degree of integration of the social groups to which the individual forms a part', and that Protestants have a much higher suicide rate than Catholics for the following reasons:

1. Catholic communities possess the stronger traditions and shared beliefs conducive to an integrated 'state of society' and 'a collective life' which restrains the suicidal tendencies endemic in industrial society.

2. The causes of suicide lie in the weakening of the power of 'collective representations' through the collapse of 'traditional beliefs' and cohesive communities in the face of industrial development and social fragmentation.

Durkheim established a positive statistical relationship between the suicide rate and educational and religious institutions. The influence of education is particularly important because the more educated a social group the more it is prone to question tradition and authority. Durkheim also provided an explanation of differential suicide rates in terms of the consciousness of those committing suicide, that is, by reference to 'collective representations'.

Superficially his argument is simple: the state of society produces either strong or weak suicidal currents and the extent to which a particular individual is affected depends entirely on the nature of the social bonds and degree of his/her integration in the social group. Discussing egoistic suicide, for example, Durkheim cited evidence showing that education and suicide were closely connected in that the more educated Protestants kill themselves more frequently than the less educated Catholics. Education fosters a spirit of free inquiry and develops a critical attitude towards traditional authorities. But Jews, who are more educated than Catholics, have a markedly lower suicide rate. Now this could mean that those Jews with a higher education kill themselves more frequently than those with a poor education. Durkheim, however, did not differentiate the different layers within a social group. By so doing he might have preserved the correlation between education and the suicide rate: but this would have meant cutting across his main argument that it is the lack of integration within a religious group which constitutes the fundamental cause of suicide, and, more particularly, the break with tradition engendered by education and individualism.

Durkheim argued that 'free inquiry' – 'the relentless spirit of criticism' – is especially marked among Protestants but this in itself is not the cause of suicide. The need for 'free inquiry', he suggested, has a cause of its own – 'the overthrow of traditional beliefs', the questioning and criticism of established authority:

> For ideas shared by an entire society draw from this consensus an authority which makes them sacrosanct and raises them above dispute. (Durkheim, 1952, Ch. 2)

High suicide rates flow from a weak social morality. And morality, for Durkheim, was closely bound up with religion. With this in mind his account of the low suicide rate among English Protestants is particularly illuminating for the statistics clearly threatened the whole thrust of Durkheim's analysis of suicide. As with the example of Jewish suicide statistics, Protestant English statistics are simply assimilated to another explanatory structure and interpreted as buttressing, not invalidating, Durkheim's argument. For the statistics are not what they seem: in England there exist laws sanctioning 'religious requirements', the power of Sunday observance and the prohibition of religious representation on the stage, respect for tradition is 'general and powerful' so much so that 'religious society... is much more strongly constituted and to this extent resembles the Catholic Church' (Durkheim, 1952, p. 161). Durkheim offers no evidence, for this assertion, but the significance of his remarks lies in the shift of emphasis from the concept of the suicide rate as a social fact, a *sui generis*, correlated closely with specific forms of social structure to a view of society that depends for its validity on the interpretation by the subject. For to argue that in England society is cohesive and regulated, that social bonds are strong notwithstanding the pervasive influence of Protestant ideology, is to postulate that this is how individuals actually perceive the social structure.

Similar problems confronted Durkheim in his analysis of Jewish suicide statistics, for having claimed an external link between the decline of traditional authority and education (the Protestants in France) he was forced to analyse these as an exception. Religious minorities, Durkheim suggested, suffering from continuous persecution, use knowledge 'not... to replace [their] collective prejudices by reflective thought, but merely to be better armed for the struggle'. In other words, education has a different meaning for Jews than it has for Protestants, and therefore Durkheim concluded that a high degree of education does not necessarily imply a weakening of traditional authority among the Jews. In effect, Durkheim has imported meanings into his sociological analysis to explain away statistics which cannot be adequately analysed in terms of external social facts and social forces.

The construction of meaning on the part of the acting subject is as significant for the analysis of suicide as the external determinations. Durkheim claimed, on the one hand, that suicide was a collective phenomenon characterised by a definite external structure and laws and, on the other hand, he stressed the internal nature of such facts thus implying some notion of meaning. As was argued earlier, Durkheim never solved satisfactorily the dualism of internal consciousness and meaning and external socio-moral determinations. Thus in *Suicide* he failed to discuss attempted suicide which is far more common than successful suicide: attempted suicide, as a 'cry for help' constitutes a communicative act involving the construction of meaning on the part of the actor and its assumed effects on those for whom the act is intended. But Durkheim was less concerned with the subject as creator of meaning than the reactions of subjects to collective social forces; *Suicide* was a paradigmatic study of the dislocations within modern society, the implications for the human community of the collapse of social bonds. There is a strong ideological thrust to Durkheim's theory of suicide exemplified in his uncritical acceptance of official statistics, his reliance on coroners' reports and their commonsense definition of suicide. The collection of suicide statistics is itself highly problematical: many social groups, for religious and social reasons, tend to under-report suicide. The statistics on which Durkheim relied were inherently biased by official definitions and method of classification, but, nevertheless, unproblematically integrated into his general theory.

Functionalism, Holism and Teleological Explanation

Although Durkheim rejected Comte's philosophy of history he accepted his attempted synthesis of science and reform. Comte's sociological positivism was based on the natural laws of social evolution governing human society and the strict application of natural science to the study of social institutions. Durkheim defined society as a social fact but also as a moral reality. As a moral structure society dominated the individual, its various parts functioning in relation, not to the individual, but to the whole. Durkheim's debt to Comte is thus clear: the holistic concept of society suggests that the basic tendency of its institutions – its parts – is the promotion of social 'health', social solidarity, stability, equilibrium. As with Comte, Durkheim defined the normal state of society as one of social harmony in which social forces work to produce conformity to the dominant norms.

By defining society as an organic whole Durkheim analysed social processes and institutions in terms of their relevant functions for the needs of the system. To explain a social phenomenon, he argued in *The Rules of Sociological Method* (1982, Chapter 5), it is necessary to separate the 'efficient cause' which produces it from the 'functions it fulfils'. Thus in *The Elementary*

Forms of the Religious Life (1961) Durkheim analysed religion in terms of its functions for strengthening social bonds and integrating the individual into society. Religious beliefs express the collective nature of society through representations, while religious rites organise and regulate its functioning. Religion expresses universal values, a role which is indispensable for the adequate functioning of all human societies. Similarly, the division of labour normally contributes to the promotion of social solidarity, while both the 'forced' (specialisation being no longer based on the natural talents of individuals) and the anomic forms are abnormal in that they fail to contribute to the development of social co-operation and cohesion. Durkheim's central argument, in his studies of the division of labour, suicide and religion, was the necessity for a moral order to regulate adequately social institutions thus facilitating the promotion of social solidarity. Functions are thus explicated in terms of the 'needs' of the social system.

One of the main problems with Durkheim's functionalism is that it eliminates the active role played by agents in the making of the various forms of social solidarity and patterns of social change. His approach ignores the question of how the moral values which hold society together are created and by whom. Thus in his analysis of collective representations such as totems, flags and ideologies, he seems to suggest that their function is one of reaffirming the underlying unity and solidarity of society. But flags are created by particular social groups seeking an identity, legitimacy and a domination over society and can be divisive producing a conflict over values (many American Indians reject the American flag, seeing it as symbol of repression). Durkheim's functionalism marginalises the role agents play, collectively and individually in the social reproduction and reproduction of cultural symbolic forms: the social forms pre-exist the individual to exercise effects on him/her. Durkheim's functionalist objectivism becomes teleological when agents disappear from the making process. To the extent that Durkheim claims only that specific institutions, such as professional associations, function to strengthen or weaken forms of social solidarity he avoids an explanation in terms of an ultimate purpose.

One result of Durkheim's holistic functionalism was a somewhat paradoxical argument of the social function of 'deviant' behaviour such as crime and suicide. Crime, for example, was 'normal' in those societies not dominated by a *conscience collective*, in which individualism has developed a sense of moral responsibility, and where some individuals will diverge from the collective norms; only in this way was moral change itself possible. Durkheim was opposed to the assimilation of the individual into the collectivity, advocating the development of personal autonomy and individual differences as the only viable basis of genuine individualism. The relation of the individual to the collectivity preoccupied his later writings as he sought to define the mediating institutions between the individual and the state. A social function cannot exist without moral discipline: economic functions, for example, are only a means to an end which is the harmonious community. Durkheim thus advocated occupational groups, or corporations, which would morally regulate economic activity and provide the basis of genuine social solidarity. In the preface to the second edition of *The Division of Labour* (1964) he described these secondary institutions as professional groupings consisting of lawyers, judges, soldiers and priests; the various industries would be governed by an elected administrative council exercising broadly similar functions to those of the old guilds such as labour relations, regulation of wages, conditions of work, promotion and so on. These groupings would also exercise a more general function, that of developing and encouraging intellectual and moral solidarity.

These proposals formed part of Durkheim's general theory that organic solidarity gradually dissolves coercive power in society so that a co-operative social order emerges regulated not by state institutions but increasingly by professional associations and their ethic of service to the community. In his *Professional Ethics and Civic Morals* (1957) he argued that these institutions were essential if the state were not to oppress the individual. The state must be subordinated to civil society although the institutions are closely related to it; state intervention is not abandoned but Durkheim's essential point was that the state could never constitute the source of moral unity for a modern complex society. It was for these reasons that he rejected Tönnies' form of state socialism, for while the intermediary institutions were largely autonomous they nevertheless were supervised by the state.

Durkheim's arguments are important because they focus on one of the central problems of sociology, that of maximising individual freedom and personal autonomy with the increasing collectivist trends of modern industrial society. A democratic society was one in which the source of moral obligation flowed out of the institutions of civil society, the source of social solidarity was immanent and not something imposed externally from above. Nevertheless, Durkheim remained within the positivist paradigm in that the mediating institutions were never defined in ways which maximised human activity and reflected popular democratic forms: Durkheim's professional associations are close to a bureaucratic structure whose function is the maintenance of social harmony; they are not institutions through which popular dissent and the conflict of interests can find expression, but the means of assimilating such elements to an underlying concern with social order. Their 'true' function lies in maintaining social cohesion but this is not their ultimate goal or purpose. Their function is quasi-religious in the sense of expressing a system of collective beliefs and practices which command obedience, the symbols and sentiments which transform society into a community in which individual differences, while significant, are merged ultimately into a higher unity. Here Durkheim is close to teleological explanation, going beyond the statement that an institution can strengthen or weaken specific features of society to an holistic position which identifies function in terms of the whole society.

For Durkheim social cohesion remained the highest principle to such an extent that his notion of mediating institutions is itself collectivist, its bureaucratic implications clearly detracting from its democratic potential. There is a sense in which Durkheim's reified concept of society finds its expression in a reified notion of mediation. Durkheim's holistic function-alism defines society in static terms, minimising the historical basis of insti-tutions as the products of human action in favour of institutions as things which regulate human action. Society was an organism and thus Durkheim writes of the 'pathological state' of modern society, its 'morbidity', 'pessimism' and 'abnormal', 'anomic' division of labour: the social organism has 'reached a degree of abnormal intensity'. Thus anarchists, mystics and socialist revolutionaries share a profound hatred of the present and 'disgust for the existing order' developing only 'a single craving to destroy and escape from reality'. Life is often harsh, Durkheim writes, 'treacherous or empty' and the task of sociology is to identify the means of establishing a collective authority which will regulate the degree of 'collective sadness' in society and prevent it from reaching 'morbid' heights' (Durkheim, 1952, pp. 360ff). Yet, as one of Durkheim's students, Maurice Halbwachs (1970) observed, if high suicide rates are found in all advanced societies in what sense can they be categorised as 'morbid?': 'Are all European societies unhealthy? Can a single society remain in a pathological state for three-quarters of a century?' (Lukes, 1973, p. 225).

4

Critique of Positivism II: Social Action

Understanding and the Social Sciences

The dominant methodological orientation of nineteenth-century sociology was positivism: society was defined in holistic, organicist terms as a system determined by the existence of specific laws which worked to promote change and cohesion through different stages of evolution. It was assumed that a fundamental continuity subsisted between the realms of nature and society. The methods appropriate to the study of the natural sciences were thus appropriate to the study of human society and culture.

In Germany the emergence of sociology as a distinctive discipline owed much to this positivist tradition, but in striving to define its own specific methodology and concept of society many of the central assumptions of positivist orthodoxy were abandoned. The major influences on the development of German sociology were philosophers – Wilhelm Dilthey (1833–1911), Heinrich Rickert (1863–1936) and Wilhelm Windelband (1848–1915) – concerned with epistemological issues and problems of methodology in the social and cultural sciences. Towards the end of the nineteenth century positivism had become an increasingly significant current of thought within German intellectual culture. For these philosophers, the Comtist notion of sociology as the queen of the sciences represented a serious threat to the study of human action and human culture. It was argued that positivism foundered, first, because human society constituted a realm of unique, not recurrent, law-like processes in which human autonomy and freedom were decisive elements; and, second, because society itself did not exist in any meaningful sense apart from the individuals who comprised it together with their unique human actions. Thus the methods of the natural sciences were considered inappropriate for social and cultural study. Effectively, therefore, the possibility of sociology as a science was rendered extremely problematic.

One of the fundamental assumptions in this critique of positivism was that the socio-historical realm could be understood only because it had been created by humanity. 'Mind can only understand what it has created', wrote Dilthey. 'Nature, the subject-matter of the physical sciences, embraces the reality which has arisen independently of the activity of mind. Everything on which man has actively impressed his stamp forms the subject-matter of the human studies' (Dilthey, 1976, p. 192). Dilthey made an important distinction between explanation and understanding: to explain an event, or an institution, assumed an external, mechanical relation between the human agent and the world of reality; explanation was conceived in terms of mechanical causation which effectively eliminated the subjective aspects of human life from the analysis. But human culture consisted also of the category of understanding, the interpretation of reality by human subjects which saturates everyday life and without which society would be impossible. Because positivism treated human agents externally, as objective data, it failed to integrate this element of understanding into its methodological framework.

From these arguments it is fairly clear that Dilthey's concept of understanding is historicist and opposed to the reduction of understanding to psychological categories and the reliving of the experience of others. Hermeneutic understanding seeks to produce *historical knowledge* – not psychological knowledge – of the part to whole. Understanding is, therefore, not a form of empathic penetration and reconstruction of individual action and consciousness, but an interpretation of cultural forms that have been created and experienced by individuals. Dilthey clearly rejected the naturalistic positivism of Comte and Spencer, the reduction of historical reality and culture to mechanistic laws and materialist concepts which excluded the category of understanding.

Dilthey's separation of the natural from the cultural sciences was a distinction between what Windelband called the *nomothetic* sciences, concerned with establishing general laws, and general phenomena, and the *idiographic* sciences which were concerned with unique and unrepeatable events. Rickert further developed this distinction by equating the scientific with the *nomothetic* methodology and the cultural with the *idiographic* methodology. The essential difference between the sciences was defined not so much in terms of subject matter or content, but rather in terms of their distinctive method: as an individualising method, the cultural sciences were concerned with the analysis of reality in terms of values not laws. Rickert emphasised that the cultural sciences explored questions of meaning in relation to the concept of culture as something produced through human action and thereby saturated with human values. The methodology of the cultural sciences was individualising and related to values (what Rickert termed 'value-relevance'). In contrast, the natural sciences investigated objects separated from values. The cultural sciences should, however, avoid value judgements seeking merely to relate objects to values. It was this concept of value relevance – or value relatedness – which played an important role in the development of Weber's interpretative sociology. Rickert did not imply the necessity to make *a priori* judgements on the value of cultural elements or actions, only that cultural forms can be analysed in terms of the values of the culture of which they form part.

Formal Sociology: Simmel and Sociation

Rickert had argued that the object of study in the cultural sciences must be constructed by the researcher through methodology, he rigorously opposed the 'naive realism' of historians by postulating a concept of reality as formless and chaotic unless ordered through theoretical categories. One result of this standpoint was to empty the concept of society of all substance other than unique individuals who comprised it. Society was no objective datum governed by laws of development, no whole exercising ontological priority over its parts. Society was defined in nominalist terms and in the sociology which emerged out of the methodological debate over the status of the cultural sciences the categories of understanding and the human subject lay at its centre.

The work of Georg Simmel (1855–1918) reflected many of these arguments. The subject matter of sociology was defined as social interaction between active human agents which always involved complex cultural meanings. It was not a question of individuals as such, but of the ways in which they act socially: thus Simmel rejected the positivist argument that society constituted an objective system dominating its members; society constituted as an intricate web of multiple interactions and relations between individuals which embody the principle of sociation; individuals connected by interaction; institutions such as the family, religion, economic organisations and bureaucracy constituted the forms taken by the social content of such interaction. The true object of sociology was thus sociation.

Simmel's work covered an enormous range of topics and issues, including problems of methodology in the social sciences: *The Problems of the Philosophy of History* (1977 [1892]) which influenced Weber's work on methodology, 'The Problem of Sociology' (Wolff, 1965 [1894]), 'How is society possible?' (Wolff, 1965 [1908]) 'The Field of Sociology' (Wolff, 1950 [1917]); contributions to cultural theory – *The Philosophy of Money* (1910), 'Philosophic Culture' (1957 [1911]), and essays and studies in philosophy, music, literature, fashion and general problems of aesthetics.

His first important sociological work, *On Social Differentiation* (1890), was written under the influence of Spencer and positivism, although the central argument that society progresses from a state of undifferentiated group existence to a condition in which human autonomy and individualism are possible, because of differentiated social structures, remained a significant element in the later anti-positivist and anti-evolutionary sociology. In *The Problems of the Philosophy of History* he defended the notion of man as the cognitive subject whose actions produce the historical world. Historical knowledge is possible, not as a simple reflection of an external reality, but as a form of human experience. The world itself becomes an object of knowledge through the analysis of forms (Simmel, 1977, pp. 16–18, 60–1). What Simmel meant by form was a category, or number of categories, through which the world of experience becomes transmuted into a taxonomy, a conceptual scheme with both epistemological and ontological status. Law, sexuality, society are thus forms in this sense. Forms provide coherence to the world of diverse and incoherent objects: Simmel suggests that the concept of form is immanent and can never be deduced from the context or from the artefact (Simmel, 1980, p. 6).

Thus for Simmel the problem of social reality was solved by recourse to Kantian philosophy. Kant had argued that knowledge was possible only through the immanent categories of the mind and not by reference to experience and context. Similarly, Simmel argued that social reality becomes meaningful only through the organising principles associated with specific, universal forms. It followed that science did not develop out of content, which was merely random, objective facts pertaining to experience; rather, science always implied interpretation and ordering according to concepts which remain *a priori* for the different sciences. In the elaboration of science, concepts have priority. There are no objective laws, no totality. Simmel rejects the hypostatised notion of society found in Comte and Spencer in favour of an active, ceaseless interaction of many elements that constitute a complex structure. He opposed those modes of sociology which reified society as a reality external to the individual existing as if it had a life of its own separate from human action. The concept of form enabled Simmel to analyse institutions and social processes objectively while retaining the notion of the active human subject. Sociation did not imply isolated individuals who lack development and therefore interaction. Without forms there is no society; forms inhere in reality itself although reality in its empirical immediacy is structureless. It is only through what Simmel calls the 'great forms' that the complex reality of human society is rendered intelligible.

There is, therefore, a structure, or order, which expresses itself in sociation. Form is rigorously separated from content. Simmel writes:

> I designate as the *content*, as the *material*, as it were, of sociation. In themselves, these materials with which life is filled, the motivations by which it is propelled, are not social. Strictly speaking, neither hunger nor love, neither work nor religiosity… are social. They are factors in sociation only when they transform the mere aggregation of isolated individuals into specific forms… subsumed under the general concept of interaction. Sociation is the form… in which individuals grow together into units that satisfy their interests. (Wolff, 1950, p. 41)

It is these reciprocal forms of sociation which constitute the object of sociology, not individual actions or isolated elements which Simmel identifies as the content or material of sociation. Through the forms of sociation individuals develop into a unity; love, purposes and inclinations become transposed from individual properties into the social through their realisation in forms. Forms of sociation include hierarchies, corporations, marriage, friendship; forms do not produce society, forms are society. If all interaction ceased then society itself would no longer exist. Simmel's distinction between form and content enables him to argue that although the content of institutions and actions may vary, the forms remain. Thus the form of sociation among a band of robbers may be the same as that characterising an industrial enterprise; economic interests may be realised in forms of competition as well as co-operation. Power becomes a sociological form through a structure of interaction which links the dominator and the dominated: absolute power, for example, always involves an interaction, an exchange between the action of the superordinate and the subordinate.

Perhaps the best known of Simmel's forms is the dyad which he defines as a relation of two individuals involved in immediate reciprocity. The dyadic form can comprise different contents such as teacher/student, doctor/patient, husband/wife, and so on, but its essential character hinges on the dependence of the whole or each individual: the withdrawal of one destroys both the relation and the whole itself. But should another individual join the group creating a triad a qualitative change occurs in which there is no longer immediate reciprocity but mediation. The dyad is not experienced as a supra-individual element, a collectivity; in contrast the triad is experienced as a social structure standing outside and independent of the individual.

In these formulations Simmel opposed the reductionism of psychology which failed to grasp the sociological fact that a change in the forms of sociation, a change in numbers, necessarily engendered the development of new properties which cannot be derived from studying the individuals alone. Similarly, in his discussion of secrecy, which he describes as 'one of man's greatest achievements', Simmel analysed it as a form which enhances, not diminishes, human life in that it produces an intimate, private world alongside the public world, a world in which the exclusion of outsiders leads to a heightened sense of moral solidarity on the part of those who share the secret. But as secrecy is surrounded by the permanent possibility of detection it therefore generates tension between the individual's capacity to keep the secret or a weakness to reveal it: 'Out of the counterplay of these two interests, in concealing and revealing, spring nuances and fates of human interaction that permeate it in its entirety... every human relation is characterised, among other things, by the amount of secrecy that is in and around it' (Wolff, 1950, pp. 118–20, 330–4).

The task of sociology, as Simmel formulated it, was thus to identify the 'pure forms' of sociation and engage both with the uniqueness of historical phenomena and the underlying uniformities. Society is the product of human activity in the sense that society is sociation, and sociation itself exists at the level of ordinary everyday life as forms which bind individuals together. Forms have no separate reality apart from content in the same way as the individual has no separate reality from society. Individuals create society and forms; and simultaneously exist externally to both. The individual's relation with society is dualistic, both within and outside it, 'both social link and being for himself, both product of society and life from an autonomous centre' (Simmel, 1956, pp. 22–3). Without sociation the human agent could hardly exist; but the forms of sociation restrict his autonomy. Simmel's concept of society is one built around the dualisms of human existence: sociation entails conflict and harmony, attraction and repulsion, hate and love, independence and dependence. Clearly this is a different sociological standpoint from the nominalism of Tarde: society is not conceived in atomistic terms but is structured through forms that realise both the individuality and regularity of human action.

Nevertheless, Simmel emphasised that human existence is real only in individuals and that to confine sociology to the study of 'large social formations resembles the older science of anatomy with its limitation to the major, definitely circumscribed organs such as heart, liver, lungs, and stomach, and with its neglect of the innumerable... tissues'. The study of major social formations constitutes the traditional subject matter of social science, and by accepting this approach 'the real life of society as we encounter it in our experience' would play no role in sociological analysis (Wolff, 1965, pp. 312–32). The object of sociology is interactions 'among the atoms of society', and in his essay, 'The Problem of Sociology' (Wolff, 1965), Simmel rejected the notion that sociology was defined by its contents. Sociology was neither a dumping pot for the other human sciences, history, psychology, jurisprudence, nor a summation of other disciplines. Sociology was defined as a distinctive method, an instrument of investigation: 'In so far as sociology is based on the facts that man must be understood as a social being and that society is the medium of the historical process, it contains no subject matter not already treated in one of the existing sciences.' The study of form clearly distinguishes sociology from the other sciences: thus sociation constitutes a form stripped of all psychological, biological and historical elements and although these latter disciplines are useful in the description of facts they always 'remain outside the purpose of sociological investigation'. As forms are not reducible to, or defined by, their content so sociology is conceived in terms of the categories of its analysis and perspective. Sociology abstracts from the complexity of social life that which is 'purely society', that is, sociation. The sociological approach is therefore its mode of abstraction, the means whereby the essential features of concrete phenomena are extracted from reality and exaggerated so that the underlying configurations and relations, which are not actually realised in reality itself, are clarified. In this way it becomes possible to compare social phenomena that have radically different contents but share a similarity of form (Wolff, 1965, pp. 312–32).

The purpose of these 'ideal types' is to facilitate the analysis of meaning. In his discussions of forms such as the dyad, secrecy and fashion, Simmel's main concern is always with the meanings of the actions that comprise the structure, understanding the modes of sociation from the standpoint of both the subject and the whole. Social interaction is always more than the sum of the actions, involving both the form or structure as well as the relations within the form itself. Society is not analysed from an holistic standpoint but from the perspective of social interaction conceived as a network of hidden relationships.

Simmel's sociological approach has been characterised as a form of sociological impressionism, the network of interrelationships constituting a labyrinth rather than system, his sociology dismissed for its failure to develop a constructive view of society as a whole. But the significance of Simmel's sociology lies precisely in the fact that it opposed the anti-humanist, scientistic approaches of positivism and vulgar Marxism and sought to recover the concept of society as the product of socially mediated human action. Thus forms explain the resilience of human society, its toughness, elasticity, colourfulness, 'so striking and yet so mysterious', the interactions that constitute sociation producing the social bonds which 'makes for the wonderful indissolubility of society, the fluctuations of its life, which constantly attains, loses and shifts the equilibrium of its elements' (Wolff, 1965, p. 328). The point is, of course, that Simmel was concerned with society as a whole, with large-scale social formations, but not as external structures stripped of their human determinations. Simmel's sociology rejected all modes of reifying social institutions and processes for while forms are external to individuals they only appear as autonomous entities. 'The deepest problems of modern life', he wrote, 'derive from the claim of the individual to preserve the autonomy and individuality of his existence in the face of overwhelming social forces, of historical heritage, of external culture, and of the technique of life' (Wolff, 1950, p. 409).

Simmel had developed a sociological perspective which exerted a great influence on subsequent German sociology especially that of Max Weber. Although Durkheim's *The Rules of Sociological Method* was translated into German and published in 1904, it had little impact and it was Simmel's notions of understanding, social action and methodology which triumphed. Durkheim's *positive* sociology contrasts sharply with Simmel's *ambiguous* sociology. In a review of Simmel's work written in 1900 Durkheim had drawn attention to what he considered an entirely arbitrary distinction between form and content: but Simmel constantly emphasised the impossibility of rigorously distinguishing form and content. It is 'impossible to avoid ambiguity', he wrote, 'the treatment of a particular problem will appear to belong now in one category, now in another'. Ambiguity even extended to methodology and Simmel argued that there existed no clear technique for the application of his fundamental sociological concept of sociation (Wolff, 1965, p. 324). It was the implication here of the arbitrary nature of sociological method, as well as the ambiguity over form and content, which clearly differentiated Simmel's humanist sociology of modernity from the nineteenth-century positivist tradition and it was these themes which were further developed in Weber's sociology.

Understanding and the Problem of Method: Weber

The sociology of Max Weber (1864–1920) sought to synthesise the positivist emphasis on causal analysis with the hermeneutic concept of understanding. Although Weber shared with Simmel a concern with integrating the human subject into the cultural sciences within a social action framework, he differed from Simmel in his emphasis on macro sociological studies of institutions and processes conceived from a broad historical perspective. Both were concerned with the fate of the individual within modern culture, but whereas Simmel focused his analysis on the atoms of society, Weber dealt with such holistic categories as the Protestant ethic, pre-industrial social structures, bureaucracy and the nation state. The range of Weber's empirical and historical studies is truly encyclopaedic covering economic history, political economy, the comparative study of religions and the methodology of the social sciences.

Originally trained in jurisprudence and the history of law, Weber's first studies examined the structure of East German agriculture and the recruitment of Polish workers; in 1896–97 he published studies of the decline of the ancient world and the stock exchange. At the outset of his intellectual career Weber was not a sociologist and rarely used the term in his first writings. At university he lectured on law and political economy and at the age of thirty-one became Professor of Political Economy at Freiburg before moving to Heidelberg in 1896. Weber thus came to sociology from economics and history; his early sociological writings reflect a concern with the methodological and epistemological issues raised by the positivist intrusions into German historical scholarship during the latter part of the nineteenth century. German social science had been strongly influenced both by the evolutionary theory of society conceived by Comte and Spencer, as well as the burgeoning Marxist intellectual culture that emerged in the 1890s. Under the leadership of Karl Kautsky and Eduard Bernstein, the German Social Democrats became the single most important Marxist political party in Europe, commanding widespread support from the German working class. The rise and institutionalisation of German sociology effectively coincided with the development of a political mass movement committed to Marxism and an intellectual culture which attempted to systematise Marxist materialism into a coherent science of society. Weber's sociology developed both as a response to evolutionary positivism on the one hand and to dogmatic Marxism on the other.

Weber defined Marxism as a form of economic determinism, a theory postulating a strict functional relation between modes of thought and economic interests: ideas, whether they were religious or political, were merely epiphenomena lacking any vestige of autonomy. For Weber, Marxism defined knowledge as ideology, as the reflection in consciousness of class and economic interests: concepts were scientific in so far as they reproduced this objective reality while pointing the way forward to the historical inevitability of socialism and communism. Society was thus a system dominated entirely by its mode of production and laws of development. Human subjects exercised no constituting role but were the passive objects of an historically evolving whole.

Weber's opposition to the concept of objective determining laws was based on the argument that such laws – whether Marxist or positivist – eliminated the active and conscious elements of a culture transforming all ideas to the status of automatic reflexes of external, material forces. Like Simmel, Weber adopted a nominalist standpoint arguing that holistic and collectivist concepts such as the state, bureaucracy and system could be analysed only as the results and modes of organisation embodied in human action. Bureaucracies do not act. The burden of his early methodological essays is to demonstrate that the fundamental task of social science lies in analysing society as a structure of meaning-endowing actions centred on the human subject.

In his essay, 'Objectivity in Social Science' (1949 [1904]), Weber outlined his approach in terms of understanding 'the characteristic uniqueness of the reality in which we move', a reality which consists in 'an infinite multiplicity of successively and co-existing emerging and disappearing events, both "within" and "outside" ourselves'. The study of so-called objective laws, or the relations between the various external elements that constitute a social system, does not, by itself, generate meaning. Weber insisted that the category of meaning is produced only through social action when the actor attaches a subjective meaning to behaviour. For Weber, history possessed no immanent meaning as historicists had suggested: history is simply the human context in which individuals and groups struggle to define and achieve certain values and goals. Weber followed Nietzsche's stoic refusal to accept the existence of universal values: there is no meaning apart from the concrete actions of human actors (Weber, 1949 [1904], p. 72).

Weber defined society in terms of sociation, 'social relationships' which 'denote the behaviour of a plurality of actors in so far as, in its meaningful content, the action of each takes account of that of others and is oriented in these terms'. Social action is oriented towards human subjects not things, the acting individual saturating the social context with meanings. Weber's concepts are relational not substantive and his concept of action assumes intentional behaviour involving motives and feelings; sociology as a cultural science is thus concerned with meaningful action rather than with purely reactive or mechanical behaviour. Sociology is defined as a science 'which attempts the interpretative understanding of social action in order... to arrive at a causal explanation of its course and effects' (Weber, 1964, p. 118). Explanation is interpretative in the sense of seeking to understand the meanings of the actor through empathy, and causal in the sense of seeking to relate the action to means and ends. Weber did not define sociology as a subjective, intuitive mode of investigation: because human action is subjective it does not follow that it is unpredictable. Social action hinges on the actor selecting means to realise specific ends and it is this rational component which separates human action from natural processes. Moreover, because Weber's focus is on action a 'probability' element is introduced. Against Marx, Weber asserts that it is important to be certain that in specific situations actors will follow a particular course of action: but the only certainty is that they 'probably' will. Hence the illusion that society is grounded in deterministic laws which eliminate this probabilistic element of social action Because action is social it is thus governed by norms relating to the means–ends continuum and it is this patterned aspect that enables the sociologist to undertake causal analysis, for without action nothing can happen: and therefore the motives impelling individuals to act must constitute part of the causal process (Weber, 1964, p. 88).

Weber argues, then, that objective knowledge is possible within the cultural sciences; the fact that the object of study is cultural values does not imply a subjectivist sociology. Weber distinguishes evaluation (*Wertung*) from value relatedness or value relevance (*Wertbeziehung*) to emphasise the point that social phenomena have significance only through their relation with a specific value system which will clearly influence the ways in which the scientist selects the object of study but not the analysis of it. Ethical neutrality forms an essential element of a valid social science, and Weber stresses that the social scientist must never impose his own values on the mode of investigation and interpretation of empirical material. Cultural science cannot evaluate ends only render explicit those ideas which underpin the ends themselves. 'It is self-evident that one of the most important tasks of every science of cultural life is to arrive at a rational understanding of these "ideas" for which men either really or allegedly struggle' (Weber, 1949, pp. 53–4). The task of social science is not to pass judgements but to isolate the structure of values within a given social context and demonstrate the relevance of these values for an objective understanding of social action. Interpretative understanding (*Verstehen*) and causal explanation are essential modes of analysis for the attainment of scientific, objective knowledge. The subjective meaning of social action is grasped through empathy and reliving, but, unlike Dilthey, Weber's interpretative understanding becomes scientific through its integration into objective, causal explanation. Thus Weber criticises Simmel for his failure to distinguish between subjectively intended and objectively 'valid' meanings which are often treated 'as belonging together' (Weber, 1964, p. 88).

Culture is the realm of values but 'empirical reality only becomes "culture" to us because and in so far as we relate it to value ideas'. Culture in this sense includes those elements which are significant because of their value relevance and it is impossible to discover 'what is meaningful to us by means of a "presuppositionless" investigation of empirical data'. Weber's argument is that not everything within culture is worth investigating for 'only a small portion of existing concrete reality is coloured by our value-conditioned interest and it alone is significant to us' (Weber, 1949 [1904], p. 76).

There is thus no whole, no 'essence' to history and society, but a constantly fluctuating culture of meaning-endowing social actions and the probability of action taking place; social relationships are conceived in inter-subjective terms as embodying purposive activity. If two individuals collide with each other on a crowded railway station this is not an example of social action; but if they begin to argue who was responsible for the collision then this involves a subjective relation to the other and hence is social action. Social structure is therefore the product of action and social collectivities such as bureaucracy, corporations and states treated as results of subjectively understandable action. Weber thus rejects the methodology 'which proceeds from the whole to the parts' arguing that this can accomplish only a preliminary analysis of reality: as there is no external, objective social world determined in its struc- ture by laws of development so there is no correspondence between scien- tific, sociological concepts and an objectively 'real' datum. Sociological concepts are pure types which do not reflect reality but, through the processes of abstraction and selection governed by value relevance and significance, embody the essential elements of different phenomena. Weber's ideal types are in effect Simmel's pure forms, analytical constructs enabling the researcher to make comparisons with many different phenomena which, although characterised by different content or material, belong to the same form. These forms are constituted through action. As there are no objective laws governing society so action must be defined in terms of 'probability' rather than 'necessity' and the structure of sociological concepts built around this probabilistic perspective.

Ideal Types and Social Action

Weber's sociology sought to combine explanation with understanding; social action was both subjective and objective; but subjective understanding was the specific characteristic of sociological knowledge. Weber did not advocate intuitive understanding, for human relationships enjoy regular and consistent patterns so that causality can be defined but only in terms of probability. Probability refers to the chances that in specific contexts human subjects will orient their behaviour to certain norms so that a given observable event will be followed, or accompanied, by another event. Social action is always probable rather than certain because the unique nature of social relationships generates the possibility of deviation from the expected course of action. The ideal type is the means of analysing the probability that actors will follow one course of action rather than another.

Ideal types are concerned with the subjective elements in social life, those unique and unrepeatable elements of culture disregarded by positivist social theory. Ideal types involve selection:

> The one-sided accentuation of one or more points of view and by the synthesis of a great many diffuse, discrete, more-or-less present and occasionally absent concrete individual phenomena which are arranged according to those one-sidedly emphasised viewpoints into a unified analytical construct. (Weber, 1949 [1904], p. 90)

The ideal type is no description of reality but a mental construction which incorporates the essential, not the average, properties of a particular phenomenon. The term ideal type implies no moral standpoint; it is a methodological concept which facilitates the understanding and explanation of social phenomena. It neither corresponds with an external objective reality nor constitutes 'essence' in the manner of an Hegelian 'spirit'. Ideal types are pure forms; some of its features will therefore be absent from its concrete forms. For Weber, ideal types were tools of analysis, their value purely heuristic, a mode of 'revealing concrete cultural phenomena in their interdependence, their causal conditions and their significance' (Weber, 1949 [1904], p. 92).

Weber's method is thus to construct unreal relations in order to analyse real historical relations; reality is known through concepts and abstractions. He identified three distinct ideal types: historical formations such as modern capitalism and the Protestant ethic characterised by their specificity; abstract ideal types such as bureaucracy and feudalism which characterise different historical and cultural periods; and finally, types of action. The level of abstraction varies with each of these ideal types although Weber argues, as we saw earlier, that social formations and large-scale institutions always designate categories of human interaction and that the role of sociology is to reduce these concepts to understandable action, to the actions of participating individuals. He identifies four types of social action:

1. Rational action (*Wertrational*) oriented to the attainment of an absolute value which may be aesthetic, religious, ethical; the goal is pursued for its own sake and not because of the possibility of success.
2. Rational goal-oriented action (*Zweckrational*) in which goal and means are rationally chosen.
3. Affectual action determined by the emotional effects on the actor.
4. Traditional action which is guided by custom and habit.

These four types of social action are defined in terms of their distance from the borderline of meaningfully oriented action: thus *Wertrational* and *Zweckrational* action both involve some measure of conscious choice in ends and means while affectual and traditional action approaches the borderline of purely reactive behaviour. Weber was especially concerned with rational action, rationality being defined exclusively in terms of the means not the ends, the latter being outside the province of science.

For Weber, action governed by rational norms is always more predictable in its possible effects than so-called irrational action. The more a value is absolute so the action corresponding to its achievement becomes irrational for 'the more unconditionally the actor devotes himself to this value for its own sake, to pure sentiment or beauty... the less is he influenced by considerations of the consequences of his actions'. The norm of rationality against which all social action is measured is the ends–means relationship, the goals defined by the acting subject as well as the choice of means necessary to attain them. Rational action is social action in so far as the subject must take account of others in his course of action. Rationality and irrationality – irrationality being deviations from the rational norm – are structured, therefore, in the concrete, existing situation, the world as it is, the world of human experience. Weber, here, approaches a positivistic standpoint. The ideal type, which does not exhaust all the possibilities of a particular phenomenon is the conceptually pure form to which actual action closely approximates, the classification being useful only in terms of its results (Weber, 1964, pp. 117–18).

Weber is arguing, then, that sociology seeks to formulate type concepts and generalisable uniformities: human behaviour, whether external or internal, displays relations and regularities which are understandable in terms of the cultural significance attached to them by the acting subject. Sociology is both interpretative understanding of the complex structures of meaning of typical social actions and causal explanation based on the probability that one event will be followed by another. Causal explanation depends on establishing a 'plausible sequence of motivation' in which the outcome or event is linked with action: he notes for example, an apparent correlation between the suicide rate and the rise and fall of the stockmarket but it is only when the sociologist has identified the motivation to suicide with the specifics of the stockmarket that a causal explanation is established. Ideal types must therefore be constructed both in terms of their adequacy on the level of meaning and causal adequacy.

The sociologist must interpret the meaning of social action as rigorously as those explanations which are offered in the natural sciences. Weber's distinction between the methods of the natural and the social sciences does not imply that the social sciences are less scientific, less objective and do not offer grounds for verifying hypotheses. Objective knowledge and certainty constitute the aims of sociology even though the nature of reality as defined by Weber makes it virtually impossible to achieve these ends. In analysing social action it is not necessary to invoke any mode of intuitive understanding or seek to grasp the whole of a person's experience: one does not have to be Caesar in order to understand Caesar. Weber's concept of understanding differentiates behaviour from action, the former lacking subjective meaning being simply habit or reactive behaviour, and he postulates two distinct modes of understanding: direct, observational understanding and explanatory or motivational understanding. By direct understanding, Weber means explanation in terms of observable, objective properties within a given context and which are immediately understandable, such as the action of someone chopping wood, or the writing down of the formula $2 \times 2 = 4$; explanatory understanding, in contrast, involves knowledge of motives, the subjective meanings attributed to the action by the actor.

This distinction is not particularly helpful, however. To take the example of the woodcutter: the action involved in cutting wood contains a referential meaning, in that the act always assumes an end to which the product of the act – wood – is to be used, for making toys, for building, for fire; this meaning is built into every act of chopping wood even in those cases where the individual is merely engaged in physical exercise. Both direct and explanatory understanding imply a context of meaning and it is virtually impossible to differentiate them in Weber's terms. Weber's ambivalent attitude to positivism is evident here: the context of meaning and its norms are given data. The ends of human action, too, are defined as falling outside the domain of science. But in criticising positivism Weber argues that before explaining why an individual followed a specific course of action it is essential to understand the meaning of the action itself. Sociological analysis must be adequate, both in terms of meaning and causality. Ideal-type categories of action, therefore, are constructions in which actors are related both to other actors, or subjects, and to the historical context; ideal-type analysis is interpretative-causal linking meanings to ends.

For Weber, sociological positivism and Marxism lacked the categories of meaning and motivational understanding other than as derivations from external laws and inevitable historical development; the human subject was determined by the workings of laws to the extent that historical events automatically occurred irrespective of the subjective intentions of the actors. In contrast, Weber emphasised that meaning is inter-subjective and not, as with Marx, systemic, the social whole conferring historical meaning on individual actions. But one such whole, capitalism, is defined by Weber as a structure of social actions and seeking an explanation of its specific and unique historical development involves the sociologist in asking the question: what motivated individuals to save and invest rather than to spend and consume?

Religion and Social Action: Capitalism and the Protestant Ethic

Weber's first major sociological study was *The Protestant Ethic and the Spirit of Capitalism* (first published in article form, 1904–5) in which he raised the problem of the sociological analysis of a unique social formation, modern European capitalism and sought to explain its historical development through the method of the ideal type. By 1904 Weber was turning increasingly away from historical studies towards sociology, although he continued to employ the concept of culture rather than the concept of society in his writings. The influence of Rickert is clearly evident in Weber's concept of cultural significance which linked the uniqueness of the historical phenomenon with its interpretation in terms of specific cultural values. Ideal types bring out the cultural significance of that particular segment of reality defined as significant; and they function, too, as heuristic tools investigating questions of cultural values. Weber emphasised particularly the historical dimension of social phenomena arguing that cultural significance can be judged only on this basis. The study of the relation of Protestant theology and capitalism is both a study in historical sociology and a methodological exercise in systematic sociology through the application of typical constructs to complex empirical material.

For Weber, capitalism was the product of a unique historical phenomenon, ascetic Protestantism, and its cultural significance was bound up in these 'ideal' origins and resulting motivational structure which effectively predisposed certain individuals to a particular orientation to work and rational social action. The relation of religion to economic activity had been widely discussed by many scholars before Weber, although it was not until the turn of the century that detailed statistical analysis which linked religious affiliation with occupation became available. A negative correlation was established, for example, between Catholicism and successful business activity. Weber was particularly concerned to demonstrate that ideal elements, such as religious ideas, were not mechanically linked to the economic structure but actively shaped the ways in which individuals carried out their ordinary day-to-day activities.

Weber's study was initially intended as a preliminary analysis, although subsequent criticism has often assumed it as a final statement. During the years following the publication of the articles, Weber replied to his many German critics and in particular began work on a vast comparative study of world religions. In 1920 he published a new introduction to the Protestant ethic study and shortly after his death further important material was published in his *General Economic History* (1923). In these writings Weber rejected the commonly held view that his study merely reversed the Marxist argument of the priority of economic forces in social change making religious ideas the causal factor in social development. In the 1920 introduction he emphasised that his analysis was treating 'only one side of the causal chain', while in the early articles he pointed out that he was not substituting for the 'one-sided' materialist approach of Marxism 'an equally one-sided spiritual-istic causal interpretation of history and culture' (Weber, 1930, p. 183). His comparative studies of world religions sought to analyse the plurality of factors which influenced the course of economic development and explored in greater detail the broad cultural implications of religious ideas on the formation of capitalism as a system. Only if Marxism is defined as a one-factor theory of social change can Weber's study be regarded as its opposite and its refutation.

The question Weber posed in his preliminary analysis of Protestantism, and in his later studies of Chinese, Indian and Palestinian religions, was why did capitalism, defined as a highly rationalised system, develop only in western Europe. In India, Palestine and China the material infrastructure of capitalism also existed – markets, division of labour, money economy, trade routes – yet only in western Europe did capitalism fully emerge out of such conditions. Weber notes, for example, that Indian geometry, natural sciences, medicine, political and historical thought, while all highly developed, lacked systematic concepts and methodology. In China science, remained unorgan-ised; there was no 'rational, systematic and specialised pursuit of science'. The existence of specific material conditions is insufficient to form a basis for capitalist development and in particular capitalist economic action 'which rests on the expectation of profit by the utilisation of opportunities for exchange, that is on [formally] peaceful chances of profit'. One of the most important points Weber makes is that if capitalism is defined loosely as a mode of money making then it is characteristic of all civilised societies, China, India and Mediterranean antiquity:

> The impulse to acquisition, pursuit of gain, of money, of the greatest possible amount of money, has in itself nothing to do with capitalism. This impulse exists and has existed among waiters, physicians, coachmen, artists, prostitutes... gamblers and beggars... it has been common to all sorts and conditions of men at all times... whatever the objective possibility of it is or has been given... Unlimited greed for gain is not in the least iden-tical with capitalism, and still less its spirit. (Weber, 1930, p. 17)

By capitalism Weber meant a system characterised by a rational organis-ation of formally free labour, the separation of business from the household, the development of rational book-keeping and rational systems of law and administration. Weber was careful to distinguish his concept of capitalism from contemporary sociologists such as Simmel and Sombart: Simmel, in his *Philosophy of Money*, assimilated capitalism to the concept of 'money economy', while Sombart, in his *Modern Capitalism* (1902), identified capitalism with economic 'adventurers' (entrepreneurs seeking to maximise their profits through courage and excessive risk taking) and high consumption particularly in luxury goods. Neither consumption nor the money economy was unique to the west: but a world view which abjures consumption and luxury demanding of those who accept its tenets that they work and invest, not to expiate sin as with Catholicism, but for the promise of salvation, is unique to western Europe. The unique, economic structure of western capitalism is thus homologous with the unique Protestant theology, especially Calvinism, which developed during the sixteenth and seventeenth centuries. Weber adds that by the eighteenth century capitalism had become effectively independent of its religious foundations.

For Weber, then, sociological explanation of the capitalist social formation, while recognising the importance of purely economic factors, identifies the modes of rationalism which are unique to it with forms of social conduct and action. The fundamental issue between Marxism and Weber's sociology lies ultimately in Weber's rejection of the Marxist philosophy of history, the view that capitalism necessarily develops through the workings of objective, economic laws determined by material forces which effectively render the subjective component – human action – irrelevant. This interpretation of Marxism assimilates meaning to historicism: human actions have meaning only in terms of the developing whole and the ultimate end of the historical process, the reconciliation of contradictions in communist society. For Weber, Marxism lacked a concept of motivation: change occurs through the workings of external, impersonal forces in which human action is reduced to the status of total passivity. But change is always change through the actions of human agents: human subjects are motivated to act in specific ways, to accept or reject the prevailing system of ideas, to reject luxury and immediate consumption, to postpone their worldly gratification and avoid all spontaneous enjoyment of life' in favour of a rigorous asceticism. It is the motivational structure of action which constitutes the spirit of capitalism, a spirit not found in India or China, but bound up with Protestant ideology.

The term 'spirit', suggests some notion of essence outside history and society, a metaphysical concept rather than sociological category. Although there is ambiguity in Weber's formulation, the weight of his argument nevertheless suggests that spirit is the active element of a world view which, in its everyday forms, structures human action. Weber defines spirit as 'a complex of elements associated in historical reality which we unite into a conceptual whole from the standpoint of their cultural significance'. The spirit of capitalism is thus a methodological concept, an abstraction 'put together out of the individual parts which are taken from historical reality... a conceptual formulation... that is the best from the point of view which interests us'. As such the spirit of capitalism is expressed in a rationalising attitude to life, in such maxims of conduct as be prudent, diligent, punctilious in repayment of debts and loans, avoid idleness since time is money, be frugal in consumption, and so on. The spirit of capitalism is a social ethic, a structure of attitudes and behaviour closely identified with ascetic Protestantism and its associated religious sects such as the Puritans and the Calvinists (Weber, 1930, pp. 47–53).

Although Puritanism, Pietism, Methodism and the Anabaptist sects exemplified the capitalist spirit, Weber particularly emphasised the significance of Calvinism. For Weber, Calvinism constituted a form of inner worldly asceticism built around the notion of worldly vocation or calling. It was Luther, however, who originally emphasised that the fulfilment of worldly duties 'is under all circumstances the only way to live acceptably to God... it alone is the will of God, and hence every legitimate calling has exactly the same worth in the sight of God'. But Luther's attitude to capitalism, argued Weber, was broadly traditional identifying 'absolute obedience to God's will with absolute acceptance of things as they were'. The individual was encouraged to remain in the station and calling which God had determined and 'restrain his worldly activity within the limits imposed by his established station in life'. Thus Lutheranism could never establish any new connection between worldly activity and religious principles (Weber, 1930, pp. 81–5).

Of all the Protestant sects it was the Calvinists who successfully combined the notion of calling with values appropriate to capitalist development. Calvinism advocated the concept of predestination which superficially suggests a fatalistic rather than positive approach to the world on the part of the believer. Weber's argument is that it was precisely because the Calvinists had to prove their election through good works that their religious beliefs acted as a dynamic and not passive element in social change: the Calvinist, he writes, 'creates his own salvation, or, as would be more correct, the conviction of it'. Hard work and the moral pursuit of a calling, while not constituting infallible evidence of salvation, nevertheless functions to assuage the fear of damnation. The Calvinists effectively required some sign, some criterion 'by which membership of the *electi* could be known'. It was not a question of accumulating good works, as with Catholicism 'but rather (of) systematic self-control' in relation to material pleasures and 'the constructive use of time'. Idleness, gambling, excessive sleep are proof only of imperfect grace. The faithful must attend not simply to their ordinary spiritual obligations, such as prayer, but strive hard in their worldly callings. Weber stresses that there was nothing especially original in the maxims of Protestantism: many religions had condemned idleness and hedonism but the Calvinists went much further in demanding adherence to their maxims of everyday conduct, not as proof of salvation, but as evidence that one may not be among the damned. Religious grace 'could not be guaranteed by any magical sacraments, by relief in the confession' but the individual must methodically supervise his own state of grace in his own conduct, and thus to penetrate it with asceticism... a rational planning of the whole of one's life in accordance with God's will... something which could be required of everyone who would be certain of salvation. (Weber, 1930, p. 153)

Weber concludes by arguing that only as long as the psychological sanctions which develop from the notion of predestination and the concept of proof remain efficacious 'does such an ethic gain an independent influence on the conduct of life and thus on the economic order'. It is not, therefore, Weber's argument that the ideas of specific theologians exercised a decisive role in the genesis of capitalism, but of the influence 'of those psychological sanctions which, originating in religious belief... gave a direction to practical conduct and held the individual to it' (Weber, 1930, p. 197). Religious leaders did not set out consciously to produce an ethic for capitalism; the unintended consequences of social action effectively led to that situation. The human subject, non-consciously but actively, transforms humanity, ideas and society.

Weber has, therefore, linked action with the social system and social development, although his stated methodological approach rejects collective concepts in favour of methodological individualism. The 'elective affinity' between the norms of ascetic Protestantism and the psychological-motivational structure of capitalist values eliminates any notion of a deterministic relation of economic 'base' and cultural 'superstructure'. It must be emphasised that Weber is not arguing that the existence of ascetic Protestant values automatically led to capitalist development – the most frequent criticism of Weber's thesis is to identify different countries, and different areas within a country, where Protestant asceticism existed but capitalism failed to develop, such as Calvin's own homeland of Switzerland and seventeenth-century Scotland – rather that the social ethic constitutes one of many elements which, through a process of mutual interaction, leads to social change.

This is not to suggest that there are no problems with Weber's formulation of a necessary link between religious ideas and economic forms. The evidence which he selects to defend his thesis is largely derived from writers who lived after Calvin such as Richard Baxter (1615–1691), John Wesley (1703–1791) and, particularly, Benjamin Franklin (1706–1790) and his analysis assumes a direct relation between the ideas expressed in their literary works and social action. He offers no independent evidence that prominent Protestant businessmen subscribed significantly to ascetic Protestant ideas, or that Protestant business communities adhered to the theological maxims regulating everyday conduct. What is more striking is Weber's failure to elucidate the precise ways in which businessmen interpreted Protestant maxims, to grasp the meanings of theological concepts for the subject. Meanings are in effect *imputed* to the subject on the basis of an interpretation of texts by the sociologist. As many critics have pointed out,

Weber offers no other evidence in support of his thesis. Finally, it has been suggested that Weber's exemplary figure of Franklin, far from embodying ascetic norms of conduct, enjoyed a private life dominated by hedonistic principles, engaging in extra-marital affairs, cultivating a taste for good food and wine, theatre and sports. Franklin was a far more complex figure than the single-minded Puritan portrayed by Weber (Kolko, 1960).

In a similar way, critics have emphasised that many Protestant businessmen were involved in 'traditional' economic activity such as war profiteering, colonial expeditions, land and currency speculation. But no evidence is advanced which relates to such individuals and groups. Weber's thesis is at its weakest here: the evidence offered in support of his thesis is largely derived from the social teaching of the Protestant sects (itself culled from Ernst Troeltsch's work on the Christian Churches and their social values) and never from the actors themselves (Marshall, 1982, pp. 116–19).

Weber's basic argument is, however, clearly against reductionist, monocausal explanation. There is scope within Weber's general approach to account for the ways in which capitalism itself affects Protestant values:

> For those to whom no causal explanation is adequate without an economic (or materialistic as it is still unfortunately called) interpretation, it may be remarked that I consider the influence of economic development on the fate of religious ideas to be very important... religious ideas themselves simply cannot be deduced from economic circumstances. They are in themselves... the most powerful plastic elements of national character, and contain a law of development and a compelling force entirely their own. (Weber, 1930, pp. 277–8)

In rejecting one-factor theories of social development Weber approaches an agnostic, pluralistic perspective: the causal chain, he argues, can run from the technical to the economic, at other times from the political to the religious. It is impossible to bring this process of pluralistic causation to a single resting point. Yet as he shows in the study of the Protestant ethic, there exists immanent properties within certain religious ideologies which successfully effect a transformation of the culture: thus although rejecting evolutionary theory, Weber seems to adopt a similar standpoint with his argument on rationalisation. The rationalising process is immanent within the Protestant religion, and as the major characteristic of western culture rationalisation constitutes a law of development. Yet Weber's study of religion stresses the active role of the subject: social development is not inevitable, the fate of humanity has not been decided in advance. Weber's sociology thus moves ambiguously between the poles of certitude and agnosticism, between the subject as active agent and society as external determining process.

Modernity and Rationality: Simmel and Weber

The sociology of culture, as it developed in the work of Weber, Tönnies, Simmel and Sombart identified culture as a unique realm of values which expressed an immanent historical process. As we have seen with Weber's study of Protestantism, culture exercised an active role in social action and the development of social formations: it could not be reduced to a reflection of economic forces. Comparing the specific and unique development of western rationalised capitalism with the failure of capitalism to emerge as a system in India, China and the Near East, Weber argued that it was the absence of a cultural orientation to the world, a motivational structure built around rational values, which accounted for the difference. Why did not all societies follow the western path to modernity? For Weber the answer lay in the specific culture of the west, in the systematic application and discipline of impersonal rules and regulations to the conduct of social life. The whole of western architecture, mathematics, science and music, he suggested, could be identified as products and as active elements of a rationalising culture. In his unfinished study of music – *The Social and Rational Foundations of Music*, written in 1912 but not published until 1921 as an appendix to *Economy and Society* (1968) – Weber attempted to show how western music, once it became an autonomous art form based on tonality, polyphony and the study of counterpoint, and modern musical notation which facilitated structural composition leaving little scope for improvisation, became highly rationalised: sonatas, symphonies, operas, together with instruments such as the organ, piano and violin were unknown in non-western cultures. Thus although polyphonic music was known in other cultures the absence of rational harmony was the decisive element (Weber, 1958b).

Weber's theme of the rationalisation of culture informs much of Simmel's work notably his *Philosophy of Money* (1978 [1900]) which, in many ways, constitutes a pioneering study of the cultural foundations and crisis of the modern capitalist economic system. Unlike Weber, Simmel was not concerned with investigating the historical genesis of large-scale social formations; Simmel's concept of sociation predisposed him to the study of the small-scale, the molecular processes involved in such significant social relationships as the dyad and secret society. But his major contribution to the sociology of culture was *The Philosophy of Money*, a work which influenced the later studies of culture carried out by the Frankfurt School.

On one level *The Philosophy of Money* is an abstract, non-historical, non-genetic, 'phenomenological' analysis of the social and cultural significance of money in modern industrial society. Simmel knew Marx's work and clearly regarded his own contribution as supplementing *Capital*, constructing 'a new story beneath historical materialism such that the explanatory value of the incorporation of economic life into the causes of intellectual culture is preserved, while these economic forms themselves are recognised as the result

of more profound valuations and currents of psychological, even metaphysical preconditions' (Simmel, 1978, p. 56). Clearly, cultural analysis required the
methods of the cultural sciences. Simmel regarded culture as irreducible to the
economic structure, a 'form' in which purposive social action finds expression.
Ultimately the world is apprehended through what Simmel calls the 'great
forms'. Forms shape the raw, unmediated reality into a coherent order. The
world is thus a totality of forms – art, science, religion – which bring together
diversity and unity: without forms there would be only 'an indifferent simultaneous juxtaposition of contents'.

The Philosophy of Money examines the ways in which the money economy
transforms cultural forms into external objects and breaks up the unity of
individual and society. For Simmel, culture is a specifically human and
meaning-endowing activity of the subject, for 'by cultivating objects, that is,
by increasing their value beyond the performance of their natural constitution, we cultivate ourselves... In refining objects, man creates them in his
own image'. Culture, as 'the supra-natural growth of the energies of things,
is... the embodiment of the identical growth of our energies'. What Simmel
terms the 'tragedy of modern culture' is the simultaneous development of
science, technology and art, the availability of knowledge and the decline of
individual culture. 'Every day and from all sides', he writes, 'the wealth of
objective culture increases, but the individual mind can enrich the forms
and contents of its own development only by distancing itself still further
from that culture.' The result is the domination of objective culture over
subjective culture, the 'frightful disproportion' between the immense
culture embodied in material things and the subject's understanding and
knowledge of this process (Simmel, 1978, pp. 446–8). Like Ferguson and
Smith, Simmel identified the division of labour as the factor responsible for
reducing the individual to a 'negligible quantity' able to cope less and less
with the growth of objective culture, becoming a 'mere cog in an enormous
organisation of things and powers which tear from his hands all progress,
spirituality, and value in order to transform them from their subjective form
into the form of purely objective life' (Wolff, 1950, p. 422). Modern culture is
essentially characterised by multiple participation in a complex of social
circles which, for Simmel constituted the most important criterion of human
development. But as modern society becomes institutionally decentred,
culture becomes increasingly rationalised and money, with its 'colourless
indifference' the common denominator of all values: the modern mind is
calculating, quantitative values replace qualitative values, the world is fixed
by mathematical formulas, dehumanised by 'stable and impersonal' time
schedules; punctuality, calculability and exactness pervade all spheres of
culture. The tension between objective culture and subjective culture
becomes increasingly marked with the development of the division of
labour and a money economy. In *The Philosophy of Money* Simmel depicts
this fragmentation and alienation as the result of a specific historical process

which transforms cultural objects, created by human subjects for human subjects, into autonomous *things* which have the appearance of 'autonomous mobility'. Modern man, he writes, 'is so surrounded by nothing but impersonal objects that he becomes more and more conditioned into accepting the idea of anti-individualistic social order (that is socialist ideas)... cultural objects increasingly evolve into an interconnected enclosed world that has increasingly fewer points at which the subjective soul can interpose its will and feelings'. The real tragedy of culture is thus the tendency to turn the creative subject into an object, to reify the products of human culture and effectively eliminate purposive human action (Simmel, 1978, pp. 296–7, 448–61).

Thus cultural development is structured around irreconcilable contradictions: the source of Simmel's cultural pessimism lay in his awareness that the realisation of human potential depends in part on the expansion of objective culture, that the growth of subjective culture with its rich inner life flows from the reification of culture itself.

Simmel's analysis of the cultural effects of economic rationality, of the increasing penetration of the money economy into social life, are echoed in Weber's account of modernity. Although noting Simmel's 'brilliant analysis' of the spirit of capitalism, Weber went much further than Simmel in grounding his analysis of rationality in comparative historical sociology. Whereas Simmel's analysis focused on the ways individuals experience the fragmentary and fleeting moments of everyday life within an increasingly rationalised culture, Weber conceived rationality as a broad, collective process existing within historical time and space.

What did Weber mean by rationality? Although he invested the term with ambiguous, multiple meanings, the core meaning seems to refer to the application of systematic and precise modes of calculation and available means in the pursuit of specific goals and ends. A comprehensively rationalised reality is grounded in rational and methodical action free of all magical influences. Weber identified Judaism as the religious source of Occidental rationality: its fundamental concepts of a rational ethic and world open to rational action were further consolidated in the inner-worldly asceticism of Protestantism. With its emphasis on discipline, depersonalisation and calculation, Protestantism rationalised religious belief itself: salvation became linked to an impersonal God, the unintended effects being growing secularisation and worldly 'disenchantment'. Rationality comes to pervade all aspects of social life, business, science, politics and law. In this way the process of rationality undermines the coherent and unified world views of the pre-modern world generating multiple, secular beliefs and values which saturate modern pluralist culture. A process of differentiation occurs as the homogeneous, unified pre-modern culture is transformed into a modern culture of partly autonomous and competing 'value spheres' – the political, economic, intellectual/scientific and aesthetic/erotic (the personal sphere) – each with its own inner logic and structure. Further, the rationalisation process makes possible 'a de-centred world', one lacking a dominant world view or ideology, a social order which enables individuals to produce meanings free of dogmatic religious constraints.

Weber distinguished rationalisation as an overall historical process, the 'iron cage', from specific forms of rationality found in law, government, economics which dealt with the ways in which actors master the social world. The study of Protestantism and capitalism had made the point that rationality constitutes the key to understanding social change through the rational pursuit of specific goals and pattern of motivation. Weber's discussion of rationality contrasts sharply with Simmel's narrowly pessimistic perspective. Unlike Simmel, Weber accepted the Enlightenment belief that the rational values of science combined with those of social justice and equality provide the basis for human emancipation. Weber distinguished two types of rationality, 'substantive rationality', based on the belief in 'ultimate values', ideals, goals, ends which are pursued for their own sake: equality, justice, freedom; and 'formal rationality' based in the calculation of means over ends, the search for the most efficient and cost effective measures to achieve narrowly defined goals. Formal rationality is not concerned with values oriented to achieving a better society only with those values which make existing structures work effectively: hence formal rationality constitutes the basis of modern market capitalism producing goods that satisfy narrowly conceived wants (consumer durables for example). But the rationalisation process is double-edged: substantive rationality becomes increasingly subordinated to the practical dictates of 'formal rationality', the application of quantitative calculation to the purposes of life. Hence the conflict between the ethic of brotherly love which is basic to all religions and the utilitarian calculating ethics of the modern market. Political parties, educational and cultural institutions, the administration of government, all become dominated by a rationally calculating specialisation. Such developments presage the triumph of the machine over human autonomy. This 'iron cage' of modernity is always possible, the total domination of bureaucratic ideals over the ideals of life (Gerth and Mills, 1948, pp. 280–93).

While the scope for human action is circumscribed by formal rationality, the ideals of substantive rationality, of autonomy and freedom, do not disappear: there exists permanent tension between the two forms of rationality, between social action guided by 'world images' created through ideas, and social action oriented to fragmented, dehumanised bureaucratic ideals. As Weber expressed it: it was not 'ideas, but material and ideal interests' which govern social conduct but quite frequently 'the world images that have been created by "ideas" have, like switchmen, determined the tracks along which action has been pushed by the dynamic of interest' (Gerth and Mills, 1948, p. 280).

The Theory of Class

Weber's theory of rationality and modernity, the development of a de-centred world is closely imbricated with his theories of class and domination. In contrast to contemporary Marxist thought Weber insisted that the political was not a secondary and derivative phenomenon but an active, autonomous element exercising a critical role in the formation of modern society. He rejected Marx's analysis of capitalism as a law-governed system structured in class struggle and internal contradictions, defining capitalism as a rational mode of organisation.

In his analysis of social class, however, Weber seems to follow Marx: property, or the lack of it, constitutes 'the basic categories of all class situations' and the factor which produces class 'is unambiguously economic interest'. However, the 'class situation' is differentiated 'according to the kind of services that can be offered in the market'. Here Weber departs from Marx in stressing that skill may constitute a form of property productive of internal class differentiation: those offering services are differentiated 'just as much according to their kinds of services as according to the way in which they make use of these services'. It is 'chance' within the structure of the market which Weber identifies as 'the decisive moment which presents a common condition for the individual's fate'. In this sense class situation is ultimately 'market situation'. Writing of Marx's fragment on class, Weber noted that 'it was intended to deal with the issue of class unity in the face of skill differentials'. Thus Weber distinguished between 'ownership classes' (those who receive rents from the ownership of land, mines, factories) and 'acquisition classes' ('typical entrepreneurs' offering services on the market such as bankers and financiers, as well as members of the 'liberal professions' who enjoy a privileged position through their ability or training). Weber described these groups as 'positively privileged' comparing their market position with 'negatively privileged' groups such as wage-labourers who have neither disposable property nor specialised skills. For Weber, classes never constituted homogeneous wholes but were highly differentiated internally embracing a number of different interests. He argued that the basic tendency of capitalism was the expansion of the 'acquisition classes' with the result a more pluralistic social structure, one increasingly built around educational qualifications.

A pluralistic stratification system thus develops involving complex differentiation within dominant, middle and working classes. Weber described the stratification system within modern capitalism as consisting of working classes, petty-bourgeoisie, 'intelligentsia' (a category lacking independent property but whose social position hinges on technical training, such as engineers, bureaucratic officials and other white-collar workers) and, finally, a class which occupies a 'privileged position through property and education' (entrepreneurs and so on). Given this complex stratification system there is clearly no simple relationship between class situation and class consciousness as conceived by Marx. Class constitutes a crucial objective factor in the formation of consciousness, affecting the 'life chances' of individuals in a variety of ways, but there exists no automatic transposition of so-called economic and class interests into solidaristic class consciousness. Weber rejected the historical relation of class to social change, the concept of historically necessary objective laws of social development. Consciousness, therefore, is structured firmly within the present, within the empirical market situation, and quite clearly Weber's sociology has eliminated such notions as 'class-for-itself' (fully conscious of its historical interests).

Social stratification is further complicated by the existence of 'status groups'. Weber distinguished classes from status groups by arguing that class situation differs from status situation by virtue of 'a specific, positive or negative, social estimation of honour'. Class situation depends on the market; status situation hinges on the judgements which others pass on his or her social position, thus attributing positive or negative esteem. Because a status group is characterised by a 'specific style of life', comprising social distance and exclusiveness, a repudiation of economic factors as the basis of membership and a commitment to patterns of non-utilitarian consumption, it approximates to a unified social class: 'With some oversimplification, one might thus say that "classes" are stratified according to their relations to the production and acquisition of goods; whereas "status groups" are stratified according to the principles of their *consumption* of goods as represented by special "styles of life".' There is, of course, a close relation between status groups and property and in this respect class and status are linked: an economically ascendant class will, through subsequent generations, achieve the position of a status group. Both propertied and propertyless individuals may belong to the same status group while economically declining groups exercise considerable social influence. Weber's point was that class and status constituted two distinct types of group formation and organisation: thus although interrelated, class and status are competing structures of stratification relating specifically to the distribution of power. Power is not a separate dimension of stratification, classes, status groups and political parties are all phenomena 'of the distribution of power within a community' (Gerth and Mills, 1948, pp. 180–95; Weber, 1964, pp. 424–9).

Weber's pluralistic model of stratification is theoretically one which assumes the existence of a strong civil society. Power, for example, constitutes an expression of the distribution of interests within civil society; but at the same time power and class cannot be assimilated to economic elements, or political parties be considered solely as the expression of class interests. The principle of autonomy is important for defining the separation from the state and bureaucracy of institutions bound up with class, status and power.

Capitalism, Bureaucracy and Democracy: Weber's Theory of Domination

Throughout his life Weber accepted the necessity for a strong nation state, its primacy in all social and political spheres. His early studies into the agricultural conditions of Eastern Germany had pointed to the problems caused by an incursion of Polish workers into German territory and their potential threat to German culture. Germany at the end of the nineteenth century had developed into a strong, centralised nation state with its own distinctive national culture. Political unification was achieved during the first stirrings of industrial development and Weber emphasised that if Germany were to become a truly modern industrial nation then it could do so only under the guidance of new political leaders. The Junker landowning class still controlled large sections of German political life, yet in Weber's terms they constituted a declining class incapable of generating the necessary dynamic leadership. As for the industrial bourgeoisie Weber depicted this class as cautious and unpolitical, wholly dominated by the Junkers. The industrial working class was equally incapable of leadership being an immature class politically, its leaders in the Social Democratic Party contemptuously dismissed as mere journalistic dilettantes. Weber defined a politically mature class as one which repudiated sectional interests in favour of the political power interests of the German nation.

Weber's attitude to questions of power was uncompromising: all modern states, he argued, demanded a structure of domination through which some individuals ruled others. Weber rejected what he regarded as Utopian political concepts such as direct democracy (he discussed the example of Soviets in his essay, 'Parliament and Government in a Reconstructed Germany', written in 1918) on the grounds that in large, complex modern societies such institutions were technically impossible. He accepted the extension of democratic rights in modern societies but argued that the process of democratising society entailed an increasing bureaucratisation and centralisation of power structured in the rational norms of a bureaucratic state apparatus. In modern society the administrative function is determined by size: the administration of mass structures is radically different from the personalised relationships of administration in small associations; administration expands with the result that those with training and experience exercise technical superiority in the carrying out of complex tasks. The classic democratic doctrine, based on the sovereignty of the people, formed no part of Weber's theory of democracy. Writing to Robert Michels, whose book, *Political Parties* (1962 [1911]), advanced similar arguments on the nature of organisation, Weber asked: 'How much resignation will you still have to put up with? Such concepts as "will of the people", genuine will of the people, have long since ceased to exist for me; they are fictitious. All ideas aiming at abolishing the dominance of men over men are "Utopian"' (Mommsen, 1974, p. 87).

One of Weber's fundamental arguments was that the rise of modern political parties – itself a democratic development – entailed increasing bureaucratisation and the weakening of human initiative and action. His ideological support for a strong German state and his general distrust of 'mass' democracy was closely bound up with his sociological studies of bureaucracy, a legal-rational form of domination described as eliminating all personal, irrational and emotional elements from administration. Bureaucratic administration subordinated the individual to the rational, specialised division of labour and an increasing rationalisation of all spheres of social life. Pessimistically Weber described this process in terms of a 'new iron cage of serfdom' and a dehumanised, 'disenchanted world'.

For Weber, parliamentary democracy was largely passive in its effects; the mass of the people were uneducated, politically ignorant and incapable of forming reasoned political judgements. The real objective of democracy was the creation of charismatic leaders who succeed in establishing leadership over the masses not through policies but by their personal qualities. In this way the inherent trends towards bureaucratisation might be checked by the emergence of a powerful personality with extra-mundane gifts who succeeds in integrating the propertyless masses into modern society. Modern mass political parties, however, are based on bureaucratic principles of organisation and the basic trend of modern society is for parties to select their leaders and offer them for election to parliament: democracy becomes increasingly a mode of selection of leadership.

Weber insisted throughout his writings that the struggle for power was an inherent feature of all social life pervading every sphere of social action. Parties exist to achieve power. It is important to understand Weber's concept of power in this context: he did not accept the crude Marxist position which defined power in terms of economic interests and class structure. Power is defined in social action terms as 'the chance of a man, or of a number of men, to realise their own will in a communal action even against the resistance of others who are participating in their action' (Gerth and Mills, 1948, p. 180). Individuals do not necessarily strive for power merely because of possible economic rewards: power, including economic power, may be valued for itself, or for the social honour it confers. There is thus no single source of power and one of the consequences of Weber's argument is that changes in the economic organisation of society do not automatically result in changes in the distribution of power. Hence his rejection of the 'Utopian' ideals of socialism. He argued that the highly specialised division of labour, which forms the backbone of a modern economy, must inevitably lead to greater bureaucratisation: bureaucratic modes of organisation, technically superior to other modes, are essential for large-scale planning and mobilisation of resources. Only through formal rational principles of bureaucratic organisation is it possible to develop the modern polity, economy and technology. The fully developed bureaucratic structure compares with other organisations as the modern machine compares with non-mechanical modes of production. Bureaucracy is characterised by the following characteristics: precision, speed, unambiguity, knowledge of the files, continuity, discretion, unity, strict subordination; the bureaucratic office has a clearly defined sphere of competence, its officials organised in a clearly defined hierarchy of positions, and appointed, not elected, on the basis of technical qualifications. All personal and irrational elements are eliminated in favour of specialists and experts. Thus under the guise of expert impartiality a bureaucracy may control the flow of information to the public: both Prussian and Russian bureaucrats used their monopoly of census statistics as the basis for proposing their own specific anti-democratic reforms (Beetham, 1974). The development of modern society demands this mode of administration for the larger the association, the more complicated its tasks and its reliance on rational organisation. In this sense the future belongs to bureaucratisation.

For Weber, the increasing bureaucratisation of social life formed the major structural form of modern capitalism: rationalised efficiency which results from bureaucratic organisation enables humanity to develop economically, technologically and politically, but this progress is achieved at some cost, 'a parcelling out of the human soul', a dehumanisation of the subject. As for socialism, rather than decentralising power, it will lead inevitably to a further centralising of institutions and the dictatorship of the bureaucratic official. Weber's pessimism is complete: modern society cannot escape from bureaucratic organisation.

Thus a contradiction is generated between the democratic trends of bourgeois society and the anti-democratic ethos of bureaucratic organisation. In Weber's analysis bureaucracy becomes the major source of authority in the modern world: 'Every domination expresses itself and functions through administration. Every administration, on the other hand, needs domination, because it is always necessary that some powers of command be in the hands of somebody' (Weber, 1954, p. 330). This is what Weber called 'imperative co-ordination', the probability that commands will be obeyed irrespective of their specific content or degree of supervision. Domination is distinguished from power in that domination carries the weight of legitimacy, that individuals obey not because of physical compliance, but through a belief in the validity of norms regulating the command. For Weber, domination was not simply the external fact of an order being obeyed, but involved a subjective component, as if those who are ruled had made the content of the command the basic maxim of their own activity. In this respect Weber differs sharply from Mosca in seeking a voluntaristic basis for power. 'It is an induction from experience', he writes, 'that no system of domination voluntarily limits itself to the appeal to material or affectual or ideal motives as a basis for guaranteeing its continuance. In addition every such system attempts to establish and to cultivate the belief in its "legitimacy"' (Weber, 1964, p. 325).

Weber identified three ideal types of legitimacy: traditional, resting on a belief in the authority of 'immemorial traditions'; charismatic, based on the prophetic pronouncements of oracles and great leaders invested with 'magical' qualities; and finally, rational, based on a belief in the legality of enacted rules and the right of those in authority to issue commands that have their basis in law. Commands, then, always carry a minimum of voluntary compliance; they are obeyed because of a belief in the legitimacy of the authority. It is, therefore, not a question of an 'organised minority', or élite, imposing its rule on an unorganised mass, but rather of the process of institutionalising the 'inner support' of subjects for the different modes of authority. Weber's sociology of domination is ultimately less concerned with the sources of power in material forces, such as property ownership, than in the ideologies which legitimate different forms of rule.

Modern society is characterised by rational-legal domination centred in bureaucracy with its hierarchy of offices and impersonal rules and norms – Weber argued that capitalist production created 'an urgent need for stable, strict, intensive and calculable administration'; in the field of administration the choice lay simply 'between bureaucracy and dilettantism'. In his lecture on socialism, given in 1918, he argued that modern democracy was increasingly a bureaucratised democracy, the administrative staff completely separated from the ownership of property; all bureaucratic enterprises, from factories to armies to schools, based on purely technical norms of efficiency and grounded in rational-legal authority, increasingly separate the individual from the means of work. Socialism would accelerate these trends and prepare the ground for 'a new bondage', a bureaucratic mode of domination stifling all freedom and independent human activity.

Weber's reflections are prescient in the light of later developments within capitalism and state socialist societies which have witnessed an enormous growth in bureaucratic administration. There can be no doubt that Weber was right to emphasise the growing autonomy of the state and the legitimation needs of modern industrial societies: thus while Weber's typology of domination can be criticised for constituting a taxonomy, a formal structure of concepts, rather than a theory which investigates the actual functioning of different modes of domination, including the repressive apparatuses of the state – police, army, and so on – it nevertheless illuminated the necessary subjective element present in structures of authority. In his lecture, 'Politics as a Vocation' (1919), he quotes Trotsky's remark that 'every state is founded on force', but adds that the modern state is never simply a repressive apparatus but a community that successfully claims 'the monopoly of legitimate violence' (Gerth and Mills, 1948, pp. 78–83).

Yet while domination implies a subjective component and a consenting actor Weber maintained a resolutely pessimistic view of modern democracy. The masses confer legitimacy purely passively: there is little sense of an active relationship between the various groups and classes of civil society and the state apparatus. Weber accepted Michels' theory of mass democracy and the inevitable rule of functionaries elaborated in his *Political Parties* (1962 [1911]). The whole question of popular democratic control is eliminated on the basis that a modern industrial society necessitates bureaucratic administration from above. But, as was noted earlier, Weber defined modernity in terms of an unresolved tension between substantive and formal rationality, a dialectical process found in forms of legal-rational domination. Thus while he depicts modern bureaucracy as an iron cage, administration actually embodies some substantive values, especially in its commitment to appointments and promotions based on merit and educational qualifications. But this process of rationalisation seems to lead inevitably to increasing centralisation and the rule of the few over the many. Here lies a fundamental contradiction in Weber's sociology between the theory of the global process of rationalisation and the different forms of rationality embodying substantive values and pointing to potential emancipation.

5

Marxism after Marx

Marxism and Sociology

When Marx died in 1883 Marxism as a distinctive body of knowledge, theory of society and scientific methodology had exercised little influence in the field of the social sciences. Discussion of Marxism was largely confined to the workers' movement and it was not until the 1890s that a wider debate was initiated involving scholars from different areas of the social sciences – economics, history and sociology. The main academic critics of Marxism – Weber, Durkheim, Pareto, Mosca, Croce, Stammler, Sorel – did not set out simply to refute historical materialism but were mainly concerned with the problems which Marx had identified within the social sciences and modern society. This growing interest in Marxism was partly the result of its increasing popularisation in the socialist movement, as well as the importance of socialism itself as an organised political trend based on the principles of class struggle, class consciousness and class solidarity.

Marxism was developed outside the academy by socialist intellectuals who defined it as a natural science of society emphasising the existence of specific laws of social development, the inevitability of class conflict, the polarisation of classes, growing economic crises and eventual collapse of capitalism. At Marx's graveside Engels had declared that as Darwin had discovered 'the law of development of organic nature, so Marx discovered the law of development of human history'. Engels' reference to Darwin and natural history is significant, for the Marxism which developed during the 1880s and 90s made no distinction between the methods of the natural sciences and those of Marxism. The Marxism of the Second International was particularly positivistic in its early phases. During the 1890s the major political party advocating Marxist theory was the German Social Democratic Party whose leaders, Karl Kautsky (1854–1938) and Eduard Bernstein (1850–1932), enjoyed close ties with Engels; the Social Democrats were responsible for the publication of many of Marx's early, and later writings such as the *Theories of Surplus Value* (1964–72), part of *The German Ideology* (1964) and the final volumes of *Capital* (1957, 1958, 1962). The party, having been legalised in 1890, polled one and a half million votes at the first general election.

Kautsky, who wrote voluminously on the history of religion, socialism, ethics and economic and political theory – he was described as the 'Pope of Marxism' – represented the orthodox wing of Marxist theory; many of his ideas were shared by the Russian, George Plekhanov (1856–1918). More than any other writers Kautsky and Plekhanov transformed Marxism into an integrated world view, defining its basic concepts in positivistic, evolutionary terms, arguing that the task of intellectuals was merely to defend Marxist thought from bourgeois theory thus preserving its theoretical purity. Following the inspiration of Engels, in his *Anti-Duhring* (1954), Marxism became codified into a set of rules and general materialist principles applicable to all social and historical phenomena.

During the 1890s the major Marxist works were largely polemical, dogmatically defending Marx's method of analysis, his general theory of laws of development and the nature of capitalism as an exploitative system of production. In 1899 Bernstein published his *Evolutionary Socialism* (1963), in which he subjected these dogmatic concepts to the test of empirical reality. Contrary to Kautsky and Plekhanov, he argued that the historical development of capitalism did not support Marx's theory of crisis, the notion of inevitable polarisation of classes or the law of the centralisation of capital. The working class was not becoming impoverished, the middle classes were not disappearing, small businesses were developing and there was no evidence that capitalism as a system was doomed to historically inevitable collapse. Bernstein concluded that history demonstrated no 'iron laws', no 'historic necessity'; socialism must be validated, not by appeals to an historically inevitable future, but rather through the ethic of socialism, the *a priori* categories of Kantian moral philosophy in which individuals are regarded, not as means or instruments, but as ends in themselves. For Bernstein the movement was everything; there was no 'ultimate goal'. The political conclusions which Bernstein drew from his analysis came to be known as 'revisionism', that as capitalism was gradually and peacefully evolving towards a more complex social structure than existed at the time Marx wrote *Capital*, so it was possible to extend democracy, citizenship and equality from within the system itself The struggle for socialism was thus conceived as a piecemeal, evolutionary process and not as the violent conquest of state power by a disciplined party apparatus.

Bernstein's critique of Marxism was immediately rejected by Kautsky who merely repeated that Marx's analysis of capitalism was correct in virtually every detail: Bernstein had misinterpreted the statistics. The revisionist controversy is important, however, because it highlighted the weaknesses of Marxism in the light of modern social science. In particular it focused attention on the changes within capitalism since the 1860s that could not be accommodated to the dogmatic prescriptions of orthodox Marxism. For all its claims as a science, Marxism had become ossified into a quasi-religious system which admitted the existence of no facts or historical evidence which might render it untenable. The revisionist debate reflected many of the criticisms which academic scholars were increasingly levelling at Marxism.

The first significant discussion between Marxists and representatives of 'bourgeois' social science had taken place in 1894 at the first International Congress of Sociology; further debates took place in the 1890s and early years of the twentieth century. The Marxist theory of inevitable social change was particularly criticised, as was the concept of laws of natural necessity and the reduction of the human agent to a product of external conditions. Marxism, it was argued, postulated a rigid, mechanical notion of the relation between the economic 'base' of society and its ideological 'superstructure', a correspondence theory of knowledge which transformed ideas into a passive reflection of class interests. Kautsky developed this model to account for the necessary development of socialist theory itself as occurring outside the workers' movement, the product of intellectuals whose privileged position enabled them to escape from the socio-economic determinism which affected all other groups. The workers attained only a limited consciousness, broadly economic and oriented to trade union matters. As capitalism intensified the objective class struggle through heightened contradictions and tensions, the working class became increasingly receptive to Marxist theory. One important consequence of this élitist position was that the state was defined as an instrument of social transformation, the result of socialist leadership from above. This passive concept of consciousness is central to orthodox Marxism and was further developed by V. I. Lenin (1870–1923) in his theory of the 'vanguard' party.

Weber, Durkheim and Simmel rejected the Marxist concept of economic laws in favour of a voluntaristic sociology which also took account of the growing complexity, not homogeneity, of modern capitalist society. Criticism of the positivist elements in Marxism, however, did emerge from the Marxist movement itself and was not confined to those intellectuals outside the socialist movement. The Italian Marxist, Antonio Labriola (1843–1904), and the French theorist of revolutionary syndicalism, Georges Sorel (1847–1922), sought to combat the concept of Marxism as a self-contained system based on natural laws of development by invoking Vico's dictum that humanity knows only that which it has created. Sorel, who wrote extensively on Marxism during the 1890s contributing an important essay on Vico, introduced Labriola's work into France especially the *Essays on the Materialist Conception of History* (1967 [1896]). Sorel, however, was much more concerned with Marxism as a theory of action than Marxism as a theory of totality and it is interesting to see how these two elements were combined in Labriola's work.

Labriola accepted the concept of society as a whole, analysing social classes and individuals as parts developing in relation to the whole; he assimilated, too, the model of base and superstructure in which ideas correspond to specific social conditions. But he went beyond naturalistic Marxism by emphasising the uniqueness of historical formations and rejecting the simple triadic schema of social change – thesis–antithesis–synthesis – in favour of a theory of change centred on human activity, consciousness and thus *praxis*. Like Sorel, Labriola attacked the whole notion of economic determinism and the theory that historical change can be explained entirely in terms of the economic factor. He defined the historical process as an historical totality in which intellectual and material culture are organically bound together and all elements of material life and intellectual culture were an expression of the historical epoch – an expressive totality – an organic unity in an all-enveloping process of historical development. There was no 'dominant' element as such: while historical events and sociological processes existed in relation to economic forces they could never be reduced to them as mere passive expressions (Labriola, 1967).

Thus reality is not a given datum but created through human activity; the goal of socialism is not lying in wait in some distant future but results from *praxis*. There is no truth waiting to be discovered only a truth which must be *made*. Sorel praised Labriola's rejection of 'vulgar Marxism' and its crude theory of economic determinism. As the editor of two influential socialist journals, Sorel proposed to examine Marxism in depth and during the late 1890s contributed a number of critical essays on such topical issues as the revisionist debate, Marxism as a science and the role of ethics in socialist theory. After 1903, however, he became increasingly disillusioned with orthodox Marxism and turned towards revolutionary syndicalism and his theory of the myth developed especially in his *Reflections on Violence* (1950 [1908]).

Orthodox Marxism, Sorel argued, had degenerated into a species of historical fatalism built around the notion of periodic and catastrophic economic crises which supposedly culminate in a general crisis of the whole capitalist system and subsequent political transformation. The reductionist formulas of Kautsky and others ignore the real 'authors' and 'actors' of history and the fact that social relationships are made by men as much as by the development of the productive forces. Sorel was a perceptive critic of vulgar Marxism: his work was influenced by what he called 'the treasures contained in the work of Vico', especially the notion of the social world as the work of humanity and that humanity understands only that which it has created. Thus for Sorel there was no natural history of society, no scientific socialism. In the debate on revisionism he sided with Bernstein arguing that 'the problem for socialism is to develop in the working classes a superior culture, which would allow them to administer the productive forces... Today, the proletariat is far from possessing this culture' (Sorel, 1976, pp. 126, 157–64). Socialism is vindicated, not through appeals to the 'final end' of historical development but by the ethical superiority of proletarian institutions and culture.

Sorel's anti-scientism and his general distrust of theories of social change which minimised or eliminated the active human subject, led him to argue against the holistic approach of Marxist methodology and advocate an atomistic concept of society structured in the voluntaristic practice of actors. His fundamental point was that change occurs through will, collectively organised within the working class, but expressing the contradictions of the present system and a longing for an alternative society. The myth of the general strike functions precisely in this way as a system of images, which invokes through intuition the sentiments oriented towards socialism that form an integral part of working-class experience.

As we shall see in the following section, Sorel influenced the Marxism of the Italian, Gramsci, especially the critique of scientistic anti-humanist materialism, although in general Sorel's writings exerted little significance for the development of early twentieth-century Marxism.

Culture and Domination: Gramsci and the Concept of Hegemony

Antonio Gramsci (1891–1937) has been described as the most original Marxist theorist of the first half of the twentieth century. Gramsci's work is characterised by a concern with problems of culture and the relation of cultural formations to political domination. One of the major problems shared by both sociology and Marxism was to develop concepts which focused on the interrelation of structure and human action and agency. Marx had dealt with the systemic nature of social formations and briefly noted the reflexive capacity of individuals but failed to develop concepts which linked the two, concentrating rather on economic categories. Gramsci was the first major Marxist to focus on the 'superstructure' and raise critical questions concerning the specific relations between the economy, culture, class and power. Gramsci was especially critical of positivistic Marxists who interpreted Marxist method as a natural science of society based on determining economic and historical laws. Gramsci argued that the methods and concepts of the natural sciences were wholly inappropriate for a dialectical science such as Marxism with its focus on problems of consciousness and *praxis*.

One of the leaders of the Italian Communist Party, Gramsci spent the last years of his short life incarcerated in Mussolini's jails producing, often in elliptical form to avoid prison censorship, reflections and reviews of Marxist theory and the relation between Marxism and political science, sociology, philosophy and history. Arrested in 1926 Gramsci wrote 3000 pages of analysis as well as hundreds of letters: his activity firmly negated the intention of the prosecutor at his trial that 'this brain must be put out of action for twenty years'.

In the years following the Second World War, the Italian Communist Party published much of this material, frequently in an abridged form to avoid embarrassing the party's rigid Stalinist standpoint. Not that Gramsci deviated widely from orthodox Leninism: he accepted the necessity for a revolutionary party and rejected his youthful advocacy of workers' councils as constituting the basis for a total reorganisation of society. His writings during the great strike wave and factory occupations in Turin from 1919–1921 parallel Lenin's reflections on the relation of state and soviets in *The State and Revolution* (1917); influenced especially by the work of Sorel, Gramsci suggested that the working class, through its own independent institutions, possessed the capacity to transform society. In 1924 he wrote that Bolshevism was the first movement to develop the conception of proletarian hegemony; in the *Prison Notebooks* he is more explicit noting that the concept of hegemony represented Lenin's 'greatest theoretical contribution to the philosophy of *praxis*' (Gramsci, 1971, p. 365). Yet there are significant differences between Lenin's notion of the dictatorship of the proletariat, with its assumption of a strong, coercive state apparatus and Gramsci's theory of hegemony. For Gramsci, hegemony is predicated on a resilient and independent civil society allowing autonomy to 'private institutions' such as education, church, political parties, trade unions, and so on, which form the source of *consent*. Equally, Gramsci's concept of Marxism differs sharply from Leninism being influenced less by Engels, Plekhanov and Kautsky than the anti-positivist elements in Labriola, Sorel and the Italian Hegelian, Benedetto Croce.

Distinguishing his approach from 'automatic Marxism' Gramsci defines Marxism as the philosophy of *praxis*, constituting the expression of the collective will of the subordinate working class striving to educate and liberate itself from exploitation and class domination. The historical process is characterised, not simply by impersonal economic laws but by human will, organised into collective forms (trade unions, political parties, professional associations, and so on) which become 'the driving force of the economy,' moulding 'objective reality' (Gramsci, 1977, p. 35). Any fatalistic acceptance of historical inevitability condemns the working class to passivity and defensive political action. Social change is thus grasped not as an automatic effect of external processes acting on an inert mass but the result of a complex historical process.

Gramsci's emphasis on will, on voluntarism is brought out vividly in one of his first significant articles, his response to the 1917 revolution, called prophetically, 'The Revolution against *Das Kapital*' (Gramsci, 1994). Written shortly after the successful October Revolution, Gramsci's article argued that the Bolshevik accession to power vindicated Marxism as a non-fatalistic, activist theory built around the concept of 'collective will' rather than objective, 'iron laws'. Throughout his early writings Gramsci continually emphasised the self-activity of the working class, arguing that fatalistic acceptance of the inevitability of socialism condemns the proletariat to passivity and defensive political action. For Gramsci, revolution was not the automatic product of external economic forces but the result of one class establishing a cultural domination over all other classes. A 'rising class', he wrote, will strive to establish its authority over other social strata both through economic, polit-

ical and military power and 'intellectual and moral leadership'. All revolutions are preceded 'by an intense work of cultural penetration' as the rising
class aims to subjugate allied and subordinate strata to its ideas. A dominant
class is thus defined as one which saturates civil society with the spirit of its
morality, customs, religious and political practices: 'The founding of a ruling
class is equivalent to the creation of a *Weltanschauung*.' If the working class is
to constitute a dominant class it must establish a culture that commands the
support of other strata; its world view, Marxism, is thus not a class ideology
as such, but the expression of the immanent structural trends of history.
Cultural hegemony prior to the act of revolution is created through collective
action. Gramsci thus distinguishes hegemony – associated with consent and
equilibrium between social classes – and domination, associated with coercion and the state. Hegemony is created within civil society and the private
institutions which mediate the individual and the state; direct domination
flows from the state apparatus, coercion through public institutions (Gramsci,
1971, pp. 77–84).

Gramsci first employed the term 'hegemony' in his *Some Aspects of the
Southern Question* (Gramsci, 1978 [1926]), where he argued that the proletariat
'can become the leading (*dirigente*) and the dominant class to the extent that it
succeeds in creating a system of alliances that allow it to mobilise the majority
of the working population against capitalism and the bourgeois state'
(Gramsci, 1978, p. 443). Hegemony is effectively a synthesis of political, intellectual and moral leadership in which a class passes from defending its own
'corporate' interests to unifying and directing all other social groups. Two
examples from Gramsci's work will illustrate his general argument. He
suggests that only the bourgeoisie and proletariat strive to establish hegemony. Feudal society, in contrast to capitalism, is dominated by a closed caste,
the dominant classes do not develop an organic passage from the other classes
to their own but remain 'technically' and 'ideologically' separate. In contrast,
the Jacobins, a specific social group, developed into a hegemonic class by
representing all the popular forces ranged against the old regime and organising a national, popular collective will. Thus although possessing certain
economic functions related to the developing bourgeois means of production,
the Jacobins passed from a merely economic phase of development to an
ethical-political stage with their own political party and *Weltanschauung*.

Gramsci, of course, was concerned with the possibility of revolution in the
advanced capitalist countries. His analysis of hegemony suggests that the
working class was not simply a passive victim of an overpowering structure
of bourgeois ideology, but actively acquiesces in the persistence of bourgeois
society. In western Europe civil society was relatively strong, thus enabling the
bourgeoisie to rule through consent. Gramsci emphasises that hegemony is
not wholly consensual but consists of a synthesis of consent and coercion, an
equilibrium in which force plays a role but is not dominant. The distinction
between civil and political society is therefore not absolute since the capitalist

social formation cannot be broken down into wholly separate and independent institutions. Thus he notes that education, while belonging as an institution to civil society, is dependent on the state both economically and ideologically. In Hegelian terms, Gramsci argues for the ethical role of the state, for while defending the economic and political interests of the dominant class, the state is nevertheless instrumental in building up the institutions which contribute to the strength of civil society such as law and education. This is Gramsci's way of expressing the problem of relative autonomy, that the state is not simply the organ one class uses to oppress another but the means whereby modern complex capitalist society is created and legitimised, not through class ideology, but a bourgeois *Weltanschauung*.

A synthesis of political, intellectual and moral elements, Gramsci's concept of hegemony is analytically valuable for its rejection of the positivistic conception of the economic as the 'basis' with ideas and culture as mere 'reflexes' or 'appearance'. Hegemony points to a voluntaristic element in the structure of class domination foregrounding the active role of agents in legitimising forms of rule. Gramsci argues that modern capitalist societies are structurally complex in that there is never one single class which dominates 'from above' by excluding and ignoring the actions of other groups and classes. A dominant class must always listen to the voices of subordinate classes and take account of the real effects these classes produce. Gramsci's model assumes a balance between persuasion and coercion, active consent and force. It is not a question, therefore, of dominant values annihilating all others, for the concept of hegemony allows for differences, alternative culture and other voices which can then become the site of resistance and revolution.

With its emphasis on the hierarchical relations between social classes and groups and the ongoing struggles over culture, politics and values, Gramsci's concept of society is defined as a field of forces in which partly autonomous classes and groups resist total and harmonious integration into the social whole, an anti-functionalist perspective which places the making of society through collective action at its centre.

Intellectuals and the Construction of Hegemony

One of Gramsci's most significant contributions to a sociology of modern society is the theory of intellectuals. For Gramsci, intellectuals exercised a critical role in the formation of both ideologies and consent. Social cohesion was as much the function of intellectuals as of social structure. The failure of Marxism in the advanced capitalist societies posed questions both on the role of leadership as well as the function of intellectuals in society as a whole.

Gramsci defined intellectuals sociologically, rejecting the conception of intellectual activity as intrinsic to a special social stratum. Such properties, he argued, were characteristic of everyone in society:

What are the 'maximum' limits of acceptance of the term 'intellectuals'? Can one find a unitary criterion to characterise equally all the diverse and disparate activities of intellectuals and to distinguish these at the same time and in an essential way from the activities of other social groupings? The most widespread error of method seems to me that of having looked for this criterion of distinction in the intrinsic nature of intellectual activities, rather than in the ensemble of the system of relations in which these activities… have their place within the general complex of social relations… All men are intellectuals… but not all men have in society the function of intellectuals. (Gramsci, 1971, pp. 8–9)

Gramsci thus rejected the idealist notion of great intellectuals: intellectuals were defined in terms of knowledge production and work function. Discussing the Italian philosopher, Croce, Gramsci described him as a 'constructor' of ideologies in the interests of the governing class, although 'interests' and 'ideologies' cannot be assimilated mechanistically to class position. Intellectuals produce knowledge and ideologies which are always more than a simple reflection of class interests. As a social stratum, intellectuals develop more slowly than other social groups and although giving expression to the interests of a dominant class they equally articulate the cultural traditions of a whole people. The development of capitalism, however, introduces a new type of intellectual, the technical organiser, the specialist who gradually replaces the older, traditional type organising society through the institutions of the state.

Gramsci defined intellectuals, therefore, as those who perform functions of organisation within the realm of production, culture, public administration. Underpinning his theory was the awareness of the specific historical development of bourgeois society towards increasing centralisation – a national educational system, local and national civil service administration, the growth of the church and the professions and especially the rapid development of the state apparatus. In Gramsci's view certain economic 'corporate' classes – classes whose own narrow interests were wholly class conditioned – must necessarily pass into hegemonic classes if they are to become a dominant class. In this process intellectuals play a critical role linking the basic economic structure and basis of a class with the wider cultural institutions:

> Every social group, coming into existence on the original terrain of an essential function in the world of economic production, creates together with itself, organically, one or more strata of intellectuals which give it homogeneity and an awareness of its own function not only in the economic but also in the social and political fields. (Gramsci, 1971, p. 5)

Gramsci argues that social classes do not develop their own intellectuals; a social class, striving for hegemony, must transform itself from its original amorphous structure into a homogeneous, ideologically unified group capable of generating, through its allied intellectuals, universal concepts. Intellectuals are defined both in terms of structure and function as well as consciousness.

Gramsci distinguished two types of intellectual: organic and traditional. Organic intellectuals belong to social groups aiming to direct the whole of society, 'experts in legitimation', who emerge as the result of changes in the mode of production; organic intellectuals express the aspirations of a class without themselves constituting a class. In contrast, traditional intellectuals evolve through a process of 'uninterrupted historical continuity' and unlike organic intellectuals are not so closely bound up with the mode of production. Traditional intellectuals are characterised by a caste-like structure; they define themselves independently of the dominant class. Traditional intellectuals are inter-class, existing within the interstices of society, linking the past with the present as an historically continuous process. Organic intellectuals produce ideas which mark a sharp break with the past. Traditional intellectuals include ecclesiastical intellectuals, lawyers, teachers, doctors, their function one of maintaining continuity between one social formation and another. Gramsci cited the eighteenth-century French clergy who, through their function in education and monopoly of religious ideology transformed themselves from traditional intellectuals into the organic intellectuals of the landed aristocracy. Gramsci's point is that any social group striving to establish hegemony must conquer and assimilate the traditional intellectuals. In Italy, the bourgeoisie failed to create an 'hegemonic phase' remaining at the corporate level, and thus used Piedmont, the northern monarchical state, as the means of domination. In Germany, the Junkers constituted the traditional intellectuals of the bourgeoisie, retaining an independent economic and political base.

Gramsci's examples are hypotheses. He could not conduct empirical research into the complex relation of intellectuals and social structure. His purpose was largely theoretical to show that while all social groups necessarily forge links with different types of intellectuals, only the political party can carry out the task of welding together the organic intellectuals and the traditional intellectuals: 'The party carries out this function in strict dependence on its basic function, which is that of elaborating its own component parts – those elements of a social group which has been born and developed as an "economic" group – and of turning them into qualified political intellectuals, leaders and organisers of all the activities and functions inherent in the organic development of an integral society, both civil and political' (Gramsci, 1971, pp. 16–17). An economic social group – the landed interest, the industrialists, the proletariat – can only develop beyond the specific 'moment of their historical development' and become the agency of national and international activity through the fusion of the two types of intellectual within the structure of a political party.

As 'functionaries of the superstructure', intellectuals mediate the worlds of culture and production producing the ideas which the masses 'spontaneously' accept as legitimate because such ideas express more than the sum of the class interests of the dominant group. In this sense intellectuals are 'organisers' of social hegemony and Gramsci emphasises their critical role in the hegemonic structures of western European civil societies in which direct forms of domination have been the exception. Gramsci's is not a pessimistic sociology of the intellectual: his concept of modern capitalism was not that of a mass society, although he noted the tendency towards bureaucratisation and centralisation, but a complex structure of independent, 'private' institutions (political parties, trade unions, church, professional associations, and so on) which formed the basis of consent and social hegemony. The vitality of civil society and the persistence of hegemony enabled intellectuals in the advanced capitalist countries to exercise their function as organisers of, and experts in, legitimation without forming a special élite dominating society from above. It thus follows that the proletariat, as a rising class striving for hegemony, must saturate civil society with its own distinct values and culture, not as simple working-class ideas or interests, but universalised as socialism – a world view – which compels the whole society and in particular the traditional intellectuals to accept *actively* the validity and historical necessity of its fundamental principles.

For Gramsci, then, intellectuals are structured in a hierarchy of functions relating to hegemony. At the apex are the creative intellectuals who produce the world views, ideologies and theoretical systems; at the base are administrative intellectuals whose function is one of diffusing the values and culture of the existing hegemony; and finally, in the middle ranges are the organisational intellectuals without which no dominant group could survive. The role of creative intellectuals is more significant in strong civil societies where they work to bring together a number of strata or groups into an 'historical bloc' (that is, the English industrialists and the aristocracy, the German Junkers and industrialists). Gramsci emphasises that the withdrawal of their allegiance to hegemony will produce an 'organic' crisis, a crisis of authority and the possibility of social disintegration. Creative intellectuals are structurally and ideologically more crucial than the second-order intellectuals, although these subaltern groups are functionally necessary if social hegemony is to work adequately and therefore they must be assimilated into the dominant intellectual bloc. The sociological value of hegemony is that it works at both the macro (system)and micro (everyday life) levels. For example, during the nineteenth century Alpine mountaineering clubs in Britain became very popular, especially after 1850, bringing together different fractions of the upper and middle classes: the landed aristocracy, industrial bourgeoisie, old and new professions together with intellectuals united around an ideology which emphasised masculine, romantic values. At this micro level the values reflected the competitive individualism of the 'rising' capitalist class. It is through these specific values that the macro and micro levels can be linked focusing both on class and power as well as culture and action (Robbins, 1987).

The concept of hegemony breaks decisively from 'totalising' theories structured in determining laws and broad historical processes: hegemony is 'made' at both the system and micro levels by agents seeking to establish new values. While hegemony focuses on the ways in which social integration is achieved – and hence the view that Gramsci represented the Durkheim of modern Marxism (Lockwood, 1988) – it points emphatically to the actual making of values through action and struggle. And although close to Durkheim, Gramsci's emphasis on the active interpretation of cultural values leads not to the harmonious integration of the individual into the social system but to a critical awareness and consciousness of the possibilities for opposition and change.

Gramsci on Sociology

Hegemony constitutes rather the triumph of consciousness, social action and *will* over external conditions: 'Structure ceases to be au external force', Gramsci wrote, 'which crushes man, assimilates him to itself' and makes him passive [but] is transformed into a means of freedom, an instrument to create a new ethico-political form and a source of new initiatives' (Gramsci, 1971, p. 367). Gramsci was sharply critical of positivistic sociology for reducing social relations to the status of inviolable natural laws. He was particularly hostile to Marxists such as Nikolai Bukharin whose text book *Historical Materialism* subtitled *A System of Sociology* (1969) originally published in Russia in 1921, exercised an influential role in the education of leading Marxists inside and outside the Soviet Union. One of the first Marxists to interpret historical materialism as a form of sociology, Bukharin sought to assimilate the burgeoning sociology of Weber, Simmel, Michels and others, to accommodate twentieth-century Marxism to twentieth-century sociology. He distinguished between 'proletarian science' and 'bourgeois science', the former assimilating the scientific insights of the latter. Yet, as Gramsci emphasised, Bukharin's conception of Marxism was close to 'bourgeois natural scientific materialism' in its attempt to reduce the dialectic to general laws of motion working objectively and independently of human consciousness.

Gramsci followed Labriola in rejecting sociology on the basis of its inability to grasp the whole historical process: Labriola had coined the term, the philosophy of *praxis* as the 'essence' of historical materialism, defining it as the 'immanent philosophy' which pervades the entire historical and social individual. As a philosophy of *praxis*, Marxism cannot be reduced to sociology which for Gramsci was a science seeking to discover social facts, the causal relations between them and the general laws of social systems through the methods of the natural sciences. Marxism, as a world view, cannot be schematised into an external body of knowledge structured around the discovery of regular and objective laws since such a standpoint assumes the passivity of the historical subject. Gramsci admitted, however, the value of statistics especially from the point of view of social planning, but his main thrust against sociology, as he conceived it, was that all statistical laws, and predictions based on these laws, defined as natural phenomena, ignored the essential component of all social situations, that of collective will. Reality is constantly changing through *praxis*; it is impossible to predict scientifically the effects of actions or the workings of elements on elements: one can foresee only in the sense that one acts and therefore contributes to the 'predicted' result.

As there were no sociological laws which facilitated prediction as in the natural sciences, so there was no 'Marxist sociology', since reality was always a created reality and the historical process an act of self-knowledge by the proletariat (an historicist standpoint and one difficult to reconcile with Gramsci's sociological and historically specific mode of analysis). For Gramsci, sociology separated theory from practice: objective laws and objective facts exist only in a process of active mediation involving an historical subject. Ultimately Gramsci argued that historical knowledge is not possible merely as the product of empirical social science: empirical inquiry must be guided by historicism and humanism.

Gramsci thus criticised Bukharin's scientism and failure to grasp that all objective economic and sociological phenomena derived from social relationships, human activity, values, culture and consciousness. Bukharin's concept of system, Gramsci argued, fetishised and hypostatised society. For Bukharin, society was defined as a system greater than the sum of its parts; it is not hegemony which transforms the different parts into a whole, but a system of mutual interactions between the different members. In this way the subject plays a role but one severely circumscribed by external forces. For Bukharin

> Each individual in his development... is filled with the influences of his environment, as the skin of a sausage is filled with sausage-meat... Like a sponge he constantly absorbs new impressions... Each individual at bottom is filled with a social content. The individual himself is a collection of concentrated social influences, united in a small unit. (Bukharin, 1969, p. 98)

The parallel between nineteenth-century positivist sociology and Bukharin's Marxist sociology is brought out quite sharply in this formulation. Society is an organism consisting of different structures; the system dominates the individual who is linked to others through mechanical modes of interaction. An homologous relationship subsists between the material and economic 'base', and the culture of society; cultural institutions, ideologies and consciousness are epiphenomenal forces lacking all autonomy. The system normally exists in a state of equilibrium, a situation facilitated by morality and customs which co-ordinate human action to prevent social disintegration. But the existence of class interests and sources of conflict necessarily lead to adjustments and change and, in extreme situations, to revolution.

The important point about Bukharin's mechanistic and abstract concept of society is that it fails totally to develop a theory of civil society and the institutions through which social action occurs, values produced, culture transformed and with it the social individual, social groups and social classes. In Bukharin's formulation, reminiscent of later sociological functionalism, the human agent is passive, the product of external forces; social change is the result of a breakdown of equilibrium within the system, of necessary adjustments and thus the development of a new systemic equilibrium. Such ahistorical, excessively abstract and mechanical conceptions of society fails to grasp, in Marx's and Engels' words, that 'civil society is the true source and theatre of all history' (Marx and Engels, 1964, p. 48).

In contrast, the explicit sociological Marxism of Austro-Marxism (a term coined by the American socialist, Louis Boudon, to describe a group of Marxists active in the years after the end of the First World War, the most prominent being Max Adler, Rudolf Hilferding, Otto Bauer, Karl Renner) was mainly concerned with the specific development of capitalism, its class structure, and state institutions: they argued, rather like Weber, that civil society was changing, the class and occupational structure leading to the emergence of a broad middle class including what Renner called 'the service class' (managers and salaried employees), and a shift in authority relations from those based on private property to bureaucracy. Perhaps the most significant empirical study of the school was Hilferding's *Finance Capital* (1980 [1910]), which influenced Lenin's *Imperialism* in its depiction of modern capitalism as a fusion of banking and industrial capital within a structure dominated by cartels, trusts and monopolies. Hilferding emphasised the role of an increasingly interventionist state which prevented capitalist economic laws working out towards crisis and collapse: his concept of 'organised capitalism' emphasises the close relation between the nation state and private capital.

Thus although focusing empirically on changes within capitalism, the Austro-Marxists reached broadly similar conclusions to those of Bukharin and orthodox Marxism. The masses were largely passive; the human agent exercised no decisive role in change other than as determined by external forces. Thus their methodological orientation explicitly rejected the *Verstehen* approach of Weber and Simmel arguing for the unity of the natural and cultural sciences: 'Nature and Society... comprise the causal regularity of events as a whole... a social scientific standpoint... is logically on the same footing as natural science.' As a 'natural science of social beings and events' Marxism studied the law-governed interconnectedness of phenomena: the link between the Austro-Marxist methodology of scientific inquiry and their social reformism is brought out in Adler's concept of Marxism as 'a system of sociological knowledge' which grounds socialism 'upon causal knowledge of the events of social life'. Marxism and sociology 'are one and the same thing', the science 'of the laws of social life, and its causal development', striving 'to deduce the development of socialism from capitalism as a matter of causal necessity (Bottomore and Goode, 1978, pp. 60–4). As with Bukharin, the Austro-Marxists defined Marxism as a closed discourse based on positivistic scientism and evolutionism. The complex pluralism of modernity, the problematic autonomy of human agency, and the creative role of values and culture were assimilated to the primacy of economic forces.

Western Marxism and the Problem of Sociology

The many attempts to define Marxism as a sociology foundered over the specific nature of Marxism as a revolutionary, critical social science. Marxism was simplified, purified of its emphasis on contradictions and the role of ideas and collective agent in social change. Similarly, the complexity of sociology was assimilated to a unified, closed positivistic discourse. In this way the tensions and ambiguities within and between Marxism and sociology disappeared. By emphasising the centralising and collectivist nature of the emerging industrial, capitalist social order, Marxist theorists tended to assimilate the concept of civil society to historicism (Gramsci) or the economic infrastructure and the causal laws of the social system (Bukharin). As was argued earlier, Gramsci's concept of civil society gives his work a sociological dimension which links system and micro levels but his historicism pulls it back both towards orthodox Marxism and what the French philosopher Merleau-Ponty termed 'Western Marxism' (Merleau-Ponty, 1973).

Whereas orthodox Marxism was locked into a mechanical base/superstructure model of necessary economic causality, western Marxists (notably Lukács, Ernst Bloch, T. W. Adorno, Max Horkheimer, Herbert Marcuse) redefined Marxism as a philosophical 'critique' structured in such humanist concepts as *praxis*, alienation, emancipation and Utopia. Western Marxism was pre-eminently a philosophy of history concerned not with laws of development but rather with the fate of culture, with values, meaning, human purposes. Social consciousness and practice were no mere reflexes of economic laws.

A Marxism of the superstructure, western Marxism owed more to Hegel's speculative philosophy than to Marx's materialist social theory, to Hegel's historicising of culture and society and the young Marx's reflections on alienation and dehumanisation. From Hegel came the concept of totality: social theory must address the problem of the whole culture of a society in its immanent development. Marx's materialist and historical category of totality, together with his analysis of social formations structured in objective, law-like processes, was dismissed as residues of nineteenth-century positivism. Bloch's *The Spirit of Utopia* (1920) is an exemplary work of western Marxism with its totalising messianic view of culture, its Utopian demand for a wholeness to heal the fragmented character of modern society. One of the most important Marxist theorists in the immediate post-1917 period was Georg Lukács (1885–1971). His work includes studies of aesthetics, literature, philosophy, politics and sociology. Lukács turned to Marxism during the First World War: his pre-war writings were informed by a strong anti-positivist outlook influenced by the work of Rickert, Simmel, Weber and Dilthey. In 1915 he belonged to a circle of Hungarian intellectuals which included Karl Mannheim, Arnold Hauser, Béla Bartók, Zoltan Kodaly and Michael Polányi, all of whom were concerned with the problems of democracy and culture. Joining the Hungarian Communist Party shortly after its founding in 1918, Lukács began writing a series of essays dealing with the question of Marxism and modern bourgeois thought.

One of the most influential texts of Marxism was *History and Class Consciousness*, subtitled, 'Studies in Marxist Dialectics', (1971 [1923]) a book which has the remarkable distinction of being banned by the Third International as non-Marxist and heretical, and yet a potent influence on the thought of such diverse thinkers as Martin Heidegger, Jean-Paul Sartre and Herbert Marcuse. Directed against the evolutionary positivism that dominated the Marxism of the Second International *History and Class Consciousness* attempted to relate Marx's social theory to its Hegelian origins in the concept of totality and dialectical method. Facts do not speak for themselves but have meaning only when integrated into a whole; the fundamental axiom of dialectical method is that the whole is prior to the parts and that the parts themselves must be interpreted in their relation with the whole; the meaning of facts lies in their mediation with the whole. Thus the 'ultimate goal' of the socialist movement is the '*relation to the totality* (to the whole of society seen as a process) through which every aspect of the struggle acquires its revolutionary significance'. The meaning of history, or truth, lies not in the study of the empirical, objective structure of capitalism but in grasping that the working-class movement and its consciousness constitutes the expression of a necessary historical progress. The proletariat simultaneously is both the subject and object of history, the knowing subject which approaches truth through 'knowledge of the real, objective nature of a phenomenon… of its historical character and the knowledge of its actual function in the totality of society'. The 'self-knowledge of the proletariat', its awareness of its position in the social structure as an exploited class, 'coincides with knowledge of the whole', its awareness that its class situation can be understood only from the standpoint of the whole society, its system of production and social relations. Thus knowledge of reality is inseparable from the class position of the proletariat (Lukács, 1971, pp. 12–23).

Marxism is, therefore, not a systematic body of knowledge based on historically objective laws and the application of natural scientific methodology, but a revolutionary *praxis* in which the individual becomes a subject not an object of the historical process. Marxism is wholly distinct from bourgeois thought, and while bourgeoisie and proletariat share the same social reality, capitalism, they comprehend it differently. Bourgeois thought is profoundly unhistorical, accepting the given, empirically immediate forms, thus conceiving change as catastrophe rather than as mediated by the structural principles of the whole. In contrast, proletarian thought is self-knowledge of the real historical situation, comprising a rejection of the immediately given forms of society in favour of the 'immanent meanings' of the historical process as a whole. Lukács concludes that proletarian thought stands 'on a higher scientific plane objectively' than bourgeois thought since it refuses to consider objects in isolation from the total process.

Thus the proletariat comprehends society as a coherent whole and, unlike the bourgeoisie, 'aspires towards the truth even in its false consciousness... and substantive errors'. Ontologically privileged, the worker is nevertheless transformed into a commodity, into an object by the nature of capitalist production so that his empirical condition corresponds to the capitalist transformation of social relations into relations between objects and things. This is reification, a process which dominates capitalist culture stamping its 'imprint upon the whole consciousness of man', a process which is total:

Reification is... the necessary, immediate reality of every person living in capitalist society. It can be overcome only by *constant and constantly renewed efforts to disrupt the reified structure of existence by concretely relating to the concretely manifested contradictions of the total development, by becoming conscious of these contradictions for the total development*. (Lukács, 1971, p. 197, emphasis in original)

Yet how is it possible for the proletariat to aspire to truth given the total penetration of reification within the culture? Lukács argues that as a commodity, the proletariat embodies the whole process of reification, but because it is an object its class situation drives it towards consciousness, 'the self-consciousness of the object', which enables it to cut through the fetishised nature of capitalism.

In these formulations Lukács comes close to abandoning Marxist materialism altogether. Historically, the worker is not transformed into a *thing*, or mere object, for while the social world of commodities penetrates consciousness, disposing the worker to grasp society as a natural, objective datum, there is always within every situation forces which work against reification. If Lukács's theory was historically accurate, it would be impossible to understand the development of specific working-class institutions such as trade unions or the struggle of the English proletariat against the nineteenth-century Factory Acts: in the most advanced industrial society of the nineteenth century the English working class should have been wholly dominated by reification, yet they created the most powerful trade union movement in the industrialising world and struggled, successfully in many cases, to improve their economic, social and political status. Lukács's conception of reification as a total process flows from his theory of totality, that the whole is prior to its parts which are organically bound together and express the inner core of the whole itself. It should be clear that this conception of totality is neither empirical nor historical but an *historicist* category in which the whole is directly expressive of the historical process. The relation of parts and whole is thus symmetrical rather than uneven and contradictory.

For Lukács, history is invested with a meaning outside its empirical, concrete determinations, its different phases expressing an essence which is the historical process conceived as a totality. Lukács' critique of positivism thus ends in idealism, the rejection of all principles of verification and empirical evidence as the basis of Marxist theory: totality cannot be reconstructed through its empirical parts, the facts cannot simply be accumulated before the whole emerges. If wholes cannot be structured in terms of the empirical but only in terms of the future, the maturation of the historical process, then all social science would seem superfluous.

Lukács' standpoint is Hegelian, for like Hegel's philosopher who could genuinely interpret the ruses of history, so Lukács' historicism allows scope for the socialist, revolutionary intellectuals to impute consciousness and grasp the meaning of the whole. But the whole must be known before facts can be integrated within it, and the only way that the whole is known is not by empirical method but by accepting the privileged historical standpoint of the proletariat. And, of course, this itself cannot be proved, only accepted as the truth of history. In Bloch and Lukács cultural critique is substituted for socio-economic analysis. Influenced by Simmel's pessimistic sociology of modernity and Weber's value pluralism, both theorists grounded historical truth in the historical process and the privileged ontology of a universal class. In his essay on reification, Lukács (1971) identified the essential antinomies of bourgeois thought in its failure to grasp totality, splitting the whole into distinct specialist studies and fragments. Bourgeois thought, with its value relativism and immediacy, contrasted with the totalising *praxis* of the proletarian perspective. Socio-economic analysis of objective laws was not the route to critical knowledge (Lukács, 1971, pp. 128–30).

But not every western Marxist shared Lukács' and Bloch's revolutionary Utopianism. In his analysis of social formations Gramsci develops the sociological principle of socio-historical specificity. The concept of hegemony focuses analytically on the genesis and structure of distinct socio-cultural-political levels of a social formation, while simultaneously identifying the collective agent as both making and being made by these forces. In the broad tradition of western Marxism there exists a failure to analyse the mechanisms whereby moral and normative elements are constituted in social action. It is this sociological problem which Gramsci addressed in his theory of hegemony. How is social integration possible other than through coercion and fraud? By appealing to the supra-historical *praxis* of the revolutionary proletariat the whole question of the variability of class consciousness and class structure could be ignored. Bourgeois ideology deflects the proletariat from its true historical tasks. And for all his historicism Gramsci postulates a sociological account of the ways in which cultural elements structure social action, the various modes whereby values are institutionalised and the complex genesis and functioning of ideologies in relation to social consciousness.

Western Marxism culminates in the critical theory of the Frankfurt School. In the work of Adorno, Horkheimer and Marcuse, many of the critical problems raised by classical sociology, in relation to modernity, the sources of social action, the role of values in social integration and political legitimacy are theorised away, explanation couched in ahistorical essentialist terms of a pervasive total ideology and a transhistorical striving for emancipation. Moreover, they failed to theorise the historically complex development of civil society, uncritically accepting the one-dimensional, finalising concept of culture advanced by Simmel and Weber. But Weber's rationality thesis embodied critical sociological implications which in the tradition of western Marxism were buried under cultural determinism, historical pessimism and anti-capitalist romantic rhetoric.

The school took its name from the Frankfurt Institute for Social Research established in Germany in 1923. Its leading members were Theodore Adorno (1903–70), Max Horkheimer (1895–1973) and Herbert Marcuse (1898–1978). Deeply influenced by German idealism, the pessimistic cultural sociology of Simmel and Weber, and the philosophically oriented Marxism of Lukács and Karl Korsch (1886–1961), the Frankfurt theorists accepted the broad arguments of Marxism but followed Lukács and Korsch in criticising its tendency towards positivism, evolutionism and scientism. Marxism was predominantly a critique of capitalist society and its forms of knowledge; thus the emphasis was placed on consciousness, *praxis* and human values. But unlike Lukács and Korsch, the Frankfurt School remained aloof from politics believing that the proletariat had become integrated into what it called 'organised capitalism' and thereby lost its revolutionary historical role.

The Frankfurt School's theory of society is profoundly pessimistic based on a theory of mass society and mass culture: capitalism, it argued, had become increasingly centralised and its social structure progressively 'atomised'. In the nineteenth century the bourgeoisie had enlarged the 'public sphere', institutions separate from the state through which it conducted its business and organised its culture. But with the development of a centralised economy and polity, collectivist ideologies emerge which emphasise conformity to the social system. The public sphere shrivels: the social structure no longer contains strong, independent institutions that guarantee individual values. The autonomous individual disappears. In this process science played an important 'instrumentalist' role: the scientistic, anti-humanist principles of bourgeois science permeate society as a whole and lead inevitably to a new mode of domination centred in technology and bureaucracy. Consciousness and culture become alienated from the realm of human action, values and *praxis*. The relation between individuals increasingly becomes a relation between things.

Critical Theory and the Project of Modernity

In his inaugural address as Director of the Institute in 1930, Horkheimer redefined historical materialism as 'critique' not science, and argued for the integration of philosophy with social science. Later, exiled in the United States of America as a refugee from German Fascism, Horkheimer coined the term 'critical theory'. Like Gramsci's notion of the philosophy of *praxis*, the term critical theory implied a Marxism which emphasised the active role of cognition and rejected the 'copy', or reflection theory of knowledge: theory was defined as an autonomous practice, a critical element in the transformation of society and culture. The leading figures of the Frankfurt School rejected Lukács's historicist identification of the proletariat with historical truth, but followed many of his other arguments such as the universality of reification within capitalism, and the methodological importance of categories such as totality, negativity, dialectics and mediation in the analysis of ideological and cultural forms (Adorno, 1967, p. 32).

In his essay, 'Critical and Traditional Theory' (1976 [1937]), Horkheimer had argued that the goal of bourgeois, positivist science was 'pure' knowledge, not action. Whereas critical theory was based in *praxis*, traditional theory (that is, positivism) separated thought and action, establishing the authority of observation over imagination, and advocating the methods of the natural sciences, especially biology, in the analysis of socio-cultural phenomena. Knowledge was thus 'fetishised' as something standing apart from and superior to human action. But this kind of disinterested research was impossible within the framework of capitalist mass society for it assumed an autonomous individual researcher. In reality, however, the researcher's perception was always mediated through social categories which in the context of modern society meant reification. Bourgeois science, including social science, was linked organically to technical control, technological domination and instrumental rationality. For Horkheimer, only in a non-reified, rational world was prediction – of the principles of positivist science – possible. The basic distinction, therefore, between critical and traditional theory, was that the former rejected the bourgeois illusion of the autonomous scientist and the goal of a politically neutral objective knowledge. Critical theory postulated an inseparable relation between knowledge and interests. But knowledge was not produced automatically; it required the active intervention of intellectuals. Only intellectuals can consciously reveal the negative and contradictory forces at work within society through their commitment to critical thought and 'emancipatory interests'.

Methodologically, the Frankfurt School developed a notion of immanent criticism: they argued that the methods of social science should be 'adequate' to its objects. Since objects are neither static nor external but made through human action and mediated by human values and subjectivity, social scientific method must start from the concepts and principles of the object itself and not from its appearances and surface reality. The concepts, however, were not identical with the object because they sought to uncover both the object's immanent tendencies as well as its relation with the wider whole. The objects of social science become known only through practice, through the subject transforming reality. Thus truth constituted a 'moment' of 'correct' practice. But what was correct practice? For Horkheimer, correct action meant action linked with emancipatory interests which were distinguished from class or group interests by their universality and authenticity (Horkheimer, 1976).

Emancipation, however, became increasingly problematic. In *Dialectic of Enlightenment* (1973 [1944]), Adorno and Horkheimer explained the failure of proletarian revolution in the advanced capitalist countries as the result of a conformist mass culture and control over social consciousness through the 'culture industry'. Following Weber, Adorno and Horkheimer argued that western culture was dominated by instrumental (formal) rationality, its goal the control over human action and society through a dehumanised science and technology. How, they asked, had the ideals of the Enlightenment, of freedom, justice, autonomy of self, led to a social world structured in conformism, the totalitarian systems of fascism and communism and the alienated administered world of modern capitalism? The answer lay in the inner tension of Enlightenment rationalism, between the universal ideals of science which freed individuals from the constraints of mythology and unreason, and the positivist, quantitative and pragmatic goals of science empirically realised in the culture of utilitarianism. This tension is mirrored in the development of bourgeois society itself: the principles of calculation and systemisation have the effect of rationalising culture, transforming science and reason into modes of technological domination which signal the eclipse of the autonomous individual.

Much of the analysis in the *Dialectic of Enlightenment* has only the most tenuous connection with Marxist social theory. In the post-war years Horkheimer abandoned Marxism altogether, while Adorno rejected the concept of totality, arguing that far from constituting the key to scientific knowledge 'the whole was untrue'. Critical theory effectively separated itself from the fundamental concepts of Marxism such as class struggle and the leading role of the working class in social change. Capitalist societies were analysed as closed systems in which all effective opposition had been assimilated and politically neutralised. All modes of social communication were monologic; the system was as perfectly integrated as the models employed in structural functionalism. And while critical theorists such as Marcuse (in his *One Dimensional Man*, 1964) did identify potentially negative and oppositional forces, these were largely marginal to society as a whole (students and blacks, for example). In general the first generation of critical theorists failed to develop an adequate sociology of modern society, the relation between capitalism as a system and its structural differentiation with the emergence of civil society as an autonomous sphere separate from the state. Thus the critical sociological problem of social integration was resolved not in terms of a complex process of a subjectively mediated interaction but rather as a simple one-way process of cultural indoctrination. Society, wrote Adorno, has come to mean the domination of things over human action, so, although the product of human activity, its historical development obstructs subjects reaching consciousness of themselves as subjects: they identify their fate with the domination of market forces:

> In mockery of all hopes of philosophy, subject and object have attained ultimate reconciliation. The process is fed by the fact that men owe their life to what is being done to them... the mass appeal of sports, the fetishization of consumer goods, all are symptoms of this trend. The cement which once ideologies supplied is now furnished by these phenomena, which hold the massive social institutions together on the one hand, the psychological constitution of human beings on the other. (Adorno, 1989, pp. 274–5)

Modern society becomes an iron cage of total administration, consumerism and resignation. Such pessimistic reflections on the state of modern mass culture are closely bound up with Adorno and Horkheimer's negative judgements on the unfulfilled hopes of modernity. In the *Dialectic of Enlightenment* (1973) Adorno and Horkheimer took up Weber's paradox that the process of Western rationalisation connoted both freedom–emancipation and bondage–reification. The *Dialectic of Enlightenment* focuses on the genesis of bourgeois culture and the goals of Enlightenment philosophy and science and the attempt to humanise society, history and the domination of nature through the application of rational principles. But Adorno and Horkheimer went further than Weber in seeing Enlightenment as a modernity split in two. For them Enlightenment is as 'totalitarian' as any system through its organising elements of calculation, quantification, formalism, utility and efficiency. The Enlightenment principles of order, control, domination and system banish all myth, subjectivity and value, with its ideal 'the system from which all and everything follows'. Formal rationality thus provides Enlightenment with the 'schema of the calculability of the world' (Adorno and Horkheimer, ibid., pp. 3–7). In an anticipation of later postmodernist critiques of reason and identification of Enlightenment with authoritarianism, Adorno and Horkheimer conclude that the totalitarian implications of Enlightenment find their most complete expression in the concept of culture industry which successfully transforms the liberating, civilising potential of rational communication into a conformist and passive mode of social control.

Part II

Modern Sociology

6

Functionalism

The Origins and Development of Sociological Functionalism

Functionalism as a distinct methodology and theory of society originated first in the work of Comte, Spencer and Durkheim, and second, in late nineteenth-century and early twentieth-century anthropology, notably the writings of A. R. Radcliffe-Brown (1881–1955) and Bronislaw Malinowski (1884–1942). Durkheim is often cited as the dominant influence on the development of sociological functionalism for his argument that social institutions exist solely to fulfil specific social needs. 'All moral systems', he argued, constitute 'a function of the social organisation', and apart from 'abnormal cases' every society, develops a morality necessary, for its adequate functioning (Durkheim, 1953, p. 56). In *The Rules of Sociological Method* he explicitly argued that the function of a social fact is social in that it necessarily produces socially useful effects. Thus:

> To explain a social phenomenon the efficient cause which produces it and the function it fulfills must be investigated separately. (Durkheim, 1982, p. 123)

For Durkheim, cause and function related to specific ends, especially those concerned with social solidarity and the maintenance of society as an organic whole. Durkheim's holistic functionalism sought to explain social facts not solely by focusing on the cause on which they depended but by showing their function 'in the establishment of... general harmony' (Durkheim, 1982, p. 125). Durkheim distinguished functional from causal analysis arguing that the efficient cause of social facts must be investigated separately from the function they fulfill socially. Causes refer to origins, functions to intrinsic properties. Thus in analysing the division of labour Durkheim established its efficient cause in preceding social facts such as changes in the population and urbanism and its function as generating reciprocity of services, that is, to integrate the social structure of modern industrial society. Durkheim's anti-nominalism clearly rejected the explanation of social facts in terms of individual desires and purposes.

Durkheim was particularly concerned to show that the function of social facts was moral: social institutions 'normally' worked to promote the goals of social solidarity. Education and religion functioned in this way promoting moral values which integrated different individuals into the social collectivity. Similarly, crime, as a 'normal' and 'healthy' feature of all societies, functions both to reinforce collective sentiments and to facilitate 'the normal evolution of morality and law'. Durkheim argued that the existence of criminal behaviour constituted an index of the flexibility of the *conscience collective*. A normal level of crime indicates that the collective conscience lacks the total authority to 'suppress' all 'divergencies' within society. Crime itself reflects the existence of social conditions which enables individuals to express themselves as individuals: 'If there were no crimes, this condition would not be fulfilled... collective sentiments would have attained a degree of intensity unparalleled in history... The authority which the moral conscience enjoys must not be excessive for otherwise no one would dare to attack it, and it would petrify too easily into an immutable form.' The existence of crime, therefore, shows that the collective sentiments are not too strong as to crush all sense of individuality and originality (Durkheim, 1982, p. 101).

Durkheim's functional approach to the study of institutions, while remaining tenuously within the framework of nineteenth-century evolutionism, tended to emphasise the synchronic, structural dimensions of society at the expense of the diachronic, the genetic and historical: the concept of society as a differentiated and integrated whole, in which the various elements exercise interdependent functions to sustain a complex unity, has the effect of separating 'function' from 'development' generating abstract, ahistorical social typologies such as mechanical and organic solidarity. In a broadly similar vein Malinowski and Radcliffe-Brown, in their studies of Pacific tribal communities (Trobriand and Andaman Islanders), rejected the evolutionary and diffusionist approach and argued for structural and systemic analysis. Rather than pose the question, how did this particular institution or custom originate, they asked how does it fit into the broader context, how does the part relate to the whole? In contrast to American cultural anthropology and German ethnology, early twentieth-century British anthropology developed a distinctive sociological approach to the analysis of social structure, defining society as an integrated system.

Radcliffe-Brown specifically abandoned the search for *origins*, the historical past of institutions and customs, arguing that each culture constitutes 'a functionally interrelated system' in which 'general laws or functions' operate (Radcliffe-Brown, 1952, p. 180). Anthropology, declared Malinowski, should deal with the totality of social, cultural and psychological elements of communal life 'for they are so interwoven that not one can be understood without taking into consideration all the others' (Malinowski, 1922, p. xvi). In this way magic was analysed as fulfilling an 'indispensable function' in primitive societies through satisfying a social need which cannot be satisfied by any other factors of primitive civilisation, while the function of the funeral ceremony 'is the part it plays in the social life as a whole and therefore the contribution it makes to the maintenance of the structural continuity'. For Radcliffe-Brown, a social system, that is, 'the total social structure of a society together with the totality of social usages', constituted 'a functional unity', a condition in which all parts 'work together with a sufficient degree of harmony or internal consistency, that is without producing persistent conflicts which can neither be resolved nor regulated'. Culture was thus an integrated whole: to explain any belief, rule, custom or institution demanded an analysis which linked the element functionally with the structure of the culture as a system (Radcliffe-Brown, 1952, Ch. 9).

This model of society stresses the elements of harmony and consistency, not those of conflict and contradiction. The functional unity of a system is defined in terms of social order. In defining society in holistic terms functionalism implies that as everything within the system is necessarily functional for the whole, then change, based on conflict, must be conceived as a threat to the basis of the system itself. The tendency to regard functionalism as a conservative sociological theory stems largely from its central concern with social integration and the frequent reference to the analogy of society as a human organism in which social 'health' is identified with social order and 'disease' with social conflict. There is also the problem of teleological explanation, that systems have particular 'needs' and that the purpose of institutions lies in satisfying such needs. But in his analysis of collective representations and symbolic forms, however, Durkheim rejected teleological functionalism arguing that sociological analysis must investigate the ways in which they weaken or strengthen society (Mouzelis, 1995, p.135).

Given its early development in Durkheim's sociology, functionalism was barely a significant presence in the mainstream of European sociology during the first years of the twentieth century. The early American sociologists – Albion Small, Robert Park, Charles Cooley and W. I. Thomas – were attracted to the individualistic, psychological approach of Tarde, and Simmel's theory of sociation, both criticised by Durkheim for a failure to grasp society as a collective phenomenon. American individualism, combined with empiricism and social psychology, effectively precluded the development of a *theory* of society in the manner of the European sociologists. A collectivist conception of society did, however, emerge in America during the 1930s in the form of a dogmatic Marxism although it failed to strike deep roots in American intellectual culture. The first significant holistic conception of society developed by American sociology, sociological functionalism, developed after 1945 as the major sociological paradigm in the work of Talcott Parsons (1902–1979) and other American sociologists as R. K. Merton, Marion Levy and Kingsley Davis functionalism became codified into a form of structural functionalism.

Talcott Parsons is the major figure in the transition from the predominantly individualistic social psychological theory of early American sociology to its post-war holistic, anti-psychological standpoint. Parsons was the first American sociologist to develop a coherent theory of society conceived as a whole in opposition to the dominant mode of anti-theoretical sociological empiricism. Yet Parsons' work during the 1930s, culminating in *The Structure of Social Action* (1961a [1937]), was not strictly speaking functionalist but a development of an anti-utilitarian, voluntaristic theory of action in which Weber and Durkheim were singled out for their insight that social integration is centred around a core of common norms and values accepted as legitimate by the members of society. And from Durkheim Parsons developed the concept of 'emergent properties', that is, the idea that the social constitutes a realm with its own distinctive reality and structure independent from individuals, their motives and interests. Equally action was not reducible to its context and that the voluntaristic theory of action which Parsons was developing emphasised choice as well as constraint.

Parsons' theory of action, which explicitly relegated Marx to a minor position in the history of social theory, emphasised the need for central values at a time in American history – the Depression years of the 1930s – when American values appeared to be under strain. Parsons' voluntarism clearly opposed what he regarded as deterministic Marxist theories of inevitable class conflict, class ideologies and class struggle. For Parsons, the answer to social disorganisation lay in the furthering of moral values which would bind society together as a cohesive unity; and by emphasising the voluntaristic aspects of action, Parsons focused on the need for individuals to act and thus create the conditions necessary for social regeneration.

During the period following the end of the Second World War, however, beginning with his article, 'The Present Position and Prospects of Systematic Theory in Sociology' (1945), Parsons' action theory adopted a systems approach. Whereas in *The Structure of Social Action* Parsons' starting point was the 'unit' act, in books such as *The Social System* (1951), the starting point became 'the empirical system' and a concept of focusing particularly on the ways in which actors become integrated through the normative culture, that is part of the action system. In his later work Parsons attempted increasingly to link the actor with the social structure within the framework of a functionally defined systems theory. In short, the actor 'internalises' values which provide the motivation for action which then reinforces the social consensus.

By the 1950s sociological functionalism was increasingly regarded not simply as one of many sociological approaches but the sociological method. In his 1959 paper, 'The Myth of Functional Analysis as a Special Method in Sociology and Anthropology', Kingsley Davis proclaimed that functionalism was the method employed by all social scientists, irrespective of whether they called themselves functionalists or not. Functionalism, he noted, related parts to whole and one part to another, a method characteristic of any science and if 'there is a functional method, it is simply the method of sociological analysis'. Critics of functionalism, however, have suggested that far from constituting an objectively neutral methodology for the social sciences, functionalism is simply an expression of conservative ideology. In seeking to explain the need for social stability and social order, sociological functionalism fails to provide an adequate analysis of social change and social conflict; the historical basis of society as a *process* and structure is assimilated to a static concept of social solidarity and social consensus. Functionalism, wrote Alvin Gouldner, resonates sentiments that favour the preservation of privilege... A social theory that takes as its central problem the maintenance of social order and is thus 'more ideologically congenial to those who have more to lose' (Gouldner, 1971, pp. 253–4).

Gouldner's critique of functionalism is broadly similar to C. Wright Mills' criticism during the 1950s which defined functionalism as an example of 'grand theory' reflecting the dominant values of American capitalism and which failed to account for the reality of power in society. In *The Sociological Imagination* (1959), for example, Mills argued that the 'normative order' which Parsons identified as the basis of every social system ultimately fails to explain the simple fact that in all societies some individuals make decisions while others obey them: Parsons' theory suggests that individuals virtually govern themselves through a social consensus which pre-empts airy consideration that consent might be manipulated (Mills, 1959, Ch. 2).

In general these criticisms miss the point: it is one thing to argue against the later Parsons that the human agent has disappeared within the framework of the social theory, and another to charge functionalism with a lack of substantive concern with power. Functionalism cannot be dismissed for ignoring power in society and the problems of social conflict and of 'vested interests'; Parsons' work includes many discussions of the sources of conflict and power, while his argument that in explaining social order he simultaneously focuses on those elements likely to produce social instability, a lack of cohesion and thus the possibilities of social change, is clearly persuasive in the sense that any sociological theory must incorporate analysis of both dynamics and statics. It is in this spirit that R. K. Merton has argued that far from embodying a conservative ideology, sociological functionalism can be radical and critical by pointing to the failures and weaknesses, the 'malfunctioning' of specific institutions for satisfying the collective needs of society. The introduction of concepts such as 'functional alternatives', 'dysfunctions' and 'moving equilibrium', and the identification, in some functionalist writings, of 'the positive functions of social conflict', its creative role in systemic change, have tended to weaken the general criticism of functionalism as a theory of system maintenance and cohesion. Thus, for Merton, functionalism is methodologically neutral, given an ideological colouring only by the politically motivated. Functional analysis, he writes, does not entail any specific ideological commitment which 'is not to say that such commitments are not often implicit in the works of functional analysts' but that they remain 'extraneous rather than intrinsic to functional theory' (Merton, 1957, pp. 38–43).

What, then, is sociological functionalism?

Sociological Functionalism: General Features

The basic characteristics of sociological functionalism can be briefly summarised:

1. Societies are wholes, systems of inter-related parts. Each part has meaning in terms of its relation with the whole, performing a specific function within the system; society is thus a system of interdependent elements all of which contribute to the integration and adaptation of the system as a whole. Social causation is thus multiple and reciprocal.

2. The concept of system, derived as a sociological concept derived from the Italian sociologist, Vilfredo Pareto (1848–1923), is central to all forms of sociological functionalism. It is the functional relation of parts to whole which distinguishes functionalism from other holistic approaches. Society is thus defined as a structure of elements possessing a patterned form; the point of departure is the system as a whole and those factors essential for its survival, evolution and adequate functioning.

3. Radcliffe-Brown and Malinowski's concept of society as a self-sustaining whole refers essentially to small-scale, relatively isolated societies in contrast to complex modern social systems which are less tightly integrated.

4. All elements which make up the social system are indispensable to the extent that they perform special functions related to the 'needs' of the system as a system. The concept of need does not necessarily suggest a teleological explanation: to argue that any functioning society 'needs' a minimum of basic institutions which regulate the provision of food, shelter, work, socialisation and so on is not to argue that this is its 'purpose'. Needs refer rather to the basic necessary conditions which must be present if society is to survive and develop. Hence social stratification has been analysed as the mechanism whereby individuals are trained to the limit of their inherent ability to fill functionally necessary positions which then rewards them with high renumeration and status. Stratification constitutes the mechanism by which societies ensure that the most important positions are conscientiously filled by 'the most qualified persons.' This is achieved by:

    a. the factual existence of functionally important occupations and

b. the need for an adequate reward system which motivates the most talented individuals. The concept of functionally important position relates to the general functionalist argument that stratification works to integrate the social system around a core of values which legitimise existing inequality.

5. Parsonian functionalism has further elaborated the notion of need by developing the concept of 'functional prerequisites' of social systems which 'refer broadly to the things that must get done in any society if it is to continue as a going concern, that is the generalised conditions necessary for the maintenance of the system concerned'. The functional prerequisites include provision for an adequate relationship of the individual to the environment, role differentiation and role assignment, communication, shared cognitive orientations and articulated goals, normative regulation of means, the regulation of affective expression, socialisation and social control of deviant behaviour. Many of these functional prerequisites are implied in any concept of society and are therefore tautologous: all societies must have modes of socialisation and means of communication since without these society as a concept would be impossible, irrespective of whether the theoretical standpoint is functionalism, social action, sociological nominalism or Marxism. Although the emphasis is clearly on social cohesion and stability, change is present in the form of structural differentiation which enables a social system to respond to its needs; with increasing complexity societies evolve new modes of integration.

6. Nevertheless, integration of all parts of the system – the subsystems – is never 'perfect'. Merton describes the postulate of universal functionalism as an ideal never found in reality: Durkheim's work, for example, stressed the instability, the extremely fragile nature of social solidarity within the advanced societies and the consequent problems of the integration of the individual into the social whole. Although the basic tendency of social systems is towards equilibrium and a harmonious balance between its various institutions, deviance, tension and strains exist moreover as 'dysfunctional' elements which tend to become institutionalised or resolved in the direction of social integration and equilibrium.

7. Social change is adaptive and evolutionary. If there is rapid social change it occurs within the cultural rather than within the economic institutions. Even rapid social change has a tendency to leave the basic institutional framework intact.

8. Social integration is achieved essentially through value consensus, 'shared cognitive orientations', that is, through a pervasive set of principles which legitimise the existing social, economic and political structure.

The Concept of System

The concept of society as a system is most elaborately developed in Parsonian functionalism. Repudiating the atomistic, individualistic theorising of early American sociology, Parsons consistently argued that a theory of society cannot be built up from facts; the data of social science itself must begin from theory, derive from theory: a fact is always a statement of experience couched in terms of a conceptual scheme. Describing himself as 'an incurable theorist' Parsons' work from *The Structure of Social Action* to *The Social System* and his later studies of social structures, culture and modernisation has consistently affirmed the principle of 'the autonomy of theory', that is, sociology develops through a rigorous analystic approach to problems of concepts and method. In *The Social System* (1951) Parsons develops the idea of a system held together by three analytically distinct systems, the personality (including motivation, beliefs, moral values all internalised by actors), the social system (roles and positions) and the cultural system (artefacts such as art, literature and knowledge comprising the core values of society). Each system is autonomous although overlapping with others; the cultural values clearly affect motivation and beliefs for example. However, if society as a whole is to function there are specific 'pre-requisites' which must be met and these Parsons groups under four headings – adaptation, goal attainment, integration and latency (AGIL for short). Adaptation refers to activities by which the system adapts to its environment modifying and controlling it in terms of the needs of the system; goal attainment refers to the mobilising of resources to attain specific goals and seeking such goals methodically; integration refers to the solidarity of the system, its survival as a cohesive whole; and, finally, latency, which refers to the accumulations and distribution of energy which takes the form of motivation (Parsons, 1967). In his later writings Parsons refers to the fourth variable as *pattern maintenance* or *tension management*. Thus analysing the social system Parsons notes that every social system consists of four major subsystems, kinship, social stratification, power and religion. The kinship system is the main socialising agency, stratification the means of distributing rewards within a differentiated social structure, and these two subsystems effectively reinforce the pattern of inequality in society:

> The consequence of this is that the combination of an occupationally differentiated industrial system and a significantly solidary kinship system must be a system of stratification in which the children of the more highly placed come to have differential advantages, by virtue of their ascribed kinship status, not shared by those lower down. (Parsons, 1951, p. 161)

These internal subsystems, the economy, the polity, socialisation and societal community (stratification, power, kinship, religion) are further subdivided into the subsystems of action (AGIL). Parsons, it should be noted is not defining society in terms of the interactions of individuals, or the totality of such interactions structurally patterned: society constitutes a structure which links individuals with the whole, a systemic approach that emphasises the factor of motivation, that actors pursue goals within a framework that is neither reducible to individuals or atomistic interaction.

For Parsons, system is an indispensable master concept, its meaning directly bound up with its relation to the concept 'environment'. The concept of subsystem enables Parsons to treat the individual in relation to this environment while still remaining part of a system of action. The system is thus highly centralised and organised around values as distinct from interests: there is little awareness of possible conflicting social worlds, with their own distinctive culture and values within a social system, that a social system, while retaining its wholeness, lacks a coherent, unifying *centre*. The biological organism or system necessarily adapts to its environment. But the social system is made by humanity, social groups and social classes each seeking to establish their own identity within the social whole and striving to remain autonomous in terms of their institutions and values. In Parsonian functionalism there is no sense of society as a decentred structure built upon the basis of different and conflicting interests *and* values. Rather, the system tends to total coherence possessing an inbuilt equilibrium which Parsons emphasises is constantly undergoing change – the 'moving equilibrium':

> The social system's own equilibrium is itself made up of many subequilibriums within and cutting across one another, with numerous personality systems more or less in internal equilibrium, making up different equilibrated systems such as kinship groups, social strata, churches, sects, economic enterprises, and government bodies. All enter into a huge moving equilibrium in which instabilities in one subsystem in the personality or social sphere are communicated simultaneously to both levels, either disequilibrating the larger system or part of it, until either a re-equilibrium takes place or the total equilibrium changes its form. (Parsons and Shils, 1962, pp. 226–7)

Parsons' imagery does present problems when related to his concern with social action. When he writes of the 'in-puts' and 'out-puts' of subsystems and systems, for example, he seems to be moving towards 'cybernetic functionalism' in which society has become a self-contained and self-equilibrating system. The concept of system needs seemingly re-inforces the general criticism of Parsonian Functionalism as based in 'an oversocialised notion of the individual' (Wrong, 1976). However, Parsons has always rejected this criticism pointing to his concept of 'the pattern variables' for providing the basis of autonomous action and choice within the system. Pattern variables can be related to the actor's orientation to objects or refer to the objects themselves.

They raise the possibility of choice by providing the actor with options over pairs, or dichotomies, of values. They include particularism/universalism (objects such as relating to others on the basis of gender, class, and so on or as a human being); affectivity/affective neutrality (actors oriented to objects to be emotionally involved in relations, or regarding it as a business arrangement); specificity/diffuseness (relations defined in terms of specific roles lawyer, teacher, or more broadly roles defined through marriage and the family; quality/performance (choosing relations because of persons, or through the ends involved) The pattern variables enable Parsons to theorise both at the action and system levels: action is a mixture of the pattern variables but it remains limited and formal with restrictions on openness and fluidity. Parsons own example of the workings of the pattern variables, the doctor/patient relationship, while involving universalism, specificity, affective neutrality also involves the possibility of doctors treating patients as sources of income in a competitive capitalist culture and, through the pursuit of a medical career, striving for status and power within an hierarchically organised medical profession.

Such action is difficult to accommodate to Parsons' schema and one of problems with the pattern variables is that they constitute highly formal/abstract and remotely unreal categories which tend to diminish the sheer 'messiness' of social life, the many-sided nature of social life, its open and fluid character. Parsons' model is too neatly symmetrical dominated by the functional requirements of the social system via the AGIL and pattern variables, to achieve equilibrium. Parsons is careful to qualify the usage of his concepts: equilibrium is not an empirical fact or reality, for no society is equilibrated in the sense that its parts 'fit' together in complete harmony. Equilibrium is an heuristic device which is employed in conjunction with the concept of inertia: the absence of change within a system of action results in stasis, but in reality systems of action are constantly modified and changed by processes involving communication, decision making and differentiation. This aspect is especially marked in Parsons' analysis of integration: since no system can be perfectly integrated it becomes essential to create institutions that mediate the possible conflict of interests, the 'internal conflict and other failures of co-ordination'; the integrative subsystem thus functions to adapt individuals to the 'goals of the social system' by generating legitimate values, 'the institutionalisation of value-patterns which define the main structural outline of society' bringing '"into line" the behaviour of system units in accordance with the integrative needs of the system, to check or reverse disruptive tendencies to deviant behaviour and to promote the condition of harmonious co-operation' (Parsons and Smelser, 1956, pp. 16–23).

Equilibrium of *all parts of the social system* comprises the normal condition of human society, with conflict, although present, an essentially residual and abnormal element. Society is thus characterised by the existence of 'value orientations' held by certain 'solidary groupings' (professional occupations such as scientists) which, over time, pass into the 'value system' of the whole society. Parsons defines value system as 'the set of normative judgements held by the members of the society who define... what to them is a good society' (Parsons, 1951, pp. 36–7). But not all members of a society would necessarily agree on what constitutes the 'good society'. In any case, irrespective of the pattern variables Parsons' own approach seems to give individuals little choice in the matter: norms, values and collective goals govern and control individual behaviour motivating and orienting the individual to the social system. Internalising the collective goals the individual is thus socialised and social order augmented, a standpoint which suggests a passive not active relation of the individual actor to values, the internalisation of norms approaching simple habit formation and thus conformism to the status quo. Through explicit socialising agencies such as family, school and community the actor successfully internalises societal goals so that social order, far from being problematical is 'normal'. Like Durkheim, Parsons emphasises that constraint is not forced on the individual but develops organically from the collective conscience, that is, from society. 'In this way', he writes, 'the moral component of the *conscience collective* is social' comprising common, shared values internalised through the agencies of socialisation (Parsons, 1967, pp. 27–9).

Culture is a critical element in this process. Writing on Marx, Parsons argues that an inadequate theory of personality led Marx to misunderstand that action 'is a function of the organisation of behaviour... in terms of generalised codes that permit the programming of widely varying particulars'; it is these 'cultural codes' which underlie the 'normative components of societies'. For, contrary to Marx's materialist theory, society is not dominated by social and class conflict; Durkheim's concept of organic solidarity is recommended as a more fruitful way of understanding modern society. For lacking adequate concepts of order and personality Marxist materialism must fail to explain what Parsons calls 'directionality of orientations to work and enterprise' – this being accomplished in Weber's study of Protestantism and capitalism. Thus remaining 'psychologically naive' Marx's social theory failed to account for the significance of cultural factors in the maintenance of social order, social integration and equilibrium (Parsons, 1967, pp. 123–35).

Parsons' critique of Marx undoubtedly focuses on one of the major weaknesses of historical materialism as it developed in the analysis of modern capitalism (*Capital*) and became codified into a world view by later generations of Marxists. The voluntaristic element is assimilated to underlying laws and external structures: yet this is precisely Parsons' own theoretical position, in which functionalism assumes a neatly ordered, closed social world, a vast filing cabinet consisting of systems and subsystems, multiple divisions and subdivisions, endless classifications which bear only the most tenuous relation with historically produced societies, a theoretical framework in which questions of who makes values, why and how, have been systematically removed.

Moreover, system changes occur not through social struggles over material resources and ideology, but behind the backs of agents through modes of internal disequilibrium and re-equilibrium. Parsons concept of actor is too one-dimensional, too easily conforming to the existing norms and values, lacking a many-sided and reflexive self capable of engaging in the strategies and practices linked to social change and to the broader issues of power. For example, although dismissing Marxism for its notion of class conflict and structural contradiction, Parsons advances concepts such as 'strains' and 'tensions' and notes that in modern society there is 'widespread' anomie, all of which suggests the possibility of structural conflict. It is, nevertheless, the system which produces strains and tensions, the failure of its regulative, socialising institutions: within the closed field of the system there is virtually no scope for autonomous social action because there are no sources of legitimate opposition to the all-embracing central values, no institutional means for expressing the possibilities of social alternatives other than in the form of 'deviance'. Parsonian functionalism, built around system integration has successfully effaced the human subject from social theory other than as supports of the system and system needs.

Functionalism and the Dialectic of Social Life: Merton

Writing on the functional necessity of religion for modern industrial society, Parsons accepted Durkheim's correlation of morality with the sacred noting his 'important insight' into the exceedingly close integration of the system of religious symbols of a society and the Patterns sanctioned by the common moral sentiments of the members of the community' (Parsons, 1954, p. 206). In a similar vein two representatives of functionalism write:

> The reason why religion is necessary is apparently to be found in the fact that human society achieves its unity primarily through the possession by its members of certain ultimate values and ends in common. Although these values and ends are subjective, they influence behaviour, and their integration enables this society to operate as a system... Even in a secularised society some system must exist for the integration of ultimate values, for their ritualistic expression, and for the emotional adjustments required by disappointment, death and disaster. (Davis and Moore, 1969, p. 499)

Criticising this extreme functional interpretation of religion, R. K. Merton (1910–) has argued that although some kind of moral agency is functionally indispensable for society, religion can be both functionally unifying and dysfunctional. He points out that the Durkheimian orientation of functionalist analysis is one rooted in the function of religion in non-literate societies and thus the effective absence of several religions. In modern society the tendency is for a plurality of religions and an increasing secularisation of values and beliefs, processes which raise serious questions on the function of religion as such to promote or produce structural unity. 'In what sense does religion make for integration of the larger society, if the content of its doctrine and values is at odds with the content of other, non-religious values held by many people in the same society?' In non-literate societies there is usually a single religion which call thus be taken as a model of functional unity. Merton goes on to suggest that in modern societies the concept of 'functional alternative', or 'functional substitute', may be of more value in analysing the relation of values to social cohesion. Although this still assumes the centrality of religious values for the concept of social unity it raises the question of the degree of unity found in the social and historical world.

Merton argues that the postulate of total functional unity is clearly contrary to social reality and an obstacle to social analysis, diverting attention from 'possible disparate consequences of a given social or cultural item' for the various social groups and individual members of groups. All human societies are integrated but few societies are characterised by that '*high* degree of integration in which *every* culturally standardised activity or belief is functional for the society as a whole'. Rejecting the whole notion of functional unity, or functional indispensability of elements, Merton advances the argument of a *net balance of functional consequences* which 'avoids the tendency of functional analysis to concentrate on positive functions' and focus on possible dysfunctional consequences. A major theorem of functional analysis, Merton concludes, is '*just as the same item may have multiple functions, so may the same function be diversely fulfilled by alternative items*'.

Merton defines function objectively as the 'observed consequences' which 'make for the adaptation or adjustment of a given system', while dysfunction is defined as the consequences which reduce the possibility of adjustment and adaptation. Further modifying the functional theory of coherence of systems, Merton distinguishes manifest from latent functions, the former consisting of the objective consequences facilitating adjustment and adaptation of the system and which are 'intended and recognised' by individuals, while latent functions are unintended or unrecognised. As an example he cites Thorstein Veblen's analysis of 'conspicuous consumption', human activity, which functions both to satisfy the needs of the individual consumers (manifest function) and to enhance social status since goods are bought not because of their utility but for their expensiveness (latent function). In this way what may appear to be irrational behaviour by members of different social groups to outsiders is actually functional for the group itself. For Merton latent functions constitute a significant development of sociological theory since they challenge all commonsense knowledge and focus on the 'hidden' components of processes (Merton, 1957, pp. 27–33, 51–8, 65–71).

Merton has sought to introduce a more flexible form of functionalist analysis, but in doing so has confused the distinction between actor and system: the concept of manifest function assumes some awareness on the part of the actor of the actual consequences of action. But does this imply that the actor is equally aware of the consequences for the system as a whole? Unanticipated consequences of action defined as latent functions are clearly systemic in nature linking the individual social actions collectively with society as a whole. Thus although he avoids employing the concept of system arguing that sociological analysis must begin from the 'units' or 'items' rather than from the system as a whole, Merton's notion of social structure, with its interdependence of parts, implies a systemic and deterministic approach. This is particularly brought out in his analysis of the latent functions of the phenomenon of 'bossism' or 'political racketeering' in American society.

Superficially, the illegitimate political machine violates all accepted legal and moral norms yet it succeeds in carrying out 'positive functions' inadequately fulfilled by other legitimate structures. Merton argues that the political machine functions first as a means of centralising the scattered bases of political power (officially devolved by the democratic ethos of the American Constitution), and second, to provide assistance for certain deprived subgroups whose access to legitimate channels is restricted. The 'corrupt political machine' effectively 'fulfils the basic function of providing avenues of social mobility for the otherwise disadvantaged... in a society which places a high premium on economic affluence and social ascent for all its members'. 'Bossism' is therefore not merely the means 'of self-aggrandizement for profit-hungry and power-hungry individuals, but... an organised provision for subgroups otherwise excluded from or handicapped in the race for "getting ahead"'. Moral disapproval is irrelevant for an understanding of the structural and functional role of the political machine (Merton, 1957).

Bossism as a structure persists, therefore, not through fulfilling a vital need for the system as a whole, but for the reciprocal relationship it generates with smaller units. It is this 'norm of reciprocity' which enables the element to enjoy autonomy; the relation of part to whole is uneven rather than symmetrical. Nevertheless, the part, or subsystem, can be understood ultimately only in terms of the wider system. In this way unintended consequences are assimilated to an underlying structure similar to Smith's 'hidden hand' and Marx's dialectic of history. 'Bossism' is more than simple corruption but a process which functions at both the micro and macro level of the social system, its latent functions dependent on the failure of other institutions within the social whole. Merton's concept of latent function is therefore predicated on systemic analysis; it also minimises the role of the subject since it is the system itself which determines the functions, and thus the ends, unintended or not, of institutions at the micro level.

The conservative implications of Merton's functionalism are thus clear: 'bossism' is *explained away* by focusing on its effects on those individuals immediately involved in its workings: but the existence of widespread political corruption constitutes a threat to the legitimacy of the democratic political order and its persistence must ultimately weaken belief in democratic processes in society as a whole. Merton's functionalism fails to incorporate a genetic dimension so that social structures are never concretely related to interests and ideology. Historically, political 'bossism' develops out of the weaknesses of civil society and a failure thoroughly to democratise society as a whole. Merton's analysis accepts as *given* what should be explained: that élitism, in whatever form, functions to promote specific interests against other opposed interests by organising society *from above*. The analysis assumes a passive population, subjects who can be manipulated by élites towards ends neither acknowledge.

Similar criticisms can be brought against one of Merton's most significant contributions to functionalism, the study of anomie and social structure. Here he presents a typology of individual adaptations to the disjunction 'between culturally induced high aspirations and socially structured obstacles to realisation of these aspirations', between the officially sanctioned cultural goal of monetary success (although Merton emphasises that American culture defines other success goals) and the legitimate institutional means of achieving such goals. Culture generates motivation; social structure constitutes the means of satisfying aspirations. But not everyone can be successful: anomie is likely to result when an acute disjunction exists between the cultural norms and goals and 'the socially structured capacities of members of the group to act in accord with them'. Merton thus considers five modes of adaptation (see Table 6.1):

1. conformity to the goals and the institutional means, the most common form without which no society could survive
2. innovation, in which the goals are accepted but non-institutional means employed for their realisation, such as white-collar crime, or the Robber Barons
3. ritualistic adaptation in which the goals are 'scaled down' but the means accepted as legitimate thus allaying status anxiety – the ritualist is one who continues to follow institutional norms compulsively, for example the conformist bureaucrat
4. retreatism is the rejection of both goals and means so while individuals may have assimilated both as norms, failure or frustration can lead to defeatism, quietism and resignation, the individual escaping into the private world of drug addiction, chronic alcoholism or vagabondage
5. rebellion, a combination of accepting and rejecting the goals and the means, as with revolutionaries who seek to set up an entirely new society, or those who have become resentful and discontented with their failure to achieve the goals (Merton, 1957, Ch. 4).

Merton argues that every society generates norms governing conduct but they differ 'in the degree to which the folkways, mores and institutional controls are effectively integrated with the goals which stand high in the hierarchy of cultural values'. Not everyone can be upwardly mobile or follow a middle-class lifestyle. Within Merton's model there are similar assumptions to those made by Durkheim on the nature of humanity – striving competitively for success rather than co-operating with others – and the function of institutions to maintain social stability and thus the status quo. Merton's analysis is effectively couched at the level of system: it assumes the necessity for a systemic ideology which is accepted uncritically and passively as the norm by the population. Institutions function not to mediate ideology but to serve as neutral means for the realisation of ideological goals. But individuals are not passively socialised into the dominant cultural norms: social class, family, trade unions, and other institutions function as mediators of 'official culture', generating co-operative values which may well include a rejection of the dominant goals and institutionalised means as defined by Merton. But this activity cannot be accommodated easily to Merton's typology which assumes social stability, or equilibrium of the social system, to rest on an 'oversocialised' notion of humanity (Merton, 1957, pp. 77–8).

Table 6.1   A typology of modes of individual adaptation

Modes of adaptation	Cultural goals	Institutionalised means
Conformity	+	+
Innovation	+	–
Ritualism	–	+
Retreatism	–	–
Rebellion	+/–	+/–

+ signifies acceptance, – signifies rejection

Functionalism, Social Conflict and Social Change

One of the most persistent criticisms of sociological functionalism, as it developed into the dominant paradigm of American sociology during the 1940s and 50s, was its failure to explain social change and the persistence of social conflict within the advanced societies. Yet Parsons has not shirked from analysing the problem of social change, revolution and anomie. In his discussion of German Fascism, written during the 1940s, he described Nazism as 'one of the most critical... social events of our times' (Parsons, 1954, Ch. 6), while in *The Social System* a substantial part of the chapter on social change was devoted to analysing Russian communism and the 1917 Revolution. In every social system, Parsons has argued, equilibrium is always precarious and its breakdown as 'scientifically important a phenomenon as its preservation' (Parsons, 1951, p. 338).

Parsons' analysis of German Fascism is based on the assumption that in modern society the common value system is always likely to break down and produce the 'strains' which result in disequilibrium and anomie. A revolutionary movement is one consequence of such strains, strains which gain ascendancy only if a number of specific conditions exist such as 'the presence in the population of sufficiently intense, widely spread and properly distributed alienative motivational elements'. Nazism succeeded because the rapid industrial and technological development of Germany created strains within the cultural subsystem leading to 'widespread insecurity' and 'a good deal of free-floating aggression, a tendency to unstable emotionalism and susceptibility to emotionalised propaganda'. In short, a process of rationalisation, a 'secularisation of religious values', undermined 'traditional and conservative systems of symbols', producing 'imperfectly integrated institutional structures, ideological definitions of the situation and the psychological reaction patterns typical of anomie'. Parsons analyses fascism and communism as movements exemplifying a 'romantic' revolt against 'the whole tendency of rationalisation in the Western World'. Rapid social change produces a state of instability in which norms no longer regulate society; anomie results with fascism and communism emerging as mass movements able to canalise the 'free-floating aggression' engendered by technology, urbanism and industry (Parsons, 1954, pp. 104–41).

Parsons is thus proposing a theory of cultural determinism and a linear theory of modernity. Although critical of Marx for failing to develop a theory of motivation, Parsons effectively proposes that a conjunction of certain cultural elements determined that Germany deviated from the 'normal' western path of industrial evolution. His analysis of Bolshevism is couched similarly in terms of an equilibrium model leaving no room for human *praxis*: the events in Russia, as with those in Germany, were inescapable. Revolutionary movements are notably 'ambivalent in structure' fusing together Utopian and realist elements, and although beginning from a perspective of total, uncompromising criticism of the existing social system, are increasingly forced to accommodate themselves to 'reality' after the revolution. No society, Parsons writes, can 'become stabilised on the basis that a fundamentally ambivalent motivational structure towards its central values and ideology became the norm'. The central values of the old society reassert themselves. Differential payments in industry and a rigid system of stratification emerge as 'the need for adaptive structures in the light of fundamental functional requirements... and the re-emergence of conformity needs associated with the old society as such'. There is thus continuity in change and Parsons concludes his analysis with the hope that industrialisation will bring with it 'a universalistic-achievement pattern' of motivation to transform Soviet Russia into a social system broadly similar to America's (Parsons, 1951, pp. 523–33).

Similarly, Parsons has never denied the factual existence of conflict in modern society: 'class conflict certainly exists... class conflict is endemic in our modern industrial type of society.' The point, however, is that class conflict for Parsons and other functionalists does not constitute the dominant structural element in a system of social stratification (Parsons, 1954, pp. 329–33). Conflict is not conceived as a source of change but rather as an indication of a breakdown of social control, a deviant response to inequalities of income, status and power. Parsons' equilibrium model minimises the importance of power and conflict; it does not deny the factual significance of these elements. Similarly, sociological conflict theory makes frequent reference to consensus and equilibrium. Both Parsons and Merton repudiate the argument that sociology can thus be divided into those theories which emphasise conflict and those which stress consensus. Using the analogy of biology, Parsons notes that there are not two distinct theories referring to the health of the organism on the one hand, and its pathology on the other. Nevertheless, sociological functionalism has tended to categorise conflict as dysfunctional, or as a 'disease', thereby shifting attention away from its important constituting role in the formation and maintenance of social structures.

Thus Lewis Coser in *The Functions of Social Conflict* (1956) has criticised Parsons' 'static' equilibrium model suggesting that 'conflict, rather than being disruptive and dissociating, may indeed be a means of balancing and hence maintaining a society as a going concern'. Rather than tearing society apart, conflict performs 'group maintaining functions in so far as it regulates systems of relationships' creating new norms and values, re-establishing unity between different groups, the boundaries between them, and redressing potentially disruptive inequalities in power and authority. Without conflict society ossifies and stagnates; Coser's concern is not with systemic conflict, with basic contradictions within the system itself and thus the possibility of revolutionary change, but conflict as antagonisms between different parts of the system, such as social groups, communities, political parties (Coser, 1956, pp. 153–7). It is an aspect which is missing from Parsonian functionalism which defines change from within the closed field of the system, as the product of disjunctions between culture and social structure, or of strains and tensions which develop independently of social groups or class interests, culture and ideology. Increasingly criticised for his failure to explain social change as a dynamic process, Parsons responded to redress this problem by attempting to develop a theory of social evolution. In his 1964 paper, 'Evolutionary Universals in Society' (Parsons, 1967), and *Societies: Evolutionary and Comparative Perspectives* (1966) Parsons introduces and defines the concept of evolution universal as a complex of structures and associated processes the development of which so increases the long-run adaptive capacity of living systems in a given class that only systems that develop that complex can attain higher levels of general adaptive capacity. (1967, p. 493)

Based on the Darwinian theory of natural selection, evolutionary universals focus on the capacity of societies to successfully adapt to their specific environment. Fundamental to Parsons is the concept of evolution as a process of differentiation in which the various units and subsystems divide into at least two other forms which differ in 'both structure and functional significance for the wider system'. Thus economic production moves from the household to the factory where it is more efficient, a process Parsons describes as 'the *adaptive upgrading* aspect of the evolutionary change cycle' (1966, p. 22). Advancing a transhistorical schema of evolution, Parsons argues that social evolution from largely self-contained primitive forms to modern complex systems in which institutions become functionally specialised. In this way resources are managed more efficiently and successfully.

All societies, including the most primitive, are structured around the universals of kinship, communication through language, religion and technology. But if societies are 'to break out' of the primitive stage then two further universals are functionally necessary: a system of social stratification (involving a complex hierarchy of social groups and classes which become relatively open generating social mobility) and a system of 'cultural legitimation' which regulates the increasingly autonomous nature of modern institutions (for modern complex societies are prone to 'strains' and 'disorganisation') Finally, four other evolutionary universals mark the transition to modernity: bureaucratic administration based on legal-rational authority which efficiently mobilises complex tasks as military operations, water control and policing heterogeneous populations; a general legal system embracing universal norms applicable to society as a whole (and not to specific segments); money and markets based on property and contracts; and finally, democratic associations embracing universal voting rights, public assemblies, secret ballot, free elections, political associations and the concept of citizenship (Parsons, 1967, p. 400). While the active presence of these universals produces a participating and pluralistic political culture, their presence varies between different societies and there is no single uniform path of social evolution. However, Parsons qualifies this by arguing that it is only by building on the presence of specific universals, notably law and democratic association, that evolution is actually possible: societies such as modern Communist China, while economically developed, because they lack these specific universals are described as 'archaic' rather than modern. There is thus a close link between social evolution and the principle of autonomy: the cultural and the social systems become increasingly independent, separate and free from state controls. And with evolution more complex patterns of social integration emerge with social life organised around the 'patterned normative order'. Parsons describes modern socialist societies with their centralised bureaucracy and economy and apparatus of political control as inherently unstable. Thus the example of the Soviet Union suggests the pertinence of Parsons' theory, for writing well before its disintegration in the late 1980s he noted that

> the processes of the democratic revolution have not yet reached an equilibrium in the Soviet Union and that further developments may well run broadly in the direction of democratic government, with responsibility to an electorate rather than a self-appointed party. (1971a, p. 123)

Yet Parsons' theory, in which development hinges on previously established structures which provide the basis for further evolution, minimises the role of agents in the making of evolutionary universals and the whole schema does not advance much beyond the systemic formalism of his earlier work. The terms remain as before – 'adaptive capacity', 'system needs' – but now combined with an evolutionary framework which emphasises the significance of cultural diffusion and two critical universal evolutionary universals, 'a well-marked system of social stratification' and a system of 'cultural legitimation'. Parsons' evolutionary schema, which culminates in the modern democratic polity, characteristically underemphasises the structural significance of conflict and power, ideology and culture of the lower social strata.

In general, functionalism assimilates conflict to an underlying process which effectively strips it of all active human components. In particular, functionalist theories of social change minimise the important reciprocal relationship between the institutions, or structures, and the human agents who comprise them; change is thus conceptualised as the disintegration of structural equilibrium and not as the result of a crisis in reciprocity and the corresponding changes in consciousness and values of the human subjects. At least on this level the frequent comparison between some forms of Marxism and functionalism is valid for both tend to reify society as an external system structured in equilibrium and class domination, a whole superior to its parts; and both seek to eliminate the active human agent as the source of social relationships and social change.

Functionalism, however, departs fundamentally from these writers by eliminating power and class interests as important and enduring structural principles in the formation of inequality. There is a great deal of evidence, much of it historical in character, which points to the divisive nature of stratification and the unequal distribution of power in modern industrial societies. Power is not a 'secondary phenomenon' but bound up with economic and class forces. Neither is the agent the passive product of the system, but an active presence involved in the production and reproduction of social life. It is over these issues that functionalism founders as a sociological explanation, attributing 'needs' and purposes to society as if society constituted an active organism rather than an historical system, a structure and a process which changes through the 'needs' and interests of the different participants.

Neofunctionalism

The high tide of sociological functionalism lasted from the immediate post-1945 period through to the 1960s when many of its fundamental silences on issues of power, conflict and action were re-theorised within new sociological paradigms: Marxism, sociological interactionism, structuralism. Yet Parsonian functionalism refused to wither away: having survived earlier critiques – Wrong's oversocialised conception of the individual, Mills abstracted empiricism – sociological functionalism enjoyed a robust revival during the 1980s and 90s notably in the work of Jeffrey Alexander (*Theoretical Logic in Sociology* (4 vols) 1981–3, *Neo-Functionalism and After* 1988) Richard Munch (*Theory of Action* 1987, *Understanding Modernity* 1988) and Niklas Luhmann (*The Differentiation of Society* 1982, *Essays in Self Reference* 1990). As Giddens and Turner (1987) in their survey of modern sociological theory noted, there was now 'a considerable revival' of Parsonian thought within modern sociology and it was Alexander who coined the term neofunctionalism to describe this return to Parsonian grand theory.

But what exactly is neofunctionalism? For Alexander, neofunctionalism sets itself the task of reconstructing the 'core' of the Parsonian tradition defined as the major macro theory of western sociology. Whereas Parsons' early work attempted to end the conflict between the different warring factions within early twentieth-century sociology through a synthesis of nineteenth- and early twentieth-century social theory, neofunctionalism aims to incorporate 'the most important advances of twentieth-century social thought' within the Parsonian project by establishing continuity with and an internal critique of its fundamental principles. Radical and critical of certain aspects of functionalism, neofunctionalism represents 'the only new theoretical movement to have emerged in Western sociology in the 1980s and constitutes one indication of a deep groundshift in the entire sociological field' (Alexander, 1998, pp. 55–6). Post-Parsonian in its striving for a new synthesis, neofunctionalism represents a radical and critical sociology.

Neofunctionalism marks a movement away from Parsons' focus on the normative elements which sustain social cohesion and solidarity by introducing the elements of power, conflict and social struggles as constituting processes within the functionalist model. Parsons' holistic systems approach, his methodological collectivism, is seen as a necessary corrective to micro sociological theories which increasingly dominated the sociological field in the 1960s and 70s (see Chapter 8 for further discussion). Micro sociology had concentrated on patterns of social interaction within small-scale institutions and everyday social life, tending to ignore, or minimise, the role played by macroscopic processes. The interactionists analysed these larger processes as simply embodying more complex forms of interaction. Neofunctionalist sociology, however, shares Parsons' view of a pre-existing collective social realm, the social system. In integrating macro and micro levels, analysis must begin from the system. However, whereas Parsons had failed to introduce an adequate concept of contingency into his theory of system, Alexander advocates a more open-ended concept of voluntarism. Parsons' work is at its weakest in terms of what Alexander describes as the 'blackbox of contingency', through his conception of social order as the result of individuals internalising culture and developing a commitment to the collective norms of social solidarity. This idealist element, however, fails to deal with the problem of material, instrumental interests (which Marx had analysed)and their role in securing social order. Neither had Parsons realised the significance of culture and symbols in developing both social order and social change. Rather, Parsons analysed culture in universal terms as a morally binding process far removed from issues of power and material interests.

Here is the most radical departure from Parsons' functionalism: by focusing on contingent action and culture, Alexander believes a more flexible open-ended functionalism is possible. The neofunctionalist critique of Parsonian functionalism focuses on its failure to develop a sophisticated approach to integrating action and system, macro and micro, the individual and the collective and thus a voluntarist concept of action (Munch, 1987, pp. 156–63). Alexander advocates three levels of analysis adopted from Parsons: the cultural (patterned meanings), the personality (psychological needs) and the social system (interaction) describing them as a 'permanent contribution' to sociological theory seeking to link actors at the micro level with the broader structural forces at the macro level. But Parsons developed his systems approach before the 1960s' 'revolution' in micro sociology and it therefore lacked an adequate sociological concept of social interaction. Parsons defined the individual in terms of roles and patterns of socialisation enabling functionally necessary action to take place. In contrast, neofunctionalism conceptualises Parsons' three levels as backgrounds, or environments, which generate and condition action in terms of the division of labour and social solidarity (social system), symbolically mediated culture (cultural system) and emotional links between individuals and objects (personality system). The environments are thus the products of action; and action is the result of such environments. Alexander makes the important point that while action refers to the 'movement of a person through time and space' all actions contain elements of 'free will', choice and, therefore, 'agency', making things happen. A voluntarist concept of action, therefore, is one which is dependent on the three structured environments of which two, the cultural and the personality, exist partly within the actor him/herself. In the process of internalising culture, there are always many different layers and meanings and thus potential conflicts over cultural values. Parsons' model linked values unproblematically with institutional regulation and control, for while his

> three system division allows us to understand culture as a relatively autonomous structure that informs social action and organisation, it does not describe culture as an internal environment of action... This allows us to understand why Parsons provides a remarkably thin theory of the internal structuring of symbolic process, despite his strenuous insistence on culture's important role. (ibid., pp. 215–18)

While introducing the idea that internalising cultural values produces, or can produce, a 'surplus of meanings,' rather than a single dominant value securing system integration, Alexander fails to deal with the genesis of culture, its relation with economic and political institutions and raise questions about the making of culture, which social groups are involved in producing values and why. And what precisely are the mechanisms of communication which enable individuals to interact with others and with the wider system? This latter question has been addressed by Luhmann who follows Parsons' thesis on the increasing differentiation of society but argues that each subsystem develops its own internal cultural values which then regulate its functioning: the military subsystem, for example, does not derive its values from the educational subsystem. There is no overarching common culture or cultural system but distinct, although related, autonomous subsystems. Substituting communication for action, Luhman argues that in a highly differentiated social world communication between the many subsystems becomes the critical factor for maintaining 'differentiated unity'. The existence of different values does not mean the disintegration of the social system:

> Functioning systems are operationally closed, self-referential systems with high sensitivity and recuperability, they care for themselves. And they can do it to an amazing extent. This is the hopeful side of the problem. (Luhmann, 1994, p. 47)

Luhmann's model of modern society is a social system differentiated into 'self-regulating systems' which means that action within any one system always involves a whole range of decisions which differentiate them from those made in other systems. The subsystems are not therefore guided by external but self-reference values. This will work as long as society generates its own unity through differences between difference. This model of differentiated unity is superficially similar to Weber's values spheres, but Weber stressed that while there existed specific internal values, the tensions between formal and substantive rationality and competing pluralistic values generated an open and fluid society. But while Luhmann rejects the concept of functional integration through homogeneous values he presents a closed model dominated by functionally specific codings and programmes within the subsystems, a standpoint which precludes open critical dialogue over values. The neatly ordered social world of Talcott Parsons has been reconstituted as complex, differentiated, pluralist, autonomous, self-governing subsystems: all modern institutions are characterised by choices and conflicts over values involving a variety of collective actors. And while Alexander, in contrast to Luhmann, introduces agency, power, conflict and contingency they function within the concept of a functionally integrated system.

It remains doubtful if neofunctionalism has resolved the fundamental problems of functionalism, especially the difficult issue of who makes the environments and who takes the decisions which produce change. The emphasis is less on the making rather on the existence of micro/macro structures and the function of power, conflict, and contingency in maintaining system integration.

7

Self and Society:
Sociological Interactionism

Action Theory and the Concept of Self: the Early and Later Parsons

A major problem of classical sociology lay in the contradiction between its emphasis on the concept of society as a system or structure governed by objective laws, and the role of the participant or actor, in the making of social structure and social change. A tension was generated within classical sociology between the concepts of agent and structure, voluntarism and determinism. Marxism, functionalism and sociological positivism tended to assimilate the active role of the agent to an underlying economic, socio-cultural system. Social action theory, as it developed in the work of Simmel and Weber, sought to redefine the object of sociology as the study of human interaction. Talcott Parsons' *The Structure of Social Action* (1961a [1937]) advanced the argument that a voluntaristic theory of action constituted the major preoccupation of Weber, Durkheim and Pareto, and although there were important differences between these sociologists, working apart from each other in their own distinctive national cultures, a real convergence of sociological theory was nevertheless taking place. For Parsons, the history of sociology was not a history of competing and opposing schools, 'that there are as many systems of sociological theory as there are sociologists, that there is no common basis, that all is arbitrary and subjective', but rather the development of 'a substantial common basis of theory' and 'sound theoretical foundations on which to build' (Parsons, 1961a, pp. 774–5). This convergence of sociological theory is towards a 'generalised theory of action'.

Parsons' broad argument was that a sociological theory of action could not develop on the basis of nineteenth-century positivism with its belief in the methods of the natural sciences. The stability of society, the existence of social order, cannot be explained solely in terms of natural laws. Social order has its basis both in the objective structure of society and in the subjective actions of individuals as they internalise the values of the culture. Thus utilitarian philosophy, with its conception of individuals seeking their own interests, embodied a strong action element. But utilitarian philosophy could not account for the persistence of social order through its central precepts of the randomness of ends, the rational orientation of individuals to such ends based on knowledge of the situation, and an atomistic conception of society. It was not sufficient for Bentham and the classical political economists to cite the 'hidden hand' which fused individual interests and ends with the interests of society as a whole and collective ends or, as with Spencer, to postulate a social contract existing between individuals as forming the basis of social order. Utilitarian rationality assumed that social order was possible through:

1. the rational recognition of a natural identity of interests thus neatly solving the problem of a possible conflict of ends
2. the voluntarist postulate of a social contract which assumed that humanity consciously recognise the utility of government and social stability.

Parsons argued that the whole utilitarian doctrine, built around an atomistic conception of society and rational norms which govern the means–ends relationship, was inherently unstable since it assumed that ends were both random and atomistic. All departures from the rational norms were regarded as irrational.

In contrast, Durkheim, Weber, Pareto and to a lesser extent Tönnies and Simmel, were concerned not with 'interests' defined atomistically, but with the norms regulating human action which, internalised by the actor, were regarded as putatively desirable and therefore worthy to be realised. The voluntaristic theory of action thus refers to a process whereby the subject actively consents to the legitimacy of specific values. The norms regulating human action are therefore not external forces or constraints (as was the case with nineteenth-century positivism and Durkheim's early work) but elements organically bound up with the human actor. There is, in other words, an active not passive or adaptive relation between individuals and norms: the relation is both creative and voluntaristic.

For Parsons, however, human action is characterised by its systemic nature. The notion of human action as a system is central to Parsons' argument that late nineteenth-century sociological theory exhibited a movement towards convergence: thus although human action assumes motives, goals and wishes it can be studied scientifically only through objective, systemic analysis. The influence of Pareto on Parsons' thought is clearly in evidence here since neither Durkheim nor Weber developed a notion of system in this sense. Action constitutes a system: society is a system of action. And in the same way as the particle relates to classical physics so does the 'unit act' relate to the social system: as particles 'can be defined only in terms of their properties, mass, velocity, location in space, direction of motion, etc., so the units of action systems... have certain basic properties without which it is not possible to conceive of the unit as "existing"'. All action constitutes a structure of unit-acts involving actors. An act, therefore, involves an agent, an end to which the process of action is oriented and a situation (the 'conditions of action') involving elements some of which the actor may control and others over which he/she has no control. Within the situation there is always a choice of alternative means to ends, a normative orientation of action (Parsons, 1961a, pp. 43–4).

A system of action can thus be broken down into parts or smaller 'subsystems'. The unit-act is the smallest unit of an action system. A system of action constitutes an organisation of the interactions between actor and situation. Social action is built around rules, norms and patterns. It was Durkheim who particularly stressed the processes whereby collective representations become internalised by individuals to promote social order and a personality structure adequate to the social structure. Parsons argues that Durkheim's critique of positivism led him to define the social milieu in terms of an integrated system of norms which involve 'the existence of a common system of ultimate-value attitudes'. A common value system is one which is institutionalised. Action is thus objectively and subjectively institutionalised:

> The most fundamental theorem of the theory of action seems to me to be that the *structure* of systems of action *consists* in institutionalised (in social and cultural systems) and/or internalised (in personalities and organisms) patterns of cultural meaning. (Parsons, 1961d, p. 342)

Thus ritual is a system of action involving sacred things performed without any utilitarian calculation of advantage and related to a symbolic means–ends relationship. Thus although the source of the sacred is the supernatural 'our symbolic representations of it are sacred things' and 'the attitude of respect to them is, along with respect for moral obligations, a manifestation of our ultimate-value attitudes which are social in so far as they are common' (Parsons, 1961a, pp. 709–13).

As an action theorist Parsons was concerned with the universality of action, the relation of the human agent or personality to the social system. *The Structure of Social Action* examined the possibilities of action in the social world by rejecting the extreme voluntarism of utilitarianism, with its focus on the freely choosing actor, and the determinism of positivism, with its emphasis on causes and effects. In short, Parsons attempted to analyse the subjective element of human society as an objective structure: ends, means and conditions were all theorised from the point of view of the actor and also as external datums. As already noted, in his later writings – *Toward a General Theory of Action* (with Shils) (1962) and *The Social System* (1951), for example – action is redefined in systemic terms. The motivation of the actor in terms of goal attainment is determined by the 'needs' of the socio-cultural system. The voluntaristic component is thus diminished: the meaning of action is located within the system and not from the standpoint of the actor. Action is organised as a necessary function of the actor's relation to the situation. The social system is thus defined as

> a plurality of individual actors interacting with each other in a situation which has at least a physical or environmental aspect, actors who are motivated in terms of a tendency to the 'optimization of gratification' and whose relation to their situations, including each other, is defined and mediated in terms of culturally structured and shared symbols. (Parsons, 1951, pp. 5–6)

In his explicitly functionalist writings Parsons describes action systems in terms of roles, stable patterns of behaviour bearing a specific status such as 'father', 'businessman', 'professional' and so on. Although in his functionalist works, action and system are combined, as was noted in Chapter 6, Parsons tends to emphasise the predominant role of the system over the agent proposing a closed rather than open system working behinds the backs of agents. Although the theory of action can be seen as a critique of nineteenth-century positivist reductionism, an attempt to bring back the human subject into sociological theory and define society in terms of everyday human actions saturated with meaning, it has led, in Parsons' work, to a reified notion of society and a conservative concept of personality. As a system of action the human personality is mediated and stabilised by a common culture involving language and socialisation: moral standards and *'all the components of the common culture* are internalised as part of the personality structure'. Thus moral standards constitute the core of 'the stabilising mechanisms of the system of social interaction' (Parsons, 1964, pp. 20–2). There is thus a 'fit' between the type of personality and the type of social structure, a standpoint difficult to reconcile with the voluntaristic theory of social action outlined in Parsons' early work. *The Structure of Social Action* made no reference to Freud or Mead, but in his later writings Parsons has stressed both the importance of Mead's 'symbolic interactionist' sociology and, more significantly, the convergence of thought in Freud and Durkheim.

It is Freud, however, who has exercised the greatest influence on Parsons' concept of personality and its relation to the social system. Freud's great discovery 'of the internalisation of moral values as an essential part of the structure of the personality itself converged with Durkheim's theory of the socially integrative role of moral norms. 'This convergence, from two quite distinct and independent starting points, deserves to be ranked as one of the truly fundamental landmarks of the development of modern social science' (Parsons, 1964, pp. 18–19). Nevertheless, Freud is criticised for an excessive emphasis on the individual and for failing to analyse personality as it interacts with others to form a system. The personality system is defined by Parsons as a system of action which functions in a relatively autonomous way in relation to its dynamic structure and needs. For Parsons, the personality does not internalise social objects individually, but rather assimilates systems of inter-action between social objects. Many of Freud's basic psycho-analytical concepts – id, super-ego, ego, the Oedipus complex – are redefined sociologi-cally by Parsons: the function of the super-ego, for example, is limited almost entirely to internalising patterns of social interaction and social roles, an inte-grative mechanism which exercises control over the personality. Similarly, the Oedipal phase of human development is linked specifically with industrial society and the nuclear family: in Freud's work the Oedipal phase was defined as a fixed, universal phenomenon of all human societies.

In relation to Parsons' attempt to sociologise psycho-analytic theory it is worth noting that many of Freud's basic concepts are made to conform with a model of social integration that eliminates negative and contradictory elements. The concept of self, for example, is stripped of Freud's emphasis on the repression of instinctual drives; human sexuality is reduced to a matter of social role and social order. A fundamental harmony is assumed to subsist between the personality and the social system. Thus the development of personality, the stages through which it passes, is separated from Freud's notion of instincts or drives and from the repressive nature of culture. While Freud grasped socialisation as deeply problematical, Parsons defines it as an integrating and harmonious process of learning experiences and internalisa-tion of dominant values.

Parsons was right to note Freud's attempt to develop an action concept of personality, with its emphasis on energy and a notion of a creative self. But the emphasis on irrational and unconscious forces together with Freud's inability to contextualise the relation of the self with society as a whole or system and to everyday life, including ideological influences, and the complex social forces that produce identity weakens his contribution to sociological thought. The role of irrational, unconscious forces in the formation of self and society further suggests the potential absence of harmony between the individual and society and this remains a striking contrast with Parsons' thought.

The Concept of the Social Self: Mead

Although the dominant trend of late nineteenth-century and early twentieth-century social theory was towards developing a concept of action, none of the major sociologists discussed by Parsons in *The Structure of Social Action* constructed an adequate notion of self. The self was defined anonymously as a disembodied actor assimilating norms and producing meanings in relation to the wider, macrosociological system. The self as a distinctive social being, as the source of action and energy, existed implicitly as the necessary volun-taristic component of an anti-positivist sociology. The self was defined in terms of institutions, ideologies, culture: but its rich complexity, its many-sided aspects, its forms of action and consciousness were largely absent. Only Simmel's sociology with its basis in sociation and interaction approached an adequate theory of the living, active social subject. And it was Simmel, not Durkheim, Weber or Pareto, who exerted the greatest influence on the theory of the self which developed in the social psychology, or social behaviourism, of G. H. Mead (1863–1931).

For much of his academic life Mead taught at the University of Chicago. The first major school of American sociology developed at the University of Chicago in the work of Robert Park, who had studied with Simmel in Germany, W. I. Thomas, Florian Znaniecki and many others all of whom were largely concerned with micro rather than macrosociological issues especially the study of social interaction in the city, the process of urbanism and the ways in which individuals construct reality. Thus Thomas and Znaniecki argued that since the personal element is a constitutive factor of every social occurrence, 'social science cannot remain on the surface... but must reach the actual human experiences and attitudes which constitute the full, live and actual reality beneath the formal organisation of social institutions' (Thomas and Znaniecki, 1927, Vol. 2, p. 1834). The Chicago-based *American Journal of Sociology* had published a number of Simmel's essays before 1914 while the first major textbook in American sociology, *Introduction to the Science of Sociology* (1921) written by Park together with E. W. Burgess, contained more references to Simmel than to any other European sociologist. Simmel's emphasis on the importance of subjectivity in social life and the deeply alienating nature of modern urban society found a ready response in the Chicago school's focus on the rootlessness of American culture, the increasing isolation of individuals from community and primary groups. 'It is plausible', writes Rock, 'that the greatly accelerated processes of capitalism in early twentieth-century America gave ontological primacy to the individual above all other categories. Theories which centred... on the European forms of class, could be discounted as irrelevant. The self became chiefly problematic' (Rock, 1979, pp. 95–6). The Chicago School developed little systematic theory, and while problematic, the self was not integrated within a sociological theory of society as a system: society was defined atomistically. Indeed, the only available theory of the subject which conceived the self anti-atomistically, as a structure, derived from the social psychological approach of Mead.

Mead published very little during his lifetime; his influence on his contemporaries flowed from his lecture courses and scattered articles. After his death the lectures were published in book form, *Mind, Self and Society* (1934), *Movements of Thought in the Nineteenth Century* (1936), *The Philosophy of the Act* (1938) and his work reached a wider audience. Mead is important because he broke from the mechanical and passive notions of self and consciousness which had dominated early twentieth-century American psychology and sociology. Mead attempted to examine the genesis of the self both in terms of its practical social experience (its external aspects), as well as its experience as consciousness (its inner aspects). The intellectual influences on Mead's thought were numerous and varied: the philosophy of pragmatism (John Dewey, William James), Darwinian evolutionism, German idealism, nineteenth-century romanticism and the sociology of Charles Cooley. Thus although the self was partly biological, in that its development was dependent on the central nervous system, it was only by adapting to its environment, and struggling continually to control it, that the human organism comes to identify itself as a subject. German idealism (Hegel, Fichte) and romanticism had both emphasised the significance of a constituting subject in the formation and development of culture, but failed to ground it materialistically in the day-to-day experience of ordinary humanity. Mead criticised Cooley, for example, for a similar failure, a too subjectivist notion of the self.

Charles Cooley (1864–1929) rejected the dualism of individual and society arguing that they both constituted 'collective' and 'distributive' aspects of the same phenomenon. The self arises out of a process of communication with others and society as a whole: the 'I' is impossible without the 'you', the 'he', without the 'they'. In his most famous formulation Cooley described the genesis of a 'looking-glass self' which consisted of 'the imagination of our appearance to the other person, the imagination of his judgment of that appearance, and some sort of self-feeling, such as pride or mortification'. Society, however, and its 'solid facts' were ultimately constituted in 'the imaginations which people have of one another' (Cooley, 1902, pp. 184, 121). By defining the self almost entirely in terms of those ideas which others entertain of it, Cooley slipped into mentalism, society defined psychologically as a psychical whole. Mead, in his assessment of Cooley's contribution to American social theory wrote:

> His method was that of an introspection which recognised the mind as the locus of the selves that act upon each other, but the methodological problem of the objectification of this mind he pushed aside as metaphysical... [But] in the process of communication there appears a social world of selves standing on the same level of immediate reality as that of the physical world that surround us. It is out of this social world that the inner experience arises which we term psychical... the locus of society is not in the mind... though what goes on in the inner forum of our experience is essential to meaningful communication. (1964, pp. 304–5)

For Mead, both mind and self were the social creations of everyday life:

> Human society, as we know it could not exist without minds and selves, since all of its most characteristic features presuppose the possession of minds and selves by its individual members. (ibid., p. 227)

Humanity, through mind and self, had the capacity to reason and to reflect. Two elements of the self which Mead analysed in great detail were its reflexive nature and ability to develop symbolic forms of communication. Moreover, the self exists only, in relation to social groups 'because the individual himself belongs to a social structure, a social order' (ibid., pp. 1–7). Mind and self, consciousness and action, were thus collaborative not individual phenomena involving social roles, social relations and social institutions.

Mead was concerned with developing a concept of symbolically mediated interaction, analysing social acts which constituted the basis of human society. Reality was not a fixed datum but constantly shifting as actors – selves – create new roles and new meanings, defining their situation in a variety of different ways all of which were 'real' to them. Communication is effected through 'significant gestures', self-conscious acts which distinguish human from non-human behaviour. The acts of dogs, about to fight each other, consist of what Mead called 'a conversation of gestures' but not of significant gestures: the animals instinctively react and adjust to the situation. Significant gestures are full of meaning because they involve ideas communicated through a system of universal symbols such as language. The self develops through the use of significant symbols: Mead emphasised the central role played by language which enables the individual to have conversation with themselves through an inner flow of speech and thus 'take the attitude of others' and in this way interpret the actions of others. Mead emphasised that the capacity of individuals to communicate through vocal gestures was closely linked to the evolution of society in which co-operative activity increasingly became the norm. Social acts were defined as acts involving the co-operation of more than one person within a framework of the group (ibid., pp. 35–42).

The self is thus individual only through its reciprocal relations with others and with the community. The self is both a subject and an object, the 'I' as the subject which thinks and acts, the 'me' as the individual's awareness of self as an object in the world existing for others. Mead's notion of the 'I' is both biological and social, a synthesis of organic drives and social experience; it is not, therefore, easily separated from the 'me'. Mead's emphasis on the role of language in the formation of the self, however, suggests that the 'me' aspect of self arises out of dialogic speech acts, out of discourse, 'the inner flow of speech'.

There is no 'I' or 'me' in a conversation of gestures: it is only through dialogic communication that self-consciousness develops:

> The 'I' is the response of the organism to the attitudes of the others; the 'me' is the organised set of attitudes of others which one himself assumes. The attitudes of the others constitute the organised 'me', and then one reacts towards that as an 'I.' (Mead, 1934)

A self only exists, then, when it interacts with itself and the other selves of the community: the self arises 'through its ability to take the attitude of the group to which he belongs' and assimilate the group's social habits, the common attitudes of the community (Mead, 1964, pp. 33–4). The individual takes not simply the attitudes of others towards him/her but seeks to integrate the 'whole social process' into individual experience. The self is finally organised into a unity by this 'generalised other'.

Thus the young girl who takes the role of mother, conversing with herself and acting towards herself as she believes mothers do, has succeeded in getting outside herself by adopting the role of a 'significant other'. For Mead, as for Freud, childhood constituted the first stage in the formation of the self. Mead points to two 'general stages in the full development of the self', first 'play' which consists of internalising and imitating certain roles (mother, racing driver, teacher, and so on) through which the child acts and participates with others; the second stage Mead describes as the 'game' which involves taking the role of the others within organised activities and understanding the relations between the different roles. Through assimilating the roles of others the child takes a collective role, the 'generalised other', the organised group. Mead illustrated this process in terms of a baseball team: the individual player must take account of the role of the whole team, its structure as a team, as a whole, which is always involved in his individual action. (Other examples were the family, education, political parties, trade unions and so on.)

Thus the self arises

> through its ability to take the attitude of the group to which he belongs – because he can talk to himself in terms of the community to which he belongs and lay upon himself the responsibilities that belong to the community; because he can recognise his own duties as against others – that is what constitutes the self as such. (ibid., p. 33)

Mead's theory of the self represented a marked advance on previous sociologies of the actor: the act and the self were structures bound up with social structure yet creative and reflexive. But as Mead's work became widely known during the 1940s and 50s it was increasingly appropriated by social theorists who tended to stress the passive nature of roles and diminish the active properties of self. The 'me' dominated the 'I' in the interests of the social system and social order. Yet there is a sense in which Mead's work inclines in this direction: through his emphasis on the collective community as a unity, a structure of commonly shared values, Mead's theory of self approaches a conservative standpoint. There is, for example, no awareness in his writings of the repressive character of culture – the generalised other – and the potential conflict between the creative, voluntaristic aspect of the self and the collective, conformist nature of modern industrial society. Mead's

fundamental concepts assume a common core of values which arise spontaneously from within the common culture and community. It is the strong
sense of community which effectively overrides the possibility of conflicting
and alternative values.

Nevertheless, Mead's emphasis on the potential creativity of the subject
constitutes a significant corrective to mechanistic and reified notions of self
and society. In particular, the category of meaning is located within the
common symbols of social groups and their modes of interaction. Mead's
voluntarism and concern with the dialogic nature of everyday life stand
opposed to the dominant assumptions of structural functionalism.

Symbolic Interactionism

Mead regarded his work as social psychological rather than strictly sociological and while other members of the Chicago school focused on the micro level
of society (with studies of the hobo, the gang, the slum) leading sociologists
such as Park and Thomas analysed the role and structure of social groups and
collectivities as communities. Park, for example, while writing extensively on
communication, failed to develop adequate concepts or a substantive theory
exploring the links between the self, communicative action and social institutions and social structure. Thus the problem posed by Parsons of how a
concept of action, while embedded within specific social contexts it is not
determined by, was never adequately theorised.

It was Herbert Blumer (1900–1987) who, in 1937, extended many of Meads
ideas to the field of social structure coining the term 'symbolic interactionism'
to refer to action through which individuals attempt to 'negotiate' the
different social situations they encounter in daily life and thus produce new
meanings. Blumer had attended Mead's lectures and was clearly influenced
by his ideas and 'genius' but while Mead had focused on language and
communication he failed to explain how meanings were actually produced,
how a voluntaristic concept of action is possible. There was inadequate
analysis of the situational and contextual basis of action in its relation with the
development of the self. Although Blumer defined sociology as a practical
natural science exploring the nature of social structure the starting point was
human action. He remained throughout his life highly critical of sociological
approaches which minimised or marginalised the role played by human
agents in the making of society:

> More and more over the years, as I have had occasion to reflect on what is
> going on in sociology, the more convinced I have become of the inescapable
> need of recognising that a human group consists of people who are living.
> Oddly enough that is not the picture which underlies the dominant
> imagery in the field of sociology today. Rather sociology assumes individ-

uals as the products of structures and completely missing the complex ways they organise their behaviour and action to cope with a variety of different situations. (Blumer, 1980, cited in Plummer, 1998, p. 85)

Throughout his academic career Blumer published sparingly: like Mead, his most famous work, *Symbolic Interactionism* (1969), was in part inspired by his students. Blumer's starting point was human action which becomes meaningful only through its relationship with what he termed the world of 'objects' and 'things' which include symbolic forms as flags and uniforms. And following Mead, Blumer argued that language constitutes the mechanism for both producing and symbolising objects. It is this process which generates specific meanings. The point Blumer makes is that meaning does not inhere in the objects themselves but arises through the ways individuals interact with each other as they utilise and interpret the symbolic forms. But interpretation always involves an awareness of and response to others, to defining and understanding their actions. It is this dialogic principle derived from Mead which forms the basis of Blumer's interpretative approach.

Meaning is not fixed but fluid, open, continually reconstituted in relation to the world of objects, a process in which individuals bring to every new situation a stock of knowledge and symbols inherited from previous patterns of interaction on which they can draw to develop shared cultural definitions and further forms of action.

Symbolic interactionism emphasises the mental and creative processes at the expense of the structural and external. Social action occurs when the self takes account of others, their values, ideas, definition of the situation in which relations are made and constituted as acknowledged accomplishments. Interactionism is a dynamic process, a becoming, not a mechanistic application of given and fixed meanings. Human society consists of 'individuals who have selves' who act 'through noting and interpreting features of the situation... that group or collective action consists of the aligning of individual actions, brought about by the individual's interpreting or taking into account each other's actions' (Blumer, 1962, p. 184). Blumer's model is thus close to Weber's methodological individualism: symbolic interactionism defines concepts such as society, social structure and social organisation, social class and division of labour as existing only through individual and collective action. Social relations are made and remade.

By focusing on meanings at the expense of the structural, symbolic interactionism defined society as 'doing things together' seeking to avoid reification and dehumanisation. Blumer followed Mead's view that individuals respond creatively and reflexively not mechanically to social life and relations. Because they interpret their situation and 'construct their action' to deal with it 'the student must take the role of the acting unit he is studying. Since the interpretation is being made by the acting unit in terms of objects designated and appraised, meanings acquired and decisions made, the process has to be seen from the standpoint of the acting unit...' Social action, therefore, must always be treated 'as it occurs in the experience' of the actor. Society is not the expression of organised structure (ibid., pp. 188–9).

In the subsequent development of symbolic interactionism two distinct schools emerged: the Iowa School with a commitment to quantifiable positivist methods for measuring relations and interactions and symbols; and the Chicago School with its concept of society as humanist project, seeking to unravel the meaningful contingent and open-ended world of objects and things.

Although Blumer employed interpretation not positivistic methods he consistently maintained that sociological thought must be a dialogue between empirical and theoretical concepts. It is the close analysis of the empirical, everyday social world which produces and refines concepts. Symbolic interactionism had effectively laid the foundations for an interpretative critique of functionalist system theory while tending to marginalise the significance of the macro sociological perspective. In Blumer's formulations society exists as a developing network of interactions and relations and not an external objective structure. But does this suggest a structureless society in which the self exists as a disembodied entity lacking anchorage in social institutions? Symbolic interactionism has tended to minimise the effects which pre-existing structures, both macro and micro, have on the formation of the self and patterns of social interaction. But in influencing a whole generation of micro sociologists, including Erving Goffman and Howard Becker, Blumer's work was extended to explore the role played by structure and cultural forms in everyday life, in the shaping of interaction and production of meaning. The weakness of Blumer's symbolic interactionism lay in its reduction of social structure to the emergent properties of interaction, that while it was made and sustained by individuals it survived as a thing in itself, an interaction order. The result was to concentrate on the production but not reproduction of culture, symbols and interaction. Blumer failed to account for larger structures and the ways in which institutions with their hierarchical structures, such as bureaucracy and social class, play an important role in shaping the individual's understanding and knowledge of the social world and providing him/her with the necessary resources to negotiate different situations. Blumer's fundamental point that meaning only arises from social interaction ignores the very real problem of how meaning is mediated through relations with external structures, how symbolically mediated interaction takes place within both micro and macro contexts.

Goffman: Interaction as Drama and Ritual

Beginning his career in the University of Chicago, Erving Goffman (1922–1982) was influenced by Blumer's work going on to produce a dazzling and idiosyncratic range of studies which radically changed the basic concerns of sociological interactionism. While Blumer's work remained within the academic discourse Goffman wrote in a style accessible to the educated reader, abjuring sociological jargon. His studies of *The Presentation of the Self in Everyday Life* (1956) and *Asylums* (1961) have often been regarded as the work of a highly original writer full of brilliant insights and exemplifying an idiosyncratic socio-logical imagination. Goffman has been criticised, however, for an unsystematic and non-theoretical approach to sociological analysis. Goffman, it is true, draws on a broad range of references from literary memoirs to scientific reports. In *Asylums*, a study of 'total institutions', he quotes the Irish play-wright Brendan Behan's description of ritual insubordination within prison which functions as a process to maintain the prisoner's identity through keeping distance, or 'elbow room' between himself and 'the social unit in which he is supposed to be participating' and while not productive of change it demonstrates 'to the practitioner if no one else that he has some selfhood and personal autonomy beyond the grasp of the organisation' (Goffman, 1961).

Goffman's work, building on Blumer, suggests that while structure is important, it cannot by itself explain the specifics of human action. A focus on structure may be at the expense both of interaction and the rules under-pinning it as well as the creative role of the agent in producing and sustaining it. In contrast to the Iowa School, which focused on the ways indi-viduals embraced not created roles, with their expectations drawn from social institutions and social structure, Goffman defines the self as creative and active, capable of performing and producing not simply a single, unified self but a multifaceted self with the ability to deal with different situations and encounters.

Following Blumer's interpretist, humanist sociology, Goffman's work demonstrates that individuals play roles 'dramaturgically', as 'perform-ances' so that 'doing sociology' is like studying theatre: society is charac-terised by its 'front', or setting, which functions in a general and fixed way determining the situation for observers (the scenery, props, decor); there exists a 'personal' front or appearance (age, gender, race); and finally there is the backstage (as individuals retire to rehearse their performance) (Goffman, 1956, p. 17). Goffman employs the concepts of 'gatherings' and encounters', social situations in which two or more individuals are present. Gatherings are largely forms of unfocused interaction, while encounters are more organ-ised and focused on specific action such as card games, ballroom competition and fist fights involving the social organisation of 'talk' which regulates who speaks, to whom and in which language. An encounter is a 'little system of mutually ratified and ritually governed face to face action' (Goffman, 1997a, pp. 231–5). Through co-presence, focused and unfocused interaction indi-viduals engage in dialogue with others, talking, listening, responding. In studying the roles individuals play Goffman is concerned only with the specific social situation with spatial and temporal boundaries and not with the wider social context.

Unlike Parsons, then, Goffman does not raise questions about the role of teachers or doctors, for example, in the wider American social structure rather his work concentrates on the forms of interaction within clearly defined micro contexts. Unlike Parsons, Goffman seems to reject the concept of the internalisation of values as part of a process that generates motivation and a personality which integrates into the social order. Goffman is more concerned with the creative roles of actors which functionalism had assimilated to concepts as 'need dispositions'. But Goffman's work is informed by a Durkheimian perspective, not the internalisation of culture, but one which identifies the roles played by individuals with 'the common official values of the society in which it occurs... an expressive rejuvenation and realisation of the moral values of the community' (ibid., pp. 20–3).

In his later work on *Frame Analysis* (1974) Goffman modified his earlier Durkheimian perspective by suggesting that individuals employ organised frames, imposed on themselves, which function to hold groups together. These forms constitute the key for understanding how the participation in games, rituals and play is structured. Framed activity is 'embedded in ongoing reality' and frames are what Goffman calls 'organisational premises' of frameworks which 'correspond in some sense to the way in which an aspect of the activity itself is organised' so that individuals 'fit their actions to this understanding and ordinarily find that the ongoing world supports this fitting'. These organisational premises or rules are sustained in both mind and activity and it is this which Goffman calls 'the frame of the activity' (Goffman, 1997c, p. 158).

What does Goffman mean by action? Agents have the capacity to understand what they do and focused interaction always involves face-to-face relations and it is important to see that Goffman is not a situationist but goes on to make inferences from the larger structure. In his late essay, 'The Interaction Order' (Goffman, 1997a [1983]) he argued that face-to-face interaction constitutes a specific order defined by its own distinctive internal properties (language, symbols, rules and moral obligations) and clear boundaries, 'an analytically viable domain... whose preferred method of study is microanalysis'. This interaction order does not reflect the macro-institutional order but constitutes 'a substantive domain in its own right'. In *Asylums* he had shown how, in the face of a depersonalising social order which dehumanised and degraded individuals by a process of classifying, labelling and treated them as objects, divesting them of moral responsibility, an interaction order nevertheless develops within such total institutions enabling individuals to both sustain a sense of identity and to engage in morally responsible social action. Goffman's point is that the interaction order always involves a moral dimension, made up of trust and tact for supporting and maintaining the order based on both cognitive and normative 'presuppositions and self-sustained restraints'. For Goffman, even the most micro situation, the train or supermarket queue, exemplifies the workings of the interaction order, with individuals accepting its inherent orderliness and basis in egalitarian principles. It is not as with 'traditional' sociology a matter of individuals passively accepting the rules (the normative consensus model) rather they 'go along with current interaction arrangements for a wide variety of reasons' and Goffman notes that lying behind the notions of' community and consensus are mixed motive games' (Goffman, ibid., p. 241).

But how is this interaction order linked with the larger social organisation? A solution to this problem is aggregation, that is, extrapolation from particular social encounters to the wider social structure. But Goffman rejects this approach as invalid since 'statements about macroscopic structures and processes can reasonably be subjected to a microanalysis but of the kind that digs behind generalisations to find critical differences between... different industries, regions, short-term periods... sufficiently so to fracture overall views, and because of face-to-face interactions' (ibid., p. 247). Thus 'macroscopic' structures can be analysed 'microscopically' – in business, for example, decision making is conducted through similar face-to-face relations as characterise the micro situation. Hence Goffman advances the concept of 'loose coupling' to deal with the interface between the interaction order and social organisation. Goffman illustrates this method by focusing on the everyday world of 'talk' attempting to show how it is loosely coupled with the wider society and social structure.

In his studies of language, *Forms of Talk* (1981), Goffman suggests that society exists and is integrated loosely through talk with everyday conversation acting as a ritual affirmation of a commonly shared reality. Talk plays a key symbolic role in defining, strengthening and maintaining the structure of social groups and patterns of interaction. Goffman analyses various 'moves' individuals make in conversation which express intentions, approval or disapproval, sympathy with a particular point of view and demand a response. Through talk a world of other participants is created in everyday conversation, in pubs and work, in public ceremonies, university seminars and learned societies, each one 'a little social system with its own boundary maintaining tendencies' (Goffman, 1981, p. 113). Thus while the self develops in relation to its social context, it is constituted at the macro level by symbolic forms and shared meanings which are common to the micro level of talk. Everyday conversation, for example, is sustained through symbolic and ritual elements of politeness which produces respect for other participants; and it is this aspect which Goffman identifies as broadly similar to the conception of the individual in religious (that is, macro) institutions. Thus the institutional and interaction orders are 'loosely connected' through sharing a common basis in symbolic and ritual forms and defining the individual as embodying sacred and moral values (ibid., pp. 73, 95).

Thus modern society is characterised by a loose coupling between the interactionist practices of the everyday world and social structures, for while social structure does not define or determine cultural practices and rituals, they 'help select from the available repetoire of them' (Goffman, 1997a, p. 251). But while ingenious, this example of the loose coupling of the micro and macro orders fails to deal with interaction within the institutional order itself. For while Goffman has argued that face-to-face interaction occurs at the macro level it does not seem to constitute an interaction order in his sense. Within a bureaucracy, for example, administrators and managers generate their own distinctive interaction order producing meanings and new ideas which affect the everyday life of those in subordinate positions, in the micro contexts of the shop floor, hospital wards and supermarkets. And this interaction order is hierarchically structured a point which Goffman, as with other interactionists, ignores. As for the argument that individuals draw on resources from institutional contexts, such as class and ethnic relations to sustain them in encounters with others, this ignores the fact that class and race play important roles in constituting the interaction orders at both the micro and macro levels. In short, while both the social structure and the institutional order can be empirically distinguished it is a tight rather than a loose coupling. Goffman's micro sociology is further weakened by a vagueness on the reflexive nature of the self. He was critical of Mead's concept of the self as unified through its relations with the 'generalised other' arguing that the self was more complex than Mead allowed. The self is not fixed or finalised but mobile, open and multi-layered. Rather than a single unified self, Goffman proposed the idea of multiple selves as individuals, in their everyday lives, constantly move in and out of varied social and linguistic contexts. However, in stressing that the self is situationally located, 'embedded' within a specific context, Goffman notes how individuals always bring a particular biography, personality and culture to each situation in which cognitive and reflexive elements play a critical constituting role. But what is missing from this analysis is the relation between such factors and the specificity of the context which enables actors to act. To play a role means that some internalisation of culture and values must have taken place. This process is part of the context, for the self can reflect critically on such values as well as the context itself. It is essential to raise questions of how individuals come to believe in certain values while rejecting others and how they act with others on the basis of such beliefs.

Ethnomethodology

By the middle of the 1960s, Goffman had published his major studies of the relation of self to social interaction and specific social institutions establishing a reputation as one of the leading figures in micro-interactionist sociology. It was at this time that a more radical micro sociology emerged influenced by Parsons, Mead and sociological phenomenology notably the work of Berger and Luckmann in *The Social Construction of Reality* (1966) and the Austrian sociologist, Alfred Schutz (1899–1959). In contrast to Goffman's impressionistic and idiosyncratic approach to empirical and theoretical analysis, the ethnomethodologists advanced a more rigorous epistemological analysis of social consciousness and cognition. Detailed statistical examination and tape-recorded conversations interviews and diaries provided the empirical basis for the ethnomethodologists' claim that the orderliness of the everyday world, Goffman's interaction order, masks its fragile and deeply ambivalent nature.

Both Parsons' action theory and symbolic interactionism had assumed that social life was securely grounded in a structure of values and subjectively mediated action. Mead's emphasis on social acts which fulfil specific needs through co-operative relations with others, deals with socialisation at the 'micro' level: as the child internalises the gestures of others by 'taking an attitude' so he/she begins to act. In Parsons' action theory the actor internalises both specific cultural values and takes account of the personality of the other in the process of interaction. Parsons rejected positivistic voluntarism for reducing action to the conditions of its context: cultural values, because they are linked with the integration of society as a whole, enshrine universal not everyday, practical principles. The common culture of society defines what is desirable and valuable for the individual; cultural values are simultaneously institutionalised in society and its subsystems, and internalised by personalities. These 'higher normative components of culture' enable individuals to transcend their particular concretisation in social institutions, their meaning realised through action which goes beyond empirical everyday experience (Parsons, 1989, pp. 577–82).

Parsons, then, does not present the agent entirely as a passive, oversocialised product of social and cultural norms. There is an active relation between a rational agent and culture. Yet problems remain. Parsons' formulation suggests that the agent realises already existing values rather than actively producing them. While the link between the actor and the system is clearly articulated, it remains unproblematic, for in the very act of realising universal cultural values the bonds between the individual and normative culture is deepened. It is this aspect of Parsons' theory which has drawn criticism for developing an unreal distinction between the normative and the empirical order, between a higher and a lower reality. Parsons' agent, for all the emphasis on autonomy, approximates to a 'judgemental' or 'cultural dope' whose actions comply with standardised expectations and 'who produce(s) the stable features of the society by acting in compliance with preestablished and legitimate alternatives... that the common culture provides' (Garfinkel, 1984 [1967], pp. 66–8).

It is ethnomethodology which sets itself the task of challenging the orthodox sociological concept of self. Developed originally by Harold Garfinkel who had studied with Parsons at Harvard in the 1940s, ethnomethodology (*ethno* – referring to the observational study of the stock of commonsense knowledge available to individuals; *method* – referring to the strategies whereby the individual makes sense of the social world and communicates meaning) was the study of those methods employed by ordinary persons to make sense of and achieve commonsense knowledge of social structures. Ethnomethodology studies such knowledge as 'an object of theoretical interest'. It is concerned with describing how 'decisions of meaning and fact are managed and how a body of factual knowledge of social structures is assembled in commonsense situations of choice' (Garfinkel, 1984, pp. 77–9). Ethnomethodology is concerned above all with consciousness and cognition, the construction and meaning of social reality.

Garfinkel took the concept of commonsense knowledge from Schutz who, in his first major work, *The Phenomenology of the Social World* (published in Germany in 1932, translated 1967), stressed the creative and active role of actors in defining social reality as a process: Garfinkel's programme was to explore the ways in which individuals sustain this process and maintain the structures of the everyday world. It was Schutz who developed the important concept of the life-world (*Lebenswelt*), the everyday world of experience, 'an inter-subjective world of culture' (Schutz, 1974, pp. 134–5). Schutz described the life-world as a process constantly reconstructed through the everyday action of individuals and followed Weber in rejecting positivist methods for its exploration arguing that the object of sociology was the meaning-endowing actions of human agents as they transform the social world, its constitution and reproduction through action. Sociology must begin its task of analysis and understanding not from a conception of a world 'out there', but from the actions and consciousness of actors who strive to construct and make sense of reality within the life-world. Meaning is, thus, not waiting passively to be discovered but requires active construction.

Schutz defined the life-world as a continuous flow of experience and action drawn from everyday life, commonsense and the social actions of ordinary individuals. Social science begins from the 'taken-for-granted' self-evident nature of the social world describing it as 'the natural attitude' one which accepts the reality of the everyday world and suspending all doubt that it can be other than it is. To understand this ordinary world the social scientist must account for the ways in which individuals define and reflect upon their situation and action (the actor's intentions and purposes), as well as examining its structure.

For Schutz the everyday world is intersubjective shared with a plurality of interacting actors whose presence influences the development of ourselves. Social reality is thus the sum total of all the objects and occurrences within the social world. But this world has a structure – it is not an atomistic world – built around social relationships which involve various modes of communication. An actor has to make sense of the actions of others by learning to interpret what the action is about. To do this requires a stock of commonsense knowledge, commonsense practical understanding, which enables the individual to structure the social world of how the world works. Thus the everyday world has its own distinctive structure which to a great extent coheres around the notions of 'cookery book' knowledge or recipe knowledge in which action becomes 'reduced to automatic habits of unquestioned platitudes' (Schutz, 1972, pp. 142–3). Schutz's description of the life-world emphasises the importance of shared meanings, the notion of the world as 'ours' rather than 'mine', a linguistic community existing through mutual symbols:

> Our everyday world is, from the outset, an intersubjective world of culture. It is intersubjective because we live in it as men among other men, bound to them through common influence and work, understanding others and being an object of understanding for others. It is a world of culture because, from the outset, the life-world is a universe of significations to us, that is a framework of meaning which we have to interpret, and of interrelations of meaning which we institute, only through our action in this life-world. It is a world of culture also because we are always conscious of its *historicity*, which we encounter in tradition and habituality... the men to whom I stand in relationships are my kind, my friends, or strangers. Language is not a substratum of philosophical or grammatical considerations for me, but a means for expressing my intentions or understanding the intentions of Others. Only in reference to me does that relation to Others obtain its specific meaning which I designate with the word 'We'. (Schutz, 1978, pp. 134–5)

It is this 'we' relationship which constitutes the basic structure of everyday life; all other relationships depend on and relate to it. Schutz argues that the social world, centred around the individual, consists of a web of relationships ranging from the immediate, personal and unique (relations with *consociates* such as family and friends) to the indirect and more anonymous 'they' relations (with *contemporaries*, *predecessors* and *successors*). Knowledge of contemporaries is largely inferential and discursive based on typical not unique features. The pure 'we' relation, in contrast, 'involves our awareness of each other's presence and also the knowledge of each that the other is aware of him' (Schutz, 1972, pp. 142–3, 168).

For Schutz, then, society constitutes a structure of 'multiple realities', a social world made meaningful through language, rules, roles, statuses. But it is a stable and conformist world:

> In order to find my bearings within the social group, I have to know the different ways of dressing and behaving, the manifold insignia, emblems, tools etc. which are considered by the group as indicating social status and are therefore socially approved as relevant. (Schutz, 1962–6, Vol. 1, p. 350)

Schutz's emphasis on knowledge, understanding, shared meanings and intersubjective relations contrasts with Parsons' definition of actors as belonging to a common culture and shared norms which function to constrain and socialise individuals and their embodiment in the personality system thus sharing a culture which provides social order. During the period when

Parsons' functionalist paradigm dominated sociology, Schutz was largely ignored and his work largely unknown. Berger and Luckmann in *The Social Construction of Reality* had briefly discussed Schutz's work but mainly in relation to the problem of socialisation and it was Garfinkel who rehabilitated the Austrian as an important modern sociologist. But while Schutz's basic ambition had been to clarify the fundamental concepts of sociology, Garfinkel was much more concerned with empirical analysis of everyday action. Schutz's notion of 'intersubjective understanding' which involves implicit assumptions which enable individuals to reach agreements becomes one of the basic principles of ethnomethodological analysis. Garfinkel in effect sought to radicalise Parsons' theory of action (and criticise Berger and Luckmann's appropriation of Schutz) by arguing that social order is not the product of socialisation but the result of 'orderly' actors who are far more active and reflexive in relation to norms, playing creative roles in the construction of values and meaning. Social life is 'an accomplishment' of 'the organised artful practices of everyday life (ibid., p. 11). When individuals choose particular goals they do so in terms of the available empirical mundane knowledge and make sense of the social world through a process of 'accounting', by observing, reporting and commenting on the different forms of action in which she/he is involved. A sociological theory of action must always include the agent's own account of that action, a standpoint missing from orthodox interactionist sociologies as they draw on commonsense knowledge and the unstated rules and assumptions of everyday life. In Parsons' schema actors share in the meaning of a common culture but the rules governing action are invisible. It is crucial to make the rules visible and it is through a process of practical social reasoning that individuals come to understand and grasp the rules governing everyday social action. Thus the importance of Garfinkel's 'breaching experiments' in which individuals were faced with the breakdown of their own expectations from particular situations. For example, Garfinkel encouraged his students to act as if they were lodgers within their own homes thus disrupting the taken-for-granted routines of everyday life and bringing to light its basis in commonsense assumptions. Within this situation individuals strove to re-establish the rules of everyday life. Hence Garfinkel's view, contrary to Parsons, that social order is not the result of the workings of 'system imperatives' or a common culture but the practical accomplishments of highly reflexive agents involving accountability to participants in the making and remaking of meanings within everyday social action. In this sense all members of society contribute to the predictable nature of the social world by making things happen.

The object of study for ethnomethodology is thus the commonsense activities of ordinary members of society. It is the emphasis on these activities as phenomena 'in their own right' as cognitive processes which distinguishes ethnomethodology from traditional sociology. In effect, ethnomethodology sought to reveal the implicit rules and planful nature of everyday life. It is a world consisting of reflexive social acts which embody a variety of meanings.

Garfinkel uses the term 'indexicality' to refer to the context-bound nature of meaning: there is no objective meaning as there is for Mead and Parsons. By constructing meaning, ordinary members are effectively 'doing sociology' and there is little to choose between the sociology of the professional and of the lay public. Social science itself is a practical accomplishment.

While ethnomethodology has posited a knowledgeable, imaginative and reflexive self it tends to overemphasise this voluntarism (agents clearly vary in their capacity for reflexivity) and to place sociological analysis too narrowly within the micro contexts of everyday social interaction. Such an approach ignores the possibility that individuals may be unaware of the ways in which social structural elements external to their immediate situation, may shape their understanding and action: class position, ideology, power relations all can influence educational, religious or political values and play a key role in determining the individuals attitude to others and to society. It is this exclusion of the macro dimension which vitiates ethnomethodology as sociology, for, as was argued in relation to Goffman, interaction occurs at both macro and micro levels. It is the complex relation of these two dimensions of social life which constitutes one of the major problems of interactionist sociology. Garfinkel has raised the question of how society is put together. For Mead it arises through common understanding, but Garfinkel is more realistic: individuals act, take account of others, plan their next moves, monitor their actions and if things collapse seek to repair the damage and restore normality.

Randall Collins (1994) has argued that symbolic interactionism 'glossed over the surface' of social life and failed to get to the heart of the interaction process and it was left to Goffman and especially the ethnomethodologists to probe beneath the apparent orderly surface of everyday life to reveal the 'abyss' which lies beneath. Without the cognitive acts of reflexive, knowledgeable actors there would be nothingness. However, later developments in ethnomethodology such as the conversational discourse analysis of Harvey Sacks and Emmanuel Schegloff have tended to reinforce the view of ethnomethodology as the ultimate trivialisation of voluntarist sociology, the reduction of action to the freely constructed meanings of atomised individuals. Parsons' concept of cultural values (however problematic) succeeded in situating action in and beyond its immediate context. Ethnomethodology reverts to a positivistic model: all values are situational values, all meaning is situational meaning as exemplified in many of the examples cited by Garfinkel, students acting as lodgers in their own home, others making offers for already priced goods, action challenging pre-established conventions. This is to transform one of the key ethnomethodological concepts of 'practical accomplishment' into an empty category, for if these examples are extended to social structures such as educational institutions making sense of them through 'accounting processes' involves knowledge and awareness of their structural properties and broad social function. Ethnomethodology has stressed the importance of agency but unlike Goffman it does not provide even a superficial sociological analysis of the constituting role structure plays. The social world is made by and through action; the result of practical reasoning and skilled accomplishments. But the social world exists also as an external structure (hierarchically organised) which maintains and survives independently of human action. In analysing talk, for example, power plays a role in deciding who speaks, who has more authority in discourse and outcome. The interaction which produces talk produces power; but power relates both to the situation of speakers and the wider context for, as Goffman noted, individuals bring with them into interaction ideas, values, culture and dispositions, drawn from their experience and position in the wider society.

8

Structuralism and Post-structuralism

Since the 1950s a new social theory has emerged which shares many of the holistic assumptions of functionalism and Marxism. Originating in the study of languages, structuralism has exerted an enormous influence in the social sciences especially in the work of Levi-Strauss (anthropology), Roland Barthes, Julia Kristeva (semiotics and literary theory), Althusser, Poulantzas (Marxism and sociology) and Godelier (economics). Although these theorists disagree about the exact nature of structuralism there is, nevertheless, a broad consensus that a structuralist approach to the study of human society and culture involves the notion of wholes (a structure is not a simple aggregate of elements), but an organised system of relations, the idea of transformation (structures are dynamic, not static, governed by laws which determine the ways that new elements are introduced into the structure and changed); and the concept of self-regulation (the meaning of a structure is self-contained in relation to its internal laws and rules). In short, structuralism defines reality in terms of the relations between elements, not in terms of objectively existing things and social facts. Its basic principle is that the observable is meaningful only in so far as it can be related to an underlying structure or order.

The Development of Structuralism: Saussure

The founder of modern structuralism was Ferdinand de Saussure (1857–1913), a Swiss linguist who taught in Paris between 1881 and 1891 and whose most significant work, *Course in General Linguistics* (1974) (based on lectures given at the University of Geneva between 1906 and 1911), was published after his death. An expert in Indo-European languages, Saussure worked on a general theory of languages during the 1890s and he followed Durkheim in regarding language as an example of a social fact. Durkheim, of course, did not regard social facts as simple, naturalistic data but rather as elements related to morality and collective representations.

The contemporary French linguist, Antoine Meillet, who studied with Saussure and Durkheim, noted the significance of Durkheim's sociology for Saussure's theory of language. And Saussure himself followed the debate between Durkheim and Tarde (which was discussed in Chapter 4) on the nature of sociological method. Saussure accepted Durkheim's methodological collectivism not Tarde's methodological individualism: thus he distinguished between language (*langue*) and speech (*parole*) in terms of the collectivist character of *langue* and the individualistic nature of speech – the utterances of *parole*. For Saussure, language constituted a collective representation, an abstract system of linguistic rules which governed concrete language use, a formal and coherent structure, the product 'of the collective mind and linguistic groups' (Saussure, 1974, p. 5). Saussure rejected nineteenth-century reductionist accounts of language arguing against historical, psychological and causal explanations. Language was not reducible to the psychology of speakers or the historical evolution of society. As a social fact, exercising constraint on individuals, language constituted a definite system, or structure, which existed independently of individual speakers whose utterances were merely an imperfect reflection of the whole. No one could retain the whole of a language system just as no one could know the legal system as a whole: language, like law, exists in everyday life within the consciousness of individuals constraining their actions, its concrete forms meaningful only in relation to its structure as a whole, as a collective representation.

Saussure drew an important distinction between the study of language conceived synchronically (its existence at a specific moment in terms of its functioning as a system) and diachronically (its development through time, that is, historically). 'The opposition between the two viewpoints', he argued, 'is absolute and allows no compromise.' Synchronic linguistics 'will be concerned with the logical and psychological relations that bind together co-existing terms and form a system in the collective mind of speakers' while diachronic linguistics studies 'relations that bind together successive terms not perceived by the collective mind but substituted for each other without forming a system' (Saussure, 1974, pp. 99–100). By psychology Saussure meant collective, not individual psychology although he remained uncertain of the exact nature of a psychology of language. His main focus was on synchronic linguistics the study of which he frequently compared with the game of chess. Chess is meaningful only in terms of its internal rules, its grammar, its network of relationships in which the value of a single piece depends on its relation with the whole; and to move a single piece is to alter the relation of the other elements to the whole. To understand chess, in other words, it is necessary to account for it as a system: 'The respective value of the pieces depends on their position on the chessboard just as each linguistic term derives its value from its opposition to all the other terms.' The synchronic facts of a language, like the synchronic facts of chess, are characterised by their systemic nature. To adopt a diachronic perspective is not to observe language as a system but rather as 'a series of events that modify it' (Saussure, 1974, pp. 88–91). The facts of diachronic, historical linguistics lack a systematic character and are thus of secondary importance in the study of language. Language is a system where all parts can, and must, be considered in their synchronic solidity.

While language is made up of words, the linguistic system consists of 'signs' characterised by two elements, a signifier or *significant* (an acoustic image) and a signified or a *signifie* (a referent). Thus the sign 'cat' can be separated into the signifier (the sound image of the spoken word cat) and the signified (the animal itself). The structural relation between these two terms is arbitrary, that is, there is no necessary link between the sound image or signifier of cat and the signified of an actual cat. There is no essential catness which the word expresses and thus the relation is arbitrary. Any word would suffice. Language is thus a self-contained, relational system in which 'the value of each term results solely from the simultaneous presence of the others' (ibid., p. 114). The units that comprise a system of language acquire their meaning from their formal position, location and function within the whole. Saussure's central argument, therefore, was that language was produced socially as a collective phenomenon, independent of human will and intentions, a system irreducible to individual utterances. Speech and communication were thus made possible because of an underlying linguistic code, a system of collective norms which give meaning to specific verbal acts. Although Saussure did not employ the concept of structure, his theory of language is structural: to explain and understand an individual utterance it must be related to the 'hidden' system of functions, norms and categories. Thus Saussure abandoned causal explanation in favour of synchronic analysis of the position and function of elements within a system. The rules of language thus explain how language itself is simultaneously unknown and present, hidden from consciousness yet structuring human action.

The Concept of Structure

Saussure's *Course in General Linguistics* was not published until 1916. His concept of language as a self-contained system and advocacy of synchronic over diachronic analysis influenced the development of language studies, literary analysis and cultural theory.

In the development of structuralism two distinct trends are apparent. The first follows Saussure's separation of synchronic from diachronic analysis; while the other seeks a more historically grounded approach. An example of the former is Vladimir Propp's study of fairy tales (*Morphology of the Fairy Tale*, 1968 [1928]) which later influenced the structural anthropology of Claude Levi-Strauss. In his research, Propp advocated the primacy of the synchronic over the genetic arguing that in the analysis of fairy tales it was possible to identify a limited number of functions (thirty-one) which could then be organised into an underlying system or structure. In this way fairy stories, origi-nating in widely differing cultures, are classified for the variety of characters in direct contrast to the limited number of functions which the characters exer-cise in the course of the action.

In contrast to Propp's synchronic analysis, the Russian sociologist Mikhail Bakhtin (1895–1975) developed an historical structuralism which defined language as social communication. For Bakhtin, language was not an abstract linguistic system as Saussure had argued, but essentially historical, acquiring its living forms 'in concrete verbal communication'. Saussure's separation of utterance (*parole*) from language (*langue*) postulated the view of language as a product passively assimilated by individuals and not as 'a function of the speaker'. Saussure's dualism was rejected. Indeed, orthodox linguistics was criticised for a failure to examine dialogic relations, the linguistic interaction of different speakers. Bakhtin rejected Saussure's binary opposition of a 'pure' language and an 'impure', historically specific, utterance defining the word as dialogic. Bakhtin distinguished between the study of language through its grammatical and logical relations and language as the product of speaking subjects in which words acquire meaning through dialogue between the self and the other(s). This is one of Bakhtin's most significant contributions to structuralist thought. He wrote:

> Language is alive only in the dialogic intercourse of those who make use of it. Dialogic intercourse is the genuine sphere of the life of language [which] is permeated by dialogic relationships. (Bakhtin, 1973, pp. 102–3)

Language as discourse is active and productive, involving social evalua-tions of the present, the past and the possibilities inherent in the future. Semantic and logical relations of language lack the dialogic aspect until they become utterances and embody the positions of various speakers. Thus discourse links individuals in a chain of communication:

> Utterances are not indifferent to one another, and are not self-sufficient. They are aware of and mutually reflect one another. Each utterance is filled with echoes and reverberations of other utterances to which it is related by the communality of the sphere of speech communication... Each utterance refutes, affirms, supplements, and relies on the others... and somehow takes them into account. (Bakhtin, 1986, p. 91)

In Bakhtin's theory of language the dialogic character of the utterance involves an active, unfinalised relation of self to other in which the self, through its practical acquisition of the languages of speech genres (highly flexible, diverse everyday modes of social conversation, for example), becomes the sum of its discursive actions. All discourse implies simultaneous understanding between the speaker who listens and the listener who speaks:

Any true understanding is dialogic in nature.
Understanding is to utterance as one line of dialogue is to the next... meaning belongs to a word in its position between speakers... realised only in the process of active, responsive understanding... Meaning is the effect of interaction between speaker and listener produced via the material of a particular sound complex. (Bakhtin, 1973, pp. 102–3)

Bakhtin's theory of dialogism is built around the notion of alterity, that the autonomy and individuality of the social self springs out of its necessary relation with the 'other', seeking an identity through dialogue with others, but maintaining individual differences. The social production of self involves action and performance, individuality as the product of open-ended practices. In Bakhtin's word, the self is the 'gift' of the other constituted in and through discourse as socially productive practice.

Bakhtin's theory of dialogism represents one of the most important contributions to the development of a diachronically grounded structuralism. The genetic structuralism of Lucien Goldmann (1913–70) follows Bakhtin's broad, humanist perspective. Basic to Goldmann's sociology was a conception of 'mental structures' such as forms of thought and ideology created and transformed by human activity. Structures were *made* through the *praxis of the collective subject*, that is a definite social group which constitutes the 'true' source of cultural production. To understand a literary and cultural work it is necessary to explain its historical genesis in the social life of the group. The cultural objects are analysed both synchronically (the work as a whole) and diachronically (the products of human action). Structures are meaningful only in relation to human action and communication. Purely diachronic study, Goldmann (1980, p. 50) argues, 'which forgoes systems and structures, is scientifically important and inadequate', reality is constantly undergoing a process of structuration and destructuration: structures are always provisional for while they result from human action in specific social contexts it is individuals who transform them and thus create new structures.

Similarly to Bakhtin, Goldmann believed that the explanation and understanding of cultural forms must include an account of their origins and development raising the question of who produced them and in which specific socio-historical context as well as analysing their internal structure.

In contrast to Goldmann's genetic structuralism, the structural anthropology of Claude Levi-Strauss (1908–) advocated a methodology based not on history but the Sausserian linguistic model which stressed binary oppositions as the constituting element of a structure. It was not a question of the 'making' of structures but rather of discovering how specific cultural systems and symbolic forms such as kinship, totemism, mythologies, ceremonies and culinary practices were linked to an underlying structure hidden from the individual consciousness and only partially expressing the wider cultural system. Levi-Strauss argued that all cultures are characterised by systems of classification based on differences such as raw/cooked, high/low, hot/cold. Analysing these classification systems uncovers their basis in particular rules and relations. Levi-Strauss' structuralism goes beyond Saussure's emphasis on language as a system of relations between signs, to postulate the concept of structure as a system governed by rules which regulate its social function. Thus the ways in which food is prepared and cooked in different cultures and defined as edible or inedible depends on the codes which underlie the relations and rules structuring the culinary practices. The cuisine of any society can be analysed

> into constituent elements... and which may be organised according to certain structures of opposition and correlation. (Levi-Strauss, 1968, p. 86)

Structuralism, then, builds on the fundamental axiom that it is the relations between the elements, not the elements themselves, which determine cultural and symbolic forms. Discussing kinship systems, Levi-Strauss noted how like phonemes in a language system kinship function through the rules which govern broad familial relations such as the exchange of women and role of uncles (the avunculate) in primitive society. He shows that the avunculate constitutes one relation within a system, a structure which 'rests upon four terms (brother, sister, father, and son) which are linked by two pairs of correlative oppositions in such a way that in each of the two generations there is always a positive relationship and a negative one' in which the structure 'is the most elementary form of kinship that can exist... *the unit of kinship*'. The position of the avunculate as a 'characteristic trait of an elementary structure' is actually hidden from ordinary observation: thus empiricism, with its focus on the surface of social life as reality, is roundly rejected for failing to deal with the 'unconscious relations' of culture.

Thus the study of collective representations, symbolic forms such as totems and ceremonies, hinges on identifying a code in which the various elements provide the linguistic means for communication. Thus the value of naming and classifying the totemic system is that it brings to light the 'codes suitable for conveying messages which can be transposed into other codes, and for expressing messages received by means of different codes in terms of their own system' (ibid., p. 75). Totemism, culinary practices, myths, collective representations are communicative practices within cultures (discourses in effect). And as Saussure sought to unlock the key to language so Levi-Strauss examined the patterns of relations and rules internal to specific cultural systems uncovering the universal and invariant structures which suggests an homology with the human mind: the deep, hidden structures of cultures are ultimately imbricated with the structures of thought itself. The conclusion would seem to be that humanity is trapped within a world of signs, relations, rules, underlying codes that function at the everyday level to produce transformations (raw food transformed culturally into 'cooked') but which lie outside the actions of agents.

Marxism and Structuralism

During the course of the 1960s a distinctive form of Marxist structuralism, resolutely anti-humanist, developed in France. Its leading theoretician was the Communist Party philosopher, Louis Althusser (1918–1990). In a series of essays and analyses Althusser proposed a radically new scientific 'reading' of Marx. Influenced by structural linguistics and the scientific rationalism of Gaston Bachelard, Althusser criticised all forms of positivist/empiricist Marxism as well as the idealist, humanist-centred approach of Lukács, the Frankfurt School and those contemporary Marxists, such as Sartre, for whom Marxism was the philosophy of *praxis* built around conscious choice of human agents. Such voluntarism can never deal with the underlying structures and the relations between the various elements which influence the ways that action can occur.

For Althusser, Marxism was the science of social formations, the study of the inner logic, the relations between its various levels, or structures. Marxism was defined as a 'theoretical practice' consisting of conceptual tools (mode of production, class formation, contradiction) and substantive theory (laws of motion, the nature of capitalism and socialism) which Althusser employs to analyse the internal complexity of social formations. The specific nature of a social formation – capitalism, socialism, etc. – is analysed from the standpoint of a complex totality consisting of economic, political-legal and ideological 'practices', the 'labour of transformation' which sets 'to work... men, means and technical method'. Althusser rejected the base-superstructure model of orthodox Marxism because it suggested an essentialist notion of society, that the social totality expresses a single, dominant element, the labour-capital relation or the alienation of humanity. This 'expressive totality' is ultimately Hegelian since it conveys the notion of unity produced through a single essence. Althusser's concept of totality, in contrast, emphasises the multiplicity of economic, political and ideological structures, their relative autonomy and, employing a concept derived from Freud, *overdetermination*. Thus the most basic contradiction, the capital-labour contradiction, 'is never simple, but always specified by the historically concrete forms and circumstances in which it is exercised... specified by forms of the superstructure (the State, dominant ideology, religion...); specified by the internal and external historical situation'. Contradictions are not pure but are overdetermined, that is, determined and determining 'in one and the same movement'. There is no single contradiction which dominates, but many possible contradictions influencing each other. Hegelian philosophy and humanist Marxism tended to assimilate the complex diversity of 'a historically given society' to a single substance, or element, which functioned to determine all other elements of as well as the social whole itself (Althusser, 1969, pp. 106–13).

The concept of structure thus refers to the ways in which relatively autonomous levels combine into the 'structural complexity' of a social formation. Causality is structural not linear. Althusser illustrates this process by analysing the 1917 Russian Revolution. No single contradiction determined the development of the revolution but multiple contradictions such as those characterising 'a regime of feudal exploitation at the dawn of the twentieth century': contradictions between the advanced methods of capitalist production in the cities and the medieval condition of the countryside; contradictions between bourgeoisie and proletariat, the liberal bourgeoisie and the feudal landowners; contradictions between the Tsarist political system and nascent political democracy (Althusser, 1969, p. 96). There is thus uneven development between the various levels of a social formation; the structure and its effects determine each other with totality defined in terms of its effects. Social formations are asymmetrical in their structure. But what of the relation between the economy and the superstructure? Is the economic merely one structure among many or is it, as Marx, Engels and other Marxists have held, dominant? Althusser suggests that although the social formation comprises relatively autonomous levels, 'in the last instance' the economic determines which is dominant. This notion of a 'structure in dominance' allows Althusser to maintain the traditional Marxist emphasis on the primacy of the economic while at the same time advancing a pluralist conception of the social formation.

One result of Althusser's work has been an increasing emphasis in Marxist theory on the concept of mode of production and its relation with the superstructure, and the theory of ideology. For Althusser, the mode of production constitutes a number of different structures including the economic. It is the way in which these structures are combined which differentiates one mode of production from another. For example, the capitalist mode of production consists of a specific economic structure (the labourer, means of production, and so on) and a rational, legal system which forms part of the superstructure. The economic structure determines the specificity of the various laws which relate to property and contract. A different combination of economy and law subsists within a socialist mode of production, the socialised economic relations determining a different set of legal principles and rights. Nevertheless, the legal system, as a structure of ideology, is relatively autonomous constituting a distinct level of the social formation. But as the English Marxist historian E. P. Thompson, in his extended critique of Althusser, has pointed out, such a formal, synchronic approach fails to grasp that law, as an historical phenomenon, was not part of a separate level but always

> imbricated within the mode of production and productive relations themselves... [including]... with religion... an arm of politics... [and] it was an academic discipline, subjected to the rigour of its own autonomous logic. (Thompson, 1978, p. 288)

Because Althusser's structuralism has separated the human subject and human action from the structures themselves, one consequence is the reification of the social formation and its levels, the dominance of the system over the individual, and a tendency for the system itself to remain closed, emptied of all dialogic communicative relations. Structures, after all, do not make laws or change them.

The rigidity of Althusser's Marxism is particularly brought out in his analysis of ideology. The traditional Marxist definition of ideology as a 'false consciousness' (adumbrated in Marx's early work, especially *The German Ideology*), a distorted picture of the external world, illusory and unreal, is rejected by Althusser for its non-scientific humanism. Such a theory of ideology is centred on the notion of a 'constituting subject' and the assumption that knowledge, formed and reflected in human consciousness, develops only through the experiences of this subject. The true source of ideology is neither experience nor the subject, but objective, material reality; as an objective structure ideology cannot be reduced to the actions and consciousness of the subject. Ideology is thus defined as 'a system of representations', 'images and concepts' which 'impose' themselves as structures on social classes and individuals. Making a distinction between 'real objects' and 'objects of knowledge', Althusser located ideology as a real object forming an 'instance' of the social totality, a partly autonomous structure irreducible to the economic or political levels. Ideology is thus a system through which the individual exists as a social being, a 'lived' relation between the individual and the world, a relation which

> only appears as '*conscious*' on condition that it is *unconscious*... not a simple relation but a relation between relations, a second degree relation. In ideology men do indeed express, not the relation between them and their conditions of existence, but the *way* they live the relation between them and their conditions of existence: this presupposes both a real relation and 'an imaginary, lived' relation. (Althusser, 1969, p. 233)

Representing the 'imaginary' relations of individuals to the 'real' conditions of their existence, ideology forms an essential element of all social formations (including socialism and communism) since social cohesion is only possible through the 'practico-social' functions of ideology. Althusser here distinguishes science from ideology: science is 'theoretical knowledge', a system of concepts, a discourse which produces the objects of knowledge and which leads ultimately to the framing of scientific generalities. There is thus an important difference between theoretical knowledge and knowledge of the external world: the former does not depend on external proofs for its validity since it is purely theoretical; the latter is involved with ideology and thus the practico-social function dominates the theoretical function.

Ideology is produced, therefore, not by the intentions of subjects but by institutions, specific apparatuses which, in modern capitalism, are increasingly state organs. Ideology is anchored within institutions which themselves are the products of ideology. In his essay, 'Ideology and Ideological State Apparatuses' (1971), Althusser, responding to criticisms that his Marxist theory of ideology underemphasised the role of class struggle, argued that ideology constituted the 'site' of class conflict. Distinguishing between the ideological state apparatus (consisting of religious, educational, cultural institutions as well as political parties) and the repressive state apparatus (consisting of the institutions of coercion such as the army, police, judiciary), Althusser argued that the ideological state apparatuses 'largely secure the reproduction specifically of the relations of production, behind a "shield" provided by the repressive State apparatus'. In pre-capitalist societies the church functioned as the dominant ideological apparatus. In modern capitalism the educational institutions have become the dominant ideological apparatus:

> It takes children from every class at infant school age, and then for years, the years in which the child is most vulnerable; squeezed between the family State apparatus and the educational State apparatus, it drums into them, whether it uses new or old methods, a certain amount of 'know-how' wrapped in the ruling ideology (French, arithmetic, natural history, the sciences, literature) or simply the ruling ideology in its pure state (ethics, civic instruction, philosophy). (Althusser, 1971)

For Althusser, the ideological state apparatuses perpetuate submission to the established order reproducing the relations of production. But the model of society which Althusser proposes in this formulation comes close to a totalitarian system in which a process of complete ideological indoctrination into a dominant ideology is secured both by the passivity of an atomised population and the absence of alternative structures. Althusser's structuralist concept of ideology is historically and sociologically inadequate: the 'private' institutions which form part of the ideological state apparatus are centred in civil society and cannot be assimilated to state practices in the way that Althusser suggests. In capitalist society education is governed both by ideological assumptions and practices as well as by its own specific laws and values, that is, education is both dependent on the mode of production and class structure, and yet partly autonomous in terms of its immanent properties.

Althusser's emphasis on education as indispensable for the organisation and discipline of capitalist societies, together with his principle of structural causality, suggest a functionalist rather than a dialectical Marxist explanation. Although functionalist analysis has been defended as legitimate for Marxist theory (Cohen, 1978, pp. 283–5), it tends to assimilate the complex interaction between active, knowledgeable agents and the social structure to an underlying, ahistorical and deterministic process. Althusser describes this as a process of 'interpellation' as individuals are prepared for specific roles in a pre-existing social structure: as with Durkheim, Levi-Strauss and Parsons, Althusser portrays individuals as mere puppets of the system. His Marxist structuralism, like functionalism, eliminates the dialogic, humanist tradition of sociological thought: men and women become mere supports of structures. In his account of the Russian Revolution, for example, Althusser fails to include as a critical factor in its genesis the contradictions within the Russian socialist movement itself, contradictions within theory between those advocating an evolutionary road through a bourgeois republic (Plekhanov) and those who favoured a direct transformation to socialism skipping the bourgeois phase (Lenin, Trotsky). In the resolution of these theoretical differences both individual and collective agents played a crucial role to become a 'voluntarist' factor in the development of the revolution; similarly with the concept of workers' council or soviet, a decentralising, plebeian form of democracy which arose out of working-class activity and culture, intellectually independent of its theoretical formulation in Marxist discourse. Both the concept and the institution can be grasped sociologically only by positing a collective agent within an historical framework which includes choices and possibilities.

Although there are clear parallels with Parsonian functionalism, Althusserian structuralism departs radically from Parsons' general theory in the central role given to the apparatus (state or ideological) which rather like the Frankfurt School's concept of culture industry, dominates society from above: there is no sense here of civil society as an independent and mediating realm of potentially autonomous institutions or of the complex patterns of social interaction through which individuals come to define their identity and self, negotiate and transform situations and produce meaning and values. Althusser offers a thin description of modern society, one deficient in the concept of structure as a complex and dynamic process which works through, not behind, the backs of individuals.

Post-structuralism and the Problem of Sociological Thought: Foucault

The promise of structuralism lay in its proposals for a more rigorous method in the social sciences, one purged of humanism, essentialism, historicism. Its advocates made much of its anti-bourgeois, anti-individualistic stance. Meaning did not inhere in the actions of a creative subject but emerged out of a process which 'de-centred the subject'. To understand a text, for example, it was unnecessary to seek out the intentions behind it. Rather than raise the question of who produced the text, structuralist analysis focused on the ways in which the relations and differences between the various internal elements, such as language, produced meaning. But in focusing on structural transformations in discourse, language and history, structuralist analysis became increasingly de-contextualised, focusing on synchronic at the expense of diachronic processes. Society and history became elusive and shadowy concepts. With the exceptions of Bakhtin and Goldmann, structuralism failed to address the complex, historical nature of social structures, their contradictions, conflicts and transformation through the practices of collective agents. The de-centring of the subject tended to eliminate the problem of choice, the possibility of alternative modes of action and thus the voluntaristic dimension of social structures, culturally mediated interaction.

Michel Foucault (1926–1984) stands mid-way between structuralism and post-structuralism, although he always maintained that his work was resolutely anti-structuralist: 'I have never been a Freudian, I have never been a Marxist and I have never been a structuralist,' Foucault claimed. He has, nonetheless, exerted a profound influence within the social sciences, ranging from literary studies, history, philosophy and sociology. His first major work, *Madness and Civilisation* (1961), explored the methods of classifying and institutionalising the mentally ill, their incarceration and 'great confinement' during the age of Enlightenment. *The Birth of the Clinic* (1963) examined the social context of medical history, theory and practice based on the development of specific 'discursive formations'. This linguistic turn in social theory is further exemplified in *The Order of Things* (1968), an examination of 'fields of knowledge' within the social sciences and an analysis of the social and historical conditions necessary to sustain and develop them. One of Foucault's major themes was the way in which the social sciences as they developed during the nineteenth century were deeply imbricated in problems of social order and control. Foucault rejected the optimistic scientific rationalism of the Enlightenment arguing that the advent of modern industrial societies and nation states led to the development of specialised intellectual fields, notably demography and statistics, with the task of generating practical knowledge relevant for the organisation and administration of an advanced society. In *Discipline and Punish* (1977 [1975]), Foucault's critique of rationalism and Enlightenment science and philosophy was extended to the study of the 'moral techniques' which increasingly defined penal theory and practice during the course of the nineteenth century and the emergence of new forms of social control. Enlightenment philosophy, with its reforming, humanitarian zeal constituted a Utopian vision wholly at odds with its disciplinary practices:

> Historians of ideas usually attribute the dream of a perfect society to the philosophers and jurists of the eighteenth century; but there was also a military dream of society... to the meticulously subordinated cogs of a machine... to permanent coercions, not to fundamental rights, but indefinitely progressive forms of training... to automatic docility. (Foucault, 1979, p. 169)

The modernity project is thus emptied of utopian hopes and replaced by Jeremy Bentham's model prison, the panopticon, where every prisoner remained in the gaze of the warders: modernity produces societies based on discipline, surveillance, normalising practices through discourse. In *Discipline and Punishment* Foucault defined modern industrial society as a carceral system built on the training and disciplining of humanity, producing docile bodies, processes of surveillance carried out by trained specialists, teachers, judges, psychiatrists.

Foucault's studies, then, embrace such broad topics as madness, psychiatry, prisons, sexuality and the history of the social sciences all examined from a broad, wide-ranging historical perspective. Although his work was clearly indebted to structuralism (the focus on language and discourse) Foucault abandoned many of the fundamental structuralist positions notably the Levi-Strauss argument of the universality of discourse and language; and more pertinently he rejected Althusser's structural concept of totality together with all totalising theories and discourses. Discourse is analysed as historical and specific to particular social groups and practices. In particular, Foucault attacked linear and evolutionary theories of history as well as the related notion of totality for eliminating the irreducible pluralism and open-ended diverse nature of historical development. Foucault's whole project lay in opening up and demystifying social wholes, to allow different discourses and practices their rightful autonomy and capacity to produce truth. The problem of holistic thought lay in its assimilation of differences to a dominant centre.

Unlike Weber and Durkheim, Foucault abandons the idea that history discloses an underlying meaning, pattern or structure and that the task of the social sciences lay in developing concepts and theories which provided coherence to this process. Such 'global discourses' Foucault describes as 'tyrannical' because they assimilate a vast range of diverse and complex practices to a single dominant structure. Foucault believed that all totalising theories (such as Marxism) reduce the autonomy of the micrological elements, the 'local, discontinuous, disqualified, illegitimate knowledges against the claims of a unitary body of theory which would filter, hierarchise and order them in the name of some true knowledge and some arbitrary idea of what constitutes a science and its objects'. It becomes essential to 'reactivate' local, minor knowledges in opposition to 'the scientific hierarchisation of knowledges and the effects intrinsic to their power'. He suggests the term archeology to describe a method of analysing these micro elements; and the concept of 'genealogy' as the 'tactics' of describing and thus bringing to light 'these local discursivities, the subjected knowledges which were thus released would be brought into play'. Genealogy constitutes the meticulous re-discovery of all micrological forces, their struggles and memories, a standpoint which 'wages war' on all forms of centralisation, on discourses claiming neutral scientific status for all discourses are imbricated with centralised, social, cultural and economic power. The task of genealogy is not to show how specific groups dominate others, but how discourses work to subjugate individuals and how individuals are constituted through 'the multiplicity of organisms, forces, energies, materials, desires, thoughts etc.' (Foucault, 1980, pp. 83–97).

These, then, are Foucault's broad themes and method. Genealogy as 'a form of history' accounts for knowledge and discourses without making any reference to a 'subject', its focus on the plurality and discontinuity of history and the role played by rationalised discourses in the maintenance of social control. Foucault's work raises the sociological problem of how social order is possible within complex industrial societies. Durkheim's master concept for examining this problem was the internalisation of norms which Foucault rejects because it assumes the existence of a subject. Social control is, rather, the result of a whole range of discourses developing during the nineteenth century which functioned autonomously within a plurality of social contexts producing decisive effects on the workings of modern society. While pre-modern societies functioned through externally imposed forms of coercive power (wielded by monarchs, for example) during the course of the nineteenth century society became increasingly reliant on forms of specialised knowledge and a burgeoning culture of experts. One of Foucault's main points is, that as there are many discourses, so there are many rationalities. Unlike Weber and the Frankfurt School, he rejects rationality as a total, global process; rationality is intrinsic to certain fields or discourses:

> I think that the word rationalisation is dangerous. What we have to do is to analyse specific rationalities rather than always invoking the progress of rationalisation in general... I think we have to refer to much more remote processes if we want to understand how we have been trapped in our own history. (Foucault, 1982, p. 210)

What is striking in Foucault's formulation is its superficial similarity with Weber's thesis on the autonomisation of 'spheres', internally structured through their own specific logic; and Foucault also shares Weber's hostility to totalising concepts arguing that society is constituted as a network of molecular processes of social action. As we have seen, in Weber's sociology there is both a global and pluralist sense of rationality. But in Foucault's work there are only rationalities which function within specific fields. Thus history (and society) works through molecular networks of rationality; society has no 'centre' only multiple microcosms. Analysis must ascend from these web-like processes.

Foucault's defines society in terms of a multiplicity of fields of knowledge, 'discursive formations,' characterised by specific rules which enable specialists and experts (doctors, teachers, scientists) to produce statements about a specific practice (such as mental illness) which are true or false only in terms of the 'discursive rules' intrinsic to and functioning within a specific field. There are no absolute, universal criteria for passing judgements on what is 'truth'. Everything is relative. To this extent Foucault advocates a structuralist standpoint seeking to reconstitute the object and explicate its rules and functions. A discourse is everything written or spoken about a specific practice based on specialist knowledge and bodies of experts which has the effect of controlling those who lack knowledge (such as the patient). In this way normalising judgements are made and experts make decisions on who is to be defined as mentally ill, criminal or sexually deviant.

Discourse is thus effectively a form of power exercised by particular social groups; discourse decides 'who' speaks and what they say, for no one has the right to say anything. Foucault cites psychiatry as 'a dubious science' which produced little objective knowledge while generating 'wise men' and moral guides who decide who is normal and who is to be committed to the asylum. Hence power and knowledge are joined. As social practices put knowledge to work it is the discourses which produce truth. Power does not inhere in a dominant ideology or property-owning class but within everyday life, below and alongside the state apparatus. In hospitals, armies and schools, discipline functions through specific social practices, the rational keeping of records, training which provides the basis for normalising judgements. In the course of the eighteenth and nineteenth centuries the keeping of records, dossiers and recording information generated a vast expansion of the methods of classifying individuals which Foucault notes was already well developed in the economic field (especially taxation) but extended increasingly as a mode of permanent surveillance on whole populations and social groups. While the state apparatus organised this process centrally it was also dispersed regionally, locally, extending to many groups. This is Foucault's point, that power does not inhere in the state but rather constitutes a process which 'passes through much finer channels'. Power is not part of an integrated social system but develops unevenly at many different levels.

Society is thus analysed as a vast, impersonal system of surveillance, mobile and diffuse, working through 'networks', 'circulating' in 'the form of a chain': 'It is never localised here or there, never in anybodys hands, never appropriated as a commodity or piece of wealth'. Foucault stresses the de-centred nature of power arguing against substantialist concepts which locate power as the possession of a social group or class. The analysis of power must begin from 'its infinitesimal mechanisms, which each have their own history, their own trajectory, their own techniques and tactics' and to trace how these become transformed displaced, colonised by forms of global domination (Foucault, 1980, pp. 98–9). In pre-modern society, for example feudal society, power functioned through signs of loyalty to the monarch, through rituals, ceremonies and levies. In contrast, modern society is characterised by 'disciplinary power', incarceration with administrative apparatuses continuously exercising surveillance. Disciplinary power is always 'the bearers of a discourse' which aims to produce 'a society of normalisation' (ibid., pp. 105–7, 125). Power is never reducible to violence or force, but is a relational process which circulates through the social body with individual actions affecting others:

> We should admit rather that power produces knowledge (and not simply by encouraging it because it serves power or by applying it because it is useful); that power and knowledge directly imply one another; that there is no power relation without the correlative constitution of a field of knowledge, nor any knowledge that dies not presuppose and constitute at the same time power relations. (ibid., p. 27)

Power is neither repressive nor global: it is micro power, mobile and decentered working through a 'force field'.

By employing these specific concepts and method Foucault clearly abandons basic structuralist methodology. The concept of force field further enhances his post-structuralist position. Discourse functions at many levels within a field of forces which Foucault defines as a multiple, open and fluid structure. By definition a force field does not constitute a totality since it lacks a unifying centre but consists of fragments, perspectives, discontinuity. In the study of history and society there is neither depth nor finality only the arbitrary, no universal but only partial truths. There exists no goal to history, for within the force field there are strategies and tactics, struggle and conflict which work to promote many possible outcomes. In his study of sexuality, *The History of Sexuality* (1984) for example, he argues that the world of discourse is never neatly divided between dominant and dominated/ accepted and excluded discourses but 'must make allowance for the complex and unstable process whereby discourse can be both an instrument and an effect of power, but also hindrance, a stumbling block, a point of resistance and a starting point for an opposing strategy'. Challenging the traditional notion that the nineteenth century repressed knowledge of sexuality, Foucault suggests that its culture generated a diverse range of discourses on sexuality, a rich variety which made possible the development of a 'reverse discourse' on homosexuality.

> Discourses are tactical elements or blocks operating in the field of force relations; there can exist different and even contradictory discourses within the same strategy. (Foucault, 1984, pp. 100–2)

Foucault's work, while richly suggestive, throws up many problems. His relational concept of power, for example, is not grounded contextually since it fails to identify the different forms of power which function at both the micro and macro levels. It is not a question of dissipated and localised forms of power which many sociologists had recognised before and after Foucault, but the problem that power is unequally distributed throughout society at both the micro and macro levels. Specific institutions, such as multinational corporations and transnational media through their control of resources and the social effects they produce have enormous concentrated power. But the existence of institutionalised forms of power does not presuppose that power is always economically and politically centralised. Macro power can and does co-exist with micro forms of power. Foucault's concept of force field admits a de-totalising approach which rejects the sociological fact that society consists of a hierarchical structure of institutions and practices and that within institutions there exist also hierarchical relations in which power is highly concentrated. Foucault's emphasis on the ubiquity of power eliminates fundamental structural relations, the ways in which different social groups seek to impose their ideas and values on others. Power is not simply a web, or a 'chain', of unequal relations but consists of institutions which effectively control the resources and technology of modern society.

A second problem concerns the making of discourses. To argue that a discourse defines the subject is to cut out ordinary routines of social life, the patterns of face-to-face interactions and the inter-subjective dimension of social action, Weber's 'subjective understanding' of others. For how are the discourses internalised? And how are they produced? To take Foucault's own examples: all modern societies discipline their members through discourses which would include the political discourse of nationalism. But in Foucault's terms how are the beliefs and values associated with nationalist identity and culture, which underpin and sustain the military power of the nation state, internalised and accepted as legitimate by subjects constituted through discourses? How do the specialists, the teachers, social workers and doctors 'persuade' the 'subjects' of the necessity for military power? To answer this question Gramsci's concept of hegemony is valuable for linking the macro and micro levels and, as was argued in Chapter 5, this approach offers a more nuanced sociological analysis of a field of forces by focusing on the making of beliefs and practices and the ways they become an integral part of everyday reality. While Foucault's stress on the micrological aspects of power represents an advance on the approach of ethnomethodologists and symbolic interactionists, it fails because it has not worked out a concept of collective action that enables individuals to produce and interpret the meanings attached to the collective symbols. Foucault notes that the technology of power in the nineteenth century 'fabricated sexuality' and represented madness. The assumption seems to be that the individual is passive, controlled and indoctrinated. Foucault's model is close to that of the Frankfurt School. How can opposition develop? In his study of sexuality Foucault (1984, pp. 100–2) argues that discourses exist both as an instrument and effect of power but they nonetheless generate opposition. The discourse on homosexuality developed specialist controls and classifications on what is perverse but it then produced a reverse discourse speaking on behalf of homosexuals and demanding new classifications. This 'reverse discourse', however, did not suddenly materialise out of a force field but was the product of collective action by groups who felt victimised and sought to establish their identity and place in society as well as those specialists in sexual matters. The reverse discourse is made through struggles over values and identity within legal, cultural and political institutions and between macro forces of government and the micro elements within small communities. If a reverse discourse on homosexuality was possible why were there no reverse discourses on the social and political use of the social sciences during the period Foucault investigates, advocating the emancipatory and humane role of scientific discourses?

Similarly with the question of bio-power: as the discourses control the body other discourses, such as feminism, emerge to challenge them. But how? It seems that there is always an ongoing struggle around prisons, sexuality and so on (Foucault, 1980, pp. 129–31) and that there are no relations of power without resistances, for like power resistance is multiple. But this raises the major problem: Foucault's work lacks an adequate mode of sociological contextualism which would tease out the links between different discourses, social groups, institutions. Although Foucault argues that his work deals with the local and micrological and not totality, he engages in broad, sweeping generalisations concerning the nature of discourses and power, the controls exerted on society. There is a lack of historical specificity, a shadowy notion of the social context in which many different discourses and practices proliferate exerting their effects on individuals. While he notes the co-existence of different fields of knowledge ranging from the economic to the political and cultural they are never grounded sociologically. There is no sense of the complexity of plural discourses and power relations within modern society: the force field becomes an empty sociological category. With discourse disengaged from the making process, a functional and teleological explanation is implied, that discursive formations constitute the needs and the purposes of modern disciplinary society.

Foucault's contribution to sociological knowledge is thus deeply ambiguous. The emphasis on language and discourse has weakened the concept of society, reducing it to discourse and discursive formations. But where do these begin and end? Is society discourse?

Sociology and the De-centring of the Subject

One of the basic tenets of structuralism, from Saussure to Levi-Strauss, was the notion that any structure must have a fixed element, a hierarchy of meanings cohering round a centre. Thus structuralist theorists such as Roland Barthes analysed striptease and fashion as signifying systems relating to specific cultural contexts and meaning (*System de la mode*, 1971). But in his later work, especially *S/Z* (1970), his famous deconstruction of a Balzac short story, Barthes argued that texts are not centred in a definite structure given to them by their use of language: rather, because a text can be read in many different ways it is structured in a multiplicity of meanings. It was Jacques Derrida who proposed that as the meaning of signs is arbitrary they neither represent nor are based on a sense of objective reality. Derrida's work has played a key role in the development of post-structuralism and in his studies of language and literature proposed the radical view that writing does not reproduce a reality but produces and reproduces multiple realities. Whereas in structuralism the centre organised the various elements into a whole, post-structuralism abandons this closed notion, what Derrida called 'the structured nature of structures' fully to embrace the implications of Saussure's contention that the linguistic system consists only of 'differences'. Meaning thus becomes a function of the differences between terms which then refer to its differences with other elements and terms: the play of infinite differences within texts produces the possibility of multiple meanings (Derrida, 1972).

Foucault's critique of totalising concepts and theories, and his notion of a 'subject' produced through discourse and discursive practices, is clearly part of the post-structuralist attack on the subject as the creator or source of meaning. Everything consists of differences with no unifying culture and a plenitude of meanings all equally valid. Sociologically, the concept of decentring can be wilfully obscure although as a distinctive sociological concept it had first been articulated in Weber's thesis on rationality. As was argued in Chapter 4, Weber proposed that modernity consisted of partly autonomous spheres regulated by specific internal values which were organised through specialists. This structured pluralism represents one of the most enduring contributions to sociological thought: a decentred social world is one shaped by cultural institutions outside the control of the state and the coexistence of many competing ideologies or world views and values. The decentring process suggests a culture of ambiguity, tolerance, pluralism and *difference*. Moreover, Weber makes it clear that in the construction of new ideologies and values agents play a part: the study of the Protestant ethic had demonstrated the links between actors, values and motivation and the social consequences of their actions. Moreover, by arguing that the rationality which leads ultimately to the modern decentred world was not the result of conscious intentions but the unintended consequences of actors pursuing the goal of religious salvation, Weber introduces the de-centring of the subject into his sociological analysis while retaining the link between action and structure.

All these elements are missing from the post-structuralist theory of de-centring of the subject. Foucault's discourses and discursive practices are disengaged from actors and complex patterns of social interaction becoming subjectless practices which function as part of the 'needs' of a modern industrial society.

Foucault's work is flawed in two ways: first his concept of de-centring fails to deal with the de-centring of structure and institutions so the development of partly autonomous spheres means that some practices and discourses are not functionally linked with the system; and second that the post-structuralist de-centring of the subject, because it disengages the agent from the practices, leads to teleological explanations of social and historical change.

9

Sociological Thought and the Problems of Agency and Structure

As I have argued in earlier chapters, classical sociology brought together a concern with developing both concepts and a substantive theory within the framework of history and empirical research combining a union of theory and research. There was, too, a focus on the structure of society as a whole and the ways individuals collectively organise their actions and their relations with institutions. One of main problems of classical sociology lay in defining the exact mechanism of action and its links with social structure and the autonomy of action and the influence of the system as a whole.

Twentieth-century sociology has been described as dominated by this issue between sociology which stressed the action/actor/cultural values pole (Weber, Simmel) which leads to micro sociology; and sociology which emphasised the macro forces, institutions and structures from Marx to Durkheim and Parsons. In his attempt to bring these strands together in a unified theory, Parsons, in *The Structure of Social Action,* argued that it was not a question of differing and opposed theories within the discipline but of a systematic convergence which excluded Marx and Marxism. In the post-war years dominated by Cold War rhetoric Parsons's view prevailed. But beginning in the 1960s, partly as a result of growing disillusionment with the dominant paradigms of Soviet Marxism and American Functionalism, sociological thought became increasingly pluralistic. The rediscovery and publication of Marx's early manuscripts provoked a humanist Marxism which rediscovered older and forgotten humanist Marxists (Lukács, The Frankfurt School); and this in turn generated a structuralist critique of humanism within the social sciences. The humanist tradition within sociology of Alfred Schutz and sociological phenomenology emerged; there was a new emphasis on micro sociologies and a concern with the everyday social world. Increasingly, the Parsonian project was marginalised; there was no convergence and unity, only many different sociologies.

202

One result was proliferation of new concepts and theory within sociology. Durkheim's classic definition of sociology as a distinct field of study was abandoned in favour of an eclectic, uncritical assimilation of concepts and theory from intellectual fields only loosely connected with sociological knowledge: post structuralism, discourse theory, postmodernism. The result was both a lack of rigour and clarity and a failure to adequately 'sociologise' these new concepts and engage in a fruitful dialogue. In the course of the 1980s and 90s new attempts to resolve these dualisms in sociology emerged: this chapter examines three important attempted syntheses which attempt to bridge the micro and macro gap, the agency and structure problem.

Habermas, Communicative Action and the Public Sphere

During the 1960s the work of the Frankfurt School became widely known and influential in the social sciences. The concepts of culture industry and one-dimensional man, the theory of modern capitalism dominated by a dehumanised rationality, seemed to offer a more salient analysis of modern society than the dogmatic prescriptions of Leninist Marxism and the rigid formulations of structural functionalism. But as Jurgen Habermas (1929–), one of a new generation of critical theorists observed, the Frankfurt School programme established by Horkheimer and Adorno assumed an objective teleology in history, the progressive unfolding of human emancipation, a standpoint which provided the normative foundation of its critique of capitalist formal rationality. Culture industry as the embodiment of formal rationality functioned to integrate an atomistic society *from above* and therefore eliminating the constituting role of social struggles in the production and reproduction of society. The historically complex, variable practices of the everyday world were thus ignored, reduced to ideological reflexes of the centralised culture industry. As Habermas argued, the Frankfurt School's highly speculative philosophy of history marginalised specific empirical analysis between the forces and relations of production in favour of teleological institutionalised rationality.

Thus their conclusions were bleakly pessimistic: culture industry worked like an 'apparatus' socialising individuals into mass conformity. Unlike Gramsci, the Frankfurt School theorised social integration as indoctrination; there was neither a concept of civil society (only an atomised mass society) and hence of social struggles and opposition, nor an adequate sociological concept of the internalisation of values. Moreover, their substantive theory postulated the untenable proposition that all forms of industrial society (capitalist, communist, fascist) were broadly similar in structure integrated around a centralised cultural apparatus.

In Habermas' view the Frankfurt School's concepts were too narrowly defined for dealing with the development of modern complex societies although their emphasis on the centrality of culture remained an important insight. The theory of culture industry, however, failed to deal with the everyday world of social interaction other than as reducing it to ideology. As noted in Chapter 8 the work of the micro sociologists has shown how complex and variable this world can be, one involving both normative and cognitive elements in social action. Rejecting the concept of an inert, alienated mass, Habermas has attempted to develop a more rounded, comprehensive sociology of modern society synthesising Marx's materialism with classical sociology and contemporary systems and interactionist perspectives. While adhering to Adorno's and Horkheimer's critique of positivism, Habermas has argued that Marxism must be reformulated by integrating systems theory (especially Parsons) with action theory (especially Weber, Mead, Schutz).

Sociological theory, he argues, must combine an emphasis on both action and structure as well as motivation and patterns of communication. 'From Hegel through Freud to Piaget the idea has developed that subject and object are reciprocally constituted, that the subject can grasp hold of itself only in relation to and by way of the construction of an objective world.' Thus social systems are 'networks of communicative actions' involving socialised personalities and speaking subjects (Habermas, 1979, pp. 98–100):

> A social-scientifically appropriate crisis concept must grasp the connection between system integration and social integration. The two expressions 'social integration' and 'system integration' derive from different theoretical traditions. We speak of social integration in relation to the systems of institutions in which speaking and acting subjects are socially related. Social systems are seen here as *life-worlds* that are symbolically structured. We speak of system integration with a view to the specific steering performances of a self-regulated system... Both paradigms, life-world and system, are important. The problem is to demonstrate their interconnection. (Habermas, 1976, p. 4)

System integration refers to the structural properties of social systems which work together producing an integrated whole; while social integration focuses on society from the perspective of the actors, the participants and therefore deals with norms, culture, action. Arguing that society must be conceived simultaneously as system and life-world, Habermas defines the life-world as the realm of culture, personality, meaning and symbols, all of which form the basis of communication: agents seek mutual understanding through the substantive reason embodied in speech and action. In contrast, action linked with instrumental reason works through the social system and its subsystems. For Habermas, modern society is characterised by, the 'uncoupling' of life-world from system (in primitive society kinship structures were largely inseparable from the economic forces; in modern society the economic institutions are differentiated from those of kinship) and with it the 'uncoupling' of social from system integration. Working through market elements, integration becomes largely automatic. But as modern society evolves, the possibility of social integration through the life-world grows, on the basis of subjectively mediated communication, not system imperatives. Nevertheless, system imperatives based on bureaucratisation and monetarisation constantly threaten to 'colonise' the life-world. The result is a permanent tension between life-world and system (Habermas, 1989, pp. 116–19).

For Habermas, the Marxist base and superstructure model lacked an adequate concept of communicative interaction, that is, action-oriented towards establishing forms of mutual agreement and understanding, a negotiated consensus governed by shared norms. Habermas's concept of communicative action emphasises both cognitive and normative elements in this process (in contrast to Parsons's overstatement of the role of the normative) arguing that it is through 'linguistically mediated interaction' that individuals reach understanding and achieve co-operation with others. Marxism had ignored the role of language in social evolution defining society in terms of a 'productivist model' based in collective social labour but society equally consists of 'networks of communicative actions' involving speaking as well as tool-making agents (Habermas 1979).

While Habermas's concept of language is based on the ideal of free and open discourse involving active agents it also assumes that language constitutes the medium of political emancipation in that it embodies universal elements – autonomy, responsibility and a tendency towards a consensus. All linguistically mediated action raises questions about the validity claims, beliefs, values, truth. Habermas posits four validity claims: that what individuals say is comprehensible, that it is true, that it is right (that is, governed by normative elements) and a sincere expression of the individuals' beliefs. These claims provide the background for a consensus between speaker and listener enabling individuals to ask such questions as Do you mean that? Is that true? Habermas employs Schutz's notion of the life-world as the realm of communicative action, the everyday world of culture, which includes shared meanings, tradition and forms of social interaction. It is through the life-world that communicatively agreed consensus is reached. Habermas introduces the concept of 'ideal speech situation' as one in which 'speech acts' lead to emancipation because it is assumed that all participants have equal and free access to knowledge; communicative action thus occurs only when one or more individuals, on the basis of shared understanding employ reason to convince others of the rightness of their arguments.

Society consists of both a life-world functioning through communicative action and a system functioning through purposive, instrumental or strategic action in which persuasion takes place through sanctions, power and money. Strategic action is oriented towards specific goals of the system and the most efficient means of realising them, system imperatives such as the maximisation of profit irrespective of consequences for the quality of life within the life-world. In contrast communicative action is oriented to raising issues over the quality of life and engaging in open dialogue with others.

Thus, although working within the field of critical theory, Habermas rejects the Adorno–Horkheimer–Marcuse theorisation of a social system free of all significant structural contradictions and opposition. The life-world generates potential sources of conflict with system imperatives in the form of new social movements (notably the ecological and peace movements) bound to a free, open discourse, to substantive values associated with the quality of life, emancipation and communicative action. Habermas's model employs the concept of 'public sphere', elaborated in the early writings of Horkheimer, to explore the ways in which cultural institutions mediate between the individual and the state, between private interests and collective power. In his book *The Structural Transformation of the Public Sphere* (1992 [1962]) Habermas traced the genesis of the public sphere to eighteenth- and nineteenth-century bourgeois culture embracing cultural institutions such as coffee houses and salons which enabled the middle class to gather publicly and claim the right openly to discuss public issues: the public sphere is defined as 'the realm of social life in which public opinion is formed', in which 'access is guaranteed to all citizens'. The public sphere embodies rational communication among free citizens: 'In the *salons* the mind was no longer in the service of a patron; "opinion" became emancipated from the bond of economic dependence' (Habermas, 1992, p. 33). In the course of the nineteenth century the public sphere expanded, a process corresponding to the growth of markets and new forms of cultural communication (newspapers and magazines) outside the state's control. Habermas' concept gives priority to political news and culture; the emphasis is on individuals reading newspapers in order to discuss contemporary issues in face-to-face conversation. But the development of capitalism threatens the integrity of the public sphere: the very forces which have brought it into being weaken its autonomy: the public sphere 'takes on feudal features' as rational criteria for achieving agreement are replaced by a consensus 'created by sophisticated opinion-moulding services' of the modern mass media. This 're-feudalisation' transforms the culture of communication into mass entertainment in which representations and appearance, the 'aura' of personal prestige, outweigh rational debate. The culture-debating public of the bourgeois public sphere committed to open dialogue over broad social issues is replaced by a culturally conservative public of passive consumers. A pseudo-public sphere emerges characterised by bureaucratically closed modes of communication (ibid., p. 195).

It is within the life-world that the public sphere exercises its critical function. As there exists conflict between the public sphere and capitalism, so this relationship is later theorised in terms of a permanent tension between life-world and system, one which becomes especially acute in modern society. System imperatives governing economic production and profitability, the steering media of money combined with an increasingly centralised state, seek to penetrate the structures of the life-world effectively distorting linguistically mediated interaction and undermining the rational and universal elements of truth embodied in language. Language becomes increasingly dominated by the functional imperatives of instrumental rationality with distorted communication, built on force and coercion, eroding the potential for rational communicative action. As the public sphere embodied the free conversation of citizens so undistorted communication is structured in the principles of co-operation, understanding and open dialogue, but system imperatives constantly seek to 'colonise' the life-world producing a centralisation of culture, growing bureaucratisation, instrumental rationality, widespread passivity and the decline of autonomy.

Habermas' model is strikingly similar to that of Parsonian functionalism: the system functions externally to agents and crises develop, not through the collective actions of social classes and groups over the allocation of scarce resources, but through the impersonal logic of system imperatives. But the life-world is actually the site of social struggles and conflict over economic the imperatives that Habermas associates with system integration. For example, at the system level collective actors within an industrial firm will frequently negotiate over economic issues: the economic organisation of work and wage bargaining between trade unionists and employers function at the system level involving different groups of actors in conflict over the allocation of resources, each committed to specific goals and forms of action. The system, in short, works through institutions and collective actors, through structure and action. But rather than clarifying the relation of action theory to systems theory, 'the question of how these two conceptual strategies... can be related to and integrated with one another', Habermas has reinforced the division between them (Mouzelis, 1991).

At the heart of Habermas' critical theory is a contradiction between a deterministic systems theory and a voluntaristic action theory. The life-world constitutes the sphere of human action and autonomy through language and communication with the 'project of Enlightenment', dismissed by Adorno and Horkheimer, remaining a genuine possibility. Individuals possess the capacity for self-reflection, understanding and knowledge. A theory of emancipation is built on a model of communication not production, with Habermas positing as an ideal state of undistorted communication the 'conversation of free citizens', action oriented towards 'truth'. The life-world as the public sphere is the sphere of free and equal discourse, of rational understanding and a 'normative consensus' that flows 'from the co-operative interpretation processes of participants themselves'. The rationalisation of the life-world signals 'a release of the rationality potential inherent in communicative action' and opens the way for genuine emancipation (Habermas, 1989, p. 146).

Habermas' avowed 'reconstruction' of historical materialism with its emphasis on 'ideal speech communities', a communicative rationality which offers the possibility of 'negotiated' consensus has the effect of separating the collective agent from social and cultural production, transforming social action into disembodied ahistorical categories: the concept of the modern life-world as a forum for undistorted communication is sociologically naive and historically untenable. It is doubtful if the modern public sphere has become refeudalised, rather it combines both formal and substantive rationality providing the basis for dialogue and criticism as well as passivity and political quiesence. Habermas's life-world/system constitutes an inadequate model of modern society providing little if any space for the constituting role of social struggles organised and carried out by collective actors whose actions occur at both micro and macro levels. The separation of system integration from collective agents reinforces the dualisms which Habermas' synthesis of Marxism, systems theory and sociological phenomenology had sought to surmount.

Giddens: Structuration Theory

Habermas' attempt to resolve the fundamental dualisms of sociological theory – action/structure, macro/micro – succeeded only in re-introducing functionalist, deterministic and speculative philosophical issues into his model of communicative action. His analysis of system and social integration is weakened by a failure to provide a sociological analysis of the role of collective actors in the processes of system integration. The problem lies with Habermas' deterministic theory of the colonisation of the life-world, for if the system imperatives of money and power – formal rationality – wholly penetrate the realm of culture and personality, then the concept of society approximates to the closed model of culture industry which Habermas had rejected. Habermas has failed to show the patterns of interactions which result in the emergence of the social self, or agent, to analyse the ways such interactions lead to distinctive modes of communication. By suggesting the substantive thesis of the colonisation of the life-world, he closes off the possibility that the dialogic relationships characteristic of the everyday world can exercise a key role in the constitution of society as a whole.

   These issues are addressd in two further attempts to theorise the agency/structure problem, Giddens' theory of structuration and Bourdieu's theory of habitus and fields. While both Giddens and Bourdieu follow Habermas in seeking to synthesise classical sociology, Marxism and aspects of modern sociological theory, they differ sharply over the nature of theory itself. Giddens adheres closely to the model of theorising established by Parsons and followed by Habermas in which theory develops autonomously, analytic concepts derived from theoretical and not empirical and historical analysis. This autonomy of theory standpoint is rejected by Bourdieu who argues that sociology is simultaneously theoretical and empirical; by refusing to separate theoretical from the empirical and historical, Bourdieu reaffirms the unity of theory and social/historical analysis which had been central both to classical sociology and to the work of Marx and Gramsci.

Giddens first announced his theory of structuration in *New Rules of Sociological Method* (1976), developing it further in a series of books and articles culminating in the definitive statement of *The Constitution of Society* (1984). Unlike Habermas' attempted synthesis, Giddens is sceptical both of Parsons's systems theory and the early Frankfurt School for providing useful analytical tools. But, as with Habermas, Giddens is seeking to find links and build bridges between the different, often conflicting schools of social theory which fragmented the field of sociology during the 1960s and 70s – humanist Marxism, structuralist Marxism, critical theory, phenomenology, symbolic interactionism, ethnomethodology. One result of this differentiation of socio-logical theory into distinct specialist areas has been to reinforce the traditional dualisms within theory itself, the macro holistic analysis of functionalism conflicting with micro interactionist sociology with its emphasis on the face-to-face nature of relationships. To unify these disparate sociologies, Giddens advanced the concept of the duality, not dualism of structure, his master concept through which it becomes possible to grasp human practices as both action and as structure, that is, while agents produce meaning through action they do so within definite social contexts: hence Giddens' argument, reminis-cent of Weber, that social institutions and structure have no meaning apart from the actions they embody.

It is important to note that structuration theory differs sharply from struc-turalism which has consistently underemphasised the making of structures, failing to grasp the constitution of social life as 'the production of active subjects' (Giddens, 1976, pp. 120–1). This concept of an active agent combined with the process of 'making', opposes structuration theory to functionalism, Parsonian system theory and all objectivist theories which constitute the social world as an independent pre-given realm of external, constraining social facts, society conceived as a system with its own specific properties. Giddens, however, does define society as a social system characterised by 'definite struc-tural principles' which produce multiple institutions stretched across space and time. Unlike functionalism, structuration theory stresses the concept of social systems as open-ended while noting, for example, that claims to legiti-macy and a sense of common identity and culture, while present, may differ quite sharply for different social groups within the system itself. One of 'the main features of structuration theory (is) that the extension and "closure" of societies across space and time is regarded as problematic' (Giddens, 1984, p. 165). Rather, structuration theory defines society as the product of skilled, knowledgeable and reflexive agents although Giddens rejects the idealist notion of agents as the source of society and the centre of meaning. Agents can act only within specific contexts which nevertheless exist apart from the actions they embody as the conditions of action. As Giddens notes: 'Human society... would plainly not exist without human agency. But it is not the case that actors create social systems: they reproduce or transform them, remaking what is already made in the continuity of *praxis*.' Hence structure is a property of social systems not as something fixed and inert but '"carried" in reproduced practices embedded in time and space' (ibid., pp. 170–1). All so-called objective structures are effectively instantiated in practices as agents produce and reproduce the structures which underpin and enable action to occur. Structures are like Saussure's concept of *langue,* existing outside time and instantiated practically only as individuals draw on the rules of speech within everyday social contexts. Giddens calls this a 'virtual order' in that individuals recall such rules through memory and 'memory traces'. Football players may know the rules of the game and which exist apart from them, but they become reality only when the game, and its rules, are put into practice. Structure is thus both medium and outcome, the duality of structure referring to social structures as structures constituted through human agency and which exist simultaneously as the medium of this constitution.

But what are the specific properties of structure? For Giddens structure carries a distinctive meaning as the 'rules' and 'resources' which agents draw upon in the production and reproduction of social systems. Rules are utilised by agents in everyday social interaction, in conversation, providing the basis of an ordered and stable social life. Rules are both formal and public – rules governing elections and teaching practices, for example – and informal rules governing relations between individuals and structuring the varied encounters that make up everyday interaction. Garfinkel's experiments with trust are cited as evidence that social life necessarily rests on 'ontological security rules provide'. Awareness of rules, however, operates on two levels of consciousness: first a tacit, or theoretical grasp of the rules involved in the reproduction of social practices (discursive level of consciousness enabling agents to understand provide reasons for their action); and second, an awareness of the skills and knowledge involved in action (practical level of consciousness enabling agents to carry out action). By resources is meant 'the modes whereby transformative relations are actually incorporated into the production and reproduction of social practices' such as power which provides the capacity for agents to command others and thus transform relations. By calling on rules and resources social life is not intentionally realised by agents but 'recursively' structured.

> The only moving objects in human social relations are individual agents, who employ resources to make things happen, intentionally or otherwise. The structural properties of social system do not act, or 'act on', anyone like forces of nature to 'compel' him or her to behave in a particular way (ibid., p. 181).

Structuration theory clearly represents an important corrective to sociological theories which either remove or marginalise the role of individual or collective agents in the production of social life. But Giddens goes further arguing that for someone to be 'a competent' member of society they must be skilled not solely in 'the practical accomplishments of social activities' but possess knowledge integral to 'the persistent patterning of social life'. In short,

Giddens shares Garfinkel's concept of the agent as someone capable of understanding the rules of social life and providing reasons for action: agents have the capacity for the self-monitoring of action. But this emphasis carries with it the danger that structure is effectively collapsed into agency, that social life, including institutions, practices and values, is the outcome of reflexive actions. This suggests, for example, that social institutions have no independent and sustaining existence other than through the day-to-day actions of individuals. Of course Giddens is right to emphasise that structures are made, but it is also the case that structures also exert themselves on those making them as objective, independent institutions: for example, in many contemporary European societies compulsory military service, administered through military and political institutions, exerts a powerful constraining influence on specific groups limiting their choices and freedom to act. While it is the case that hierarchical military institutions, values and practices are made through collective social action, they pre-exist, endure and function objectively apart from those agents whose actions instantiate the workings of the institutions. There is an inherent duality of structures which both pre-exist agents and their actions while also the enduring beyond the everyday encounters of social life (Mouzelis, op. cit., pp. 119–24).

A further problem with structuration theory lies in its failure to specify the properties of agents and structure and the mechanisms whereby they are linked together other than in highly abstract and overtly voluntaristic terms (imagination, creativity and so on). The ways in which action transforms structures is unclear and the concept of agent highly elliptical, and as a flesh and blood reality, impoverished.

Bourdieu: The Theory of Fields and Habitus

The third approach to theoretical synthesis, Pierre Bourdieu's 'reflexive sociology' attempts to situate the creative, active, inventive capacities of human agents within objectively existing socio-cultural contexts. Bourdieu describes his approach as *genetic structuralism*, 'the analysis of objective structures' which are inseparable from the genesis of subjective 'mental structures' which allows individuals to make sense of and act within the social world (Bourdieu, 1990, p. 14). In contrast to Giddens, however, Bourdieu's *genetic structuralism* develops sociological concepts which link the empirical/historical with the theoretical rejecting systems theory (Parsons, Habermas) and critical theory (as both teleological). Alexander's neo-functionalist standpoint that theory develops independently of empirical and historical analysis, and Merton's re-appraisal of functionalism are seen as tendencies which merely reinforce the dualism between 'theory' and 'empirical research'.

From his early work in French higher education (*Reproduction in Education, Culture and Society*) (1970) to his later studies of culture and class (*Distinction,*

1979) and the higher civil service (*The State Nobility*, 1984), Bourdieu (1929–) has argued that empirical work is always theory-laden and it is only in its current phase that sociology has separated empirical from theoretical analysis. Marx, Durkheim and Weber embraced the unity of theory and empirical research, and Bourdieu draws on their work for some of his fundamental concepts: Weber's differentiation of spheres (which becomes the concept of fields), Marx's concept of social struggles as a constituting characteristic of fields and Durkheim's concept of mental frameworks through which individuals absorb experiences to provide a coherent form through which to make sense of the social world. Bourdieu has also produced a number of theoretical works which advance his own specific concepts and method while engaging in a critical dialogue with other theoretical perspectives: *Outline of a Theory of Practice*, (1970) *The Logic of Practice* (1980) and *An Invitation to Reflexive Sociology* (with Wacquant) (1993). Bourdieu aims to resolve the agency/structure issue (together with other dualisms such as macro/micro, objective/subjective which have plagued modern sociological theory) by developing a theory of a 'force field' and 'socialised subjectivity,' what he calls habitus. He is critical both of structuralism (although his work has clearly been influenced by structuralist concepts) and some of the dominant tendencies of modern orthodox sociology. The strength of structuralism lay in its 'objectivism', with its weaknesses in a failure to deal with problems of consciousness, practice and agency. Sartre's existentialist philosophy with its focus on the consciousness of agents and criticism of mechanistic Marxism constituted the other intellectual tradition influencing the development of Bourdieu's sociology. Bourdieu argued that it was not either/or, a question of making a choice between objectivism and subjectivism but rather of preserving the gains of both traditions. His task lay in unifying the subjective and objective in sociological analysis (Bourdieu and Wacquant, 1992, p. 135). His fundamental objectivist concept is field which is 'tied to structural ways of thinking'. Advocating a structuralist objectivism, which includes the concept of 'social space', Bourdieu distinguishes between 'relational thinking' that is analysing the connections and positions individuals occupy in social fields, from substantialist thinking.

Bourdieu describes his sociology as methodological relationalism because it places emphasis on 'the primacy of relations' and a relational notion of the whole. He rejects the concept of society as a system, a seamless unity, unified and integrated through a common culture or dominant ideology. Rather, society constitutes a network of objective relations structured in social space and specific microcosms which he calls fields. Social context is defined as multi-dimensional space differentiated into distinctive fields, networks of objective positions which agents occupy by virtue of possessing different forms of capital – economic (material skills, wealth), cultural (knowledge, intellectual skills) and symbolic (accumulated prestige and a sense of honour).

Fields constitute 'the true object of social science', a socially structured space of positions, a system of power lines, 'a magnetic' field analysed both genetically (historically) and synchronically (focusing on its internal structure). Education, religion, political parties, the arts, are thus fields characterised by internal differentiation, hierarchisation and social struggles. Fields are not 'apparatuses' which dominate society from above and which eliminate all social struggles. Culture industry and the ideological state apparatus are examples of the latter which Bourdieu describes as 'pathological' notions of a field. All fields have their own distinctive logic, principles and body of specialists who adjudicate practices, knowledge and products. Bourdieu emphasises that fields become increasingly autonomised with the development of modern complex industrial societies, a process of relative autonomy which is slow and piecemeal occupying many years as fields establish their own specific institutions, rules and practices.

Fields are the product of modernity: Bourdieu identifies the historical development of fields with modern complex societies, and their processes of internal differentiation and autonomisation a standpoint which seems close to Parsons's sociology; but social change occurs through struggle, conflict and competition, and it is struggle which produces the differences within a field. Fields can further be subdivided into subfields (the cultural field contains the subfields of the novel, painting, music). It is important to note that it is not individuals who produce differences within a field but the objective positions occupied by agents and institutions. All fields, however, share a general law: those agents occupying dominant positions will necessarily adopt defensive and conservative 'conservation strategies' to preserve their status, while newcomers to a field develop 'subversion strategies' aiming to overthrow the governing rules although at the same accepting the field's legitimacy. This is effectively the precondition for entry to any field, a recognition of the 'values at stake' within it which both limit criticism and lead to 'partial' not total revolutions, to action which destroys a particular hierarchy but not the 'game itself'. Hence, while striving to monopolise and differentiate themselves from others, rivals, such as an economic firms, fashion designers, writers, architects, individuals are guided by strategies (individual and collective) which change and preserve the field itself.

Unlike Giddens, Bourdieu advocates an objectivist concept of structure in that fields are defined as 'systems of relations that are independent of the populations which these relations define', objective relations existing independently of consciousness. But to avoid reifying the concept of structure it is essential to include a subjectivist dimension in which the agent is conceived as creative, imaginative and active. Thus while structuralism emphasises relational thinking it lacks an adequate theory of action: to adopt a structuralist concept of field, for example, is to situate the agent and his/her actions as the passive products of specific relations and to ignore the precise way and the elements involved in action itself. Relational analysis must be enriched by theorising the specific properties which motivate different courses of action within distinctive fields.

What, then, is the role allocated to agents in the construction of fields? How successful is Bourdieu in combining his objectivist notion of field with a subjectivist notion of action? He argues that it is the specific internal properties of fields which enable agents to act for unlike an apparatus fields develop through the practices of active not passive agents. Bourdieu makes the point that agents become socialised into fields, not through norms, but cognitively by a process of internalising the social structure of the field itself. In short, agents transpose the objective properties of a field (the hierarchy of positions, traditions, history, institutions) into 'mental structures', or 'frameworks', which then work to condition the ways the field is perceived, grasped and understood. In this way, the possibilities for action inherent within is enhanced.

To act, however, requires more than cognitive frameworks. Agents make choices over this or that course of action, whether to engage in practices which may transform both the field and themselves. It is not a question of free will but of choices made within a definite structure and agents possessing the necessary properties to 'play the game' and be effective; they are not cultural dopes. But what are these properties? Bourdieu employs the concept of habitus, 'socialised subjectivity', not a habit, but rather a system of 'durable dispositions', or properties, enabling agents to understand, interpret and act in the social world. Habitus both organises practices and allows for the perception of practices. As an acquired, autonomous and permanent set of dispositions durably incorporated in the body, habitus enables agents to adapt and adjust to widely different contexts. Neither co-ordinated nor governed by specific rules, habitus is inculcated during childhood and structured by the social context becoming ingrained as both generative and transposable dispositions. A system of lasting and transposable dispositions which incorporates past experiences, functioning at all moments as a matrix of perceptions and actions making possible an infinitely diversified tastes, expectations, aspirations. Habitus produces practices and a perception and appreciation of practice. Habitus is clearly bound up with social class: individuals will share a common culture and taste (such as the working class preferring red meat, the middle class fish; the working class choosing realist art, the middle class modernist art). In his study of photography, Bourdieu shows that while the higher and lower professions are both conscious of photography as an art form the working class see photography in practical, functional terms, as a means of cataloguing family rituals and practices: only 10 per cent classify photography as an art form while two thirds of photographs are seasonal greetings celebrating family festivals, social gatherings and summer holidays that function to integrate the family into a sense of identity and history providing symbolic value. The photograph joins the circuit of gifts which are chosen specifically for their high symbolic yield.

Habitus thus assumes a reflexive agent whose orientation to the social world is grounded in practical knowledge and Bourdieu cites Marx for the argument that between 'the conditions of existence' and the variety of social practices the 'structuring activity' of human agents intervenes. It is not a question of human agents adapting passively to a pre-given social world but of active creative agents open to many possibilities, able to employ knowledge and skills in maintaining and advancing their position within fields. Moreover, agents act through 'practical sense' in which goals and ends are not determined solely through conscious, deliberate and rational practice but flow from the socially constituted 'feel for the game' (Bourdieu and Wacquant, 1992, p. 126). Hence when confronted with routine everyday situations habitus tends to reproduce, but when confronted with novelty it will innovate.

Thus habitus functions practically as 'structuring structures... as principles which generate and organise practices and representations'. Although they can be modified by later experience, the system of dispositions become ingrained, internalised as 'second nature'. Thus within the field of diplomacy the dispositions linked to an upper-class family background and public school education enables individuals to move with confidence and style in a highly formalised social world dominated by pomp and official ceremony This is the practical sense which enable the individual to act with a minimum of reflection and energy:

> The relation between habitus and field to which it is objectively adjusted... is a sort of ontological complicity, a subconscious and pre-reflexive fit. This complicity manifests itself in what we call the sense of the game or feel for the game (practical sense), an intentionality without intention which functions as the principle of strategies devoid of strategic design, without rational computation and without the conscious positing of ends... In a number of social universes, one of the privileges of the dominant, who move in the world like a fish in water, is that they need not engage in rational computation in order to reach the goals that best suit their interests. All they have to do is to follow their dispositions, which being adjusted to their positions 'naturally' generates practice adjusted to the situation. (Bourdieu, 1990, pp. 108–9)

Habitus thus preserves a sense of continuity working as non-conscious structuring principles governing the ways that the past plays an active role within the present. Each individual contains the individual of yesterday acquiring through past experience the necessary capital that enables him/her to function within a specific field. This is the problem of history; the field structures the habitus and is the product of the embodiment of the immanent necessity of a field as individuals normally encounter situations which confirm their habitus.

Analytically the concept of field assumes the distribution of economic, cultural and symbolic capital and social struggles between classes and fractions of classes each pursuing distinctive goals and strategies: fields are fields of struggle, 'force fields' in which agents occupying specific positions aim to transform or maintain the established balance of forces. For Bourdieu, socio-logical theories of system erode the dynamic principles of fields – struggle, conflict, competition, and the active role of opposition and resistance – force fields are always open and developing, never finished and frozen in time. Although never wholly autonomous (the market for example, constantly exerts an important, external effect), the more they approach autonomy the more completely they fulfil their internal potential. At the same time fields are historically specific their internal differentiation the product of particular historical development and grounded in time and space and not, as with some Marxist and Parsonian theory, governed by transhistorical laws. Fields are thus linked with modernity for less complex undifferentiated societies lack the 'uncoupling mechanisms' which enable fields to separate from centralised political, religious and ideological institutions.

In analysing the complex ways in which fields work, Bourdieu emphasises both the theoretical/critical and empirical/historical dimensions arguing that as each field is unique it must be reconstituted each time in research. Each field must be investigated anew; fields do not provide 'ready made answers' and therefore must be reconstructed by new thinking both theoretical and empir-ical. The sociological study of fields involves both conceptual tools and substantive perspectives: Bourdieu is concerned with the general historical trend towards the autonomisation of fields and identifying mechanisms which produce change. In describing his standpoint as genetic structuralist, he iden-tifies the dynamic principles producing change as the relation of habitus to field in which dispositions oriented agents both to the past and the present.

One of the fundamental problems with other sociological theories of agency-action/structure is their tendency to theoretical and empirical vague-ness regarding the precise socio-cultural physiognomy of agents and the modes of situating them within dynamically developing contexts. Bourdieu resolves this problem through the concept of mental structures and it is this which provides a bridge between the poles of subjectivism/habitus and objectivism/field. The habitus is a mental, cognitive structure. The self is not socialised through normative culture but actively engages with under-standing, interpretation and practice: what Bourdieu provides is both the reflexive and cognitive emphasis of ethnomethodology and the contextual-ising of the self within definite social structures. In this way Bourdieu advances an explanation of both the genesis of fields and the complex ways that agents contribute and relate to their structure and transformation. Yet while marking a distinct advance on the work of Parsons, Habermas and Giddens notably for reuniting the theoretical/conceptual with the empir-ical/historical, Bourdieu's sociology generates a number of problems. The concept of habitus, for example, suggests a narrow and somewhat impover-ished notion of the social self, one based in selfishness and egoism, concerned entirely with the pursuit of goals that enhance status and position. Moreover, because Bourdieu has theorised fields as sites of struggle over scarce resources, the notion of 'interest' functions as a crucial element in determining the practices which aim at monopolisation and domination. It is not a question of agents agonising over values, principles and fundamental beliefs in a critical and reflexive mode but of action which is wholly instrumental. Specific practices enable agents to maintain or increase their assets thus enhancing social status – 'reproductive strategies' – or transform one type of capital into another (economic into cultural or symbolic capital) – 'conversion strategies' – thus advancing claims to legitimacy.

Indeed, Bourdieu argues that the logic of practice itself always conforms to economic calculation even when it might suggest 'disinterestedness'; the logic of fields effectively corresponds to the reproductive structures of capitalist economy, class struggles and ideology. The field of education, for example, reproduces capitalist class relations, generates a legitimating ideology and continually leads to the conversion of economic into cultural capital. An homologous relation is thus posited between the internal and external struggles so that the educational field embodies the conflicts and clash of interests between different social classes and fractions of classes.

Field theory further assumes modes of communication but Bourdieu's model marginalising inter-subjective elements. All action, for example, takes place through 'positionality' not 'interaction', for Bourdieu's standpoint is that structures cannot be reduced to interactions and practices through which structures express themselves. In short, communicative practices arise entirely on the basis of positions occupied within a field not through the subjective properties inherent in forms of interaction. But without a concept of interaction there can be neither dialogue nor communication, no living exchange of ideas, judgements, and aspirations and no real grasp of the ways in which agents actually change and develop their sense of social and cultural identity. How can reflexivity constitute an integral part of Bourdieu's sociological project if the conditions which enable a reflexive agent to pursue creative and voluntaristic action are theorised away? Because Bourdieu has conceived action in instrumental terms there is no room for the partial autonomy of ideas and values, no critical thought within the different fields other than as means of achieving status and domination. Thus for all its strengths Bourdieu's sociology shares with other contemporary sociological and Marxist theories a deficit of subjectivism, voluntarism, reflexivity and a failure to develop an adequate theory of inter-subjective communication.

10

Postmodernity and Sociological Thought

Modernity and Postmodernity: Differentiation and De-differentiation

As earlier chapters suggested the concept of modernity is closely bound up with the rise and development of classical sociology and its analysis of the complex transition from pre-modern societies to modern industrial social systems. Modernity constituted the cultural logic of an urban-based capitalism in which highly differentiated structures – political, economic, cultural – increasingly separated themselves from centralised institutions, a process exemplified in Gramsci's concept of civil society and the Frankfurt School's notion of the public sphere. As Kumar has noted, modernity was not simply about innovative ideas but embraced intellectual, political and social forms linked historically with capitalist modernisation, industrial technology and economic life 'a speeding up of economic evolution to the point where it took on revolutionary proportions' (Kumar, 1995, p. 82).

It was Max Weber who first employed modernity as a sociological concept arguing for its basis in the Enlightenment project of reason, science and human emancipation. The historical genesis of the term has been widely discussed and its origins traced back to the middle ages to the concept of *modernitus* – modern times – and *modernity*, men of today (the philologist Erich Auerbach noted fourteen different meanings in Latin), to the famous seventeenth-century dispute between the Ancients and the Moderns and, more pertinently, to the Renaissance discovery of time and the differentiation of history into Ancient, Medieval and Modern periods. By the end of the eighteenth century the concept of society had become embedded in a sense of historical time, its development conceived in terms of a dynamic unfolding process involving distinctive evolutionary stages (primarily economic for Adam Smith and Adam Ferguson, philosophical and cultural for Kant and Condorcet). The contemporary meaning of modernity is thus imbricated in Enlightenment reason, the belief in progress and positive science. Modernity signifies a culture of innovation, a rational ethos challenging traditions and rituals in the name of critical thought, empirical knowledge and humanism.

But while bound up with this Enlightenment project of human emancipation, modernity became widely used by nineteenth-century writers to refer both to changes in society and culture as well as fundamental transformations in human experience. It was the French poet Charles Baudelaire (1972) who defined modernity as 'the transient, the fleeting, the contingent; it is one half of art, the other being the eternal and immutable', describing it as the alienated experience of the 'fragmented' nature of modern urban life. As the concept of modernity captures the 'fleeting' moment, the 'snapshots', so modern painting breaks from tradition and the past by emphasising the fragmentary and ephemeral yet exploring the hidden truth, the 'eternal' and the 'poetic' which lie beneath the chaos and impressionistic surface of everyday life. It is Baudelaire's concept which later sociologists, notably Simmel, assimilated into their theorising as well as thinkers linked with the Frankfurt School, notably Walter Benjamin and Siegfried Kracauer, who transformed it into a social theory of modernity focusing on the micrological, the transitory and fragmentary nature of modern culture. In contrast Weber described modernity as the growing autonomy of spheres, or fields, which produce experts and specialised knowledge, a development which carries with it a darker side, that the application of science may lead not to knowledge and emancipation but to the triumph of formal rationality over substantive rationality.

As distinct from the Baudelarian-Simmel concept of modernity, with its anticipations of postmodernist experience, Weber advanced a structural concept dealing with the transformation of whole societies, ideologies, social structure and culture. Modernity confirms the promise of scientific reason to unmask irrational forces and point to necessary social change. Similarly Giddens has argued that modernity implies historical awareness, a consciousness of historical continuity of the ways the past continues to live in the present. This concept of modernity emphasises that it is agents and their actions which make history and social change possible through the specific properties of modernity itself – increased purposiveness, conscious collective action and the ability to engage in 'reflexive monitoring' in relation to possible alternatives (Giddens, 1987, p. 223). Thus the sociological concept and basis of modernity as an historical process lies in the development of new social movements during the nineteenth century, providing the institutional basis for new ideas and forms of collective action, political movements such as socialism and anarchism, movements embracing sexual liberation, feminism and culture (avante garde art and modernism), all challenging traditional ideas and urging collective action to achieve substantive goals. But modernity also signals the expansion of highly centralised societies based on the nation state, a universal educational system, a common language and national culture, a national division of labour, factory-based commodity production and a regimented and disciplined work force. In this latter sense modernity signifies homogeneity and the marginalisation of differences within national cultures and societies.

Both classical sociology and Marxism theorised these developments although in sharply contrasting ways. For Marx modernity implied permanent upheaval and transformations in human wants and desires: the focus was on the dynamic principles inherent in the present with capitalist society described as a 'revolutionary' system of production undermining the apparent solidity of bourgeois society, a new kind of society characterised by shocks, collisions, crises and contradictions in all spheres. In *The Communist Manifesto* Marx and Engels wrote of the

> constant revolutionising of production, uninterrupted disturbance of all social relations, everlasting uncertainty and agitation, distinguish the bourgeois epoch from all earlier times. All fixed, fast-frozen relationships... are swept away, all newly formed ones become obsolete before they can ossify. All that is solid melts into air, all that is holy is profaned, and men at last are forced to face with sober senses the real conditions of their lives and their relations with their fellow men. (Marx and Engels, 1962, p. 37)

While Marx and Engels celebrated modernity as embracing an enlarged human capacity to change the world, Weber pessimistically portrayed it as the progressive rationality of the social world, a disenchantment with the increasing domination of formal rationality and the iron cage of depersonalised administration. Weber's theory of modernity is closely tied up with the Enlightenment project and the emancipatory potential of science and reason to change the world for the good and put in place a firm commitment to substantive values. In Weber's view modernity enshrined a tension within Enlightenment reason itself, between the goals of freedom and the practical necessity to adapt to the pre-determined functions and purposes of the system, to utilitarian modes of calculation concerned with making the existing institutions work efficiently.

It is this meaning which becomes increasingly important for the theory of postmodernity. Rationality produces a differentiation of value spheres, the break up of the traditional, pre-modern unified world view and the emergence of a pluralist structure of partly autonomous fields and competing values. As the first sociologist to fully grasp and understand the significance of this 'decentring ' of the modern world, Weber argued that each sphere and its activity must be judged by its own internal values so that each sphere becomes the preserve of specialists whose expert knowledge and competence allow them to reach legitimate conclusions and which other, non-specialists must accept. Rationality invades the state, bureaucracy and culture, personality: coherent and rigorously systematic ideas replace the irrational and magical elements characteristic of pre-modernity (Gerth and Mills, 1948, p. 328). In contrast, Simmel tended to produce an unstructured vision of modernity as fragments, 'snapshots' of fleeting experiences in which individuals lose all sense of belonging to a whole, fated to a tragic resignation and passivity. Rather than a structured concept, Simmel's notion of modernity is based in feelings and mental outlook. But in describing modern culture as one characterised by permanent changes and diversity in cultural forms, fashion and artistic styles Simmel anticipated many of the fundamental elements of postmodernity.

The differentiation thesis, however, remained at the core of sociology during the first half of the twentieth century, in the work of Karl Mannheim (1893–1947) on the sociology of knowledge and culture, in the sociological functionalism of Parsons, Merton and symbolic interactionism. During the 1960s and 70s, the rise of new social theories (humanist Marxism, semiology, structuralism, poststructuralism, discourse theories, together with the growing importance of cultural studies, and feminism), sociological thought became increasingly fragmented, dominated by a scepticism towards its classical heritage, the grounding of theories in a distinctive conceptual framework and a clearly defined field of study. The fundamental object of sociology, society defined precisely as forms of social organisation based on differentiated, hierarchically ordered institutions, became problematic. It was the Frankfurt School whose concept of critical theory provided the first systematic critique of the pluralist and differentiation thesis by advancing a theory of modern society centrally organised around technology, economics and politics in which the formal, instrumental rationality of culture industry eliminated all independent pluralist structures. But while Adorno and others noted the increasing economic commodification of culture and the tendency for boundaries between structures (the economic, political, cultural) to collapse, they retained the classical Marxist and sociological principle of society as a hierarchically structured system of institutions clearly defined by specific boundaries (their distinction between high and low culture for example).

Increasingly, however, the notion of separated and partly autonomous spheres seemed outdated: the aesthetic, cultural and political were being colonised by the economic. This de-differentiation process further suggested the collapse of the principles of hierarchy and clear boundaries between institutions and practices. The 'legislators' and specialists associated with modernity and the national state and culture, were now replaced by 'interpreters,' that is, by intellectuals who offered scepticism and tolerance of many points of view, not certainty and cultural security. Modernity had assimilated into one homogeneous whole all the voices which make up society and its culture (ethnic, gender, class, regional) integrated around a centre which might be described in terms of a dominant ideology, hegemony, value system or common culture. It was argued that the culture of experts and legislators impoverished rather than enriched society by encouraging the accumulation of specialist knowledge in narrow spheres with a commitment to the 'truth'. In contrast de-differentiation encourages the plurality of voices, the re-assertion of difference, diversity, open and fluid structures, scepticism and relativism in values.

The Origins of Postmodernity: the Problem of Meta-narratives

Originating in Enlightenment philosophy and the transition to new forms of social organisation, the concept of modernity was built around universals, the idea of progress and evolution, the unfolding of reason and the expansion of human freedom and emancipation. Marx went further, portraying modernity as the historically necessary development of capitalism bringing with it challenges to old traditions by new class-based ideologies and the promise of 'real' history in the classless society of communism. A pessimistic note was struck by Durkheim and Weber with modernity co-existing with anomie and the formal rationality of unfreedom within an iron cage. Marx, Weber and Durkheim grounded their theories of socialism, rationality and organic solidarity within the larger historical framework of historical change presenting a specific 'narrative' to historical development: the emancipation of the working class, the triumph of reason, and the progressive evolution of human society, 'grand narratives' which provided history with meaning, direction and purpose.

Belonging firmly to the era of modernity, these grand narratives have provided the target for postmodern theorists. With the dominant Marxist narrative of emancipation in his sights the postmodern philosopher J. F. Lyotard (1924–) has argued that the persistence of struggles against communism from within communist states themselves, combined with their totalitarian character has rendered such narratives 'barely credible' (Lyotard, 1989, p. 318). In his hugely influential *The Postmodern Condition* (1979) Lyotard argued that in pre-modern societies narratives were mainly the preserve of storytellers, a culture of oral tradition and custom in which knowledge, legitimated from within by the community, reinforced a sense of social unity. Modernity, by substituting science for custom and tradition, promoted the idea of knowledge as something to be legitimated externally by appeals to institutions and norms. Thus the Enlightenment theory of human reason and progress is legitimated by appeals to the impersonal norms of a positive and objective science; the Marxist narrative of socialism through class struggles legitimises and judges as historically true diverse actions such as trade union solidarity and mass mobilisation leading to the dictatorship of the proletariat. Lyotard proposed that modernity became increasingly dominated by these grand narratives and their sense of history as a totalising process structured in an absolute truth or truths. Modernity designates 'any science that legitimates itself with reference to a metadiscourse' such as the Enlightenment's appeal to the goal of universal freedom. Such meta-narratives, he argued, are rooted in a nostalgic yearning for organic unity, wholeness, harmony. But there is no collective, universal subject seeking emancipation and freedom. The concept of the whole is totalitarian and 'terroristic' in that it seeks to exclude others from participating in its idealised community. Meta-narratives always appeal to the interests of particular communities with their basis in homogeneity and common purpose. The postmodern rejects all totalising conceptions and is defined precisely as an 'incredulity towards metanarratives' (Lyotard, 1989, p. 318). Lyotard thus attacks Enlightenment reason, universal history and the idea of wholes: 'Let us wage war on totality' he cries, on all attempts to forge order and sense out of the flux of multiple and discontinuous events.

Postmodernity is thus defined as the rejection of 'narratological' knowledge, that is, the assumption that 'truth' is grounded in a specific subject such as a social class, human nature or reason. In place of the 'foundational' knowledge of modernity, postmodernity embraces relativity and uncertainty: knowledge is always incomplete and indeterminate, there are no universal standards and criteria to make absolute judgements, only differences and ambiguity, multiple paradigms and conceptual frameworks. This sceptical pluralism is linked with the de-centring of modern society, the absence of a common culture and shared ideology: the postmodern condition is one of micro contexts and micro struggles in which a variety of social groups attempt to 'wage war' against the totalising and centralised power of the modern state, multinational companies and bureaucratised science and technology.

Lyotard's work represents one important strand of postmodern theory. It is clearly indebted both to the post-structuralist theories of the subject as well as the general malaise on the political left, the collapse of socialist beliefs and ideals. But does it offer anything for sociological knowledge? In this book I have looked at the developing tensions between Weber's methodological individualism and totalising theories such as Marxism as well as the ongoing critique of grand theory by the sociological interactionists. There is nothing original in a critique of totalising social theory from within sociology. Lyotard's success and influence lies in giving voice to disquiet about all totalising theories (mainly philosophical and political) and the related substantive issue of the centralised power of the modern nation state. The socio-cultural context, the historical background of the rise of postmodernity was one characterised by the rise of new social movements based on micro politics and their rejection of holistic categories of identity based on class, in favour of gender and ethnic elements. Implicit is the view that traditional sociology is irrelevant for its fundamental concepts of class, nation common culture are no longer salient and must be replaced by postmodern concepts embracing difference, ambiguity and heterogeneity.

Postmodernity and Post-industrial Society

The term postmodern had originally been invented in the 1940s and 50s, used first in architecture to designate an ultrafunctionalist and standardised form of housing; and second, by a number of American literary theorists to characterise the disappearing boundaries between high and popular culture. In sociology C. W. Mills, in his *The Sociological Imagination* (1959), had used the term the 'postmodern period' to designate a new epoch following 'the modern age' with its Enlightenment ideals of reason and freedom: the 'ideological mark' of the 'postmodern period', Mills noted, was that 'increased rationality may not be assumed to make for increased freedom' (Mills, 1959, pp. 166–7). More generally, the concept of the postmodern signified both a new social formation supplanting industrial capitalism and the ideologies associated with the 'modern age', liberalism, socialism and Marxism. As the term postmodern became increasingly popular within the human and social sciences so, too, did the related sociological concept of post-industrial society.

During the 1950s sociologists, such as Daniel Bell, S. M. Lipset, Raymond Aron and Ralf Dahrendorf arguing against what they saw as the static, ahistorical bias of functionalism and the worn-out ideological historicism of Marxism by advanced the concept of post-industrialism (although the term varied from one sociologist to another – 'post-capitalist', 'post-bourgeois society', the 'technological society', the 'knowledge society' – in essentials it suggested the priority of technology, science and culture over private property and class divisions). Post-industrial society was contrasted with nineteenth-century capitalist society and twentieth-century industrial society in terms of the transformation of social structure: post-industrial society constituted a social formation in which private property, class interests and class conflict had lost their centrality as 'axial principles'. While the social structure of capitalism had been largely organised around the axis of private property; post-industrial society is organised around the axis of 'theoretical knowledge'. In *The Coming of Post-Industrial Society* (1976), Bell argued that the 'energising principle' of modern societies is increasingly centred within the educational, scientific and governmental institutions. The traditional business firm and the entrepreneur are in the process of being replaced by scientists, economists and engineers. The source of innovation and policy making is no longer the business enterprise but the university.

Bell's general thesis rests on the Weberian argument that modern society is organised into three separate although related realms: the economy, the polity and the culture. The polity regulates the distribution of power and the different interests in society; the culture, as the realm of self-realisation, establishes meaning through the expressiveness of art and ritual: the economic realm relates to the social structure. Each is ruled by different axial principles: self-realisation in culture, equality in politics, efficiency in economics. Thus society as a whole is not organised around one dominant element or integrated into a single system. There is always a disjunction between the different realms so that culture, for example, may repudiate the axial principle of economic efficiency and rationality in favour of irrational, hedonistic modernism with its rejection of tradition and established institutions. Similarly, the axial problem of the polity 'is the relation between the desire for popular participation and bureaucracy' (Bell, 1976, p. 115). Each of these spheres has its own inner logic and contradictory nature. Prediction and forecasting generally in the cultural and political realms is thus hazardous and Bell's main emphasis is on the economic sphere. Thus:

> The concept of a post-industrial society is not a picture of a complete social order; it is an attempt to describe and explain an axial change in the social structure (defined as the economy, the technology and the stratification system) of the society. But such a change implies no specific determinism between a 'base' and a 'superstructure'... it is likely that the various societies that are entering a post-industrial phase will have different political and cultural configurations. (Bell, 1976, p. 119)

Bell concludes that a new post-industrial culture is emerging, one based on pleasure, anti-nomianism and anti-institutionalism, a 'rage' against order and bourgeois values. This postmodern culture celebrates a hedonistic world of mass consumption, fashion, photography and travel, a consumptionist culture built on play, fun and display (Bell, 1979, pp. 46–7, 71). While this new culture abandons many of the fundamental principles of capitalist modernity (economic growth based on massive capital investment, technical innovations, factory-based, labour-intensive production with the correlative expansion of markets and consumption) it comes into conflict with the pluralist structures of post-industrialism which remain based in a national state, national culture, a national division of labour and hierarchically organised institutions. In Bell's view, post-industrial society is not a de-centred society, for while it has become transformed from one largely dominated by the production of goods to one dominated by the production of theoretical knowledge, a new social structure emerges. In modern societies, theory dominates empiricism in the areas of science, economics and information technology. The scientist, the mathematicians, the computer technologist and the economic theorist rise to prominence to form what Bell calls a distinct 'knowledge class'. At the heart of post-industrial society is a professional class embodying norms of social responsiveness derived from an ethics of service to the community. The profit motive has no place within the burgeoning research institutes and universities. This professional-scientific class will eventually saturate society with its professional values: Bell distinguishes his position from earlier writers such as Saint-Simon by defining the new class as those who apply their knowledge to the organisation of society as a whole. It is not a question of technocrats exercising power, but rather the production of new values and principles of organisation.

While Bell's work describes many of the basic changes which are occurring within modern industrial societies, it is clearly an example of what Lyotard would describe as a meta-narrative with rational, scientific knowledge legitimised by a new 'knowledge class' and the inevitable historical development of planned, centralised, rational and bureaucratic social systems as the logic of industrialism. In contrast to Bell's post-industrial concept of modernity, a number of later writers, including Marxists David Harvey and Frederic Jameson and sociologists Z. Bauman and Scott Lash, have attempted to develop homologies between the broad contours of post-industrialism and postmodernism. In *The Condition of Postmodernity* (1989), Harvey describes postmodern society and culture as constituting a continuity with modernity. Technology and innovation have produced a dispersed, de-centred mode of production characterised by flexible labour processes and markets. Harvey employs the concept of flexible accumulation which is characterised 'by the emergence of entirely new sectors of production, new ways of providing financial services, new markets, and, above all, greatly intensified rates of commercial, technological and organisational innovation' (Harvey, 1989, p. 147). New technology allows for a rapid turnover of goods for unlike mass production assembly lines (the Fordist model) production is broken up into segments which involve extensive subcontracting. Postmodernity is thus defined as a spatial system characterised by parallel branches and subdivisions and not a hierarchically organised space of production, a de-centred space of flows in which consumer durables are increasingly supplanted by the production of 'events', 'spectacles' with an instant turnover and a resulting sense of the ephemeral and fragmentary. Postmodernity 'celebrates difference, ephemerality, spectacle, fashion, and the commodification of cultural forms' (ibid., p. 156–7). By accelerating the pace of social life spatial barriers are overcome with

> a disorienting and disruptive impact upon political-economic practices, the balance of class power, as well as upon cultural and social life. While historical analogies are always dangerous, I think it no accident that postmodern sensibility evidences strong sympathies for certain of the confused political, cultural and philosophical movements that occurred at the beginning of this century (in Vienna, for example) when the sense of time-space compression was also peculiarly strong. (ibid., p. 284)

Harvey's concept of time–space compression is the defining feature of postmodernity working within an increasing global economy determined by multinational corporations in which economic co-ordination functions outside the boundaries of the nation state.

Like Harvey, Jameson in *Postmodernism: The Cultural Logic of Capitalism* (1992) contextualises postmodernity, describing the development of capitalism through three stages: market capitalism, monopoly capitalism and multinational capitalism. On the basis of Ernest Mandel's theory of three capitalist epochs (Mandel, 1975), Jameson describes the post-1945 period as 'late capitalism', which constitutes 'the purest form of capital yet to have emerged, a prodigious expansion of capital into hitherto uncommodified areas' (Jameson, 1992, pp. 35–6). A new form of social life and economic order has emerged as a 'purer and more homogeneous expression of classical capitalism' in which postmodernism is effectively a mode of production and not simply a cultural category (ibid., p. 406). Postmodern cultural production thus penetrates to all areas of late capitalist society breaking down the boundaries between different structures so that, for example, the economic and the cultural begin to merge.

Jameson rejects Weber's differentiation thesis, the separation of spheres, arguing that the concept of the relative autonomy of culture belongs to the early stages of capitalism for with the expansion of global, multinational capital, culture expands 'prodigiously' through all social realms 'to the point at which everything in our social life – from economic value and state power' is cultural 'in some original and yet untheorised sense' (ibid., p. 48). Within postmodern society everything has become commodified: Andy Warhol's representations of Coca-Cola bottles and Campbell's soup tins synthesise the aesthetic image with commodity fetishism and Warhol's images, like all commodities, have a depthless quality which for Jameson constitutes their strength as exemplars of the new postmodern culture.

Unlike Weber's differentiation of cultural spheres, postmodernism is dedifferentiation with all social levels acculturated, a process in which culture 'impacts' back into social, economic and political life 'in ways that make any independent... extra cultural form of it problematic' (ibid., p. 277). For Jameson postmodernism constitutes a cultural force field in which co-existing and 'diverse' elements are brought together in a structural unity. A cultural dominant functions hegemonically to integrate heterogeneous forces into a totality. But while claiming that other, non-postmodern tendencies co-exist within the structure of the force field Jameson fails to explain how other forces within the field can develop a partial autonomy from the dominant culture. Moreover, there is no analysis of the complex relation between different forms of cultural production within the force field. Indeed, there is little sense in Jameson's model of any complex play of forces at work within the field, rather that such forces become assimilated and integrated through a totalising process which connects the different postmodern forms, from architecture to film and painting, to the mode of production. As was suggested in Chapter 9 when discussing Bourdieu's concept of field, a totalising model will emphasise integration rather than dispersion and struggle. A force field is structured in difference, opposition and struggle; the specific forces at work produce changes in the structure of the field itself and the cultural artefacts produced. But Jameson's model offers no principles of change at work within the force field, no analysis of the specific groups involved in the different forms of cultural production and reproduction, the positions they occupy and the relations between them.

In effect, Jameson reduces the highly complex, differentiated and hierarchical structure of modern capitalist society, the institutions and practices and struggles of agents within different forms of production, to a deterministic historical narrative which blindly unfolds behind the backs of agents them-selves. There is, too, the problem of periodisation. Mandel's concept of late capitalism is located within the post-1945 period, but Jameson's postmod-ernism emerges in the 1960s. Moreover, capitalist production passed through a number of distinctive phases from the 1940s to the 1990s, from the centralised governmental intervention linked with Keynsian economics to the free market associated with Reagan and Thatcher. And as noted earlier David Harvey has pointed to the post-Fordist phase of the 1970s involving smaller and flexible economic units than those associated with 'organised capitalism' (Harvey, 1989, Ch. 10). In Jameson's analysis the specifics of capitalist economic production are vaguely and abstractly articulated, with postmod-ernism linked broadly and directly with the productive process. In late capi-talism culture has become the central productive force, no longer separate from the economic. The concepts of the cultural and the economic

> thereby collapse back into one another and say the same thing, in an eclipse of the distinction between base and superstructure (so that) the base, in the third stage of capitalism, generates its superstructures with a new kind of dynamic. (Jameson, 1992, p. xxi)

But there is little compelling evidence to support this argument: as with many postmodern theories Jameson offers virtually no sociological analysis of institutions and processes, no concepts to elucidate the relations between and within different forms of production. As a Marxist analysis it necessarily assumes that modern society remains hierarchically structured, its institutions generating inequalities of income, property and culture but fails to integrate this fundamental sociological fact into the analysis.

Both Jameson and Harvey describe postmodernity as the further develop-ment of modernity extending many of the major economic and cultural forces associated with capitalism. Whereas classical sociology and Marxism devel-oped concepts linking material with ideal forces, postmodern theory reverses this order promoting cultural forms as the fundamental principle of social life. This theme of the centrality of culture to modern society had first been theo-rised by the Frankfurt School but postmodern theorists go beyond the classical principles underpinning the concept of culture industry (a synthesis of Marx and Weber) by characterising modern society as one saturated by images with the media generating a 'non-material', a dematerialised concept of reality. The French sociologist Jean Baudrillard (1924–) has forcibly argued that it is no longer possible to describe modern society in terms of concepts derived from modernist discourses and going beyond both Jameson and Harvey he aban-dons Marxist theory to celebrate postmodernity as signalling a decisive break from modernity itself.

Baudrillard's early works *The Mirror of Production* (1975), *The System of Objects*, (1968) *Consumer Society* (1970) proposed a critique of Marxism through a structuralist and semiological perspective. For Baudrillard, the decisive issue lay in Marx's productionist model of society, his emphasis on the role of labour and consequent reduction of the 'superstructure' to a reflection of the material infra-structure. Echoing Adorno's comment that Marx's vision of society was as a giant workhouse, Baudrillard argues that modern society is now increasingly structured by signs and symbols: Saussure, not Marx, offers a more reliable conceptual guide to understanding modern culture.

All objects can be analysed in terms of binary oppositions which then reveal the rules and internal relations which structure the object. Marxism had ignored the ways in which commodities are signifiers not simply material objects, that is, the commodity constitutes a sign which provides individuals with cultural identity. Signs work through referential value for they designate something against which they can be exchanged. But Baudrillard notes that within this modernist framework, signs 'constitute a distinct material reality' which are used for prestige, status and social differentiation. It is this classical configuration which postmodernity abandons (Baudrillard, 1993). While Marxism assumed a 'metanarrative' of developmental stages of history, Baudrillard advanced a developmental theory of the sign. In premodern society, what he calls 'symbolic societies', social relations are organised around 'symbolic exchange', a process occurring during festivals, rites and rituals in which the exchange of gifts, for example, reinforces the social order: here the sign has a clear referential function. With the emergence of productionist societies a fixed and stable hierarchy of signs clearly distinguish the 'real' from the 'unreal' so that 'the sign and the real' are equivalent, commodities such as clothes conferring social status: culture is organised around a social world in which word, sounds and images have a direct relation with objects and reality: the code produces coherent meanings and elicits particular responses. But with the rise of postmodern culture, signs and their codes become autonomous, producing their own intrinsic meanings with no reference to an objective reality. Advocating the political economy of the sign, Baudrillard notes that

> neither Saussure nor Marx had any presentiment of all this: they were still in the golden age of the dialectic of the sign and the real, which is at the same time the 'classical' period of capital and value. Their dialectic is in shreds, and the real has died of the shock of value acquiring this fantastic autonomy. Determinancy is dead, indeterminacy holds sway. (Baudrillard, 1993)

Referential value has been annihilated, replaced

> by a total relativity, general commutation, combination and simulation – simulation, in the sense that, from now on, signs are exchanged against each other rather than against the real... The emancipation of the sign: remove this 'archaic' obligation to designate something and it becomes

finally free, indifferent, and tally indeterminate, in the structural and combinatory play which succeeds the rule of determinate equivalence. (Baudrillard, 1993)

In this new postmodern 'semiurgic' society the codes function as the organising principles generating new forms of communication and social order. In his later works, notably *Simulacra and Simulations* (1981) and *Fatal Strategies* (1982), Baudrillard describes a social world dominated by the media and a correlative explosion of images. In modernity copies or models represented real objects and events, the age of the simulacrum, but in postmodernity the copy or the simulacra produces reality, objects, events. The whole notion of representation is abandoned:

So here is something more than that which is peculiar to our modern media images: if they fascinate us so much it is not because they are sites of the production of meaning and representation... it is on the contrary because they are sites of the disappearance of meaning and representation, sites in which we are caught quite apart from any judgement of reality, thus sites of a fatal strategy of denigration of the real and the reality principle. (Baudrillard, 1993, p. 194)

It becomes increasingly difficult to distinguish the real from the unreal: hyperreality takes over. Images bear no relation with reality: the hyperreal is constantly reproduced through the electronic media, so that, as Baudrillard notes in 'The Ecstasy of Communication' (1983) advertising and television invade all the 'most intimate processes of our social life'. Reality collapses into hyperreality:

The meticulous reduplication of the real, preferably through another reproductive medium such as advertising or photography. Through reproduction from one medium into another the real becomes volatile... becoming the real for its own sake, a fetishism of the lost object which is no longer the object of representation, but the ecstasy of denigration and its own ritual extermination: the hyperreal. (Baudrillard, 1993, pp. 196)

Today reality is hyperreal and beyond representation. De-differentiation suggests there is no difference between news and entertainment (hence his view that the Gulf War was media circus and spectacle and never happened), advertisements and culture: the individual is seduced by a social world structured around the circulation of signs and meanings. In this semiurgic society traditional sociological concepts – class, nation, ethnicity – which provided the bedrock of a sense of identity are irrelevant.

Baudrillard presents a social landscape emptied of all structural processes, institutions and agents: society consists of a vast, phantasmagoric superstructure of signs and images to which the individual has neither an objective nor alienated relationship. There are no active agents only disembodied individuals as terminals of multiple networks including television, computers, telephones, micro-satellites. Modern mass culture with its 'useless hyperinformation fabricates non-communication in that no active exchange occurs between the production of images and their reception, the mass media forcing silence on the masses and plunging them into a state of stupor' (Baudrillard, 1983).

In his essay, 'The masses: the implosion of the social in the media' (1994), Baudrillard pessimistically depicts a world of simulations and information saturation which is emptied of referents, beyond the boundaries of representation. In this world the only response of the individual is passivity and silence. But while focusing on the 'new', the centrality of media to modern society, Baudrillard's work goes beyond the frameworks of sociological thought. As with Jameson he fails to make any connections between the processes of consumption and the productive process. Within the media, for example, there exist highly complex chains of authority, hierarchical relations in which some individuals, the 'macro actors', have more power than others in the making of signs. Who makes decisions on what is produced? Are all signs and codes equal within the media and within society. Baudrillard's model is close to cybernetic thinking not sociological thinking, depicting society as a closed system in which events simply happen and are not the result of an interaction process within institutions involving the possibility of different values, perspectives and courses of action.

Postmodernity has been described as the culture of surfaces, the play of images which lack depth and historical meaning. Postmodernity emphasises discontinuity, the fragmentary and ephemeral. While there are many problems in adequately theorising and contextualising postmodernity, postmodern theory has generated important sociological insights into the nature of modern culture and society notably in its delineation of difference, its critique of the centralising and unifying tendencies of the modern state which may marginalise alternative voices and for focusing on sexuality, gender, ethnicity as autonomous realities which resist assimilation to traditional concepts of class domination, common culture and system prerequisites. But these advances, however, should not lead to calls for the abandonment of all classical and modern sociological concepts such as social control, social system, hegemony, even society itself (Bauman, 1992). To replace then with new and up-to-date concepts based on ambiguity and indeterminacy is to abandon sociological thought altogether. The danger lies in presenting a one-sided view of the social world, the concentration of specific trends within the culture which are then built into a law with everything opposing ignored.

In contrast, Giddens (1991) proposes the concept of 'high modernity', not postmodernity to capture the open nature of modern social life, its pluralism of contexts and actions with identity a project of 'reflexively organised life planning. a process facilitated by the availability within everyday life of expert knowledge (of sexuality, psychology, health, and so on). High modernity is characterised by the separation and emptying out of time/space, the disembedding of social institutions and social relations with their 're-articulation across indefinite tracts of time/space'. To live in this world is like 'riding a juggernaut' with accelerating rates of social change, risks woven into the social fabric of social life (risks from nuclear waste, genetically modified foods and so on) (Giddens, 1991, pp. 14–28; Beck, 1992). Modernity in this view is not exhausted: the postmodern is more a mood than a new social order: 'To speak of postmodernism as superceding modernity appears to invoke that very thing which is declared… impossible: giving some coherence to history and pinpointing our place within it' (Giddens, 1991, p. 47). The globalising dynamic of high modernity, however, should not disguise the resilience of local and national institutions. Unlike postmodern theory, modern sociological thought is characterised both by a concern with an emerging polycentric world based in differences and a world constituted though separate and historically unique societies structured in culturally specific institutions (for example, sociology must explain why French educational system differs from the American system although sharing similar structures and values), traditions, values and hierarchical relations of inequality and power. While difference exists it does so within these larger forms: the plural voices of postmodernity coexist with permanent institutions which both provide the basis for any possible autonomy and their integration within the larger society.

Habermas and the Modernity Project

Since the collapse of sociological functionalism as the major paradigm of western sociology, only Marxism, in its various forms, and the mass society thesis have attempted to develop a social theory of modern industrial society. The theory of post-industrial society constitutes the single exception but it has yet to be developed as a general sociological theory comparable with Parsonian functionalism or Marxism. While postmodernity shares the broad substantive themes of post-industrial theory it rejects its totalising, centralising bureaucratic meta-narrative. In Bell's theory the planners and the technocrats, basing their policy decisions on theoretical knowledge and a professional ethos, effectively neutralise popular democratic forms and active political institutions. A bureaucratic, administrative relation subsists between rulers and ruled: the logic of post-industrial society is thus to eliminate all dialogic modes of communication and the ambiguity of human discourse and action. It is precisely these forces which postmodernity celebrates, the open and fluid concept of society, the development of new social movements based on gender, ethnicity, sexuality – the hybrid nature of modern culture, the differences of many voices. But postmodernity was a critique of Enlightenment reason. Advancing a different perspective from those of Harvey, Jameson and Baudrillard, Habermas has offered an alternative view of postmodernity, one which seeks to salvage the positive values and elements from the Enlightenment project.

In his critique of the *Dialectic of Enlightenment* Habermas castigates Adorno and Horkheimer for oversimplifying the concept of modernity and failing to do justice to its rational content exemplified in bourgeois ideals. Adorno and Horkheimer ignored the fundamental elements of modernity which suggest alternatives to the domination of formal rationality. The *Dialectic of Enlightenment* remains rooted in a deterministic and pessimistic perspective. The development of autonomous spheres and experts does not necessarily suggest the triumph of instrumental rationality, for the 'validity claims' made by and mediated by specialists must justify the specific principles and practices inherent in each sphere. The values of each sphere are not automatically legitimated: they must be argued over in critical discourse and command consensus from non-specialists. In short, Habermas argues that the real potential of each sphere lies in going beyond mere technical and formal knowledge to raise issues which strike at the foundations of modern society, problems of law and morality, political constitutions, economic organisation and aesthetics. The result is the production of substantive not formal values and it is this which constitutes the unfulfilled emancipatory core of the Enlightenment project.

In arguing for the project of enlightenment Habermas follows Weber's concept of modernity but criticises his pessimistic rejection of its potential:

> The project of modernity formulated in the eighteenth century by the philosophers of the Enlightenment consisted of their efforts to develop objective science, universal morality and law, and autonomous art according to their inner logic. At the same time, this project intended to release the cognitive potentials of each of these domains from their esoteric forms. The Enlightenment philosophers wanted to utilise this accumulation of specialised culture for the enrichment of everyday life – that is to say, for the rational organisation of everyday social life. (Habermas, 1985, p. 9)

Thus the accumulated knowledge of the three spheres does not automatically lead to the enslavement of humanity but opens up the emancipatory possibilities inherent in science and knowledge. But this is feasible only if Weber's model and that of Adorno and Horkheimer incorporate a theory of communicative action based on the collective practices which enables the project to be realised by relinking modern culture with everyday life. Both Weber's critique and the Frankfurt School's blunt rejection of the emancipatory logic of rationality effectively reduce the prospects of 'self-conscious practice', self development and 'self-realisation'.

For Habermas, the rationalisation and differentiation of spheres, with their concomitant specialised culture, opens the way to the production of knowledge, criticism and communication. Moreover, this normative content of modernity effectively becomes part of the life-world, entering institutions and helping to shape different practices. Specialised knowledge, Habermas concludes, must always remain sensitive to the 'highly ambivalent' content of cultural modernity (Habermas, 1990, p. 338).

The value of Habermas' defence of the modernity project lies in its grasp of the historical and cultural specifics of modernity, grounding it in a theory of historical change. But as we have seen, it is precisely this argument on the progressive rationalisation of western society which has promoted the suspicion and criticism of postmodern theory. For Habermas modern sociological theory represents the renewal of the unfulfilled potential of 'the Enlightenment project'. The 'signature' of modernity lies in purposive activity and 'a concept of a communicative reason ingrained in the use of language oriented to reaching understanding'. Habermas' concept of modernity is based on the 'uncoupling' of a progressively rationalised life-world from the system domains of the economy and the state administration. The tension between life-world and system is both an index of potential crisis and emancipation (Habermas, 1989, pp. 303–6). But as was argued earlier in this book, Habermas' concept of system is as closed as that proposed by Parsonian functionalism, action being subordinated to the dehumanising logic of system imperatives. Communicative rationality fails to deal adequately with real historical agents, with open, unfinalised modes of dialogic interaction.

Habermas' theory of modernity stresses its sociological character: postmodernity he rejects for its reactionary philosophical basis in subjectivism, relativism and unreason. The concept of postmodernity is linked historically with the post-industrial thesis with its emphasis on the decline of industrial production, class structure and interests, rise of consumerism, technological modes of communication and differentiated status structure. Whereas modernity separated the cultural from the social sphere and led to a fundamental division between mass culture and critical, 'high' culture, postmodernity unifies popular/mass 'commodity' culture with the forms of modernist aesthetics. The subversive, critical principle at work within modernity is assimilated to a bland, pluralist culture which has neither centre nor structure.

11

New Directions in Sociological Thought

The Rise of New Social Movements

As I have argued in previous chapters, the rise of sociology was closely linked with the historical project of modernity, capitalist industrialisation, new national states and new social movements. During the course of the nineteenth century collectivist social movements based on both instrumental and substantive values developed: socialism, anarchism and the labour movement; liberal political and cultural movements institutionalised within the bourgeois public sphere and the practical concerns of communicating knowledge of economic and political life; and the first 'wave' of the feminist movement originating in the USA and Europe (especially Britain, France and Germany) with its demands for economic, political and sexual freedom. The 'suffrage movement', characteristic of British feminism at the end of the nineteenth and beginning of the twentieth century, exemplified the pluralism of modernity: in the movement, dominated intellectually by the Pankhurst family, Mrs Pankhurst stood for equal political rights including universal suffrage; one daughter, Sylvia, advanced economic liberation, equal opportunity and pay; while the other, Christabel, called for sexual revolution and freedom. The nationalism unleashed by the First World War, however, lessened the impact of both the women's and the workers' movements: extension of the suffrage in 1918 and 1928 and the rise of the Labour Party functioned to integrate these movements into modern British capitalism. The economic crises of the 1930s and the rise of European fascist and communist regimes, the Second World War followed by the ensuing Cold War and ideological conflict between the capitalist west and Soviet-style communism all had the effect of consolidating and stabilising post-1945 capitalist democracy and eroding the structural and ideological basis for the further development of broad social movements. Moreover, during the 1950s and 60s secondary and higher education expanded offering new occupational opportunities for women, while the post-war affluence generated a consumerist culture, developments which obscured the persistence of structural inequalities both between social classes and men and women.

235

Paradoxically, however, these were the forces responsible for the new critical voices raising questions about the direction and values of modern capitalism. When the French students occupied Paris University in 1968 their slogans of opposition to consumer capitalism and the centralised state looked back to older social movements which had also demanded economic and sexual liberation. In America the anti-Vietnam War and the Civil Rights movements led to a resurgence of radicalisation, and the slogan of 'liberation' became one of the key words of the 1960s and early 1970s. With orthodox Marxism no longer commanding a broad intellectual constituency, liberation meant freedom in racial, sexual and *political* issues. The title of one radical symposium, *The Dialectics of Liberation* (1970), sums up this new mood of challenges to traditional orthodox ideas and theory. There was no one dominant theory and the various movements were deeply sceptical of totalising ideas and reductionist concepts stressing the importance of local, 'micro' struggles around such issues as sexuality and ethnicity, questions of identity and decentralising forms of power. Both the American 'liberal' and the European movements shared in this sense that the old categories of social analysis were now redundant. Marxism and functionalism, for example, were rejected for their tendency to assimilate micrological practices and the concepts of ethnic and sexual identity to totalising categories such as class and system prerequisites. The new social movements based around the issues of race, sex, gender, ecology and peace proclaimed the principle of autonomy, practices independent of old-style class politics. Moreover, these movements were in many ways the structural, institutional basis for the politics and sociology of *difference*. The subjugated and the marginal, those whose voices had been drowned by the dominant discourses or simply forgotten, were rehabilitated sociologically and historically to engage in a dialogue between the past, the present and the future.

The second wave of feminism, beginning in the late 1960s, abandoned many of the received sociological and psychological categories, notably the idea of an 'essential' natural femaleness, or the binary opposition built into the norm of heterosexuality which defined the roles of men and women thus establishing clear-cut boundaries between them. Rather, the concept of gender was theorised as deeply problematic, the product of social, political, cultural and historical forces and human action: gender was never finished and complete but made and remade within specific social contexts. Second-wave feminism had its intellectual origins in the work of several feminist writers from Simone de Beauvoir (*The Second Sex*, 1949), Betty Friedan (*The Feminine Mystique*, 1963) and Kate Millet (*Sexual Politics*, 1968) all echoing de Beauvoir's famous phrase that 'one is not born, but rather becomes, a woman'. It was modern culture which promoted and reinforced various myths of women as wives and mothers.

Although there had been women sociologists before the rise of modern feminism (the British socialist, Beatrice Webb (1858–1943), the American, Jane Addams (1860–1935)) sociology had provided little of real substance and intellectual rigour in analysing issues of sexuality and gender. The work of Parsons and the Frankfurt School, for example, tended to reproduce the traditional dualisms of the binary division between men and women while research into homosexuals, another subordinate group, centred on homosexuals as outsiders and victims of discriminatory practices. Recent developments in the sociology of gender notably the emergence of 'queer theory' within sociology reflect the break up of the unitary concepts of sexual identity which had dominated the sociology of sexuality and the influence on social theory of new collective movements based on the substantive values of individual autonomy and complex and fluid identities.

Feminism and the Sociology of Gender

The history of the feminist movement has been neatly divided into three periods: liberal feminism (which largely accepted the existing social system attempting to integrate women on an equal basis with men into its public institutions); radical feminism (based around a critique of the social production of gender inequality centred on the family and its role in socialising women into a male-dominated culture and social order); and socialist feminism (based on a critique of the ways in which capitalism production generates a class-based society stratified in economic and political inequality).

One major point made by virtually all radical and socialist feminists is that, historically, sociology failed to engage with the problems of defining and analysing women's position in society other than through the categories of traditional sociological discourse such as domination, class, socialisation. Weber, for example, identified patriarchy as a variant on traditional forms of domination resting on male authority over the household and children with women dependent on men 'because of the normal superiority of the physical and intellectual energies of the male' (cited by Waters, 1994, p. 253). While Marx wrote little specifically on women Engels in his *The Origin of the Family, Private Property and the State* (1942 [1884]) argued that the basis of gender inequality between the sexes lay primarily in the capitalist exploitation of the working class by the bourgeoisie: the degradation of women under capitalism was the product of the capitalist division of labour with monogamous marriage enabling the ruling class to exercise domination over the population. Engels' functionalist explanation in terms of 'needs' of the capitalist system has been widely criticised for conflating economic and social reproduction within the family and for reducing patriarchy to the status of a mere epiphenomenon of capitalist social relations and mode of production. In her critique of Marxist theories of gender, Barrett (1993) suggests that situating women's subjugated status as 'functional for capital' reduces gender relations to an 'effect' of capital, a standpoint which fails to explain the wide variations in forms of male domination in different societies. Neither is it clear, she argues, 'why any relationship should obtain between specific forms of male dominance and, for instance the interests of capital, or at least this cannot be seen as self evident in any existing Marxist analysis' (Barrett, 1993, p. 24). This is a criticism which can be levelled at Althusser's functionalist Marxist and teleological formulation of the family as an ideological state apparatus socialising children into necessary roles in the capitalist division of labour and productive system, although Barrett, as is noted below, accepts Althusser's structuralist standpoint (Althusser, 1971).

A similarly functionalist explanation for women's social status is advanced by Parsons: increasing structural differentiation leads to different, although equal, sex roles within the family. Women's roles are 'expressive', bound up with the family and the affectual and emotional elements associated with social solidarity; men's roles are 'instrumental', concerned with external institutions and activities based around work, leadership, politics. For women it is socialisation and the childbearing processes which establishes 'a stronger presumptive primacy of the relations of mother to the small child and this in turn establishes a presumption that the man, who is exempted from these biological functions, should specialise in the alternative instrumental direction' (Parsons, 1955, p. 23). Parsons' distinction between expressive and instrumental roles assumes a binary division between men and women, fixed and unchanging socially and historically.

Gender differences are thus reproduced within the family and reinforced by women's occupational status, which for the most part is secondary to that of men. Parson's theory has been widely criticised by feminists who point to the external social organisation of work as largely determining patterns of gender inequality and the specialisation of sex roles. In contrast, symbolic interactionists, rejecting the Parsonian model, argued that sexual roles were socially constructed and not the product of internalised normative patterns. The interactionist standpoint clearly emphasised sexual identity as an ongoing accomplishment, a social process in which a reflexive self interacts with others and the social world. Goffman (1997b), for example, used the concept of *gender display* to explain how individuals within different encounters provide 'interactional portrayals, dramatic performances to convey feminine and masculine identities'. Gender display refers 'to conventionalised portrayals' of the 'culturally established correlates of sex', forms of ongoing activity embedded in everyday forms of interaction. This notion of gender as socially constructed through micro interaction is further reflected in Garfinkel's study of Agnes, a transsexual who identified herself as female even though she had a penis and was brought up as a male. Agnes, indeed, accepted the 'commonsense' idea that biological criteria distinguish men from women. Through her personal appearance (type of clothes worn, hair style, and so on) Agnes conveyed a normal female identity and Garfinkel points out that in the everyday world it is accepted that 'in the final analysis' there are either males or females (Garfinkel, 1984, p. 122).

Thus the binary division of men and women into distinct social roles is characteristic of both Marxist and Parsonian sociology as well as micro sociologies with their focus on the making of gender. Some feminist theorists argue that while sociology has explored the relation between males and females both holistically and micrologically, its contribution has been marginal for the development of a sociology of gender; the work of many leading sociologists such as Habermas, Bourdieu and Alexander has largely ignored the subtle ways that patriarchy and heterosexuality function as mechanisms of social identity and social control. It is this absence which has led some feminists to argue that sociology constitutes a male-dominated discourse. Dorothy Smith (1926–), widely regarded as a major contemporary feminist sociologist, has defined sociology as an ideological project which marginalises the concept of a 'gendered order' to sustain sociology's patriarchal nature:

> The profession of sociology has been predicated on a universe grounded in men's experience and relationships and still largely appropriated by men as their 'territory'. Sociology is part of the practice by which we are all governed; that practice establishes its relevance. (Smith, 1990, p. 1)

Sociology, she argues has neglected both women's experiences of everyday life and their position within the macro context of capitalist society. All social relations, she argues, are 'saturated' by gender and women's gender experience based around the family, household work and social reproduction. As a Marxist sociologist, Smith's basic concept, 'relations of ruling' focuses on both institutions which organise and regulate society, 'a complex of organised practices', including government, law, business and education as well as the 'discourses in texts' that further enhance capitalist power (Smith, 1987, p. 3). Patriarchy is thus the dominant organised structure of modern capitalism existing at both the institutional and the textual levels of discourse. Smith shares the interactionist emphasis on constructionism arguing that identity is produced through the use of records, documents and modes of classification which define the individual as sick, mentally ill, sexually deviant, and so on. In contrast with earlier feminist writers (for example as in Firestone's *The Dialectic of Sex*, 1974) who identified the family household and social reproduction as the fundamental basis of women's subordination, Smith provides a more rounded and comprehensive theory linking everyday experience and practices with broader issue of power. While she shares some of Foucault's concerns Smith does not conceive power as de-centred, for while there exist, 'multiple sites of power' it is always concentrated in specific institutions and practices which maintain capitalist social order.

Smith's focus is on everyday life, a standpoint which other Marxist writers reject as a form of empiricism. Barrett, for example, identifies 'women's oppression' with 'the family household system' as 'an organising principle of the relations of production for the social formation as a whole' providing 'a uniquely effective mechanism for securing continuity over a period of time' (Barrett, op. cit., pp. 211–12). However, she argues that the concept of patriarchy is limited in its analytic usefulness: gender inequality is more the product of ideologies of the family which emphasise women's 'natural' essence, reinforced by education and socialisation. Gender inequality is not simply the product of women's 'experiences' but flows from ideology, a process hinging on the ways in which women and the family are 'represented' in the media and culture. Representations are gendered and ideological: the 'subject' is thus constituted through a process of ideological representation. In contrast, Walby (1990) advances a more institutionalised notion of patriarchy arguing for the co-existence of both patriarchal and capitalist modes of production. The patriarchal mode of production, however, is contingent on particular relations existing in other social spheres. She notes that while women were excluded from the nineteenth-century public sphere they now participate, although remaining subordinate to men. The public sphere is gendered through its patriarchal mode of production. And in the private spheres of the family a patriarchal mode of production also predominates. It is the interlocking of the public and private patriarchal modes of production which provides the clue to women's subordinate status, with patriarchy functioning to exclude women from specific occupations and careers forcing them into marriage, domestic life and childrearing.

These broad examples of feminist sociological thought illustrate the point that while radical and socialist feminism was largely issue-led, sociological thought about women must be theorised as rigorously as sociology in general. The private and public spheres, ideology, rules of relations are valuable concepts which focus on structure and process. Smith, for example, explores how distinct dimensions of reality such as the textual (including those specialists who produce the dossiers and records) and the everyday social world of social practices intersect with each other. Her point is that texts mediate power in subtle and hidden modes: the act of completing a social security form, tax return, and so on links the individual obliquely with the power of the state. As society becomes more complex so there occurs an explosion of administrative knowledge geared to formal non-substantive rationality. Through the discourses and practices within everyday life the dominant class sustains gender and class inequalities.

Smith's model, however, is problematic on a number of points. Her assumption is that all women experience the same effects of power relations in everyday life. But everyday life is highly structured in hierarchies of status and social relations: for everyday life covers both that of decision makers and supermarket checkout clerks. Social class and position within a field play crucial roles in enabling actors both to make sense of the discourses encountered and to respond to them. Hierarchically structured interaction forms the basis of identity, an aspect missing from Smith's analysis. The model tends to collapse the different experiences of women within different hierarchical structures, such as women in the media, in business, education, and so on to one homogenous effect. Moreover, it is not at all clear why is only women who experience these discourses 'negatively': men also fill in forms and applications administered by the state. Relations of ruling constitutes a valuable conceptual tool but not if used to privilege women's experience generally. As Layder has pointed out, the real problem is that Smith begins analysis exclusively from the micro level extending analysis to the macro level but lacking concepts which link the two and

> somewhat ironically, despite this starting point... has little to say about interaction as such; she is more interested in the consciousness and experience from the standpoint of women. (Layder, 1994, p. 163)

To begin sociological analysis, however, from the standpoint of 'subject' as actor and 'knower' minimises the important constituting role the macro context and macro institutions play in shaping social consciousness for both men and women. Smith's work reproduces the same theoretical problems encountered with Goffman's concept of the interaction order, a failure to develop concepts which bring together different social realms. A feminist sociology can generate specific concepts for analysing gender and prising open areas traditional sociology has ignored: but such concepts apply both to men and women as well as to changes occurring within the family and marriage and to developing ideologies of sexuality and love. A dialogic relation subsists between the sexes and sociology must be sensitive to the nuances of meaning and action within it.

Queer Theory: Sexuality and Identity

Characteristic of sociological approaches to feminism has been a tendency to situate women's social position within the existing structures of patriarchy and gender relations and to accept a binary division between the sexes. In recent years the postmodern challenge to conventional sociology has made significant impact on the sociology of gender and the concept of identity. Basing many of their ideas on the post-structuralist critiques of the subject postmodern feminists reject the notion of a stable, unified and *centred* self: gender identity is defined as fluid, ambiguous, multiple, *de-centred*. Earlier feminist analyses such as Chodorow's work on the sociology of mothering (1979) are now regarded as underpinning strategies designed to reinforce the existing social hierarchies. Fraser and Nicholson (1993), for example, advocate a postmodern critique of the concept of common gender identity and trans-historical theories of gender. They are especially critical of Chodorow's reworking of the Parsonian model of socialised sex roles. In *The Reproduction of Mothering* (1979) both Parsons and the Frankfurt School are noted as contributing to the analysis and understanding of social reproduction across generations, the role of the family and 'especially the organisation of parenting'. The Frankfurt School focused on the decline of family authority in modern mass society while Parsons analysed the development of personalities which stabilise the larger social structure. Although critical of Parsons' 'conservative bias', Chodorow argues that the pattern variables help to explain the different roles played by men and women. Women's 'first association is within the family' which Chodorow defines as 'a relational institution' involving emotional and psychological responsibilities, 'relational capacities and needs', inter-personal relations intrinsic to the domestic sphere (Chodorow, 1979, p. 38). Women are defined primarily through particularistic relations 'concern with affective goals and ties, and a diffuse unbounded quality' as wives and mothers while 'masculine occupational roles and men's primary definition in the sphere of production are universalistically defined... and are less likely to involve affective considerations'. She concludes:

> The production of feminine personalities oriented toward relational issues and masculine personalities defined in terms of categorial ties and the repression of relation fits these roles and contributes to their reproduction. (ibid., p. 180)

Fraser and Nicholson argue that while 'mothering' differs across cultures, Chodorow's concept assumes a universal self constituted in early childhood through its relations with parents, a process which cuts across race and class lines. But as they point out:

> The idea of a cross-cultural, deep sense of self, specified differently for women and men, becomes problematic when given any specific content. Chodorow states that women everywhere differ from men in their greater concern with 'relational interaction.' But what does she mean by this term? Certainly not any and every kind of human interactions, for example, those which have to do with the aggrandizement of power and wealth. (Fraser and Nicholson, 1993. p. 425)

Chodorow has adopted an essentialist standpoint: concepts such as sexuality, mothering, reproduction vary widely across and within societies and cultures. The task of a postmodern feminist theory is to deal not with the universal but with diversity, abandoning 'grand narratives' of gender and sexuality. In her influential *Gender Trouble* (1990) Judith Butler argues that feminism has tended to reinforce the binary gender order it criticises by accepting the concept of a coherent gender identity. Drawing on post-structuralism and psychoanalysis, she argues that this dualism results from uncritically adopting the norms of heterosexuality on which the binary order depends. While all feminists accept that gender is social not natural, many have embraced the concept of core identity. Thus while de Beauvoir saw gender as socially constructed 'there is nothing in her account that guarantees that the "one" who becomes a woman is necessarily female (Butler, 1990, p. 8). No society or set of norms produces this essentialist notion of identity. The insistence on a coherent and unified category of woman effectively ignores 'the multiplicity of cultural, social, and political intersections in which the concrete "array" of women are constructed' (ibid., p. 14). Rather, gender identity arises out of *performance*. The task is one of subverting constructions of gender identity, to reveal the social and imitative nature of gender itself thus denaturalising the body and sex.

Butler's argument is close to Bakhtin's ideas on the subversive role of dialogism for undermining all fixed notions of self and other: within hetero-sexual, bi-sexual, gay and lesbian contexts 'gender does not necessarily follow from sex, and desire, or sexuality generally'. Through acts, gestures and desire an illusion is created of 'an interior and organising gender core, an illusion maintained for the purpose of the regulation of sexuality within the obligatory frame of reproductive heterosexuality'. Butler points to the parodies of 'primary gender identity' within 'the cultural practices of drag, cross-dressing, and the sexual stylisation of butch/femme identities'. Thus, while drag may create a unified picture of a 'woman', 'in imitating gender, drag implicitly reveals the imitative structure of gender itself – as well as its contin-gency'. Gender, in other words, is 'a construction that regularly conceals its genesis' (ibid., pp. 135–40).

Butler's performative approach highlights the complex, many-sided prac-tices which go into the 'making' of gender (and simultaneously its unmaking) but it does present problems of contextualising such activities within social institutions. The concept of identity as subversive assumes a high level of reflexivity not shared by everyone. A reflexive self, moreover, can perform only within institutions and a knowledge of sexual practices. Giddens (1993) points out that modern society is characterised by 'high reflexivity' and a more 'open' notion of self-identity generated by 'institu-tional reflexivity.' Knowledge about how society works constantly enters everyday life through, for example, the media. Public debates on the nature of sexuality and health contribute to 'an accelerated reflexivity on the level of orderly, everyday practices'. The modern self becomes a 'reflexive project' (pp. 28–30). Giddens points to the concept of the self as an autonomous 'accomplishment'. Much of the current theorising on homosexuality, for example, reflects this new approach. Thus early sociological studies of homosexuality (labelling theory and the sociology of deviance) focused on the 'homosexual role' to the detriment of the complex ways in which homo-sexuality reproduced itself through discourses. One of the first studies of homosexuality (McIntosh, 1996 [1968]) advocated analysing homosexuality as a social, not medical, category, as a social process, thus enabling the soci-ologist to raise questions concerning the organisation and function of various homosexual groups. It was not a question of the 'homosexual condition' but rather of the social role played by the homosexual. In contrast to this functionalist standpoint, which defines the role as reinforcing ideas of the 'normal' from 'threatening' sexual practices, Weeks (1977) argued for a social constructionist perspective in which the homosexual developed a unique identity and homosexuality generated its own history and meanings.

Plummer (1981), working within an interactionist framework, argued that homosexuality constituted a process 'emerging through interactive encounters (part of which will include a potentially hostile reaction) in an intersubjective world'. Homosexuality was not a fixed condition but rather part of 'an ongoing accomplishment'. The emphasis here is on the making of gender identity placing it historically and contextually; one is not born a homosexual but becomes one. Plummer focused on the micrological contexts in which individuals learn about sexual desire and 'come out' to acquire and affirm a homosexual identity.

As with post-structuralism the interactionist approach to the analysis of homosexuality abandons the idea of a core coherent identity and fixed meanings; interaction emphasised multiple, created identities and fluid meanings. However, the interactionist concept of multiple identity (analysed by Goffman for example) tended to accept the binary division of the sexes although emphasising the making of gender identity. Butler's concept of gender as performance draws attention to the fragile notion of gender boundaries, and queer theory similarly subverts all constituted categories which leaves a centred identity intact. Butler describes heterosexuality as an act of 'elaborating itself because it is perpetually at risk, that it knows its possibilities of being undone' (ibid., p. 23). The development of queer theory builds on this concept of multiple, shifting sexual identities in which culture and discourse play key roles.

Equally influential in developing a 'queer sociology' was Foucault's broad historical work: the categories of heterosexuality, homosexuality and other sexual types defined as products of power and knowledge and the ways a proliferation of discourses on sex produced the category of the homosexual. Foucault's point was that while homosexual practices have always existed the category of homosexual has not; the development of discourses about homosexuality, inversion, pederasty were linked with law and psychiatry, making possible the 'reverse discourse' in which the homosexual found his own voice using the same vocabulary and categories 'by which he was medically disqualified' (Foucault, 1980, p. 101). Both Foucault and Butler, however, ignore the impact on sexuality of wider social forces which shape sexual identity, especially the interaction process and the internalisation of culture and values. These omissions point to serious problems with queer theory as sociology. While sociological feminism succeeded in developing concepts which could be incorporated into sociological knowledge and theory, queer theory has generated no new concepts other than those derived from post-structuralism, philosophy and literary theory and postmodernism. It is therefore surprising to find one sociologist arguing:

In practice sociologists have tended to relegate the study of 'sexual minorities' to the analytical sidelines rather than treating such study as a window onto a larger world of power, meaning and social organisation. The challenge that queer theory poses to sociological investigation is precisely in the strong claim that no facet of social life is fully comprehensible without an examination of how sexual meanings intersect with it. (Seidman, 1998, p. 156)

Ultimately the question remains that although opening up discussion and posing questions, queer theory has failed to translate its concerns and concepts into sociology. As with feminism it must analyse the role played by race, class and gender, beliefs and values in shaping identity the ways in which these elements interact within different contexts and historical time. Having formed itself in the 1980s, with roots in sociology, feminist theory and post-structuralism, queer theory has yet to enter the mainstream of sociological knowledge.

Conclusion: Sociology and the Modern World

At the beginning of the twentieth century classical sociologists had defined their object of study as the transition from premodernity to modernity, society as the nation state based on industrial production, a national division of labour and a strong centralised state,. Cultural identity was non-problematic based on a national culture, a common language and national educational system. Society was defined in terms of specific borders and boundaries.

In recent years sociological perspectives defining society as a bounded system, a whole, have given way to a range of postmodern theorising based around theories of globalisation and the development of a new world society connected through electronic media and transnational economic and cultural forces. Castells (1997) and Giddens (1991) identify the emergence of a new global society in which economic, political and cultural institutions are lifted above the boundaries of the national state and national culture. Social change is characterised by a greater dynamism and speed than ever before. Castells calls globalisation 'the network society' built around new technology and forms of information such as the internet which shape and fragment individual lives. The process of globalisation means that everyday life is increasingly affected by the impact of external contexts and events occurring on the other side of the world. Globalisation constitutes a movement away from the classical concept of society to one defined across distance and time scale. Space is crossed quickly, in a wink, by fax and email: space is annihilated through time.

Globalisation, postmodernity and multiple identities suggest a new kind of de-centred society, pluralistic, a hybrid culture of multiple surfaces, depthlessness, a rejection of meta-narratives and a movement from a bi-polar to a polycentric world which erodes the immediacy and intimacy of face-to-face interaction. Yet does all this suggest a new transformation of society, new experiences? The impact of globalisation on sociological knowledge, however, remains deeply ambivalent. Throughout this book I have suggested that the era of modernity was one characterised by the struggles of marginal, opposition and suppressed groups and classes against the dominant voices of centralised power. Identity was shaped by both large- and small-scale institutions and practices, not simply by discourses but by structures. It is understanding this struggle between the centred and de-centred processes which constitutes the challenge of sociology in the twenty-first century. Obscuranist notions of de-centred identities and discourses with no foundation in historical and social contexts will not do.

To conclude:

In July 1999 the French President, Jacques Chirac, rejected a request from his socialist prime minister to give limited official recognition to France's seven regional languages: the language of the Republic, he stated, is French (*Observer*, 4 July 1999). Stuart Hall has neatly summed up the problem:

Since cultural diversity is, increasingly, the fate of the modern world, and ethnic absolutism a regressive feature of late-modernity, the greatest danger now arises from forms of national and cultural identity... which attempt to secure their identity by adopting closed versions of culture and community and by a refusal to engage... with the difficult problems that arise from trying to live with difference. The capacity *to live with difference is... the coming question of the twenty first century.* (Hall, 1993)

Further Reading

1 *Modernity, Industrialisation and the Rise of Sociology*

One of the most thorough works on the history of sociology (Szacki, 1979) traces the development of sociological thought from its intellectual origins in the philosophy of Plato and Aristotle, Renaissance thought and Vico, to modern social theorists such as Mead, Mannheim, Parsons. Nisbet (1967), Hawthorn (1976) offer general histories and idiosyncratic interpretations, while Aron (1965, 1968) examines the major sociological figures from Montesquieu to Weber. Coser (1971) is especially valuable for relating sociological theory to social context and biography and Seidman (1998) provides a valuable critical overview of the state of sociology at the end of the twentieth century.

Shils (1980) offers a wide-ranging interpretation of the main traditions in sociology while a valuable collection of essays on the history of sociology is Bottomore and Nisbet (1979).

The most comprehensive study of Enlightenment philosophy and its relation with social thought and early sociologists such as Montesquieu and Ferguson is Gay (1967, 1970).

Vico's major work has been translated into English (Vico, 1948). A good discussion is Berlin (1976) while Montesquieu (1949) includes a penetrating introduction by F. Neumann.

A general overview of the Scottish Enlightenment is Chitnis (1977) while Swingewood (1970) and Therborn (1976) analyse the specifically sociological aspects. Ferguson's essay has been republished (1966) while Millar's *Origin and Distinction of Ranks* is included in Lehmann (1960). For good discussion of Ferguson's contribution to sociology see Kettler (1965), while a useful collection of writings, including Ferguson, Kames, Robertson, Millar, is Schneider (1967).

Useful histories of positivism include Simon (1963), Giddens (1977, Ch. 1), Halfpenny (1982). The relation of the French Revolution to the development of sociology is discussed by Nisbet (1967) and Gouldner (1971). A critique of Nisbet's thesis identifying sociology with conservative thought is advanced by Giddens (1977, Ch. 6).

Saint-Simon's writings relating to social theory have been translated in two collections (Taylor, 1975; Ionescu, 1976). Saint-Simon's importance to both nineteenth-century sociology and socialism is examined by Durkheim (1958) and his relation with the Enlightenment by Manuel (1962). Hayek (1955) has interpreted the works of Saint-Simon and Comte as laying the foundations for modern totalitarianism and methodological collectivism, while Bell (1976) explores the sources of the concept of industrial society in relation to Saint-Simon.

Comte's work was translated into English during the nineteenth century (Comte, 1877, 1896). His early essays have also been republished (Fletcher, 1974). Two useful selections of Comte's sociological and philosophical writings are Andreski (1978) and Thompson (1976). Marcuse (1954) develops a critical Marxist perspective of Comte's sociology. J. S. Mill's study is still worth reading (Mill, 1961). A short, lucid account of Comte's relation with nineteenth-century statistics and social surveys is Halfpenny (1982). For a recent re-evaluation of Comte's sociology, see Pickering (1993).

Mill's *System of Logic* is widely available: a good, recent edition is edited by Fletcher (Mill, 1976).

The most succinct introduction to Spencer's voluminous works is the popular *Study of Sociology* (Spencer, 1965). Spencer's opposition to collectivism, his advocacy of the organismic analogy in social science is best approached through the essays (Spencer, 1969a). Selections from Spencer's works include Carneiro (1967), Andreski (1971), Peel (1972). The most thorough discussion of Spencer's work which places it within the context of English non-conformity is Peel (1971). A recent discussion is Haines (1997) and the wider debate on evolutionism is examined by Burrow (1966) and critically evaluated by Hirst (1976).

2 *Marxism: A Critical Science of Capital Development*

Marx and Engels's collected works are currently being published (Marx and Engels, 1975) but there is a useful two-volume edition which includes many of their most important writings including *The Communist Manifesto, The Civil War in France, The Eighteenth Brumaire of Louis Bonaparte* (Marx and Engels, 1962). The Penguin editions of *Capital* (Marx, 1976–80), *Grundrisse* (Marx, 1973) and the political writings (Marx, 1974–6) are highly recommended.

Selections from Marx's and Engels's writings include Bottomore (1964) for the early works, Bottomore and Rubel (1961), McLellan (1980a).

The most exhaustive and stimulating study of Marxism is Kolakowski (1981) while a more sympathetic series of essays is McLellan (1983). One of the best defences of the Hegelian, humanist Marx is Avineri (1968). Cohen (1978) rejects the humanist core of Marxism arguing that concepts such as mode of production, rather than alienation, are more central to Marx's scientific project. He emphasises the role of technology in social development minimising the role of ideas and the subject. Other anti-humanist interpretations include Althusser (1969, 1971), Hindess and Hirst (1975). These works should be read in conjunction with Rosdolsky (1977) which contains a thorough analysis of the *Grundrisse* and its relation with the early and later works. Marx's writings on domination are contained in Marx and Engels (1962, 1971). For Marx's early writing on the state and his critique of Hegel see Bottomore (1964). Marx's comments on Bakunin's *Statism and Anarchy* are included in the Penguin edition of his *Political Writings* (Marx, 1974–6).

For Marx's relation with sociology see Gouldner (1980), Bottomore and Nisbet (1979), Therborn (1976), Worsley (1982), Lockwood (1992) Craib (1997) and Postane (1997).

3 *Critique of Positivism I: Durkheim*

The general social and intellectual background to the development of Durkheim's sociology is examined by Clark (1973) and Lukes (1973). Wolff (1964) includes a number of essays dealing with the social and political context that shaped Durkheim's sociology.

Durkheim's most important works have all been translated into English. There is a new edition of *The Rules of Sociological Method* (Durkheim, 1982) which includes some of Durkheim's articles relating to methodology and sociological theory. Other works include the study of suicide (Durkheim, 1952), studies in philosophy and social theory (Durkheim, 1953, 1964, 1965), the study of economic organisation (Durkheim, 1964, new translation 1984), professions (Durkheim, 1957), religion (Durkheim, 1961), precursors of sociology (Durkheim, 1958, 1965).

Selections from Durkheim's work include Giddens (1972b), Bellah (1973), Traugott (1978) and Thompson (1985).

The most thorough analysis of Durkheim's relation with nineteenth-century positivism remains Parsons (1961a). Other valuable discussions include Coser (1971), Giddens (1971), Aron (1968), Lockwood (1992), Lehmann (1993) and Craib (1997). The relation of Durkheim's theory of society to contemporary science has been discussed by Hirst (1975), to contemporary French Marxism by Llobera (1981) and his theory of politics analysed perceptively by Giddens (1977).

Douglas (1967) has advanced a phenomenological critique of Durkheim's use of official French suicide statistics. This argument should be read in conjunction with Pope (1978) and Taylor (1982).

4 *Critique of Positivism II: Social Action*

For a good, general survey of the *Verstehen* tradition in social theory see Rickman (1967) and the stimulating historical and critical account of the reaction to positivism in late nineteenth-century and early twentieth-century social thought by Hughes (1959). Outhwaite (1975) is short, lucid and critical.

Dilthey (1976) is a useful selection and an important essay is included in Gardiner (1959). Rickert's major work is available (1962). For German sociology see Aron (1964).

Many of Simmel's works are now available in English translation: the early study of history (Simmel, 1977), studies in interpretative sociology (Simmel, 1980), conflict (Simmel, 1956), the role of money in the development of culture (Simmel, 1978), the theory of modern culture (Simmel, 1957) as well as selections from his essays (Wolff, 1950, 1965). Recent discussions of Simmel's importance for modern sociology include Featherstone (1997), Craib (1997). Durkheim's assessment is reprinted in Coser (1965).

Weber's major works are all available in English translation: on interpretative sociology (Weber, 1968), the methodological essays (Weber, 1949, 1975, 1977), the specialised histories (Weber, 1923, 1976), the studies of religion (Weber, 1968, 1951, 1952, 1958a). Useful selections from his work include Runciman (1978), Gerth and Mills (1948). General discussions of his work include Bendix (1963), Giddens (1971), Wrong (1970), Parkin (1982), Albrow (1990), Craib (1997), Callinocos (1999).

The critical literature on the Protestant ethic is enormous but a good, recent survey is Marshall (1982). A negative argument is advanced by Samuelson (1961).

Weber's writings on class and domination are widely available: Weber (1968) consists of three volumes which includes the important essay, 'Parliament and Government in a Reconstructed Germany'. The essays on 'Socialism' and 'Politics as a Vocation' are in Gerth and Mills (1948).

Weber's politics and concept of domination are ably discussed by Mommsen (1974), Beetham (1974), Giddens (1972a). A Marxist critique is presented by Therborn (1976). Weber's relation with Marxism has been widely discussed but see especially Lowith (1982), Aron (1968), Giddens (1971, 1977), Craib (1997) Seidman (1998).

Pareto's major work has been translated into English in four volumes (Pareto, 1963).

5 *Marxism and Sociology*

A lucid, critical account of the development of Marxism after Marx is offered by McLellan (1983). Kolakowski (1981) Volume 1 is indispensable. Anderson (1976) is a short, idiosyncratic account.

Bernstein (1963) is the main text for the revisionist debate. Sorel's major theoretical writings are available in English translation (Sorel, 1950, 1969). There is a good selection of his essays on Marxism and the revisionist debate (Sorel, 1976). Labriola's essays have been translated (1967, 1980) and there is a good discussion in Kolakowski (1981) Volume 2, Ch. VIII.

Many of Gramsci's writings have now been translated into English and published in three volumes (Gramsci, 1971, 1977, 1978). The important critique of Bukharin and sociology is in 1971, while the essay on the Southern Question, in which the first formulation of hegemony is advanced, is in 1978.

Lukács' early political writings, including the critique of Bukharin, are available (Lukács, 1972) as well as the difficult essays on dialectics and history (Lukács, 1971). For Lukács' relation with sociology, see Gouldner (1973), while Kilminster (1979) discusses the relation of Gramsci, Lukács and the Frankfurt School to Marx's social thought.

There is a useful selection of writings of the Austro-Marxists (Bottomore and Goode, 1978) and Hilferding's major work is now available in translation (Hilferding, 1980). There is a short, lucid account of the relation between Marxism and sociology, with reference to Lukács, Gramsci and the Austro-Marxists in Bottomore (1975).

For the Frankfurt School see the accounts in Jay (1973, 1988), Kellner (1988), Slater (1977), Held (1980). The most thorough account is Wiggershaus (1994). A good selection of essays is Connerton (1976) and Bonner and Kellner (1989). Bronner (1996) reviews the contributions of the major Frankfurt School theorists and assesses their relevance for modern social theory. The critique of positivism is developed in Horkheimer (1972, 1976). A negative assessment is advanced by Shils (1972).

6 *Functionalism*

Functionalist anthropological formulations are represented by Malinowski (1922) and Radcliffe-Brown (1952) while Merton (1957) advances a sociological approach. Gouldner (1973) includes the indispensable essay on reciprocity and autonomy in functionalist theory. Other useful discussions include Mulkay (1975), Rex (1961), Strasser (1976), Alexander (1998).

Parsons' writings are widely available: the difficult study of the social system (1951) is in sharp contrast to the more readable and stimulating essays (Parsons, 1954, 1961b, 1964, 1967). The key article on pattern variables, first published in 1960, is included in Parsons (1967) while a succinct theoretical view of the social system is in Parsons (1961b). Difficult texts which seek to reconcile action with systems theory include Parsons and Shils (1962) and Parsons and Smelser (1956). Parsons (1955) discusses the relation of the nuclear family to industrialism.

During the 1960s Parsons developed an evolutionary perspective: an early statement on 'evolutionary universals' is reprinted in Parsons (1967) and further argument is in Parsons (1966, 1971a). One of his last statements sums up his attempt to develop a systematic and voluntarist social theory (Parsons, 1981).

Critical discussions of Parsons' work include Black (1961), Gouldner (1971) Part Two, Menzies (1977), Mills (1959), Rocher (1974), Bourricaud (1981), Mouzelis (1995) and Scott (1995).

A valuable collection of essays which discuss functionalism and conflict is Demerath and Peterson (1967). Coser (1956, 1967) attempts to synthesise conflict sociology with functionalism, while Lockwood (1964) distinguishes system from social integration in a difficult but rewarding essay.

A classic statement by Aberle *et al.* on the functionalist theory of stratification is reprinted in Demerath and Peterson (1967). Davis's early statement is still available (Davis, 1949). The whole debate is critically discussed by Wrong (1976) and Tumin (1968).

7 *Self and Society: Sociological Interactionism*

The major statement of action theory is Parsons (1961a): a shorter statement is Parsons (1961d). A more general view is Parsons (1978). For Parsons' attempt to integrate psychology into action theory see his essay on Freud (Parsons, 1971b) and the essays on psychological and social structure (Parsons, 1964). Useful discussion of Parsons' theory of personality includes Rocher (1974).

Cooley's writings are an important source of social interactionism (Cooley, 1902, 1956) and are ably discussed by Coser (1971). The major study of the Polish peasant contains much of value for sociological theory (Thomas and Znaneicki, 1927). Mead's works are widely available (Mead, 1934, 1936, 1938) and a useful selection from them is Mead (1964) which includes an essay on Cooley.

Recent discussions include Rock (1979), Joas (1993) and Collins (1994). Gouldner (1973) Ch. 11 argues that Chicago sociology was largely romantic, intuitive, anti-rationalist. Blumer (1981) is a succinct summary.

A good selection of Goffman's writings is available (1997a, b, c) while his importance for modern sociology is ably discussed by Collins (1994), Giddens (1984) and Layder (1994).

Schutz's major work is available in English (Schutz, 1972). There are three volumes of essays (Schutz, 1962–6) and two studies of the life-world and meaning structures (Schutz, 1974, 1982). For ethnomethodology, see Garfinkel (1984), Heritage (1984), Giddens (1976), Sharrock and Anderson (1986).

8 *Structuralism and Post-structuralism*

Saussure's lectures are widely available (Saussure, 1974). A good account of his work and its importance for social theory is Scott (1995) and Seidman (1998).

There are English translations of the most significant early structuralist works: Propp (1968), Bakhtin (1968, 1973).

Goldmann's approach to structuralism is best approached through his early study of methodology, and theory (Goldmann, 1969) and his substantive study of Racine and Pascal (Goldmann, 1964).

For Althusser see especially his early essays on Marx (Althusser, 1969), the painstaking reading of *Capital* (Althusser, 1970) and the essays on ideology and state apparatuses (Althusser, 1971, 1972, 1976). The most extensive critique of Althusserianism is Thompson (1978) and other analyses include Kolakowski (1981) Vol. 3. Other structuralist works which examine class structure include Poulantzas (1973, 1975), Hindess and Hirst (1975).

A good selection of Foucault's writings is Rabinow (1986) while the selected essays and interviews introduce his main ideas and theory (Foucault 1980). For Foucault's significance for modern sociology see Layder (1994) and Seidman (1998).

9 *Sociological Thought and the Problems of Agency and Structure*

Habermas' writings are widely available in English translation: they include philosophical and theoretical studies (Habermas, 1971), studies in the theory of the modern state and public sphere (Habermas, 1976, 1992), studies in language, communication and historical materialism (Habermas, 1984, 1989). Excellent introductions to Habermas' thought include Held (1980) and Outhwaite (1994) There is a volume of essays discussing all the aspects of Habermas' thought (Thompson and Held, 1982).

Giddens (1984) is the most lucid statement on structuration theory. Scott (1995) Mouzelis (1991, 1995), and Layder (1994) offer lucid and critical appraisals.

The most accessible of Bourdieu's works is Bourdieu and Wacquant (1992), a collection of interviews and statements on the basic concepts and methodology. Good critical accounts include Alexander (1995) and Fowler (1997).

10 *Postmodernity and Sociological Theory*

Excellent accounts of the origins of postmodernism include Rose (1991) and Kumar (1995). Bertens (1995) provides lucid and critical analyses of the major figures and debates in contemporary postmodern thought while Harvey (1989) examines the relation of postmodernism with culture and social theory. Habermas (1990) defends the Enlightenment project through an extensive critique of the main figures in the debate; his contribution is analysed by Outhwaite (1994).

The theory of post-industrial society is developed by Bell (1976) in relation to economic and political structures, technology and science. Bell's book contains a valuable analysis of the concept of industrial society as it emerged in the work of Saint-Simon, Marx, Weber and Sombart. The discussion of culture in post-industrial and industrial society is developed in a later, stimulating volume (Bell, 1979). For criticism see Kumar (1978) which includes an excellent bibliography. Other studies of post-industrial society include Touraine (1971) and Dahrendorf (1959).

11 *New Directions in Sociological Thought*

Good accounts of contemporary debates in feminism and the sociology of gender include Walby (1990, 1997), Barrett (1993), Waters (1994), Seidman (1998).

Dorothy Smith's work is ably discussed by Seidman (1998) and Layder (1994).

Queer theory is placed within a sociological and historical framework by Seidman (1996, 1998), Plummer (1992) and more generally by Fuss (1991).

Bibliography

Adorno T. W. (1967) *Prisms*, (London: Spearman).

Adorno T. W. (1989) 'Society', in Bonner S.E. and Kellner D (eds) (1989).

Adorno T. W. and Horkheimer M. (1973 [1944]) *Dialectic of Enlightenment* (London: Allen Lane).

Albrow M. (1990) *Max Weber and the Construction of Social Theory* (London: Macmillan).

Alexander J. (1995*) Fin de Siècle Social Theory* (London: Verso).

Alexander J. (1998*) Neo-Functionalism and After* (Oxford: Blackwell).

Althusser L. (1969) *For Marx* (London: Allen Lane).

Althusser L. (1970*) Reading Capital* (with E. Balibar) (London: New Left Books).

Althusser L. (1971) *Lenin and Philosophy* (London: New Left Books).

Althusser L. (1972) *Politics and History* (London: New Left Books).

Althusser L. (1976) *Essays in Self-Criticism* (London: New Left Books).

Anderson P. (1976) *Considerations on Western Marxism* (London: New Left Books).

Andreski S. (ed.) (1971*) Herbert Spencer: Structure, Function and Evolution* (London: Nelson).

Andreski S. (ed.) (1978) *The Essential Comte* (London: Croom Helm).

Aron R. (1964) *German Sociology* (New York: Free Press).

Aron R. (1965, 1968) *Main Currents in Sociological Thought*, 2 Vols (London: Weidenfeld & Nicolson).

Avineri S. (1968) *The Social and Political Thought of Karl Marx* (Cambridge: Cambridge University Press).

Bakhtin M. M. (1968) *Rabelais and His World* (London: MIT Press).

Bakhtin M. M. (1973) *Marxism and the Philosophy of Language* (published under the name of V. Volosinov) (London: Academic Press).

Bakhtin M. M. (1986) *Speech Genres and Other Late Essays* (Austin: University of Texas Press).

Bales R. F. and Shils E. (eds) (1962) *Working Papers in the Theory of Action* (New York: Harper Torchbooks).

Barthes R. (1967) *Elements of Semiology* (London: Cape).

Barrett M. (1993) *Women's Oppression Today* (London: Verso).

Baudelaire C. (1972) *Selected Writings* (Harmondsworth: Penguin).

Baudrillard J. (1983) *Simulations* (New York: Semiotext).

Baudrillard J. (1993) 'The evil demon of images and the precession of Simulcra' in Docherty T. (ed.) (1994).

Baudrillard J. (1994) 'The masses: the implosion of the social in the media ' in *The Polity Reader in Cultural Theory*.

Barthes R. (1973) *Mythologies* (London: Paladin Books).

Bauman Z. (1992) *Intimations of Postmodernity* (London: Routledge).

Beetham D. (1974) *Max Weber and the Theory of Modern Politics* (London: Allen & Unwin).

Beck U. (1992) *Risk Society* (London: Sage).

Bell D. (1976) *The Coming of Post-Industrial Society* (Harmondsworth: Penguin).

Bell D. (1979) *The Cultural Contradictions of Capitalism* (London: Heinemann).

Bellah R. (ed.) (1973) *Emile Durkheim on Morality and Society* (Chicago: University of Chicago Press).

Bendix R. (1963) *Max Weber: An Intellectual Portrait* (London: Heinemann).

Bendix R. and Roth G. (eds) (1971) *Scholarship and Partisanship: Essays on Max Weber* (Los Angeles: University of California Press).

Benton T. (1977) *Philosophical Foundations of the Three Sociologies* (London: Routledge).

Berlin L. (1976) *Vico and Herder* (Oxford: Oxford University Press).

Bernstein E. (1963 [1899]) *Evolutionary Socialism* (New York: Schocken).

Bertens H. (1995) *The Idea of the Postmodern* (London: Routledge).

Black M. (ed.) (1961) *The Social Theories of Talcott Parsons* (New Jersey: Prentice Hall).

Blumer H. (1962) 'Society as symbolic interactionism' in Rose A. (ed.) *Human Behaviour and Social Process: An Interactionist Perspective* (Boston: Houghton-Mifflin).

Blumer H. (1969) *Symbolic Interactionism* (New Jersey: Prentice Hall).

Blumer H. (1981) 'George Herbert Mead' in Rhea B. (ed.) (1981).

Bonner S. E. and Kellner D. (eds) (1989) *Critical Theory and Society* (London: Routledge).

Bottomore T. B. (ed.) (1964) *Marx: Early Writings* (London: Watts).

Bottomore T. B. (1975) *Marxist Sociology* (London: Macmillan).

Bottomore T. B. (1984) *The Frankfurt School* (London: Routledge).

Bottomore T. B. and Goode P. (eds) (1978) *Austro-Marxism* (Oxford: Oxford University Press).

Bottomore T. B. and Nisbet R. (eds) (1979) *A History of Sociological Analysis* (London: Heinemann).

Bottomore T. B. and Rubel M. (eds) (1961) *Karl Marx: Selected Writings in Sociology and Social Philosophy* (Harmondsworth: Penguin).

Bourdieu P. (1990) *In Other Words* (Cambridge: Polity).

Bourdieu P. and Wacquant L. (1992) *An Invitation to Reflexive Sociology* (Cambridge: Polity).

Bourricaud F. (1981) *The Sociology of Talcott Parsons* (London: University of Chicago Press).

Bramson L. (1961) *The Political Context of Sociology* (Princeton: Princeton University Press).

Bronner S. E. (1996) *Of Critical Theory and its Theorists* (Oxford: Blackwell).

Buci-Glucksmann C. (1981) *Gramsci and the State* (London: Lawrence & Wishart).

Bukharin N. (1969 [1921]) *Historical Materialism* (Ann Arbor: University of Michigan Press).

Burrow J. A. V. (1966) *Evolution and Society* (Cambridge: Cambridge University Press).

Butler J. (1990) *Gender Trouble: Feminism and the Subversion of Identity* (London: Routledge).

Callinicos A. (1999) *Social Theory* (Cambridge: Polity).

Camic C. (ed.) (1997) *Reclaiming the Sociological Classics* (Oxford: Blackwell).

Carneiro R. L. (ed.) (1967) *Herbert Spencer: The Evolution of Society* (Chicago: University of Chicago Press).

Cassirer E. (1951) *The Philosophy of the Enlightenment* (Boston: Beacon).

Castells M. (1997) *The Information Age: Economy, Society and Culture* (Oxford: Blackwell).

Chitnis A. (1977) *The Scottish Enlightenment* (London: Croom Helm).

Chodorow N. (1979) *The Reproduction of Mothering* (Berkeley: University of California Press).

Clark T. N. (1973) *Prophets and Patrons: The French University and the Emergence of the Social Science* (Cambridge: Harvard University Press).

Cohen G. A. (1978) *Karl Marx's Theory of History: A Defence* (Oxford: Oxford University Press).

Collins R. (1994) *Four Sociological Traditions* (Oxford: Oxford University Press).

Comte A. (1877*) System of Positive Polity* (London: Longmans Green).

Comte A. (1896) *The Positive Philosophy* (London: Bell & Sons).

Connerton P. (ed.) (1976) *Critical Sociology* (Harmondsworth: Penguin).

Connerton P. (1980) *The Tragedy of Enlightenment: An Essay on the Frankfurt School* (Cambridge: Cambridge University Press).

Cooley C. H. (1902) *Human Nature and the Social Order* (New York: Charles Scribner).

Cooley C. H. (1956) *Social Organisation* (New York: Schocken).

Coser L. A. (1956) *The Functions of Social Conflict* (London: Routledge).

Coser L. A. (ed.) (1965) *George Simmel* (New Jersey: Prentice Hall).

Coser L. A. (1967) *Continuities in the Study of Social Conflict* (New York: Free Press).

Coser L. A. (1971) *Masters of Sociological Thought* (New York: Harcourt Brace Jovanovich).

Craib I. (1997) *Classical Social Theory* (Oxford: Oxford University Press).

Croce B. (1913) *Historical Materialism and the Economics of Karl Marx* (London: Howard Latimer).

Dahrendorf R. (1959) *Class and Class Conflict in Industrial Society* (London: Routledge).

Davis K. (1949) *Human Society* (London: Routledge & Kegan Paul).

Davis K. and Moore W. (1969) 'Some principles of stratification' in Heller, C. (ed.) *Structured Social Inequality* (London: Collier-Macmillan).

Demerath N. and Peterson R. (eds) (1967) *System, Change and Conflict* (New York: Free Press).

Derrida J. (1972) 'Structure, sign and play in the discourse of the human sciences' in Macksey R. and Donato E. (eds*) The Structuralist Controversy* (London: Johns Hopkins University Press).

Dilthey W. (1976) *Selected Writings* (Cambridge: Cambridge University Press).

Docherty T. (ed.) (1994) *Postmodernism: A Reader* (Oxford: Blackwell).

Douglas J. (1967) *The Social Meanings of Suicide* (Princeton: Princeton University Press).

Douglas J. (ed.) (1973) *Understanding Everyday Life* (London: Routledge).

Durkheim E. (1952 [1897]) *Suicide* (London: Routledge & Kegan Paul).

Durkheim E. (1953) *Sociology and Philosophy* (London: Cohen & West).

Durkheim E. (1957) *Professional Ethics and Civic Morals* (London: Routledge).

Durkheim E. (1958) *Saint-Simon and Socialism* (London: Routledge).

Durkheim E. (1961 [1912]) *The Elementary Forms of the Religious Life* (London: Allen & Unwin).

Durkheim E. (1964 [1893]) *The Division of Labour* (New York: Free Press).

Durkheim E. (1965) *Montesquieu and Rousseau* (Ann Arbor: University of Michigan Press).

Durkheim E. (1982 [1895]) *The Rules of Sociological Method* (London: Macmillan).

Durkheim E. and Mauss M. (1967) *Primitive Classification* (London: Routledge).

Easton L. D. and Guddatt K. (eds) (1967) *Writings of the Young Marx on Philosophy and Society* (New York: Anchor).

Engels F. (1942 [1884]) *The Origin of the Family, Private Property and the State* (New York: International).

Engels F. (1954) *Anti-Duhring* (London: Lawrence & Wishart).

Featherstone M. (ed.) (1997) *Simmel on Culture* (London: Sage).

Ferguson A. (1966) *An Essay on the History of Civil Society* (Edinburgh: Edinburgh University Press).

Feuerbach L. (1969) 'Preliminary theses on the reform of philosophy', *Arena*, No. 19.

Fisher B. M. and Strauss A. L. (1979) 'Interactionism' in Bottomore T. B. and Nisbet R. (eds) (1979).

Fletcher R. (ed.) (1976) *The Crisis of Industrial Society: The Early Essays of Comte* (London: Heinemann).

Foucault M. (1977 [1975]) *Discipline and Punish* (London: Penguin).

Foucault M. (1979) *Michel Foucault: Power, Truth, Strategy* (Sydney: Feral Publications).

Foucault M. (1980) *Power/Knowledge: Selected Interviews*, ed. Campbell C. (Brighton: Harvester).

Foucault M. (1982) 'Afterword: the subject and power ' in Dreyfus H. and Rabinow P. *Michel Foucault: Beyond Structuralism and Hermeneutics* (London: Chicago University Press).

Foucault M. (1984) *The History of Sexuality* (London: Penguin).

Fowler B. (1997) *Pierre Bourdieu and Cultural Theory* (London: Sage).

Fraser M. and Nicholson L. (1993) 'Social criticism without philosophy: an encounter between feminism and post-modernism' in Docherty T. (ed.) (1994).

Frisby D. (1981) *Sociological Impressionism: A Reassessment of George Simmel's Social Theory* (London: Heinemann).

Frisby D. (1985) *Fragments of Modernity* (Cambridge: Polity).

Fuss D. (ed.) (1991) *Inside/Outside, LesbianTheory/Gay Theory* (London: Routledge).

Gane M. (1988) *On Durkheim's Rules of Sociological Method* (London: Routledge).

Gardiner P. (ed.) (1959) *Theories of History* (New York: Free Press).

Garfinkel H. (1984) *Studies in Ethnomethodology* (Cambridge: Polity).

Gay P. (1967, 1970) *The Enlightenment: An Interpretation* (London: Weidenfeld & Nicolson).

Gerth H. H. and Mills C. W. (eds) (1948) *From Max Weber* (London: Routledge).

Giddens A. (1971) *Capitalism and Modern Social Theory* (Cambridge: Cambridge University Press).

Giddens A. (1972a) *Politics and Sociology in the Thought of Max Weber* (London: Macmillan).

Giddens A. (1972b) *Emile Durkheim: Selected Writings* (Cambridge: Cambridge University Press).

Giddens A. (1976) *New Rules of Sociological Method* (London: Hutchinson).

Giddens A. (1977) *Studies in Social and Political Theory* (London: Hutchinson).

Giddens A. (1984) *The Constitution of Society* (Cambridge: Polity).

Giddens A. (1987) *Social Theory and Modern Sociology* (Cambridge: Polity).

Giddens A. (1990) *The Concept of Modernity* (Cambridge: Polity).

Giddens A. (1991) *Modernity and Self-Identity* (Cambridge: Polity).

Giddens A. (1993) *The Transformation of Intimacy* (Cambridge: Polity).

Giddens A. and Turner J. (eds) (1987) *Social Theory Today* (Cambridge: Polity).

Goffman E. (1956) *The Presentation of Self in Everyday Life* (New York: Doubleday).

Goffman E. (1961) *Asylums* (New York: Anchor).

Goffman E. (1981) *Forms of Talk* (Oxford: Blackwell).

Goffman E. (1997a) 'The interaction order' in Lemert E. (ed.) *The Goffman Reader*, (Oxford: Blackwell).

Goffman E. (1997b) 'Gender display' in Lemert E. (ed.) *The Goffman Reader*, (Oxford: Blackwell).

Goffman E. (1997c) 'Frame activity' in Lemert E. (ed.) *The Goffman Reader*, (Oxford: Blackwell).

Goldman L. (1964) *The Hidden God* (London: Routledge).

Goldman L. (1969) *The Human Sciences and Philosophy* (London: Cape).

Goldman L. (1980) *Essays on Method in the Sociology of Literature* (St. Louis: Telos).

Gouldner A. (1971) *The Coming Crisis of Western Sociology* (London: Heinemann).

Gouldner A. (1973) *For Sociology* (London: Allen Lane).

Gouldner A. (1980) *The Two Marxisms* (London: Macmillan).

Gramsci A. (1971) *Selections from the Prison Notebooks* (London: Lawrence & Wishart).

Gramsci A. (1977, 1978) *Selections from the Political Writings* (London: Lawrence & Wishart).

Gramsci A. (1994) Pre-Prison Writings in Bellamy R. (ed.) (Cambridge: Cambridge University Press).

Habermas J. (1971) *Knowledge and Human Interests* (London: Heinemann).

Habermas J. (1976) *Legitimation Crisis* (London: Heinemann).

Habermas J. (1979) *Communication and the Evolution of Society* (London: Heinemann).

Habermas J. (1984, 1989) *The Theory of Communicative Action*, 2 Vols (Cambridge: Polity).

Habermas J. (1985) 'Modernity: An Incomplete Project' in Foster H. (ed.) *Postmodern Culture* (London: Pluto).

Habermas J. (1990) *The Philosophical Discourse of Modernity* (Cambridge: Polity).

Habermas J. (1992) *The Structural Transformations of the Public Sphere* (Cambridge: Polity).

Haines V. A. (1997) 'Spencer and his critics' in Camic C. (ed.) (1997).

Halbwachs M. (1970) *The Causes of Suicide* (London: Routledge).

Halfpenny P. (1982) *Positivism and Sociology* (London: Allen & Unwin).

Hall S. (1993) 'Culture, community and nations', *Cultural Studies* 7(3): 239–63.

Harvey D. (1989) *The Condition of Postmodernity* (Oxford: Blackwell).

Hawthorn G. (1976) *Enlightenment and Despair: A History of Sociology* (Cambridge: Cambridge University Press).

Hayek F. (1955) *The Counter-Revolution of Science* (New York: Free Press).

Held D. (1980) *Introduction to Critical Theory* (London: Hutchinson).

Heritage J. (1984) *Garfinkel and Ethnomethodology* (Cambridge: Polity).

Hilferding R. (1980 [1910]) *Finance Capital* (London: Routledge).

Hindess B. and Hirst P. (1975) *Pre-Capitalist Economic Formations* (London: Routledge).

Hirst P. Q. (1975) *Durkheim, Bernard and Epistemology* (London: Routledge).

Hirst P. Q. (1976) *Social Evolution and Sociological Categories* (London: Allen & Unwin).

Horkheimer M. (1972) *Critical Theory* (New York: Seabury).

Horkheimer M. (1976 [1937]) 'Traditional and critical theory' in Connerton P. (ed.) (1976).

Hughes H. S. (1959) *Consciousness and Society* (London: MacGibbon & Kee).

Ionescu G. (ed.) (1976) *The Political Thought of Saint-Simon* (Oxford: Oxford University Press).

Jameson F. (1992) *Postmodernism: The Cultural Logic of Capitalism* (London: Verso).

Jay M. (1973) *The Dialectical Imagination* (London: Heinemann).

Joas H. (1993) *Pragmatism and Social Theory* (Chicago: University of Chicago Press).

Joas H. (1996) *The Creativity of Social Action* (Cambridge: Polity).

Jay M. (1988) *Fin-de-Siècle Socialism* (London: Routledge).

Kahn J. S. and Llobera J. (eds) (1981) *The Anthropology of Pre-Capitalist Societies* (London: Macmillan).

Kautsky K. (1983) *Selected Political Writings* (London: Macmillan).

Kellner D. (1989) *Critical Theory, Marxism and Modernity* (Cambridge: Polity).

Kettler D. (1965) *The Social and Political Thought of Adam Ferguson* (Columbus: University of Ohio Press).

Kilminster R. (1979) *Praxis and Method: A Sociological Dialogue with Lukács, Gramsci and the Early Frankfurt School* (London: Routledge & Kegan Paul).

Kolakowski L. (1981) *Main Currents in Marxism*, 3 Vols (Oxford: Oxford University Press).

Kolko G. (1960) 'Max Weber on America', *History and Theory*, Vol. 1.

Kumar K. (1978) *Prophecy and Progress* (Harmondsworth: Penguin).

Kumar K. (1995) *From Postindustrial to Postmodern Society* (Oxford: Blackwell).

Labriola A. (1967 [1896]) *Essays on the Materialist Conception of History* (New York: Monthly Review Press).

Labriola A. (1980) *Socialism and Philosophy* (Washington: Telos).

Lash S. (1990) *Sociology of Postmodernism* (London: Routledge).

Layder D. (1994) *Understanding Social Theory* (London: Sage).

Lehmann W. (ed.) (1960) *John Millar of Glasgow* (Glasgow: Glasgow University Press).

Lehmann J. (1993) *Deconstructing Durkheim* (New York: Routledge).

Levine D. (ed.) (1971) *Simmel: On Individuality and Social Forms* (Chicago: University of Chicago Press).

Levine D. (1981) 'Sociology's quest for the classics: the case of Simmel' in Rhea B. (ed.) (1981).

Levi-Strauss C. (1968, 1977) *Structural Anthropology* (London: Allen Lane).

Lively J. (ed.) *The Works of Joseph de Maistre* (London: Allen & Unwin).

Llobera J. (1981) 'Durkheim, the Durkheimians and their collective misrepresentation of Marx', in Kahn J. S. and Llobera J. (eds) (1981).

Lockwood D. (1964) 'Social integration and system integration', in Zollschan G. R. and Hirsch W. (eds) (1964).

Lockwood D. (1988) 'The weakest link in the chain? Some comments on the Marxist theory of action' in Rose D. (ed.) *Social Stratification and Economic Change* (London: Hutchinson).

Lockwood D. (1992) *Solidarity and Schism: The Problem of Disorder in Durkheimian and Marxist Sociology* (Oxford: Oxford University Press).

Lowith K. (1982) *Karl Marx and Max Weber* (London: Allen & Unwin).

Luckmann T. (ed.) (1978) *Phenomenology and Sociology* (Harmondsworth: Penguin).

Lukács G. (1971 [1923]) *History and Class Consciousness* (London: Merlin).

Lukács G. (1972) *Political Writings: 1979–1929* (London: New Left Books).

Lukes S. (1973) *Emile Durkheim: His Life and Work* (London: Allen Lane).

Luhmann N. (1994) 'An interview' in *Theory, Culture and Society* 2(2).

Lyotard J. F. (1989) 'The Lyotard reader', ed. Benjamin A. (Oxford: Blackwell).

Malinowski E. (1922) *Argonauts of the Western Pacific* (New York: Dutton).

Mandel E. (1975) *Late Capitalism* (London: Verso).

Manuel F. (1962) *The Prophets of Paris* (New York: Harper).

Marcuse H. (1954) *Reason and Revolution* (New York: Humanities Press).

Marcuse H. (1962) *Eros and Civilisation* (New York: Vintage Books).

Marcuse H. (1964) *One Dimensional Man* (London: Routledge).

Marshall G. (1982) *In Search of the Spirit of Capitalism* (London: Hutchinson).

Marx K. (1957, 1958, 1962 [1867]) *Capital* (London: Lawrence & Wishart).

Marx K. (1961 [1847]) *The Poverty of Philosophy* (London: Lawrence & Wishart).

Marx K. (1963[1843–4]) *Economic and Philosophical Manuscripts* (London: Lawrence & Wishart).

Marx K. (1964–72) *Theories of Surplus Value*, 3 Vols (London: Lawrence & Wishart).

Marx K. (1971 [1859]) *A Contribution to the Critique of Political Economy* (London: Lawrence & Wishart).

Marx K. (1973 [1953]) *Grundrisse* (Harmondsworth: Penguin).

Marx K. (1974–6) *Marx: Political Writings*, 3 Vols (Harmondsworth: Penguin).

Marx K. (1976–80) *Capital*, 3 Vols (Harmondsworth: Penguin).

Marx K. and Engels F. (1956) *The Holy Family* (London: Lawrence & Wishart).

Marx K. and Engels F. (1962) *Selected Works* (London: Lawrence & Wishart).

Marx K. and Engels F. (1964 [1846]) *The German Ideology* (London: Lawrence & Wishart).

Marx K. and Engels F. (1971) *On the Paris Commune* (London: Lawrence & Wishart).

Marx K. and Engels F. (1975) *Collected Works* (London: Lawrence & Wishart).

Marx K. and Engels F. (n.d.) *Selected Correspondence* (London: Lawrence & Wishart).

McIntosh M. (1996) 'The homosexual role' in Seidman S. (ed.) (1996).

McLellan D. (1969) *The Young Hegelians and Karl Marx* (London: Macmillan).

McLellan D. (1973) *Karl Marx: His Life and Thought* (London: Macmillan).

McLellan D. (ed.) (1980a) *The Thought of Karl Marx* (London: Macmillan).

McLellan D. (1980b) *Marxism after Marx* (London: Macmillan).

McLellan D. (ed.) (1983) *Marx: The First Hundred Years* (London: Fontana).

Mead G. H. (1934) *Mind, Self and Society* (Chicago: University of Chicago Press).

Mead G. H. (1936) *Movements of Thought in the Nineteenth Century* (Chicago: University of Chicago Press).

Mead G. H. (1938) *The Philosophy of the Act* (Chicago: University of Chicago Press).

Mead G. H. (1964) *On Social Psychology* (Chicago: University of Chicago Press).

Menzies K. (1977) *Talcott Parsons and the Social Image of Man* (London: Routledge & Kegan Paul).

Merleau-Ponty M. (1973) *The Adventures of the Dialectic* (London: Heinemann).

Merton R. K. (1957) *Social Theory and Social Structure* (New York: Free Press).

Michels R. (1962 [1911]) *Political Parties* (New York: Collier-Macmillan).

Mill J. S. (1961) *Auguste Comte and Positivism* (Ann Arbor: University of Michigan Press).

Mill J. S. (1976 [1843]) *A System of Logic* in Fletcher R. (ed.) (1974).

Mills C. W. (1956) *The Power Elite* (New York: Oxford University Press).

Mills C. W. (1959) *The Sociological Imagination* (New York: Oxford University Press).

Montesquieu C. (1949 [1748]) *The Spirit of the Laws* (New York: Haffner).

Montesquieu C. (1965 [1734]) *Considerations on the Greatness of the Romans and their Decline* (New York: Free Press).

Mommsen W. (1974) *The Age of Bureaucracy: Perspectives on the Political Sociology of Max Weber* (Oxford: Blackwell).

Mosca G. (1939) *The Ruling Class* (New York: McGraw-Hill).

Mouffe C. (ed.) (1978) *Gramsci and Marxist Theory* (London: Routledge).

Mouzelis N. P. (1991) *Back to Sociological Theory* (London: Macmillan).

Mouzelis N. P. (1995) *Sociological Theory: What Went Wrong* (London: Routledge).

Mulkay M. (1975) *Functionalism, Exchange and Theoretical Strategy* (London: Routledge & Kegan Paul).

Munch R. (1987) *Theory of Action* (London: Routledge).

Munch R. (1988) *Understanding Modernity* (London: Routledge).

Nisbet R. (1967) *The Sociological Tradition* (London: Heinemann).

Oberschall A. (ed.) (1972) *Empirical Social Research in Germany 1848–1914* (New York: Harper & Row).

Outhwaite W. (1975) *Understanding Social Life: The Method called Verstehen* (London: Allen & Unwin).

Outhwaite W. (1994) *Habermas: A Critical Introduction* (Cambridge: Polity).

Pareto V. (1963) *The Mind and Society: A Treatise on General Sociology* (New York: Dover).

Parkin F. (1982) *Max Weber* (London: Routledge).

Parsons T. (1951) *The Social System* (New York: Free Press).

Parsons T. (1954) *Essays in Sociological Theory* (New York: Free Press).

Parsons T. (1955) *Family, Socialisation and Interaction Process* (with R. F. Bales) (London: Routledge & Kegan Paul).

Parsons T. (1961a [1937]) *The Structure of Social Action* (New York: Free Press).

Parsons T. (1961b) *Structure and Process in Modern Societies* (New York: Free Press).

Parsons T. (ed.) (1961c) *Theories of Society* (New York: Free Press).

Parsons T. (1961d) 'The point of view of the author' in Black M. (ed.) (1961).

Parsons T. (1964) *Social Structure and Personality* (New York: Free Press).

Parsons T. (1966) *Societies: Evolutionary and Comparative Perspectives* (New Jersey: Prentice Hall).

Parsons T. (1967) *Sociological Theory and Modern Society* (New York: Free Press).

Parsons T. (1971a) *The System of Modern Societies* (New Jersey: Prentice Hall).

Parsons T. (1971b) 'The interpretation of dreams by Sigmund Freud', *Daedalus*, Vol. 103, pp. 91–6.

Parsons T. (1978*) Action Theory and the Human Condition* (New York: Free Press).

Parsons T. (1981) 'Revisiting the classics', in Rhea B. (ed.) (1981).

Parsons T. (1989) 'A tentative outline of American values', *Theory, Culture and Society*, 6(4).

Parsons T. and Shils E. (1962) *Toward a General Theory of Action* (New York: Harper).

Parsons T. and Smelser N. (1956) *Economy and Society* (New York: Free Press).

Peel J. D. Y. (1971) *Herbert Spencer: The Evolution of a Sociologist* (London: Heinemann).

Peel J. D. Y. (ed.) (1972) *Herbert Spencer on Social Evolution* (Chicago: University of Chicago Press).

Pickering M. (1993) *Auguste Comte* (Cambridge: Cambridge University Press).

Plummer K. (1981) *The Making of the Modern Homosexual* (London: Hutchinson).

Plummer K. (ed.) (1992) *Modern Homosexualities* (London: Routledge).

Plummer K. (1998) 'Herbert Blumer' in Stones R. (ed.) (1998).

Pope W. (1978) *Durkheim's Suicide* (Chicago: University of Chicago Press).

Popper K. (1963) *The Open Society and its Enemies*, 2 Vols (London: Routledge).

Postane M. (1997) 'Rethinking Marx in a post-Marx world' in Camic C. (ed.) (1997).

Poulantzas N. (1973) *Political Power and Social Classes* (London: New Left Books).

Poulantzas N. (1975) *Classes in Contemporary Capitalism* (London: New Left Books).

Propp V. (1968 [1928]) *Morphology of the Fairy Tale* (Austin: University of Texas Press).

Rabinow P. (ed.) (1986) *The Foucault Reader* (London: Penguin).

Radcliffe-Brown A. R. (1952) *Structure and Function in Primitive Society* (London: Routledge).

Rex J. (1961) *Key Problems of Sociological Theory* (London: Routledge).

Rhea B. (ed.) (1981) *The Future of the Sociological Classics* (London: Allen & Unwin).

Rickert H. (1962) *Science and History* (New York: Van Nostrand).

Rickman H. R. (1967) *Understanding and the Human Sciences* (London: Heinemann).

Ringer F. (1969) *The Decline of the German Mandarins: The German Academic Community 1890–1933* (Cambridge: Harvard University Press).

Robbins D. (1987) 'Sport, hegemony and the middle classes' *Theory, Culture and Society*, **4**(4).

Rocher G. (1974) *Talcott Parsons and American Sociology* (London: Nelson).

Rock P. (1979) *The Making of Symbolic Interactionism* (London: Macmillan).

Rosdolsky R. (1977) *The Making of Marx's Capital* (London: Pluto).

Rose M. (1991) *The Postmodern and the Postindustrial* (Cambridge: Cambridge University Press).

Ross D. (1991) *The Origins of American Social Science* (Cambridge: Cambridge University Press).

Runciman W. (ed.) (1978) *Weber: A Selection* (Cambridge: Cambridge University Press).

Sahay A. (ed.) (1971) *Max Weber and Modern Sociology* (London: Routledge).

Salamon L. (1981) *The Sociology of Political Praxis* (London: Routledge).

Samuelson K. (1961) *Religion and Economic Action* (London: Heinemann).

Saussure F. (1974) *Course in General Linguistics* (London: Fontana).

Sayer D. (1978) *Marx's Method* (Hassocks: Harvester).

Schneider L. (ed.) (1967) *The Scottish Moralists on Human Nature and Society* (Chicago: University of Chicago Press).

Schumpeter J. (1961) *Capitalism, Socialism and Democracy* (London: Allen & Unwin).

Schutz A. (1962–6) *Collected Papers*, 3 Vols (The Hague: Mouton).

Schutz A. (1972 [1932]) *The Phenomenology of the Social World* (London: Heinemann).

Schutz A. (1974) *The Structures of the Life World* (with T. Luckmann) (London: Heinemann).

Schutz A. (1978) 'Phenomenology and the social sciences', in Luckmann T. (ed.) (1978).

Schutz A. (1982) *Life Forms and Meaning Structures* (London: Routledge).

Schwendinger H. H. (1974) *The Sociologists of the Chair* (New York: Basic Books).

Scott J. (1995) *Sociological Theory* (Cheltenham: Edward Elgar).

Seidman S. (ed.) (1996) *Queer Theory/Sociology* (Oxford: Blackwell).

Seidman S. (1998) *Contested Knowledge: Social Theory in the Postmodern Era* (Oxford: Blackwell).

Sharrock W. and Anderson B. (1986) *The Ethnomethodologists* (London: Routledge).

Shils E. (1972) *The Intellectuals and the Powers* (Chicago: University of Chicago Press).

Shils E. (1975) *Centre and Periphery* (Chicago: University of Chicago Press).

Shils E. (1980) *The Calling of Sociology* (Chicago: University of Chicago Press).

Simmel G. (1956) *Conflict and the Web of Group Affiliations* (New York: Free Press).

Simmel G. (1957 [1911]) *Philosophic Culture* (New York: Putnam).

Simmel G. (1968) *The Conflict in Modern Culture and Other Essays* (New York: Columbia University Press).

Simmel G. (1977 [1892]) *The Problems of the Philosophy of History* (New York: Free Press).

Simmel G. (1978 [1910]) *The Philosophy of Money* (London: Routledge).

Simmel G. (1980) *Essays in Interpretation in the Social Sciences* (Manchester: Manchester University Press).

Simon W. M. (1963) *European Positivism in the Nineteenth Century* (New York: Cornell University Press).

Slater P. (1977) *The Origin and Significance of the Frankfurt School* (London: Routledge).

Smith A. (1976) *Theory of Moral Sentiments* (Glasgow: Glasgow University Press).

Smith A. (1970) *Wealth of Nations* (Harmondsworth: Penguin).

Smith D. (1988) *The Chicago School* (London: Macmillan).

Smith D. (1987) *The Everyday World as Problematic* (Boston: Northeastern University Press).

Smith D. (1990) *The Conceptual Practices of Power* (Boston: Northeastern University Press).

Sombart W. (1967) *Luxury and Capitalism* (Ann Arbor: University of Michigan Press).

Sorel G. (1950 [1908]) *Reflections on Violence* (New York: Free Press).

Sorel G. (1969) *The Illusions of Progress* (Berkeley: University of California Press).

Sorel G. (1976) *From George Sorel: Essays in Socialism and Philosophy* (New York: Oxford University Press).

Spencer H. (1965) *The Study of Sociology* (New York: Free Press).

Spencer H. (1969a) *Man versus the State* (Harmondsworth: Penguin).

Spencer H. (1969b) *The Principles of Sociology*, Andreski S. (ed.) (New York: Macmillan).

Stones R. (ed.) (1998) *Key Sociological Thinkers* (London: Macmillan).

Strasser H. (1976) *The Normative Structure of Sociology* (London: Routledge).

Swingewood A. (1970) 'The origins of sociology: the case of the Scottish Enlightenment', *British Journal of Sociology*, June.

Swingewood A. (1991) *A Short History of Sociological Thought*, 2nd edn (London: Macmillan).

Szacki J. (1979) *History of Sociological Thought* (London: Aldwych).

Sztompka P. (1993) *The Sociology of Social Change* (Oxford: Blackwell).

Tawney R. H. (1926) *Religion and the Rise of Capitalism* (London: Allen & Unwin).

Taylor K. (ed.) (1975) *Saint-Simon: Selected Writings on Science, Industry and Social Organisation* (London: Croom Helm).

Taylor S. (1982) *Durkheim and the Study of Suicide* (London: Macmillan).

Therborn G. (1976) *Science, Class and Society* (London: New Left Books).

Thomas W. I. and Znaniecki F. (1927) *The Polish Peasant in Europe and America*, 2 Vols (Chicago: University of Chicago Press).

Thompson E. (1978) *The Poverty of Theory* (London: Merlin).

Thompson J. B. and Held D. (eds) (1982) *Habermas: Critical Debates* (London: Macmillan).

Thompson K. (ed.) (1976) *Auguste Comte: The Foundations of Sociology* (London: Nelson).

Thompson K. (ed.) (1985) *Readings from Emile Durkheim* (London: Routledge).

Tiryakin A. E. (1979) 'Emile Durkheim' in Bottomore T. B. and Nisbet R. (eds) (1979).

Tönnies F. (1971) *On Sociology: Pure, Applied and Empirical* in Cahmann W. J. and Merberle R. (eds) (Chicago: University of Chicago Press).

Touraine A. (1971) *The Post-Industrial Society* (London: Wildwood House).

Traugott B. (ed.) (1978) *Durkheim on Institutional Analysis* (Chicago: University of Chicago Press).

Tumin M. (1968) *Social Stratification: The Forms and Functions of Social Inequality* (New Jersey: Prentice Hall).

Turner B. (1981) *For Weber* (London: Routledge).

Vico G. (1948 [1725]) *The New Science*, Bergin T. and Frisch M. (eds) (New York: Cornell University Press).

Walby S. (1990) *Theorising Patriarchy* (Oxford: Blackwell).

Walby S. (1997) *Gender Transformations* (London: Routledge).

Waters M. (1994) *Modern Sociological Theory* (London: Sage).

Weber M. (1923) *General Economic History* (London: Allen & Unwin).

Weber M. (1930 [1904–5]) *The Protestant Ethic and the Spirit of Capitalism* (London: Allen & Unwin).

Weber M. (1949 [1904]) *The Methodology of the Social Sciences* (New York: Free Press).

Weber M. (1951) *The Religion of India* (New York: Free Press).

Weber M. (1952) *Ancient Judaism* (New York: Free Press).

Weber M. (1954) *On Law in Economy and Society* (New York: Free Press).

Weber M. (1958a) *The Religion of India* (New York: Free Press).

Weber M. (1958b) *The City* (New York: Free Press).

Weber M. (1963) *The Sociology of Religion* (Boston: Beacon Press).

Weber M. (1964) *The Theory of Social and Economic Organisation* (New York: Free Press).

Weber M. (1968) *Economy and Society*, 3 Vols (Towata: Bedminster Press).

Weber M. (1975) *Roscher and Knies: The Logical Problems of Historical Economics* (New York: Free Press).

Weber M. (1976) *The Agrarian Sociology of Ancient Civilisations* (London: New Left Books).

Weber M. (1977) *Critique of Stammler* (New York: Free Press).

Weeks J. (1977) 'The construction of homosexuality' in Seidmann S. (ed.) (1996).

Wiggershaus R. (1994) *The Frankfurt School* (Cambridge: Polity).

Wolff K. (ed.) (1950) *The Sociology of Georg Simmel* (New York: Free Press).

Wolff K. (ed.) (1964) *Emile Durkheim: Essays on Sociology and Philosophy* (New York: Harper & Row).

Wolff K. (ed.) (1965) *Simmel: Essays on Sociology, Philosophy and Aesthetics* (New York: Harper & Row).

Worsley P. (1982) *Marx and Marxism* (London: Routledge).

Wright E. O. (1978) *Class, Crisis and the State* (London: New Left Books).

Wrong D. (ed.) (1970) *Max Weber* (New Jersey: Prentice Hall).

Wrong D. (1976) *Skeptical Sociology* (London: Heinemann).

Zeitlin I. (1968) *Ideology and the Development of Sociological Theory* (New Jersey: Prentice Hall).

Zollschan G. R. and Hirsch W. (eds) (1964) *Explorations in Social Change* (London: Routledge).

Index